PALO ALTO

A CENTENNIAL HISTORY

PALO ALTO
A CENTENNIAL HISTORY

Ward Winslow
and the Palo Alto Historical Association

Publications Committee
Gain A. John, Chair
Lois C. Brenner
Gloria R. Brown
Betty J. Rogaway
Steven A. Staiger
Ruth Wilson

Published by
the Palo Alto Historical Association

Endorsed by the
Palo Alto Centennial Committee

Author: Ward Winslow
Editors: Gain A. John, Lois C. Brenner,
Gloria R. Brown, Betty J. Rogaway,
Steven Staiger, Ruth Wilson
Publishing Consultant:
Stanford Publication Services,
Stanford, CA 94305
Art Director: Sue Cretarolo
Designer: Marti Somers
Copy Editor: Ellen Lehman

First Edition
Library of Congress Catalog Card Number: 93-85698

Winslow, Wardell V., 1927 —
Palo Alto: A Centennial History/Ward Winslow
and the Palo Alto Historical Association

Includes bibliography and index
ISBN 0-9638098-3-0

Published in Palo Alto, California
Manufactured in the United States of America

*The Palo Alto Historical Association
gratefully acknowledges the following persons,
foundations and trusts for their contributions to help
the Association finance publication of this book:*

Sponsors

Edward P. "Ed" Ames
Anonymous
Anne V. Becker
Florence R. Bogner
Allan F. and Marilyn S. Brown
Gloria R. Brown
Robert V. and Pat Brown
Martha Gates Commons
Shirley and Leonard Ely
Crystal D. Gamage
Marion and Bob Grimm
Billy Prior
Betty J. Rogaway
Constance L. Sonnichsen
Anne and Gordon Wright

Grant Donors

Ambassador L. W. "Bill" Lane and Mrs. Jean Lane
The Francis F. North Trust
The David and Lucile Packard Foundation

*In addition, contributions in cash or in
kind have been made by numerous members
of the Historical Association, including bequests
from Ruth Steinmetz and Clifton Slonaker.*

Table of Contents

Dedication

Boyd J. Haight was a truly devoted Palo Altan, and one who believed in bringing the city's history into full view.

Born in 1923 in Montana, he came to Palo Alto in 1927 with his family. They lived in College Terrace; his father worked for Stanford University. Boyd was graduated from Mayfield Grammar School and Palo Alto High School, and attended San Jose State College before serving for three years in the Army Signal Corps during World War II. Returning home, he took his bachelor's and master's degrees in journalism at Stanford University, and became a *Palo Alto Times* reporter in 1947. After a stint of teaching and public information work at California State Polytechnic College in San Luis Obispo, he became Stanford's assistant director of information.

Boyd rejoined the *Times* in 1951 and two years later became city editor, directing local news coverage during the area's years of great growth. Active in the Y's Men's Club, he was honored by the Palo Alto Junior Chamber of Commerce in 1956 as the city's "Young Man of the Year." In 1961 the *Times* promoted him to assistant editor.

Boyd originated many retrospective news spreads and history stories run by the paper. In those days, City Historian Guy C. Miller worked part-time at the *Times*, keeping up its files. Two years after Guy's death in 1955, Boyd wrote a column urging the placement of markers at the historic sites to which Miller had led tours, pointing out how quickly such landmarks were being overgrown. Although the scene of radio pioneering at 913 Emerson Street had been marked, he wrote, "there are scores of other historic sites unmarked and recalled only in the memory of old residents or the papers of the historical collection. And somebody needs to do something about it." At his urging, plaques were placed at many sites in the 1960s.

Boyd became editor of the daily *Sunnyvale Standard* in 1963, then city editor of the old *San Jose News* and later assistant city editor of the *Mercury News*. In 1980 he began teaching reporting at San Jose State University as an added task. That formalized his mentor relationship with generations of emerging journalists who admired his know-how, sincerity and kindly, patient manner.

All the while he kept up a keen interest in Palo Alto affairs, past and current. He had found his second wife, Polly, presiding over the newspaper clipping files Guy Miller had left. To his two sons and her three children they added two daughters and three adopted sons.

Boyd Haight was an enthusiastic and inspiring leader in the Palo Alto Historical Association project to publish a new city history. Deeply engaged in it, and in his editing, teaching and parenting at age 66, he died at his *Mercury News* desk one April morning in 1989.

In gratitude for all he set in motion to perpetuate the city's history, we dedicate this book to the memory of Boyd Haight.

Preface

The seed from which this book grew was planted in 1913. In that year a Palo Alto historical association first organized — its stated purpose to prepare a local history. The organization could not withstand the impact of World War I, however, and lapsed after four years. Harry C. Peterson, the founding president and a City Council member, lost his position as curator of the Stanford Museum and later left town. But the collection that had been started, with Guy C. Miller as historiographer, was preserved and enhanced in the Palo Alto Library.

No full-scale local history was published until 1939, when Dallas E. Wood brought out the *History of Palo Alto*, written together with Norris James. Wood had been editor of the *Palo Alto Times* for 19 years before handing that job on to Elinor V. Cogswell in 1938.

After World War II, townspeople had a fresh vision of the need to preserve the recollections of vanishing pioneers and to save the stories of places significant in Palo Alto's growth. Thus the Palo Alto Historical Association was reborn in 1948, with historian Miller the father and editor Cogswell the midwife. Together with the Palo Alto Chamber of Commerce and Civic Association, the Times and the library, the Historical Association bolstered support for Guy Miller's work on the files, and staged annual Memory Parties to capture early residents' recollections.

In 1952, Guy Miller, aided by Hugh Enochs, brought forth *The Palo Alto Community Book*, building upon and enhancing Dallas Wood's history. Meanwhile, in 1950 the Historical Association began issuing occasional pamphlets called *The Tall Tree — The Story of Palo Alto and its Neighbors*. This series served to commit to writing vital aspects of Palo Alto's past. Issues were prepared primarily by the Publications Committee of the Association.

Two Tall Tree issues merit special note. In 1955, Hugh Enochs wrote a booklet titled "The Dawn of the Electronics Age," which in 1958 was recast as "The First Fifty Years of Electronics Research" and published by the Chamber of Commerce. In 1960, a concise history by Elinor Cogswell, titled "Palo Alto — Its Backgrounds, Beginnings and Growth," was published jointly by the Chamber, the Historical Association and the City of Palo Alto. It went through ten printings and remains in use in the public schools to this day.

Two other histories later emerged: Arthur Coffman's *An Illustrated History of Palo Alto* (1969) and Pamela Gullard and Nancy Lund's *History of Palo Alto — The Early Years* (1989). Coffman's book, notable for large-format photographs, traced events from newspaper files and disregarded personalities. Only 600 copies were printed, and the book soon joined the Wood and Miller histories in the out-of-print and hard-to-obtain category. The Gullard and Lund book illuminated numerous aspects of the years up to 1925, using many photographs from the Historical Association files.

Meanwhile, several more Tall Tree pamphlets proved popular and remain in print: "Mayfield — 1850-1925," by Ruth Wilson, Lucy Evans and Dorothy Regnery (1976, reprinted 1990); "Streets of Palo Alto" (1979, revised 1991), by Wilson, Regnery and Georgiana Kjerulff; and "Parks of Palo Alto" (1983), by Marthe-H. Cohen and others.

In 1986, directors of the Historical Association perceived a need to update or replace Elinor Cogswell's concise history. As considerations progressed, the feeling grew that there should be a major revision of the previous works, bringing the city's history up to date at the 100th anniversary of Palo Alto's incorporation.

The Publications Committee first approached this task by farming out to selected local writers subjects with which they were especially familiar.

James H. Stone, Ruth Wilson, Lois Brenner, Boyd Haight, Gary Fazzino, Betty Rogaway, Jay Thorwaldson, Steve Staiger (successor to Ruth Wilson as Association historian), Gain A. John, Ward Winslow, Paul Gullixson and Gail Woolley all wrote pieces. Boyd Haight coordinated the project until his sudden death April 24, 1989.

Early in 1990, the Publications Committee completed a 10-chapter draft and sent it for comment to those just named and to a few others. From their critiques the committee concluded that the manuscript was far from ready for publication. It needed more work.

Ward Winslow was selected in mid-1990 to rewrite and expand the history. Working closely with the Publications Committee, headed by Gain John and including Lois Brenner, who acted as recorder, Gloria Brown, Betty Rogaway, Steve Staiger and Ruth Wilson, he did extensive new and verifying research and lengthened the manuscript to 20 chapters. He sought to focus on the century of cityhood.

A word about the scope of this book: It is a Palo Alto history, and necessarily parochial. Its shapers are well aware of Palo Alto's close affinities with neighboring cities and institutions, yet have not attempted to tell their stories at length. They are mentioned only when required to explain some facet of Palo Alto development.

The Historical Association's files and past publications have been the single most important source of material for this book. Other major sources have been the Stanford University Library's Department of Special Collections (cited as the Stanford University Archives in photo credits); the files of the *Palo Alto Times* and its successor in April 1979, the *Peninsula Times Tribune*, the *Palo Alto Weekly*, the *San Jose Mercury News* and other newspapers and periodicals; the collections of Mountain View, Menlo Park and Stanford history groups; oral histories and interviews with city leaders; and books by local authors, listed in a bibliography.

Gloria Brown played the leading role in locating and selecting the photographs, often taking photos herself when none were available, while Steve Staiger drafted the captions — with active involvement of the entire Publications Committee, which met weekly over many months to review manuscript materials intensively. Many of the added chapters stemmed from Lois Brenner's suggestions and study. The work was greatly enhanced by Ruth Wilson's painstaking research and by the intimate knowledge she and Steve Staiger have of the Association files.

In the final processing of this work, Stanford Publication Services — notably art director Sue Cretarolo, designer Marti Somers and copy editor Ellen Lehman — served as the publishing consultant.

Many other contributors will be thanked in the acknowlegements.

This book is the Historical Association's most ambitious project to date. If it helps readers to appreciate Palo Alto's remarkable past, and inspires others to join in recording local history to enlighten future generations, it will have achieved its purpose.

A steam locomotive crosses San Francisquito Creek into Palo Alto in 1951. El Palo Alto, the symbol of both the city and Stanford University, stands to the right of the bridge.

1

Overview: Vision and Reality

The name Palo Alto derived from a once-towering redwood by the banks of San Francisquito Creek, where Captain Gaspar de Portola and his exploring party camped in November 1769 — six and a half years before the Declaration of Independence was signed. The name has borne many different meanings in succeeding eras:

A creek crossing... possible mission site... a rancho... a picnic spot for celebrating the opening of the San Francisco-San Jose railroad in 1863... the finest trotting horse farm in the world... the setting for a breath-taking plan to create a university... a subdivision now called College Terrace ... a railroad station for the new campus... a college town... a subregional commercial and cultural center... a thriving city renowned for its climate and beauty and as a center for education, good government, fair play, high technology, advanced medicine, research, politics and culture.

In the century since its incorporation as a city in April 1894, Palo Alto's population has grown from 800 to nearly 56,000, and its area from 737.55 acres (1.15 square miles) to 25.98 square miles.

These raw numbers fail to disclose the true 100-year story; indeed, Mountain View and Sunnyvale — the neighbor cities to the southeast — far outstrip Palo Alto's population. Still, Palo Alto stands as the mid-Peninsula's leading municipality — a wellspring of innovations, a collector of amenities, a repository of quality. Year after year, the city has ranked at the top in quality-of-life surveys. Challenge after challenge has been met by its citizens in creative ways, generating facilities and institutions that are widely emulated. Palo Alto's magnetism exerts a strong pull in the surrounding communities, where many people feel a lasting connection based on ties of occupation, schooling or past residency.

Stanford University is clearly the prime difference between Palo Alto and its neighbors. As Palo Alto grew to nurture the university and its faculty and students, so the university has sustained the town, feeding it intellectual fare, culture, business and thrilling sports spectacles.

The interconnection of the city and the university has been the most important force shaping the community's character. Other independent influences bear upon the city, of course, and neither Stanford or Palo Alto has dominated the other. Yet, their symbiotic relationship is very pervasive — probably more so than those in other long-lived California town-and-gown pairs such as Berkeley and Claremont. The two entities share revenue production from a research park and a shopping center, the city supplies Stanford's fire protection and sewage disposal service and Stanford Hospital still is bound to provide some medical care for Palo Altans. Together, the two corporate bodies have acted to realize the vision of the man who founded the university and co-founded the town.

Palo Alto, often spurred by resident Stanford faculty and graduates, has compiled an impressive list of distinctions:

- *The first municipality in Santa Clara County to own all of its public utilities.*
- *The cradle for development of radio telegraphy, electronics, many computer innovations and, lately, artificial intelligence.*
- *A unified school district that has led the way to numerous educational advances.*
- *An outstanding set of amenities, paced by the early creations of a Children's Theater,*

1

Children's Library and Junior Museum, and later a fine set of parks offering exceptional learning experiences in the foothills and baylands.
- *One of the nation's most highly patronized library systems.*
- *A groundbreaking role in peace movements, encounter groups, environmentalism and refining of the local political process.*

Once Palo Alto had the same sort of rough edges that mark many western college towns; today it has a distinctive sophistication. Once it was both a college town and a bedroom community for commuters to San Francisco; later its Stanford Shopping Center dimmed San Francisco's allure for shoppers. Once it went on a rocket-ride decade of growth; in the following decade it became a battleground for pro- and anti-growth advocates of every stripe. Once it was a stronghold of progressive Republicans; later it became an electoral citadel of liberal Democrats. Once it was dry, liquor-wise; today it has a winery, a brewery and many a place serving alcoholic beverages.

These swift transitions were recent, however; change occurred much more slowly in earlier times. For most of what history we know, Palo Alto's land base was peopled by Ohlone Indians. Then Spanish exploration and settlement directed from Mexico overwhelmed and obliterated the Ohlones. Next, Mexico cast off Spain's yoke and secularized the missions, loosening their tenuous toehold. The rancho period with its vast cattle herds ensued, but its dusty romanticism was soon upset. Americans grabbed Alta California for their own and rapidly won statehood.

Farming and lumbering came next — indeed, wheat was king in the Santa Clara Valley from 1865-75. Towns sprang up at the crossroads of routes for stage coaches and wagons drawn by horses or oxen. One was Mayfield, centered at today's El Camino Real and California Avenue.

Construction of the San Francisco-San Jose train line gave impetus to acquisition of large Peninsula estates by San Francisco's merchant princes, mining bonanza kings and railroad empire builders. By a curious twist of fate, what later became Palo Alto's original site was left a hayfield amid the manors: Mark Hopkins, one of the Central Pacific Railroad's "Big Four," had an option to buy the land from rancher Henry Seale, but Hopkins died in 1878 before he could exercise the option.

Leland Stanford moved from Sacramento to San Francisco in 1874. The foremost of the four men who had pushed through the western part of the first transcontinental railroad, Stanford had amassed a fortune, and enjoyed widespread respect for having served as California's Civil War governor. Although commercial transportation was his core business, horses were his passion. Within two years he had found an ideal country property, the former estate of George Gordon by the banks of the San Francisquito. There he built his celebrated Palo Alto Stock Farm — stables and tracks for training trotting horses, which in that pre-automotive age fascinated sports-minded males across the nation. Continuing to buy ranches, he expanded his estate to over 8,000 acres.

Governor Stanford and his wife, Jane Lathrop Stanford, made a grand tour of Europe in 1883-84 with their only child, Leland, Jr. — a lad of great promise. The boy contracted typhoid fever and, in Italy, died a protracted death, two months short of his 16th birthday. His grief-stricken parents felt the light had gone out of their lives. On the night after his death, the father had a vision of the boy telling him to "live for humanity." The next morning the couple settled on what they would do as a memorial to Leland, Jr.— endow and create a university.

Although the founding grant was promulgated in November 1885, the project took time, and Stanford insisted on making the major decisions himself. His election by the California Legislature as United States senator in 1886 added to his workload. So did the extent of his ideas for the university, which, a devoted trustee wrote later, were "almost unbounded" and "utterly impractical" unless the institution incorporated the whole school system of a community.

Stanford's concept was not only for a university but for an entire educational system from kindergarten through graduate school, incorporating a village on the campus. At first he envisioned a village on his lands nearest Mayfield. Then he decided that the village should not be on the university lands, although there would still be faculty housing on leased lots. In 1886 or 1887, according to legend supported by presumptive evidence, Stanford offered to make Mayfield the college town if its dozen or so saloons were closed — and was refused. As a politician being boomed for president at a time when prohibitionist sentiment was high, he was sensitive about his public image, and wanted a clean town serving the university.

For all his wealth, Stanford had money troubles that dogged construction of the campus. The project dragged, and despite avid interest among families hoping to send students there tuition-free, there were rumblings in the press that the university would never be built and that Stanford aimed to pocket more money by leasing housing. The sting of this accusation may have prompted him to turn development of the village over to someone else.

Timothy Hopkins was a perfect choice. A junior associate of Stanford's in the operation of the railroads, he was also overseer of the Mark Hopkins family fortune, and he lived just across San Francisquito Creek in Menlo Park. What's more, Hopkins held an option to buy a tract of land along the bayward flank of the campus.

So Stanford asked Hopkins to develop the land. Hopkins prepared to exercise the option and add an adjoining parcel. Then a change in his family circumstances rendered the funds he had expected to use inaccessible. Hearing of the problem, Stanford offered to guarantee a bank loan for Hopkins. Hopkins had the town platted and by 1889 was ready to sell lots. Meanwhile, Stanford had asked Hopkins to make sure no whiskey was made or sold in the town. Hopkins

did so through a deed restriction providing that violations would result in the land reverting to him. In addition to selling Palo Alto lots — and soon paying off the loan Stanford had underwritten — Hopkins laid out the streets and planted trees, and for years was the biggest property owner.

Stanford University drew copious publicity owing to its record endowment and the idea of tuition-free education. The selection of Indiana University President David Starr Jordan to be founding president of the new campus gained widespread notice. So did the opening ceremonies on October 1, 1891, with an unexpectedly large number of students — some 440, about 25% women, rather than the expected 10% — in attendance. In the second semester the count reached 559.

Exciting news about Stanford's plans attracted people who not only desired college educations for their children but who hoped to help staff the lower schools or the university. Although Stanford did not, finally, provide them, lower schools sprang up — Herbert Hoover received tutoring at one of them before entering the university's pioneer class. Since 1891, many private schools have been founded in and around Palo Alto, and the community itself gradually developed a unified and excellent public school system. Stanford's third president, Ray Lyman Wilbur, took the lead in enabling Palo Alto High School to lease Stanford land, and also pushed for a local junior college for undergraduate studies.

The village grew with a vigor that surprised observers such as Stanford Registrar Orrin Leslie Elliott and his wife, Ellen Coit Elliott. In 1894 she wrote for a magazine:

> *The town of Palo Alto, a mile from the college buildings, consisting then (in 1891) of a couple of houses, a land agent's office and an extensive network of little white posts of the surveyor, now presents to the astonished eye the aspect of a good-sized, flourishing village, with churches, schools, 'business blocks,' and all the other paraphernalia of corporate civilization.*

rants, and put steam behind a lawsuit that succeeded in 1970 in breaking the downtown liquor sales ban.

High-rise construction began with the 101 Alma apartments in the '50s, and climbed with the 15-story Palo Alto Office Center at 525 University Avenue. A proposal to build a mid-rise Civic Center downtown carried 2 to 1; the issue split residentialist forces, who the next year were put down in an all-council recall election of Palo Alto's own special devising. The high tide of incivility in the early '60s ebbed; less extreme and more independent council members came in, and since then the clashes have been subtler.

In the early 1970s, voters struck down two intensive development projects. Palo Alto Medical Clinic sought to build a high-rise hospital, intending in part to repair the Palo Alto-Stanford Hospital cooperation that had ruptured when Stanford took over the hospital. Professorville joined residentialists in opposing it, and the Clinic plan lost. "Superblock," a massive downtown development proposal, was also rejected. The city reached build-out — open space for subdivisions or large multiple-unit construction had been used up. Battles raged over how to balance housing and jobs better, but scant land was left to work with.

One issue did unite a solid local majority in the '60s: the fight for open housing and against racial or color bias in real estate sales. After that, scattered instances of discrimination cropped up but fair housing held its place as Palo Alto's ideal.

Environmentalism, first noted in the late '60s, pervaded local discourse after Earth Day 1970 sounded widely heard alarms. It mixed with strident opposition to the war in Vietnam to produce street politics and angry confrontations with authorities. Fears of wanton property destruction and violence from both left and right ran rampant.

With the city government based downtown again, the Newell-Embarcadero building took on a new role as a cultural center, symbolizing the devotion of Palo Altans to the creative and per-

forming arts. The old police and fire station at 450 Bryant became a senior center. Meanwhile, the city staff took up team management.

Barron Park, the neighborhood that stayed independent the longest, submitted to annexation by Palo Alto in 1975, after exacting official promises not to spoil its semi-rural quality. Even this population gain could not keep the 1980 census total level with that of 1970. Lifestyle changes, dispersal of the Baby Boom generation, housing communes and other factors had lowered the demographic average. Scandals tainted a city-sponsored center designed to curb drug usage, and residentialists took the punishment at the polls. It didn't last; by 1980 residentialism stood clearly dominant, if muted.

Palo Alto had strongly supported woman's suffrage in state elections in 1896 and 1911. Although a few women had held Palo Alto offices from 1918 on, female political participation blossomed in the '80s, and by mid-decade women held four of the nine council seats. In Santa Clara County's Fifth District, which includes Palo Alto, the office of county supervisor has, since 1974, been filled by three women in succession.

Environmentalism doomed Palo Alto Yacht Harbor, because there was no good place for dumping dredging spoils, and advocates of restoring salt marshes prevailed. A 1980 vote to close the harbor withstood a reconsideration demanded by boaters. Attempts to oust Palo Alto Airport, a base for small business craft as well as light planes, so far have failed.

Declining school enrollment forced wrenching decisions on the Board of Education as to which schools to close. Ultimately a rebellion by school district voters led to cancellation of a planned second high school closure, and secured the reopening of the previously closed Jordan Middle School. In late 1987, city and school district leaders combined to sponsor a utility tax to finance city programs under leases at some abandoned schools.

In another city, many tracts of relatively low-cost homes built in the '50s might have been expected to decay in 40 years and invite massive redevelopment. No such thing has occurred in Palo Alto, one of the first California cities hit by near-hyperinflation of housing prices. Homes built in 1950 for less than $10,000 sold in the 1980s for $300,000 or more. Indeed, most of those modest homes have been enlarged and improved. Throughout the city, some remodelings from the late 1980s on grew so massive that neighbors objected and officials rewrote the rules to limit expansion possibilities.

The mills of government, now involving a sizeable bureaucracy as well as ardent citizen participants, grind finer than ever. But the tone of local politics has quieted. An influx of Asian immigrants may play a part in the relative stillness, for most of these newcomers have yet to master the assertiveness common in city politics. Indeed, Palo Alto's melting-pot aspect, existent during most of the past in limited batches, is more evident than ever, markedly in the schools. It is fed by the global scope of numerous local industries, and by foreign students studying at Stanford. Also, the agglomeration of people of professional background has meant fewer class problems.

In several downtown census tracts the proportions of elderly and very elderly residents run to record highs. This phenomenon has prompted programs for care and recreation arranged by a Senior Coordinating Council. Experiments in retirement housing, with varied intensities of medical care, are thriving, notably at Channing House, Lytton Gardens, Adlai Stevenson House and Webster House.

Palo Altans have spun off hundreds of special-purpose groups, some of them charities, others of vocational or social nature. Charitable foundations set up by entrepreneurial superstars have often provided funds to seed new programs or sustain ongoing ones. Work by volunteers has given life to many such activities, but now some observers fear volunteerism may shrink even more under the economic pressures that tend to make two-salary couples the modern married norm. Palo Alto is a favored address for association head-

quarters representing myriad fields. It has been home base, too, for idealistic activism by groups such as Beyond War and Earth Day 1990, successors in spirit to the causes of early Stanford presidents — David Starr Jordan's world peace promotion and Ray Lyman Wilbur's Save-the-Redwoods League leadership. Although a chrysanthemum growers association finally decamped from Palo Alto, a cryonics society has moved in.

Growth pressures continue. Near the end of Palo Alto's first century there have been sizeable enlargements of Stanford's medical and science facilities, and of the federally funded Stanford Linear Accelerator Center. Multi-story condominium and apartment construction has lifted the profile of housing near business districts. Hewlett-Packard, grown from the garage of '39 to a $17 billion-a-year global giant, may not much further expand its Palo Alto headquarters and research operations, but high-tech startups still look for research or production space in Stanford's shadow, near the economic sustenance of the region's venture capitalists.

Whether these pressures will burst through residentialist walls, perhaps hurled by shifting economic tides, remains to be tested. City leaders have talked of trying regional government and in a few cases have built joint projects, for example, a tri-city tertiary wastewater treatment plant. Yet a countertradition of independence has persisted since the days when Palo Alto spurned county services and had its own health officer and its own assessor. Ceding of significant local control is not likely to come easily.

Readers who envision progress as an evolutionary spiral that periodically circles around to revisit issues, and sometimes needs new lift to regain or maintain its upward thrust, will find ample evidence in Palo Alto-Stanford history to support their view.

Mrs. Stanford's belief that the founders' munificent endowment would do the job forever soon became a hindrance. Ultimately the university resorted to unprecedented fund-raising efforts

— and hiked tuition to stratospheric levels — to fulfill its mission.

Palo Alto's municipal functions were operated largely by volunteers for a long time, yet eventually officials with extensive expertise took charge. The civic infrastructure has periodically been rebuilt, just as University Avenue has been restyled.

Industry has burgeoned and then changed character, spinning off production and focusing research, development and headquarters functions in Palo Alto. Ample tax proceeds that once encouraged a luxurious municipal style are currently stretched thin.

Eras of boom, then consolidation — or retrenchment — repeat. Growth has been brought into a keenly watched tension with the need to preserve a livable environment. Limits may seem to have been reached, but there are those who believe they can be extended — and push for it.

The processes of change are in constant flux, and as crises build, the need to reinvent, or at least redirect, a locality's major institutions recurs.

Whatever the future, the community can expect to go on enjoying a climate that has often moved plain-spoken people to poetic praise.

Fr. Francisco Palou, in his diary of the 1774 expedition, wrote of the environs of *El Palo Alto*:

To both the commander and me the camp site appeared suitable for a mission. ... It enjoys many and good lands for raising crops, pasturage, firewood, timber and water. Indeed, from this arroyo (San Francisquito Creek), although it flows very deep, since it comes down from the canyons of the high range, its water might easily be conducted for the irrigation of this plain.

Palou overestimated the water supply, which is why the mission site was shifted to Santa Clara. But Leland Stanford, who understood the water problem, stated:

It is an exceedingly healthy locality. ... I think the climate cannot be excelled anywhere in California. The place feels the influence of the ocean breeze, but never so strongly as to make it disagreeable. The trees all grow up straight; they do not show the steady direction of the wind as they do in San Francisco.

Palo Alto has been built in response to a vision, even if its reality proved to be less than the dreamer foresaw — and far more. One might reasonably expect practical visionaries to pass this way again, and to realize new dreams capable of enhancing the old.

	POPULATION — U.S. Census	
1890	Mayfield Township	1,100
1900	Palo Alto	1,658
1905	Mayfield *(estimate)*	1,500
1910	Palo Alto	4,486
	Mayfield	1,041
1920	Palo Alto	5,900
	Mayfield	1,127
1925	Palo Alto	9,199
	(local count)	
	Mayfield	1,700
	(pre-election estimate)	
1930	Palo Alto	13,652
	(after merger)	
1940	Palo Alto	16,774
1950	Palo Alto	25,475
1953	Palo Alto	33,753
	(special census)	
1958	Palo Alto	48,003
	(special census)	
1960	Palo Alto	52,287
1970	Palo Alto	56,040
1980	Palo Alto	55,225
1990	Palo Alto	55,900

Lights made this Palo Alto sign over University Avenue, erected in 1911, visible from trains passing at night.

Embarcadero Road in 1900.

2

The Beginnings

"We followed the [San Andreas] valley till we came to the end of it. Here terminate the hills which we have had on our left hand between us and the estuary. At the same time the mountains on the right hand... suddenly turn to the east, and enclose the estuary in a spacious valley. We traveled a little farther in the same direction, and in a short time halted on the bank of an arroyo [San Francisquito Creek] whose waters descend from the mountains and run precipitously to this estuary."

— Fr. Juan Crespi's diary entry for November 6, 1769

The foothills, the bay, the broad valley, the creek, the mountains — these terrain features had marked the Palo Alto area for untold centuries before the first Europeans came. Crespi, in his explorer's journal, said it plainly, excluding only the redwoods near which Don Gaspar de Portola's party camped.

More romantic descriptions flowed later from the pens of relatively new settlers charmed by the place. Few have exceeded Orrin Leslie Elliott, Stanford's first registrar, in lyric appreciation. In *Stanford University and Thereabouts*, 1896, coauthored by O.V. Eaton, Elliott wrote:

The Santa Clara Valley has long been famous for its beauty, fertility and the excellence of its climate. Easy of access to the metropolis of the coast, free from the rigors of Eastern winters and the extremes of Eastern summers, sheltered from the fogs and harsh winds of the coast, and from the intense summer heat of the inland valleys, with a rare ocean quality always in the air, the students at Palo Alto have one long succession of springtime and autumn.

The buildings are placed in the broad plain sloping up from the bay to the foothills. ... The ground is high enough so that glimpses of the water are seen through the trees...

Just behind are the foothills, covered with a straggling growth of live oak, and beyond again are the mountains whose heights look down upon the Pacific over long stretches of redwood forest.

Later, taking his readers on a tour of the seasons, Elliott notes how late on hot afternoons "a gentle breeze insinuates itself... and crisp, bracing evenings force porch loiterers quickly indoors. The nights are cold and damp, and an occasional fog creeps up from the bay to defy the sun for an hour or two in the morning."

Spring unrolls vast carpets of wildflowers through the foothills. In May, after the rains wear out, "trade winds may rise by afternoon to an irritating intensity" — irritating, at least, to a bicycling enthusiast, which he was.

He neglected to mention the dry-season dust and wet-season mud, along with the ubiquitous poison oak, fleas and mosquitoes.

Others have recorded more prosaic facts. Palo Alto is at approximately 37 degrees 27 minutes North latitude and 122 degrees 8 minutes West longitude. The climate is Mediterranean subtropical, of the coastal Mediterranean subgroup, with advection fogs.

Geologically, the area is an elongated trough, the largest structural depression of the Coast

Range. Elevations range from sea level to 2,600 feet. The San Andreas Fault zone, at 300-foot to 800-foot elevations, separates the foothills from the mountains, trending northwestward. The foothills climb from 150 to 900 feet.

On the 21.6 square mile alluvial fan of the San Francisquito, rainfall varies from 14 inches in the flatlands to 42 inches near the Skyline. December, January, February, March and November are the rainiest months, in that order, with Palo Alto's official long-term precipitation average near 15.34 inches. Mean monthly temperatures vary from 46.5 degrees Fahrenheit in January to 65.8 degrees in July.

Palo Alto native Herbert Dengler, relying on plant zone compendiums and his own knowledge as a Jasper Ridge guide, has listed nine distinct San Francisquito Creek watershed zones of flora:

SALT MARSH — *cord grass, pickleweed, saltbrush, salt grass, sea lavender.*

FRESHWATER MARSH — *cattails, tules, knotweed, rushes and sedges.*

GRASSLAND — *a complex of introduced annuals such as the dominant Mediterranean wild oat, brome grasses and forbs. There are many native annual and perennial grasses and forbs.*

OAK WOODLAND — *live oaks, valley oaks and blue oaks are the principal forms in a mosaic including openings of valley grassland, a woodland savanna with a shrub understory.*

FOOTHILL WOODLAND — *oaks, laurel or bay, madrone, shrubs, vines and grasses. The tree canopy is quite closed.*

CHAPARRAL — *chamise, manzanitas, buckbrush, buckthorn and scrub oaks.*

MIXED EVERGREEN FOREST — *douglas fir, oaks, tanoak, madrone, laurel or bay, coffeeberry, hazel, toyon, shrubs, grasses and ferns.*

REDWOOD FOREST — *coast redwood, douglas fir, tanoak, hazel, huckleberry, low ground cover and ferns.*

RIPARIAN WOODLAND — *willows, cottonwoods,*

alder, maple, boxelder, creek dogwood and a dense shrub understory.

So it was and had long been, in far more profusion than today, when the white man came.

Prehistoric Settlers of California

Eons earlier, as the glaciers of the Ice Age receded, a trickle of Asians migrated across the Bering Sea land-bridge between Siberia and Alaska. Perhaps 20,000 years ago, and certainly at least 5,000 to 10,000 years ago, settlements appeared in California, where wooded lands and wildlife abounded. In the late 1700s when the Spaniards arrived, California's Indian population numbered 250,000 to 300,000.

San Francisco Bay's shoreline afforded an alluring habitat. In the mid-1770s, scholars estimate, 23,000 Indians lived near the coast between San Francisco and San Luis Obispo. Among them were about 8,000 dwelling near San Francisco Bay in scattered camps and villages of 100 to 200 inhabitants. Each self-sufficient village had limited contact with neighboring groups but stayed secure enough to avoid major conflict.

The bay supplied these Indians much as the Great Plains nurtured the bison hunters, and forests and rivers served tribes of the North and East. Tides and runoff from many streams flowed into marshes bordering the bay. With much open countryside, travel was simple and everything needed lay within a day's walk. For gathering peoples who kept busy, honed their skills, lived frugally and ate omnivorously, the bay region proved a generally healthful environment.

Yet their way of life wasn't easy, for hunger and hard times loomed as constant threats. Even so, a village could recover rapidly after a setback by harvesting a heavy crop of acorns and catching migrating waterfowl from the teeming flocks that stopped to feed in the bay marshlands. Thus favored by nature, a way of life dating back five millennia or more survived little changed until the late 18th century. To European observers, the Indian lifestyle looked placid and indolent; in

Drawing depicts a tule boat used by Ohlone Indians to hunt in the marshes and sloughs of San Francisco Bay.

FROM *THE OHLONE WAY* BY MALCOLM MARGOLIN/ DRAWING BY MICHAEL HARNEY

actuality, it happily matched human needs and environmental providence.

The Ohlone Lifestyle

The Ohlone Indians dwelling in the Palo Alto area were called the Costañoans by early Spanish diarists. Other small tribes lived nearby. Their appearance and indigenous ways are known mainly from descriptions by explorers and missionaries, and from modern study of human remains and artifacts recovered from village sites 2,000 to 4,000 years old.

Mounds rising several feet above ground level contained the bones. Forty such mounds have been discovered in the vicinity of Palo Alto, although few of them received thorough scientific explorations before roads or buildings covered them. (One village site is marked by a plaque near Webster and Middlefield.) Stanford University is studying archaeological sites near San Francisquito Creek off Sand Hill Road, and, in response to requests from present-day Native American groups, has agreed to return the remains of hundreds of Ohlones for reburial.

The Ohlones had dark brown skin and eyes and straight black hair. They stood moderately tall. One early observer's sketches show them as sturdy people with rounded features. Most of their men wore beards, a diarist noted, and they were very friendly.

Gathering and preparing food occupied much of their time. From the bay, they harvested plants, birds and fish. Early travelers told of seeing the sky darkened by flocks of ducks and geese, the bay carpeted by floating waterfowl, the marshes raucous with noisy feeding birds. Shellfish thrived in the shallows, and the salmon runs were prodigious. Afloat on reed canoes or rafts, the Ohlones caught their prey with nets. Stranded seals and whales provided rare treats.

On drier land, Ohlone boys and men hunted rodents, rabbits, birds, deer and elk with light bows and stone-headed arrows. They gathered bird eggs, snakes, lizards and insects and their larvae. A staple of their diet was the nutritious acorn, collected from the many oaks that made the valley seem a park to early visitors. Ohlone women ground acorn meal in stone mortars, then leached it and cooked a gruel. The acorn had a special virtue: storability.

Europeans Begin to Explore

Soon after Hernando Cortes conquered Mexico in 1519, Spain began to explore the land to the north.

Sailing for Cortes, Francisco de Ulloa reached the head of the Gulf of California in 1539. Then and for years afterward California was believed to be an island, but de Ulloa was convinced it was not. In 1542, Juan Rodriguez Cabrillo, following the coastline, sailed as far north as San Francisco Bay but missed discovering it. English sea captain Sir Francis Drake landed on the California coast in 1579, and in 1602, Sebastian Vizcaino discovered Monterey Bay. From 1565 onward, Spanish galleons sailed along California's coast on voyages between Manila and Mexico.

Although California had been fabled as a land of treasure, it was political danger that prompted Spain to colonize it. In the late 18th century, rival empires threatened Spain's claim to western North America. England won Canada from France in 1763. Previously, Vitus Bering, exploring for Peter the Great of Russia, had sailed along the Alaska mainland. Upon his return to Russia, Bering adver-

tised prospects for fur trading, and soon adventurers had occupied the Aleutian Islands and begun probing south. By 1765, New Spain was in jeopardy, and King Carlos III moved to reorganize the colonial government.

The Portola Expedition

Among the new leaders Carlos appointed was the energetic Jose de Galvez. Ordered to repel invaders, Galvez quickly launched colonizing expeditions from Mexico. In 1769, Gaspar de Portola led a party — part military, part missionary — to what is now San Francisco. With him were Franciscan Fathers Junipero Serra and Juan Crespi; 40 well-armed soldiers, including Sgt. Jose Francisco de Ortega; and a number of Christianized Indians.

After establishing the first mission at San Diego, and leaving Serra there, Portola marched on July 14 with Fathers Francisco Gomez and Crespi. They looked for Monterey Bay, described

PENINSULA TIMES TRIBUNE FILE PHOTO

Painting depicts Portola party's discovery of San Francisco Bay on November 4, 1769. The group later camped alongside San Francisquito Creek near El Palo Alto.

long before by Vizcaino, but they failed to recognize it. Wearily they struggled northward throughout October. Looking west from the hills, they saw the outer San Francisco Bay — the Gulf of the Farallones. From its configuration they knew they had missed Monterey Bay, and resolved to retrace their steps. But first they paused to rest, and Portola sent out a scouting party under Ortega's command. During the next two days, Ortega and his men saw San Francisco Bay proper, the Peninsula grasslands and smoke from the fires in many Indian villages.

Camping by a Tall Redwood

On November 4, Portola's main group crossed Sweeney Ridge near present-day San Bruno, affording all a view of the bay, and traveled down the Peninsula. From November 6-11, the expedition camped along San Francisquito Creek at a site marked by a tall redwood tree. Early references to this landmark fail to mention the twin trunk that *El Palo Alto* was later shown to have had until it fell during a winter storm in the 1880s. For many years the surviving tree has been the living symbol of the City of Palo Alto, and remains so today.

From the camp, Ortega reconnoitered south, then up the east side of the bay to Niles, where hostile Indians forced his squad back by setting a grassfire. Portola decided to end the search for the Monterey harbor, and the expedition retraced its route up the Peninsula and across to the ocean. Going down the coast, they again failed to recognize Monterey.

Others soon followed Portola. His lieutenant, Pedro Fages, explored the Santa Clara Valley and the south bay in 1770. In 1774, Father Francisco Palou set up a cross at *El Palo Alto* to mark a possible mission site. Two years later, Juan Bautista de Anza and Father Pedro Font, accompanied by Lt. Jose Joaquin Moraga, mapped the area. Font described and sketched a redwood with one trunk (an anomaly never explained), estimating its height as over 135 feet and its girth as over 15 feet. Because the creek often dried up in summer, Font and De Anza rejected Palou's mission site choice

PALO ALTO HISTORICAL ASSOCIATION/I.W.FABER

El Palo Alto was a twin redwood until one trunk fell in a winter storm in the 1880s. This view is looking south from the San Mateo County side of San Francisquito Creek toward present-day Palo Alto.

as flawed. Instead they founded the Mission de Santa Clara de Asis, 15 miles to the southeast, on January 12, 1777. Just across the Guadalupe River from the mission, they established the Pueblo of San Jose, which became the center of colonization in the Santa Clara Valley. The mission era had begun, and, until the mid-1800s, first Spain and then Mexico ruled what now is Palo Alto.

The Mission Era

The Franciscan fathers intended to convert the Indians to Christianity and teach them the manners, morals and crafts of Europe so they could settle on the land and become loyal subjects of the church and the Spanish crown. Despite the padres' best intentions, the venture came to grief. Although the Indian men were trained in farming and construction skills, they did not become self-sufficient. The women found the European household arts tedious and useless, and the work of the garden and poultry yard sheer drudgery. Once in a while the mission Indians were allowed to scatter into the countryside to gather food, or to stage their dances and game ceremonies, but it was not enough to preserve their culture. Their conversion to Christianity remained superficial.

Disease also made rapid inroads in the Indian population, and in fewer than 70 years between 1769 and 1836, Costañoan culture and society simply perished. The Indians lacked the organization and arms to oppose Spanish force, and could not escape removal to the missions at Santa Clara and San Francisco. There, with as many as twenty tribes and languages jumbled together, their ways of life and thought shattered under rod and rule. When mission life ended, the surviving Ohlones were cast out to fend for themselves. Western systems of land control, farming and commerce, reinforced by American hostility and contempt for the indigenous people, left no chance that the hunter-gatherers could restore their communal life.

When control of the missions passed from church to civil authorities between 1834 and 1836, most of the surviving Indians drifted to ranchos or to town fringes, homeless as well as landless. In the Palo Alto area, some lived on sheep and cattle ranches. Southeast of Palo Alto, three villages specializing in cloth manufacturing existed for a time under Chief Lopez Ynigo.

Under Mexican Rule

Mexico's new independent government ended the Spanish policy of retaining land ownership by the crown, and instead granted land to citizens outright. Even so, settlement and development proceeded slowly. By 1848, over 800 California land grants had been recorded, but most came after 1840, and nearly half were claimed by Americans and Europeans swarming into the area. Although the law permitted Indians to seek grants, few did. Why? Because land ownership was alien to their tradition.

California ranchos supported the first cattle kings. Thousands of longhorns roamed their extensive reaches. Behind the pride, beauty and wealth so often depicted as the rancho scene were the smelly cartloads of hides and tallow that rolled off to ports. Yet for a few decades, the larger, more prosperous ranchos exuded the charm and color that modern residents view as the zenith of a romantic past.

On February 2, 1848, in settling a two-year war, Mexico ceded Alta California to the United States. Another epochal event had occurred just nine days earlier: the discovery of gold in the Sierra Nevada foothills. This attracted a rush of adventurers and settlers, some of whom soon surged beyond the Mother Lode and San Francisco to the Peninsula's oak-studded plains.

In absorbing California after the Mexican War, the United States promised to guarantee existing land rights. The Land Commission formed in 1851 to settle confused, conflicting, or poorly documented claims approved roughly 75 percent of these claims. However, many claim awards were contested in court, and a time lag of 30 years until final settlement was not unusual.

Five Land-Grant Ranchos

Five Mexican land grants underlie Palo Alto's history: Rancho Rinconada del Arroyo de San Francisquito, Rancho Rincon de San Francisquito, Rancho San Francisquito, Rancho Corte de Madera, and Rancho La Purisima Concepción. (See map.)

Rancho Rinconada del Arroyo de San Francisquito, more than 2,200 acres in all, included the original Palo Alto town site. *El Palo Alto* stood at its northwest corner; a point between today's Stanford Stadium and College Terrace marked its southwest corner. It ran along San Francisquito Creek to the bay, then south to about where the projected line of Colorado Avenue intersects Bayshore Freeway. From there the boundary ran southwest, crossing El Camino Real at about Park Boulevard.

San Jose-born Don Rafael Soto, whose father came with De Anza's 1776 party, first held this

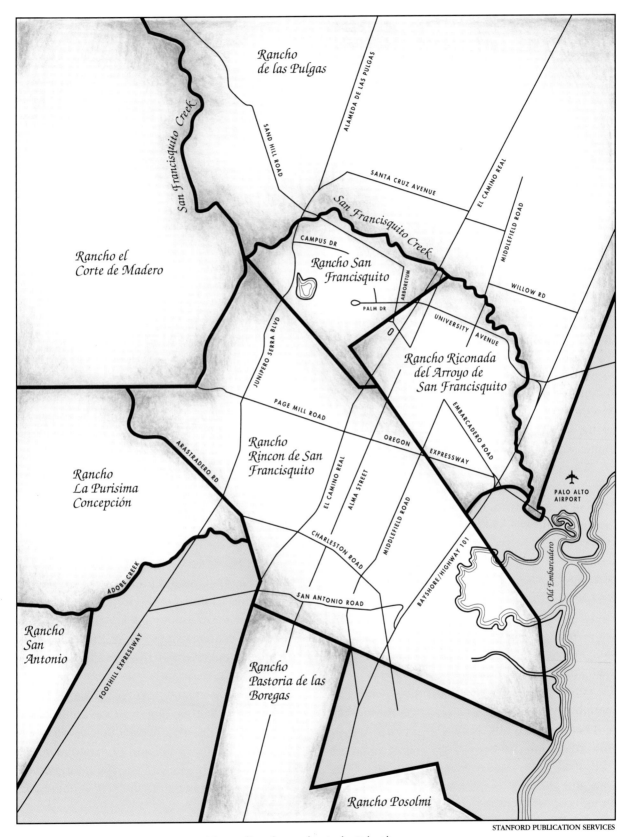

Map outlines the ranchos in the Palo Alto area.

17

grant. He settled beside the creek near the present University Avenue crossing, and established a landing for loading and unloading small boats near the present Newell Road crossing. Wagon roads carved by ox carts hauling lumber and hides to this embarcadero followed generally the modern Embarcadero and Newell roads. Soto's widow received the grant in 1841, and one daughter, Dolores, acquired a 120-acre portion of the rancho near where Newell and Hamilton Avenue now intersect. Another daughter, Maria Luisa, took possession of the rest of the rancho. Maria married John Copinger, a former British naval officer, who soon obtained a grant, Rancho Cañada de Raymundo, on the north side of the creek. He and Maria lived there until his death in 1847, after which she returned to the Soto home. In January 1850, she married Captain John Lucas Greer, an Irish seafarer.

The Greer and Seale Families

Almost immediately, Captain and Mrs. Greer had to defend their claim to the Soto rancho, for it had been disqualified by the Land Commission. They sought the help of Thomas Seale, an Irishman who, with his brother Henry, arrived in San Francisco in 1850 and set up a road grading business. The Seales wanted land in and around Palo Alto for its high-quality hay — to feed their work horses. The Greers pledged half of the land to Thomas Seale, provided he could secure title to the entire rancho for them. Thomas Seale conveyed this pledge in 1861 to his brother, whose legal effort succeeded in 1865. Henry W. Seale's reward was title to some 1,400 acres — what is now essentially central Palo Alto.

While litigation clouded the Soto grant, the Greers moved to Rancho Cañada de Raymundo and became founders and leaders of Greersburg, now Woodside. Twenty years later they returned to the Palo Alto rancho. When their home near Alma Street and Churchill Avenue was threatened by a claim that it infringed on neighboring property, they moved the 22-room, hotel-like house over the railroad tracks to the northwest side of

Embarcadero Road, across from today's Palo Alto High School. With other Greer buildings, it stood there until 1952 when the land was leased for Town & Country Village Shopping Center. Site-clearing operations demolished the main house, but a smaller Greer house still stands at 51 Encina Avenue. Meanwhile, Joseph Greer, Soto's grandson, built a home in 1905 that remains intact at 1517 Louisa Court.

Secundino Robles' Rancho "Santa Rita"

Rancho Rincon de San Francisquito, widely known by the nickname Rancho Santa Rita, adjoined the Greer property, extending south to San Antonio Creek (now called Adobe Creek). Covering 8,500 acres, it swept from the foothills to the bay. Joseph Peña, a veteran soldier from the San Francisco Presidio, acquired grazing rights to the land in 1822, and title to the rancho in 1841. In 1847, Peña sold it to Don Secundino Robles and his brother, Teodoro. Don Secundino, a native of Santa Cruz, built a two-story hacienda (at a site marked approximately by a plaque at Alma Street and Ferne Avenue). It served as the center of the region's rancho high life until the mid-1850s, providing a place for dances, to the delight of the hospitable family's 29 children, and a ring for bullfights and bearbaitings. Then the land was sold off. With some of it, Elisha O. Crosby developed Mayfield Farm. Jeremiah Clarke of San Francisco bought another portion, and also acquired the nearby Soto Landing at the foot of Embarcadero Road. Today's Colorado Avenue follows the private road Clarke built to connect his home with what became known as Clarke's Landing.

Squatters Occupy Rancho San Francisquito

Rancho San Francisquito, 1,500 acres on higher ground, covered what is now the Stanford University campus, golf course, medical center and shopping center. Juan Bautista Alvarado, governor of Mexican California in 1836-42, rewarded one of his supporters, Antonio (or Antonino) Buelna, with the grant. Buelna's adobe house, called El Paso del Arroyo, stood where Sand Hill Road

Captain John Greer, an Irish seafarer, arrived in San Francisco Bay in 1849.

The Greer family home at the corner of El Camino Real and Embarcadero Road was razed in 1952 to make way for the Town & Country Village Shopping Center.

Seale family and friends posing in front of their residence in the late 1880s. The home was located near the intersection of Byron Street and California Avenue.

PALO ALTO HISTORICAL ASSOCIATION/W.H. MYRICK

During the 1850s and '60s the Robles family adobe was a center of social life in the Santa Clara Valley. A plaque at Alma Street and Ferne Avenue marks the approximate site.

crosses San Francisquito Creek. After Buelna's death in 1853, squatters moved onto the rancho, and for a time huge ovens erected there converted magnificent oak trees to charcoal for the San Francisco markets. Francisco Casanueva, a San Francisco lawyer, attempted — mostly by deceit — to obtain the land. In 1864, thwarted by squatter resistance, Casanueva sold his claim to George Gordon, a San Francisco merchant, for $500. Gordon then quieted the claims and counterclaims. It was Gordon's "Mayfield Grange" property that Leland Stanford acquired in 1876 for his Palo Alto Stock Farm.

At that time much of the Palo Alto foothills was part of Rancho Corte de Madera — 3,500 acres including such lands as Stanford's Jasper Ridge, Searsville Lake, Westridge, Ladera and Alpine Hills. In 1833, Governor Jose Figueroa granted this rancho to Domingo Peralta and Maximo Martinez. Martinez bought out Peralta and enlarged the rancho sixfold. After many changes of ownership through family descendants and buyers, 2,000 acres of the property was purchased by Dr. Russel V.A. Lee in 1941, and eventually became the city's Foothills Park.

In the 1850s, Felix Buelna, a nephew of Antonio Buelna, built a tavern on two acres of land along Alpine Road. Don Jesus Ramos leased it in 1867. Today a landmark plaque identifies the Alpine Beer Garden, also known as Rossotti's, as

the oldest tavern in continuous operation in California. Mexican-Americans ate, drank, gambled and met there in the 19th century, and Stanford students adopted it as a favorite hangout during the 20th century.

Rancho Purisima Concepción was granted in 1840 to two Indians, Jose Gorgonio and Jose Ramon, who had been living on the land in a small house they built. A few years later they sold the 4,400-acre property to Juana Briones de Miranda, who had lived for a time in San Francisco after separating from her husband, Apolinario Miranda, a Presidio soldier. Senora Miranda had gained a reputation as a nurse and midwife — and a mother, for though their marriage was unhappy, the couple had seven children. Moving to her cattle ranch and its dwelling, she ministered to sick ranchers and Indians alike. Two of her daughters married sons of Juan Prado Mesa, owner of San Antonio Rancho to the south (the site of present-day Los Altos) and former commandante of the Monterey Presidio. One of the couples, Ramon and Manuela Mesa, built a home where Alta Mesa Cemetery is now, but later moved to Mayfield so that their children could attend its school. Juana Briones de Miranda died in Mayfield in 1890, and two of her grandsons continued to live there until the mid-20th century.

Ranching Gives Way to Farming

The rancho era ended in the 1860s. Its free-roaming cattle were not compatible with the thickening settlement, and rancho owners who found they needed cash sold land to wheat farmers and other settlers.

For the next two decades, Palo Alto's hay and grain fields and oak-studded flatlands lay quiescent between the slow-growing villages of Menlo Park and Mayfield. Mountain View, a small farming town, lay farther southeast. However, an enterprise begun in 1861, the building of the San Jose & San Francisco Railroad (later absorbed by the Southern Pacific Company), gradually opened a new era. Tracks from San Francisco to Mayfield were completed in 1863, and well-to-do San

Francisco families began to think of real estate investments and country estates in the mid-Peninsula oak groves.

A curious episode in the 1870s suggests the area's ripeness for development by those with capital, know-how, energy and vision. A Frenchman who called himself Peter Coutts arrived in 1874 with his invalid wife, two children and Eugenie Clogenson, their governess. Later his true identity as Jean-Baptiste Paulin Caperon was revealed; a liberal banker and publisher, he had fled France to escape harassment for his opposition to the government, using the name and papers of a cousin's dead Swiss husband.

Coutts bought land near Mayfield (now occupied in part by Stanford's Escondido Village), calling it Ayreshire Farms. He imported fine Ayreshire cattle; built his family a home and library on Escondido Road; laid out irrigation dams, pools and conduits; and erected a mysterious brick tower that still stands beside Old Page Mill Road.

Then Coutts — or Caperon — left suddenly in 1880 with his family. Several generations of Palo Altans gossiped about the mysterious Frenchman before journalists and historians revealed who he was and why he had departed so abruptly: There had been a change in the political situation in Paris in his favor.

The change proved to be a windfall for Governor Leland Stanford, who had purchased the Gordon estate, formerly Rancho San Francisquito, in 1876. Stanford was able to add the Coutts property at a distress sale price, disposing of the cattle but keeping the racehorses. He had bought other adjacent tracts previously, and the Coutts purchase increased his holdings to more than 8,000 acres in all. Within a few years he had become the major landowner in a locale that was sometimes called San Francisquito, sometimes Palo Alto. The only land he could not acquire, now called College Terrace, belonged to two Mayfield farmer-settlers who held out for a high price.

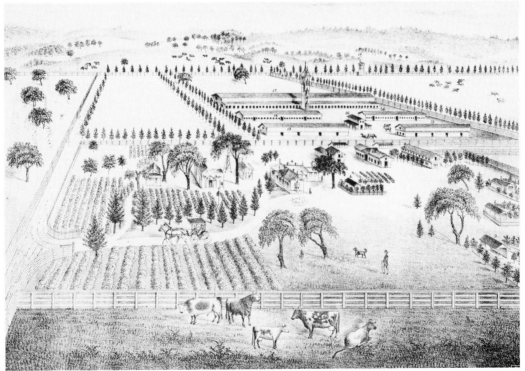

FROM THOMPSON & WEST'S 1876 HISTORICAL ATLAS OF SANTA CLARA COUNTY

A drawing of Ayreshire Farms, the home of Peter Coutts whose brief stay in Santa Clara County created mystery and legend. The property was later purchased by Leland Stanford to expand his Palo Alto Stock Farm.

Mayfield's University Brass Band at Dornberger's Grove on July 4, 1889.

3

Neighboring Mayfield

*Weekly newspaper editor T.B. Scott blasted former Mayfield
residents who had "taken a roost with the Pallyalteans down
by the creek" as "traitorous and disloyal."*

Mayfield was an established community, about 40 years old, in the early 1890s when the village of Palo Alto began to take shape less than two miles to the north. Its citizens looked on with amusement as the upstart town hung its fortune on the uncertain success of the new university on the Stanford stock farm, miles from any large population center. Palo Alto's move in 1894 to form its own government seemed preposterous. Many Mayfield residents doubted that the new town or the university would thrive, or even survive.

In the 1890s Mayfield was a maturing village. Like many other small Bay Area communities, it lay somewhat isolated, dependent on farming, lumbering and the construction at Stanford, with a social life bound up with its schools, churches and fraternal lodges. Its saloons also played a role, one that changed the community's future.

The first settlers who became identified with Mayfield bridged the years from the rancho era's ending to the town's first stirrings.

Jesus Ramos, who at age 19 came to California from his native Mexico to hunt for gold, settled early in what later became Mayfield. He worked for Don Secundino Robles at Rancho Rincon de San Francisquito and remained as Robles' foreman for several years. In 1883, Ramos bought two acres of land on Page Mill Road, which he farmed for the rest of his life. The street named Ramos Way marks approximately where his home was located. Don Jesus Ramos Park in South Palo Alto is named in his honor.

Mayfield Farm

In 1853, Elisha Crosby, a former New York lawyer living in San Jose, bought 250 acres of the Rancho Rincon de San Francisquito from the Robles brothers for $2,000. He called his land Mayfield Farm.

Mayfield began as a town in 1853 about a mile north of the Mayfield Farm. Opinions differ as to the exact location where James Otterson, a 48-year-old Scotch-Canadian, built a public house, but no one doubts that it was near where California Avenue and El Camino Real now intersect. Soon called "Uncle Jim's Cabin," it has been described as an inn, a saloon and a stage stop. Two major roads crossing nearby made the location choice: one, the newly surveyed stage road between San Francisco and San Jose; the other, Searsville Road, which ran down from the redwood lumber camps to the town of Searsville and then across the flatlands to the stage route.

By 1855, Uncle Jim's Cabin was serving as a mail stop with Otterson as postmaster. When the Post Office Department asked for a name for the postal stop, Otterson is credited with suggesting Mayfield, most likely after the Mayfield Farm. Not many months later, Mayfield began to look like a village with a blacksmith shop, a general store, a butcher shop, a cobbler's shop and its first school.

From Pioneer to Suffragist

Of all Mayfield's colorful pioneers, Sarah Armstrong Montgomery Green Wallis lived perhaps the most fascinating life. Born in 1825 in Ohio, she moved as a girl to the fringe of Indian Territory

James Otterson built "Uncle Jim's Cabin" in 1853 as the first building in the new community of Mayfield. Later enlarged, as shown here, it stood near the present intersection of California Avenue and El Camino Real.

in Missouri. After marrying Allen Montgomery, a gunsmith, she joined Elisha Stephens' 1844 party. Their wagon train reached the Sierra Nevadas as snow began, and she rode a horse across the mountains, settling on the American River near Sutter's Fort. At a remote cabin, she gave California's first quilting bee in 1846. Wintering over at the fort in 1846-47 while her husband joined American revolutionists in Los Angeles, she learned to read by listening as a woman taught a 5-year-old. After the Montgomerys moved to San Francisco, her husband abandoned her, though rumor had him lost at sea.

As a respectable "widow," Sarah rented rooms, fed boarders and washed and sewed clothes to survive. In 1849 she and Talbot H. Green were married. He was campaigning in 1851 for mayor of San Francisco when a newspaper accused him

of bank fraud and having abandoned a family in Pennsylvania. Vowing to clear his name, Green departed, leaving Sarah — 6 1/2 months pregnant — with an allowance. In 1855, he came into some money and agreed to "deal liberally" with Sarah.

The "Wedding Cake House"

She had sought a divorce and in mid-1854 married Joseph S. Wallis, a clerk whom she encouraged to study law. Wallis adopted Green's son. Sarah sued to recover more than $10,000 Elisha Crosby owed her, and in 1856 received title to Crosby's 250-acre Mayfield Farm. The couple moved there, built an elaborate home often called the "wedding cake house" and raised five children.

Wallis was elected justice of the peace in 1857 and state senator in 1862. Later he served as associate judge of the county's Court of Sessions.

*The "Wedding Cake" residence built by Sarah Wallis and her husband in 1856 was later owned by Edward Barron,
who enlarged it and whose name became associated with the surrounding neighborhood, Barron Park.*

Sarah Wallis became the founding president of the Mayfield Woman's Suffrage Association in 1870 and The California State Woman Suffrage Educational Association in 1873. The Wallises entertained suffragist leaders Susan B. Anthony and Elizabeth Cady Stanton in 1871 and President U.S. Grant in 1877.

In 1857, a man destined to become Mayfield's civic godfather arrived on the scene. William Paul had tried to do business at the nearby port town of Ravenswood, but soon saw that Mayfield, farther inland, offered more opportunities. So he bought out its only general store and established his own emporium. He also acquired land west of Main Street (now El Camino Real) and grew vegetables there.

The 1860s brought more residents and businesses to little Mayfield. Many from the East Coast

of the United States and from several European countries had headed west when they learned of the California gold rush. After failing to "strike it rich," they looked for a place where they could farm successfully, or a town where they could become part of the business community. Those locating in Mayfield built new hotels, a drugstore, another blacksmith shop, a livery stable, a lumber yard and a brewery. Farmers saw opportunity in some of the richest croplands in Santa Clara County; wheat and barley, celery, onions and strawberries grew abundantly there.

Townsite Laid Out

Storekeeper-farmer Paul, a lifelong bachelor who had been born in Scotland, made the decision of the decade in 1867: He acted to establish a townsite. It happened that he had built a house near Stanford Avenue and El Camino. Then Paul learned that someone meant to build a house right in front of his. Worrying about being hemmed in and losing access, he bought two 22-acre lots abutting his property and had them surveyed and platted — laid out in streets and building lots — by the Santa Clara County surveyor. These lots became Mayfield's original plat, filed with the county recorder on March 20, 1867. Influenced by the recently ended Civil War, Paul named the streets running northeast and southwest for war heroes: Lincoln (now California), Sherman, Grant, Sheridan and Washington.

Builders of the railroad that reached Mayfield in 1863 had placed a station near today's Churchill Avenue, not far from the Greer residence. Sarah Wallis thought the depot belonged farther south, and began agitating for a change. William Paul clinched the shift by offering free land for the new depot (where the California Avenue station now stands). He later became the town's first philanthropist by giving the lots for Mayfield's first school and for the Methodist church. Then he sold his store and took a fling at mining in Nevada.

Returning soon from the diggings, Paul ran for an at-large seat on the Santa Clara County Board of Supervisors. He won, and served for four years.

PALO ALTO HISTORICAL ASSOCIATION

Mayfield's civic godfather William Paul platted the original townsite in 1867, naming the streets for Civil War heroes.

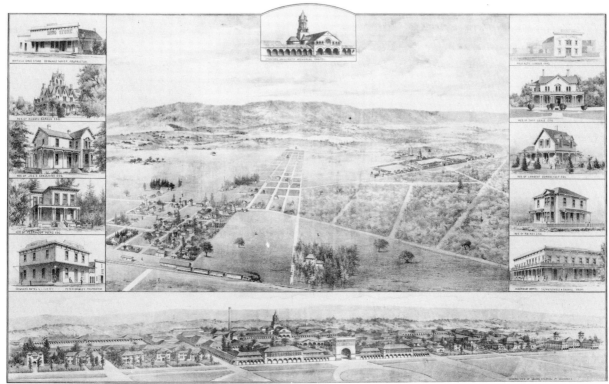

An 1889 view of Mayfield with an artist's vision of the new Leland Stanford Jr. University to the northwest of town.

(Paul's term and that of Fourth District Supervisor John Wesley Boulware, also of Mayfield, partly overlapped.) At that time and for long afterward, a supervisor wielded great power, as the county board governed unincorporated areas and its members had a decisive say over roads and other public works in their districts. In 1875, Paul sold his farm to Peter Coutts. Three years later he revisited Scotland, then returned to Mayfield for his sunset years, dying there in 1891.

Clarke's Granary and Landing

Another important figure in the Mayfield district's early years was Jeremiah Clarke, who had been the attorney for the Robles brothers. He bought some of their land in the late 1850s and later acquired more. Clarke lived away from the village center, near Matadero Creek east of Middlefield Road, where he built a home, barn and granary. He developed Clarke's Landing on Mayfield Slough

as a private boat dock, and built a private road to it generally along the route of Colorado Avenue. Like Paul, Clarke disposed of most of his Mayfield property in the 1870s. In 1878, Captain Charles G. Wilson leased the boat landing and thereafter it bore his name.

In Mayfield's first major street name change, Washington became Page Mill Road, named for William Page, a New York-born lumberman who had bought property in the hills containing good stands of timber. Page Mill Road was built as a public highway in order to bring lumber into Mayfield where Page and Alexander Peers operated a lumber yard. In 1868, St. Aloysius Church was built on Page Mill Road on land donated by Jeremiah Clarke. A new, two-story school house was constructed on Birch Street on the land given by William Paul.

After suffering financial reverses, the Wallises sold Mayfield Farm in 1878 to Edward Barron, a retired San Francisco financier. Barron added substantially to the house and acreage, and his name continued to be associated with the house long after his death. The Barron Park neighborhood, annexed to Palo Alto in 1975, also was named for him. Sarah Wallis and her husband moved into Mayfield — Sarah Wallis Park is on the site of their town home at Ash Street and Grant Avenue. Mrs. Wallis became known for arranging revival meetings, mainly to give local performers a showcase for their talents, although a few hymns were on the program.

Shipping's Decline Brings Stagnation

A half-century afterward, Elizabeth Ann Boynton Peers, wife of Alexander Peers, recalled 1871-78 as Mayfield's most prosperous time, due to the shipping of lumber and grain. But came the 1880s and the local economy stood almost still. Few buildings went up. Only the saloon trade thrived as owners slaked the thirst of ranch hands, drovers and travelers. Ugly scenes of shootings in bar brawls and blatant public drunkenness soon gave Mayfield an unsavory reputation.

In 1870, Frederick Weisshaar and Peter Spacher, two friends from Germany, had bought 120 acres of the former Robles rancho, covering what is now College Terrace, and each farmed 60 acres. This tract adjoined Leland Stanford's Palo Alto Stock Farm on the south after Stanford had bought out Peter Coutts. Stanford tried to acquire it, but Weisshaar and Spacher held out until the late 1880s, and then sold to Alexander Gordon. The new owner subdivided it into lots — some only 25 feet wide — and gave it the name "Palo Alto," advertising it as the "town of Leland Stanford Junior University." Senator Stanford objected and filed a lawsuit, and Gordon changed the name to "College Terrace" after receiving a settlement offer from the senator. College Terrace became part of Mayfield in 1891.

Construction of the university gave Mayfield new life late in the 1880s, and its social organizations flourished in the '90s. The Independent Order of Odd Fellows (IOOF) dedicated a new two-story building, still standing at California Avenue and Ash Street. IOOF functions occupied the upper floor and two stores took space on the lower floor. The Mayfield Parlor of the Native Sons of the Golden West was formed. Boats of the Mayfield Yacht Club sailed to San Francisco, and the Social and Cycling Club staged outings and gatherings. The Women's Social Club organized, and the Druids, a secret society based on old Celtic beliefs, grew prominent.

Merry Times at Dornberger's Grove

Most of the clubs held outdoor meetings at Dornberger's Grove, located at Page Mill and Park Boulevard. The eucalyptus woods that served as the town's park belonged to Lambert Dornberger, a local farmer and dairyman. Clubs marched to the grove led by a musical aggregation that adopted the name University Brass Band with Senator Stanford's approval. The bandsmen's big moment came when they played for President Benjamin Harrison during his visit to Stanford University in 1891.

Until Senator Stanford's death in 1893, the university founders' relations with Mayfield remained cordial. The senator had promised to extend a water line to the town, as he had to Palo Alto. Still, Palo Alto got most of what university

The IOOF Hall in Mayfield, dedicated in 1890, still stands at the corner of California Avenue and Ash Street.

PALO ALTO HISTORICAL ASSOCIATION/ W. H. MYRICK

Recreation in Mayfield in the late 1880s included dancing at Seghers' and Spellman's Dancing Academy.

business was done locally. The senator's passing hit Mayfield hard because it halted construction on campus, where many of the townsmen had worked.

Mayfield residents and outsiders alike often decried the eyesore quality of two rows of board shanties at El Camino and Stanford Avenue, called Chinatown. The Chinese people living there had been employed on the Stanford and Coutts horse farms, or as cooks on the campus; some had first come to California as railroad builders. Later the shacks were abated as a nuisance, and the local Chinese community relocated, mostly to the southeast quarter of town.

A Mapmaking Slight

In the early 1900s, Mayfield residents were abashed to learn that the name of their town had been left off maps of the region sent out by the San Jose Chamber of Commerce. Perceptive citizens realized that the town needed to incorporate to gain control of its progress. In 1903 a delegation from Mayfield requested incorporation from the county Board of Supervisors. The board approved in May, and in July Mayfield citizens voted 102 to 26 for incorporation. Elected to the first Board of Trustees were A.B. Clark, a professor of art at Stanford University and a resident of College Terrace, and Leonard Distel, Peter Towne, Alexander Peers and Christopher Ducker, all local businessmen who had come to Mayfield in the 1860s. Clark's colleagues named him the first mayor.

The new Board of Trustees established a Board of Health and a Board of Trade. Voters passed water bonds, and on March 18, 1904, re-

then, the town soon felt the heat of editorial criticism about a shoddy paving job.

As a result of the highway controversy two groups developed around a new issue: annexation to Palo Alto. As early as 1907, businessmen had been in favor of annexation. In 1918, another annexation attempt shaped up, perhaps encouraged by Mayfield's inclusion in the Palo Alto Union High School District two years earlier. Then the merger boomlet fell through for lack of support.

Industry Arrives with a Cannery

Although real estate development slowed down during this period, one positive project got going in 1918: the Bayside Cannery, an early Mayfield industry. Thomas Foon, owner of an Alviso cannery, purchased four acres of land on what is now Park Boulevard, and erected his second cannery at a cost of $200,000. The company played an important role in the community as it processed summer crops of fruits and vegetables from the Santa Clara Valley. Inexperienced workers were paid 20 cents an hour for an eight-hour day with others earning as much as $4.75 a day. Seasonal employment ran from 250 to 300 persons. In the mid-1920s the plant was sold to Safeway Stores and operated as Sutter Packing Company. As the valley's orchards disappeared under the surging growth of business and housing, produce had to be trucked to the plant from farther and farther away. Eventually Safeway found it cheaper to buy canned goods from competitors, and closed the plant in 1949. The building later housed a soft-drink bottling plant, then the Maximart store, and in the 1980s became the home of Cable Co-Op and Fry's Electronics.

Annexation came to the fore again in the 1920s. One Mayfield group felt it would be wise to join Palo Alto. Another faction upheld the importance of retaining Mayfield's identity and urged residents to make improvements in their city without help from Palo Alto. Consolidation first reached the ballot in Mayfield in October 1924 — and lost by 26 votes. The losers blamed transient cannery workers and engineered another election

after the cannery season had ended. Before the second vote, a joint committee of nonpartisan citizens of the two communities studied consolidation and reported finding no technical difficulties.

Among the fiercest foes of annexation was the *Mayfield Weekly News*, which contended in hot rhetorical blasts that the town could make it on its own. Mayfield had had weekly newspapers dating back to 1869-70 when the *Mayfield Enterprise* was published in English and Spanish. Subsequently, the town's events were chronicled by correspondents for papers in San Jose, Moun-

SUTTER PACKING CO.

HELP FEED YOUR FIGHTING MAN

100 Women Needed to Pack Tomatoes

AT ONCE!
ON NIGHT SHIFT!

Either Full or Part-Time
Shift Starts at 7 P.M.

It's no picnic—peeling, coring and grading wet tomatoes—but there's no better way of directly helping YOUR MAN in the service! The Armed Forces consider TOMATOES both FOOD and DRINK for their high food value.

This is one of the most vital war jobs that you can do . . . don't neglect it—we NEED YOU NOW!

20 MEN also needed on NIGHT SHIFT to UN-LOAD TRUCKS, especially from 1 a.m. to 6 a.m. Even 3 hours will help at lot!

Apply
Sutter Packing Co.
Employment Office
First St. and Portage Ave., South Palo Alto.   Phone 6188
EMPLOYMENT OFFICE OPEN 7 A.M. TO 9 P.M. DAILY
or U.S. Employment Office, 441 Emerson St.

PALO ALTO TIMES

Sutter Packing Co. newspaper advertisement seeking seasonal employers during World War II.

Mayfield's Main Street (now El Camino Real) in 1909 with an interurban trolley car in the distance.

tain View and San Francisco. A second weekly was established in 1889 by Frank Bacon, who later became a nationally celebrated stage actor. Bacon's *Weekly Palo Alto* metamorphosed into the *Mayfield Republican* and next the *Mayfield News.* T.B. Scott bought and ran the paper from 1911-16, then leased it to Thomas B. Nichols. Scott took pride in the paper being "fearlessly independent," and in it berated former Mayfielders who had "taken a roost with the Pallyalteans down by the creek" as "traitorous and disloyal to their early love."

Mayfield's Last Decision

In May 1925, Mayfield citizens again cast ballots on annexation to Palo Alto. This time they approved by a margin of 69 votes — 357 for, 288 against. Palo Alto had a population estimated at 9,000, and on July 2 its voters approved consolidation of the two towns, 1,094 to 441. So on July 6, 1925, May-

field's 1,700 residents officially became Palo Altans. When the consolidation had fully jelled, Mayfield had added 0.83 square miles to Palo Alto's existing 2.34 square miles, 5 linear miles of paved streets to Palo Alto's 28, and an assessed valuation of $1 million to Palo Alto's $8 million.

The area began to be known as South Palo Alto but for years a school and some businesses perpetuated the name of Mayfield, including a slim weekly newspaper called the *Mayfield Citizen.* The business district developed along California Avenue, where some of the finest homes in Mayfield had stood. (Lincoln, the name taken over by California Avenue, had been a consolidation casualty, for Palo Alto already had its own Lincoln Avenue.)

Officially, the Town of Mayfield had passed into oblivion. Yet even two-thirds of a century later, its imprint remains strong in the minds of history-conscious Palo Altans.

Leland and Jane Lathrop Stanford pose with their son, Leland, Jr.

4

Stanford and Hopkins Found
a New Town

*"On the night following Leland's death,
Governor Stanford was lamenting that he had
nothing to live for when in a vision his son came to him,
saying: 'Papa, do not say that. You have a great deal
to live for; live for humanity, father!' "*

— *Noted interviewer George Alfred Townsend,* Cincinnati Enquirer, *October 21, 1887*

P alo Alto came to life in the 1890s for an uncommon reason. Unlike cities built by important waterways or where main roads crossed, and unlike boom towns near gold, oil or other rich natural resources, Palo Alto emerged in its present location because of a business tycoon's choice of a country home.

In 1876 when Governor and Mrs. Leland Stanford acquired the George Gordon estate across San Francisquito Creek from the village of Menlo Park, they had no plans to found a town. Stanford wanted a trotting horse farm and a retreat not too far from their Nob Hill mansion in San Francisco. As one of western railroading's "Big Four," he presided over the Central Pacific's main offices in San Francisco and often traveled around the state or across the country in his private railroad car. But he sometimes listed his occupation as farmer, and horses captivated him.

Stanford had thought of donating part of his fortune to a public institution. A family tragedy reshaped and enlarged that notion in 1884 after the couple's only child, Leland, Jr., died in Italy. His grieving parents decided to endow a university in his memory, and to locate it on their Palo Alto Farm, which the youth had loved. That momentous project led to establishment of the town of Palo Alto.

Leland and Jane Stanford

Leland Stanford (1824-1893) and Jane Lathrop Stanford (1825-1905) were both born in upstate New York. They married in 1850, two years after Leland started a law practice in Wisconsin. But the Gold Rush had drawn his brothers to California, and Leland joined them there in 1852, quickly succeeding as a merchant. As a founder of the new Republican Party in California in 1856, Stanford championed the presidential candidacy of Abraham Lincoln in 1860. In 1861, he joined Charles Crocker, Mark Hopkins and Collis P. Huntington — the "Big Four" — in organizing the Central Pacific Railroad, which later built the western portion of the first transcontinental U.S. railroad. That same year, Stanford was elected California's Civil War governor, for a two-year term. Much later, the California Legislature elected him twice to serve in the United States Senate, from 1885 until his death in 1893.

A Renowned Horse Trainer

On the Gordon estate, which he renamed the Palo Alto Stock Farm, Stanford developed an exceptional stable of trotting horses. The most famous, Electioneer, purchased in 1876, sired nine of the 13 champions bred there. Stanford employed more than 150 craftsmen, builders, stablemen and

Leland Stanford's Palo Alto Stock Farm circa 1892. A portion of the stable complex in the background is still used today.

laborers on his farm, and many others on the adjacent Coutts' estate, where he bred English race horses. His better breeding and training methods won Stanford world renown. After concluding that all four hooves of a horse trotting rapidly are off the ground at one time, Stanford brought in photographer Eadweard Muybridge to record the locomotion. By taking progressive photographs of a horse in action, Muybridge demonstrated the accuracy of Stanford's observation, and in doing so, without realizing it, he and Leland

Stanford helped pave the way for the motion picture industry.

The Death of an Only Child

Governor and Mrs. Stanford made a grand tour of Europe in 1883-84 with their son, Leland, Jr., a child born late in their married life whose many interests had delighted them. The boy developed a sore throat after an outing in Athens, and grew sicker as they went on to Italy. Confined for three weeks in a darkened room in Florence, he finally

Eadweard Muybridge's series of photographs taken in 1878 at Stanford's Stock Farm demonstrated for the first time that at one point in its gait a trotter has all four feet off the ground. Muybridge's studies were a step toward the motion picture industry.

died of typhoid fever. He was 15 years and 10 months old.

Heartbroken and exhausted, the parents felt the light had gone out of their lives. That night, according to several varying accounts he later gave to interviewers, Stanford had a dream or vision of his son telling him not to spend his life in vain sorrow, that he had much to live for — "live for humanity, father!" The governor had previously contemplated the idea of a substantial gift for a museum; now it took firmer shape as a memorial to Leland, Jr. Before leaving Paris six weeks after their son's death, the Stanfords had drawn up a new will, providing for the projected university.

Endowing the University

Three large landholdings, including the Palo Alto farm, became the initial endowment. Later they were supplemented by cash bequests and other gifts. Working out the founding grant and the Stanfords' stated aims, and getting the necessary enabling legislation passed to reserve their lands for the university in perpetuity, took much of the next year. On November 14, 1885, the 24 men appointed by Stanford as trustees heard the deed of grant read and saw the couple sign it, declaring: "The children of California shall be our children." Distinguished as the trustees were, they had almost no role to

The Stanfords in 1887 at the ceremonial laying of the cornerstone for the new university.

The University's Main Quad is shown under construction in 1888. A railroad track spur was laid to bring in building materials.

play until 1902, for the founders retained control of the endowment.

Stanford made the big decisions himself, and said plainly he intended to do so. But he needed advice, especially as he had just been elected U.S. senator, and had duties to perform in Washington, D.C. He engaged General Francis A. Walker, president of the Massachusetts Institute of Technology, to help him develop the plans. Walker brought in Frederick L. Olmsted, the landscape architect who had designed New York City's Central Park, and the Boston firm of Shepley, Rutan and Coolidge, successors to the acclaimed architect Henry H. Richardson.

This team made major plan decisions in 1886 at the Palo Alto Farm. Stanford's concept was not only for a university but for an entire educational system from kindergarten to graduate school, incorporating a village on the campus. Years later, one of the university's most devoted trustees, George E. Crothers, commented:

" . . . Senator Stanford's ideas. . . were almost unbounded in their breadth and scope, and were utterly impractical and impossible of execution in any one institution, unless it should incorporate within itself the whole educational system of a community." The presentation of Stanford's ideas in brochures and the press would, Crothers added, "tend to lead anyone purchasing a lot in the university town to believe that Stanford would supply all educational facilities for the children of the community."

A Village on Campus?

At first Stanford envisioned the village on his lands nearest Mayfield, and Olmsted's plan, published in many periodicals, showed roads angling toward the oval in front of the Quadrangle from both Mayfield and Menlo. The plan also showed the Main Quad with its long axis north and south. Not many weeks before the cornerstone-laying in May 1887, Stanford ordered the Quad rotated 90 degrees so that its long axis ran east and west and faced north, with the view through the arcades focusing on the projected church. Then, or later in 1887, he decided that the village would not be on the university lands, although there would still be faculty housing and housing for students' relatives on leased Stanford lots. By 1888, he called for an avenue (Palm Drive) leading to a proposed train station.

Why Stanford abandoned an on-campus village scheme is unclear. Orrin Leslie Elliott, Stanford's first staff employee and long-time registrar, ascribes it in his book on the university's first 25 years to "various reasons." Professor Paul V. Turner, major author of *The Founders and the Architects* (1974), suggests that in turning his dream into actuality Stanford "realized that the construction of the university itself was difficult enough."

Indeed, for all his wealth, Stanford found his assets illiquid during the construction period. Collis P. Huntington, Stanford's archrival among the Big Four, disliked the project. Huntington controlled the pursestrings of a key holding company, and when Stanford asked for money he was apt to say it was all loaned out.

Mayfield Declines

Construction at Stanford brought scores of workmen to the area. Some lived in a temporary camp on the farm. Others secured their meals and housing in Menlo Park or Mayfield. After abandoning the plan to incorporate the village into the campus, the Stanfords looked ahead to the arrival of students and faculty. The prevalence of saloons in both neighboring towns worried them. Though not teetotalers themselves, they wanted to set a high moral tone for the students.

Legend verging on established fact has it that in 1886 or 1887 Stanford offered to make Mayfield the college town if its saloons were closed — and was refused. One account, written about 35 years later by T.B. Scott, who from 1911 to 1916 edited the weekly *Mayfield News*, said Stanford, accompanied by his wife, stopped their carriage at Lincoln and Main streets (now California Avenue

and El Camino Real), outlined their plans for the university, made the offer, and called on Mayfield people to do their part, "as a saloon town would not surround the students with the right kind of influence." After what the ex-editor branded "a heartless and selfish investigation," a Mayfield committee notified the Stanfords that the town "was willing" to keep its saloons and hence could not accept the offer.

Additional reasons may have weighed upon Stanford. He was one of America's most famous men, because of his millions, his trotters and their stable, and, not least, because his plan to spend $20 million creating a university far eclipsed all earlier philanthropy. Moreover, he was talked of as a possible candidate for president. Sensitive to public opinion, he had reaped mainly praise from the university project, but a few critics had charged that it would never be built and that Stanford aimed to pocket more money by leasing housing. That cutting accusation could have caused him to look to someone else to develop the village.

Timothy Hopkins Steps In

Timothy Hopkins was ready and willing. Through his association with Mark Hopkins, Stanford had known Timothy since he was a child, because from age 3 the fatherless boy had been raised in the Hopkins home. However, he was not formally adopted by Mrs. Hopkins until 1879, a year after Mark Hopkins died. From her, Timothy and his wife Mary had in 1888 received the former Latham estate in Menlo Park, 280 acres extending from San Francisquito Creek to Ravenswood Avenue and from the railroad to Middlefield Road. They in turn honored Mrs. Hopkins, born Mary Francis Sherwood, by renaming it Sherwood Hall.

After Mark Hopkins' death in 1878, Timothy Hopkins became overseer of his family's money interests. He began work for the Central Pacific Railroad, became its treasurer in 1883, and when the Southern Pacific was created in 1885, he became the SP's treasurer. Stanford presided over both railroads, with Hopkins his close ally. Thus when Stanford decided that a town separate from

Timothy Hopkins purchased land from both the Seales and the Greers, and laid out the new town, which was originally named University Park.

that he was not interested in the West and would not finance the land deal.

Years later Timothy Hopkins related that he then asked Seale to release him from the contract, and offered a bonus, but Seale needed cash and wanted the sale to stand. So Hopkins went to Stanford for advice. Stanford told him it would be unwise for a young man to repudiate a contract early in his business career, and offered to sign for

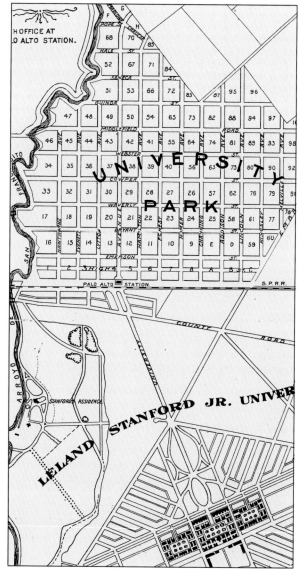

University Park, Palo Alto in 1889, with streets named by Timothy Hopkins was marketed as a "tract of beautiful oak-park land."

the campus was needed, Hopkins was well-positioned to provide it. He could exercise the long-term option Henry Seale had given to the late Mark Hopkins on 697.55 acres across the creek from Sherwood Hall.

So the two men agreed that Timothy Hopkins would establish the town. Hopkins negotiated a deal with Seale, and added about 40 acres by purchases of former Greer lands. Then a difficulty loomed. While redecorating her Nob Hill mansion in 1883, the widow Hopkins became acquainted with Edward F. Searles, an interior decorator formerly employed by a fashionable New York firm. Some accounts say she soon asked Searles — 22 years her junior — to marry her, but he demurred. In any case, they did marry in November 1887, when she was 66, he 44. Searles took charge of his new wife's fortune, and he soon told Timothy Hopkins, who had opposed the marriage, a bank loan. This was readily arranged — Hopkins as the railroad treasurer often floated loans when Stanford needed cash. The amount of the bank note remains unclear, as Hopkins was rather private about his business affairs. In his 1939 *History of Palo Alto,* editor Dallas E. Wood said it was $300,000, a figure land values of the 1880s seem to support. However, city historian Guy Miller said in his 1952 *Palo Alto Community Book* that the note was for $60,000.

Hopkins evidently had the town platted in 1887 before the money hitch arose, but the map was not recorded until 1889. In the interval whole blocks were sold. The deeds carried a clause requested by Stanford providing that if intoxicating beverages were ever made or sold on the property, it would revert to Hopkins. (Three decades later, Hopkins donated these reversionary rights to the university.)

Hopkins platted the town and put the grid of lots on auction in 1890. "University Park," as it was first named, extended from the creek to Embarcadero Road and from the railroad to northeast of Middlefield Road. According to a report in the *Mountain View Register,* 3,000 people from all over the state attended the auction and bought 106 lots, the highest priced at $287, the lowest $122.50.

University Park Is Renamed

Returning from the East, Senator Stanford was surprised to find the town called University Park, not Palo Alto, a name Hopkins had thought Stanford wanted reserved for his stock farm. To complicate matters, developers who had bought what is now College Terrace from the two farmers who would not sell to Leland Stanford had named their subdivision "Palo Alto." It took long negotiation and payment of $1,000 by an agent for Stanford to persuade them to give up the name, and lot buyers in both tracts had to approve the name change.

Thus Timothy Hopkins carried out Leland Stanford's wish to create a clean community to serve Stanford University's students, faculty and staff. Taking its name from the senator's stock farm, "Palo Alto," the town grew up entwined with the university, although most of the campus remains outside the city boundaries today.

Troubles Beset Hopkins

The cash crisis was part of a run of troubles that had beset Timothy Hopkins. In 1888, Mrs. Hopkins-Searles revised her will several times, first reducing Timothy's total inheritance to one-half, then cutting him out entirely in favor of Searles. After her death in July 1891, Timothy Hopkins contested the will. The heat of a single day in court wilted Searles, whose lawyer made an out-of-court settlement with Hopkins in 1893. It was said to have been between $2 million and $6 million.

Hopkins had resigned his railroad posts in 1892. Presumably he did so at the age of only 33 because he lost his power base when Searles gained control of the Hopkins holdings. Searles' support had enabled Huntington to oust Stanford as SP president in 1890.

At his Menlo Park estate, Hopkins grew violets, chrysanthemums, roses, apricots and prunes for the San Francisco market. In 1893, he changed the name of Sherwood Hall Nursery to Sunset Seed and Plant Co., an interesting precursor of today's *Sunset* magazine, based on part of what used to be his estate. Hopkins suffered heavy losses of San Francisco income property in the 1906 earthquake and fire. In addition, Sherwood Hall closed due to disruption of the lines from its private gas-generating plant, so from 1906 on, the family used the coach house near Ravenswood Avenue as their country home.

As a life trustee named by Stanford among the original 24, Timothy Hopkins served until his death in 1936, and set a pioneer example as a donor to the university. In addition to selling lots in Palo Alto, Hopkins laid out the streets and planted trees, and for years was the town's biggest property owner. In 1907, he gave the city a 1.5-mile strip of land flanking the creek for park use.

High Hopes

Only three houses, all dating from the 1870s, stood

View of University Avenue looking eastward from The Circle, 1893.

on the townsite land Hopkins subdivided, but soon new settlers began to arrive. Education offered by the university drew some of them, Stanford's employment opportunities attracted others, and the prospects of serving and profiting from the town as it grew accounted for a third segment.

Some of the newcomers clearly had high expectations. From the first word about it, Stanford University had drawn unprecedented publicity. "When the plan of the institution, with its proposed endowments, was given to the public, there was enough in the greatness of its conception and possibilities to fire the popular imagination," Elliott wrote later. Copious news coverage continued through the cornerstone-laying, the selection of Indiana University President David Starr Jordan to be founding president, and the opening ceremonies on October 1, 1891. The Inner Quadrangle was completed in time for Stanford's first students — 559 men and women. By then, 15 professors had been hired, and a few faculty houses had been built on campus.

Often the articles quoted Senator Stanford on his kindergarten-up plan, and on his belief that a college education should have a large practical quota from the outset. His mail ran heavy with letters from parents, asking what requirements a bright child would have to meet to be admitted for tuition-free study. The news attracted people who not only desired college education for their offspring but who themselves hoped to help staff the lower schools or the university.

The actions of the Stanfords seemed to bear out their intention of providing a complete educational system, however preposterous that idea sounded. Mrs. Stanford had sponsored free kindergartens in Mayfield and Menlo Park, along with others in San Francisco, all run on the basis of learning by doing. The Stanfords also arranged classes in reading and singing for employees at the stock farm. They were building a university and they had considered where to locate grammar and high schools.

Several cases illustrate the mind-sets of some early arrivals. Plucky Anna Zschokke, one of the first settlers in Palo Alto, built the first high school on her own when it became clear that the community would not; after the school outgrew her building and the public provided larger quarters, she lived in it. Stanford President Jordan encouraged two young women to start a school at Adelante Villa, two miles upcreek from the Quad. Herbert Hoover received tutoring there before entering the pioneer class. The proprietors subsequently moved the school to Kingsley Avenue in Palo Alto, where it became Castilleja Hall, a forerunner of Castilleja School.

Mayme Bass Suiter, principal of the first Palo Alto school in 1893-94, recalled the nature of her charges many years later. "The children came from all over the world," she said. "They were mostly younger brothers and sisters in families who had come here so their older offspring could attend Stanford."

Building a Town

The first families to winter through in 1890-91 were those of Mrs. A.P. Zschokke, P.B. Kimball, Mrs. George Andrews, Lawrence Gillan (a mason working at Stanford), Mike Lynch (head gardener at the Hopkins estate) and the Arragons. Rapidly these and later settlers built homes and businesses, started churches and schools, opened boarding houses for students, and formed an improvement club to foster public works and utility services.

Anna Zschokke, a recently widowed mother of three children, recorded these events, enriching Palo Alto's early history. She carefully noted the names of new residents, their first address, the location of their property, the type of house and number of rooms, and the name of the builder. In addition, she recorded new businesses, births, deaths, marriages, civic improvements, and important events in the lives of the early residents. Late in 1896, the *Palo Alto Live Oak*, one of several weekly newspapers that carried news of the town's early days, published Mrs. Zschokke's "Pioneer History of the Town of Palo Alto." (In 1914, the daily *Palo Alto Times* republished her account.)

By the end of 1891, Palo Alto's population had grown from 37 to 96; in 1892, it rose to more than 300 permanent residents and 400 students. Some of the influx came from close by. Early in 1892, Mrs. Zschokke noted, a stream of emigration from Mayfield began, bringing such families as that of stone mason Richard Werry, whose Mayfield-born son Alfred in 1988 became the first lifelong Palo Altan to reach the age of 100. By the end of 1894,

PALO ALTO HISTORICAL ASSOCIATION/CAROLYN CADDES

Alfred Werry, born in Mayfield in 1888, moved with his family to the new town of Palo Alto as a small child. His Werry Electric Shop operated for more than 50 years in Palo Alto.

Hopkins had sold most of his tract and used the proceeds to repay the loan Stanford had signed for. Even then, many blocks remained to be subdivided, because sales had been made not only by the lot but by the block, half-block and quarter-block.

"The end of the year 1893," Mrs. Zschokke summed up in her pioneer history, "found us with a greatly increased number of buildings; 750 inhabitants (318 last year); there had been 16 births, 1 death, 5 weddings. Three denominations were holding regular services. The incorporation of the town was assured."

Then, with the disdain of the recently settled for the newly arrived that has reverberated through Palo Alto affairs ever since, she added: "Those who settled here from this time on can hardly claim to be pioneers."

City Halls of Palo Alto

On Ramona Street, 1907.

With second story added, 1922.

At Newell and Embarcadero, 1952.

The present Civic Center at 250 Hamilton Avenue was opened in 1970. The peristyle was later removed.

5

Politics, Power and Progress

*"The people are willing to face up to problems before you
have to break your back in solving them."*
— Palo Alto City Manager Jerry Keithley,
quoted in a front-page Wall Street Journal *article, August 10, 1956*

Voters made incorporation official in the spring of 1894 — Palo Alto became a general-law city, one of only a few dozen in the state.

Ever since Palo Altans began to move onto the property Timothy Hopkins subdivided, they have debated public policy. At times they agitated the question (to use a favored term of the 1890s) quietly and deliberately; at other times, loudly and angrily.

During the community's first few years, debate had centered on creature comforts such as water, sewers, sidewalks and street signs. By 1892 some residents deemed it important to consider incorporation in order to secure good municipal services. Others felt concern that city status would mean less individual control over property and more taxes and fees to pay for new services.

By 1894, this political struggle took formal shape. Much of the support for official incorporation came from residents living between University Avenue and Embarcadero Road, a growing number of them Stanford professors. North of the avenue, where many tradespeople and small business proprietors lived, support for cityhood was weakest. Economic and political differences marked the two groups — at one public meeting, a north-of-University resident accused the townspeople with Stanford ties of forming a ring to run the city.

After incorporation petitions had been signed, the Santa Clara County Board of Supervisors set April 9, 1894, as the election date. Voters — males only, at that time — approved incorporation 98 to 21, with surprising support from both sides of University Avenue. County and state authorities put their seals of approval on the townspeople's action and Palo Alto officially became an incorporated California city of the sixth class as of April 21, 1894. In the same election, the voters chose a five-member town council, then called the Board of Trustees. In a demonstration of independent thinking foreshadowing many a future election, the voters seated only two of the men endorsed by the Palo Alto Improvement Club, which had led the incorporation campaign. The *Palo Alto Times* remarked that this result disproved the claim that a Stanford ring was in control.

Victory Sparks Celebration

Embarking on the adventure of cityhood called for celebration. Stanford students, many of them rooming in Palo Alto, helped the townspeople hail the new. The polls had closed at 5 p.m., and the result had been announced at 6:30. At dusk, horse-drawn wagons loaded with empty boxes and barrels rolled along University Avenue and dumped the wood in a vacant lot at the corner of Emerson Street. The pyre, large as a house, soon blazed as a victory bonfire. Salutes were fired on anvils (then cannon substitutes), and the Stanford band marched in to play, serenading each successful candidate at his home. The winners bought cigars for the bandsmen, and Joseph Hutchinson — soon to be the first elected leader — sent the whole crowd to eat candy and drink soda at his expense.

Nortree Hall, built by W.E. Norris and C.L. Crabtree on University Avenue, was the site of the first town government. The second story of this building served many civic, social and religious functions.

"A rousing jubilee and nearly everybody happy," said a headline in the next edition of the *Times*.

On April 28, the Board of Trustees held its first meeting at Nortree Hall (located where Liddicoat's now stands at 340 University Avenue). The board elected Joseph Hutchinson president — in effect, mayor. One of the board's first actions was to declare "the shooting of firearms in the city illegal."

First Order of Business

Water — quite in keeping with western American history — was the biggest issue early on. Who would supply it? And from what sources? Wells and windmills served some homes. In late 1892, H.G. Wilson, who had sunk a 175-foot well and built a 14,000-gallon wooden tank over it to supply the livery stable, began laying pipes to newly founded businesses. J.F. Parkinson constructed a system in his neighborhood (bounded by Forest, Cowper, Homer and Waverley) from which, as Anna Zschokke noted, "water could be rented." There were other private systems; in the area now known as Professorville, bounded by Addison and Kingsley avenues and Ramona and Waverley streets, a cooperative well with a tank house was maintained by Professors Charles B. Wing (civil engineering), Frank Angell (psychology), Charles D. "Daddy" Marx (structural engineering) and W.W. Thoburn (biology; also the Methodist minister). Others bought water from a horse-drawn tank wagon that plied the alleys.

The Improvement Club, formed in October 1892, had looked into obtaining water from the Menlo Park Water Company and from Ashby's

Palo Alto's history of municipally owned utilities began with its water supply in 1896. This city water tower was built at the eastern end of Rinconada Park to supplant the early collection of wells, tanks and distribution pipes.

artesian well. But no interim answer seemed suitable, and ultimately the club backed incorporation as a way to solve the water problem. It took the fledgling city almost two years to arrange to buy the scattered private systems and set up a central water system — a $40,000 bond issue for those purposes passed on April 2, 1896. This step initiated Palo Alto's tradition of municipally owned utilities.

Generating Electricity

Two years later, a $40,000 bond issue for sewers passed almost unanimously. These bonds not only served the purpose of sanitation but also, because installing the sewers left $12,000 unspent, figured in the city's taking over the electric utility.

Electricity had come to Palo Alto late in 1896,

provided under franchise by the private Peninsula Lighting Company of Redwood City. Marx and Wing soon asserted publicly that the firm's 20 cents per kilowatt-hour rate was too high, and claimed the city could build a plant to supply current for half that rate. The Board of Trustees asked Town Engineer E.C. Moore to cost out a new plant; the price came out at $12,000, a manageable sum as there was just that much left over in sewer bonds.

The story of Palo Alto's adventures in firming up its hold on the electrical utility and acquiring its natural gas distribution system is told more fully in the chapter on utilities. Only enough will be related here to fill in the context of the municipality's governmental and political development.

After 130 residents signed a petition for city-owned power, Moore installed a generating unit in the water plant building near today's Rinconada Park swimming pool. Residents soon were supplied with cheap electricity from dusk until midnight. Undercutting its own rates to 8 cents per kwh, the Redwood City firm began a price war. Palo Alto responded with a $1,000 license fee — a fee levied on its own plant, too. That prompted the private company to increase its rate to 10 cents.

Although it is not uncommon for cities to own their waterworks, municipal electric power is relatively rare. Marx and his coterie had created a yardstick by which the private Pacific Gas and Electric Company often has been measured. They had also laid a foundation for earning surplus revenues to use for other municipal purposes.

About a decade later, manufactured gas was added, but not without a struggle. The Board of Trustees had wanted to install a city-owned plant, but their proposal lost when three incumbents were unseated in an election. The new board awarded the gas franchise to a private firm, which laid a piping system to deliver gas purchased from PG&E.

In 1912, the city fathers sought first to control the rates and then to condemn the private gas system. This required action by the state Railroad Commission, which set rates and plant values as a forerunner of today's Public Utilities Commission.

Ultimately Palo Alto won the right to buy out the private system on favorable terms, and in 1917 a new municipal gas plant was dedicated. With that, the City of Palo Alto owned its three key utility systems outright.

A Merchant Leader Emerges

One of Palo Alto's central figures in the early years, John F. Parkinson, came from merchant rather than professorial ranks. In 1892 he had come west from Iowa with his father and uncle. Starting a lumber yard and hardware business, and later dealing in land development, Parkinson became a major force behind the establishment of many outstanding city services; some called him "the father of Palo Alto." He served on both the Board

PALO ALTO HISTORICAL ASSOCIATION

John F. Parkinson was an early civic leader in Palo Alto.

of Education and the Board of Trustees, and as mayor when the 1906 earthquake struck he performed heroically, firmly blocking any gouging of the victims. After the Woman's Club of Palo Alto founded the pioneer library, Parkinson traveled east to persuade the Carnegie Foundation to grant the town $10,000 for a library building. But his string of triumphs was about to become frayed.

Townspeople were content with local government in the early years, although in 1904 and 1906 incumbent trustees failed to be re-elected. That had little to do with local issues, however. In '04, a union movement streaked through the region, pushing workers into politics and affecting state and local elections. In part it was a reaction to employers' tactics in the 1901 San Francisco teamsters and waterfront strike. This labor-management clash spawned pro-union and anti-union slates in Palo Alto and elsewhere. The pro side unseated incumbents on the strength of an exceptional north-of-University voter turnout. But the movement soon lapsed and city issues came to the fore again.

The 1909 Charter Controversy

Between 1905 and 1909, utility system developments held a great deal of attention. By 1908, support was growing to give the town government more power. Until then, Palo Alto had been governed under state general-law provisions, which limited the city's authority. A charter city could cast off many of those limits, so a committee was named to consider charter status. Backing its "yes" recommendation, proponents argued that, under its own charter, the city could be better managed and made more responsive to citizen concerns.

J.F. Parkinson took a contrary view. Already he had had to sell the streetcar franchise he had obtained in 1903 because of opposition to his plans by Mayfield and the Southern Pacific Company. Now he said a larger government would mean more bureaucracy and higher taxes. Parkinson vigorously led the opponents of a charter, attacking the proposal in the *Palo Alto*

Tribune, a weekly and at times daily newspaper he published from 1905 to 1910 to promote his interests.

The showdown at the polls came in January 1909. Voters approved the charter measure 355 to 225, authorizing a "council-commission" system. A 15-member City Council replaced the five-member Board of Trustees. Dr. John Spencer's name had been left off the ballot inadvertently, but because of the mistake he was declared elected — and then was named mayor by the council. Day-to-day responsibility for the operation of city services was delegated to citizens serving on two appointive boards, Public Works and Public Safety. The small paid city staff consisted of the city engineer, treasurer, clerk, police chief, health officer and a few others.

Later, other boards were established, chief among them the Planning Commission, which, from 1918 on, advised on planning and zoning. A less customary body, the Board of Commercial Amusements, ruled for nearly four decades on what movies Palo Altans could see.

City Council elections under the 1909 charter generally pitted candidates living north and south of University Avenue against one another. The larger south-side group, with its contingent of Stanford faculty, usually prevailed. In 1913, this bloc pushed through an ordinance banning the sale of tobacco within 1,000 feet of a school, despite objections by small-business owners and tradespeople that it infringed on private rights and would sink some commercial firms.

Save the Oaks!

Trees have often been a disputed topic in Palo Alto, but never more so than in 1914-16, the heyday of the live oak issue. When the streets were laid out, oaks were left in many a roadway. Then automobiles began to run into trees, and a number of out-of-town drivers sued the city successfully for damages. Their claims strained city finances, so the council proposed to cut down all trees more than one foot from a curb. Angrily, the community rallied to defend the oaks. More than a hundred

Palo Alto's original street grid left many oak trees standing in road beds. This was not a problem in the horse and buggy era, but the speedy new automobiles and their careless drivers developed a propensity to collide with the trees.

school children signed save-the-oaks petitions, and one partisan pronounced the trees "a means of safety behind which one might dodge speeding machines." Bowing to the pressure, the council delayed action for 2 1/2 years before approving a compromise plan to remove 75 percent of the live oaks and to paint white stripes around the trunks of those left in streets. As late as the 1980s, faded white stripes could still be seen on oaks in the old part of town.

The live oak issue was a salient factor in 1915, when many City Council incumbents were unseated. It symbolized the kind of place Palo Alto was becoming: an intellectually and environmentally oriented town. In 1916, Mayor Robert Swain, a Stanford chemistry professor who later served as the university's acting president, declared: "The council will continue to resist building factories, for Palo Alto is an education factory, and wants to remain that way."

Six years before the 1915 upheaval nearly half of the council lived north of University Avenue. By 1917 only one councilman from the north remained. In 1919, Emma Blair and Denison Wilt Thomas became the first two women elected to the council.

During the 1920s and '30s the town was

Palo Alto City Council of 1919 including its first two women members, Denison Wilt Thomas and Emma Blair.

dominated politically by Stanford professors — men such as Swain, Arthur Cathcart, Charles Wing and E.A. Cottrell. Businessmen also enjoyed leadership roles on the jumbo-size council, C.H. Christensen, Charles P. Cooley and J. Byron Blois among them. Cooley, a farmer-turned-banker, organized his neighbors in 1914 to pave their block (400 Webster Street) where the mud "in winter was six inches deep, 36 feet wide and 400 feet long." In 1921 Cooley took office as county supervisor, staying 28 years and, by his estimate, paving 85% of the Fifth District's 350 road miles.

PALO ALTO HISTORICAL ASSOCIATION

Paving the streets and sidewalks of Palo Alto was an important early civic task as the dust of summer and the adobe mud of winter made travel difficult.

Early Civic Controversies

The city government continued to expand services during the 1920s. It established the Community House near the train depot, entered into an agreement with Stanford University to operate a hospital at Embarcadero and Cowper, and developed the Palo Alto harbor area. But the decade had a dark side; Palo Alto endured some of its worst civic discomforts in the mid-'20s.

The city had its initial run-in with the Ku Klux Klan, a white supremacist group given to terror tactics, in 1923. Robert Burnett, a graduate student

in engineering from Texas, organized the first gathering, mainly of Stanford students. University President Ray Lyman Wilbur soon sapped much of the group's potential by denying Exalted Cyclops Burnett the use of campus buildings.

In 1924, a citizens' committee aimed 25 charges at Police Chief C.F. Noble and sought his removal. Among the charges were allegations of skimming funds from police bicycle auctions and using the money for personal purposes. Noble, who kept the accounts in his head, denied the charges and branded them the work of the Klan.

The Board of Public Safety investigated the charges and initially exonerated the chief, who then resigned. But after a stinging public scolding by Mayor A.M. Cathcart, the board rescinded Noble's resignation and dismissed him for insubordination. The City Council split 6-5 against a motion of confidence in the Board of Public Safety, with Councilwoman Josephine Duveneck forcing the roll call vote. The board soon resigned, as did most of the police force.

Howard A. Zink replaced Noble as police chief and served with distinction until 1952. Zink also tangled with the Klan, but fought and won against accusations like those leveled at his predecessor. He upgraded the Police Department by getting salaries raised, setting up the first training courses and fitness standards for officers, bringing in new equipment, tightening traffic controls and hiring one of the first policewomen on the West Coast.

Joining Forces with Mayfield

The other major political event of the '20s was Palo Alto's annexation of Mayfield. Two decades earlier, some factions in Mayfield had advocated a merger of the two towns, just a mile apart. After Mayfield had finally shed the taint of its saloons and gone somewhat dry, Palo Alto leaders actively sought to bring the area into the city. It took two elections for Mayfield to agree, and after Mayfield's vote in 1925 carried, Palo Alto ratified it.

The major Palo Alto opponent of annexation was W.C. Peet, son of a famous San Francisco minister. He claimed it would cost the city too much to provide services to Mayfield. Later Peet became a leading advocate of city manager government for Palo Alto, and regularly lectured the council and ran unsuccessful slates of candidates in city elections to promote his cause.

During the 1930s and 1940s, local controversy took a back seat to the Great Depression and World War II. In 1931, the City Council donated $500 to support The Shelter, a local organization that fed and housed unemployed men. Ample precedent existed: Before the turn of the century the town had had a "friendly woodyard" where tramps could earn a supper, and in the World War I era a hostel was set up for itinerants in need of meals (average cost: 6 1/2 cents) and a warm place to sleep, with stays limited to 48 hours.

A Clouded Era's Silver Linings

Works Progress Administration funds were used to make street, sewer and airport improvements. A beautiful new Community Center was donated by Lucie Stern. Railroad grade separations at Embarcadero and Alma Street and at University Avenue and El Camino Real eased traffic problems and made pedestrians safer.

During World War II, the city imposed emergency blackout rules, invested in U.S. Savings Bonds, and allowed residents to offer more rooms for rent in a tight housing market. "Victory Gardens" were planted to stretch the food supply. Except for a controversial "curb your dog" campaign in 1943 (dogs were not curbed), and various proposals to extend the University Avenue commercial district past Cowper Street, local politics stayed fairly quiet until the 1950s.

At the 50th anniversary of its incorporation in 1944, the city was absorbed in its war effort. Right after the war ended, attention turned to overcoming shortages and regaining an even keel. But no such tranquility awaited; the late '40s were a mere prelude to what the '50s brought: a startling period

PALO ALTO HISTORICAL ASSOCIATION/DAN BAKER

Palo Alto's civic duty included war bond drives during World War II. This jeep was part of a rally at the Stanford Theatre.

City Manager Jerry Keithley, right, Mayor Noel Porter, center, and Vice-Mayor James Marshall inspect the site of Foothills Park before its purchase in 1959. Keithley, the first city manager under the new charter, was instrumental in meeting municipal service demands of the post-World War II growth in Palo Alto.

PALO ALTO TIMES/GENE TUPPER

of growth and development. The city's second 50 years would bring expansion with daunting new orders of magnitude.

An effort to annex Barron Park into the city was defeated in 1947 because of that area's liquor stores and roadhouses. Despite this result, expansion of Palo Alto was imminent.

A Great Expansion Period
From 1948 to 1960, annexations and home-building were to push the city's southerly fringe out by miles and add thousands of newcomers to the populace. A few leaders who foresaw this surge realized that the quaint 1909 charter government could not deal with it. In 1948 the City Council asked Stanford political science Professor E.A. Cottrell, a former mayor, to draft a modern charter.

Although Cottrell appreciated what volunteer council members and commissioners had accomplished under the old charter, he judged that with subdivisions multiplying and industry moving in, the day of the unpaid hobbyists was done. They lacked the availability and the skills needed to run an increasingly complex city on a day-to-day basis. The time was ripe for a professional city manager.

So, in 1950, the voters adopted the new charter without much opposition. The City Council remained a 15-seat body, but the Boards of Public Safety and Public Works were dropped. A city manager took charge, with other department heads who had long been accustomed to running their own shows reporting directly to him.

New Charter, New Manager
Jerome Keithley, enticed away from Stockton, became Palo Alto's first city manager. "We hired someone to tell *us* what to do," Mayor Walter Gaspar quipped at the time. The council anticipated growth, and wanted someone to manage it. Keithley became a strong manager — highhanded, his critics often charged — and played a leading role during the explosive growth of the '50s and early '60s.

Jerry Keithley's arrival also touched off a political and philosophical struggle that lingered into the 1980s. The big issues were growth, traffic

Palo Alto's Most Complex Election Tuesday

Showdown Nears In 10-Year Political Feud

SAN JOSE MERCURY NEWS/DICK FLOOD

This political cartoon from the May 4, 1967 edition of the San Jose Mercury News *reflects the most bitter political campaign in Palo Alto's history.*

reached a virtual stalemate on all civic issues. Residentialists retorted that the establishment had hatched the recall idea in a desperate attempt to stave off loss of power and an end to unbridled growth. The recall sponsors, claiming that disruption and the council's inability to make policy were the only issues, endorsed all of the establishment candidates.

An exceedingly bitter campaign ensued. In May 1967, the voters upheld the disruption allegations and unseated all but two of the residentialists: Kirke Comstock and Enid Pearson. Those ousted were replaced by members who turned out to be more moderate than many had feared, although development proposals continued to win approval.

As antipathy to the Vietnam War boiled up in the late '60s, Palo Alto was confronted by — and reacted to — war protests, the drug culture, student activists and self-styled "revolutionaries." The latter group included a gang known as Venceremos, which regularly disrupted City Council meetings and led most of the violent street mob rumbles. The council passed an anti-commune housing ordinance, approved a curfew law and set up a program to prevent drug abuse.

Meanwhile, police relations with the angry segment of the community deteriorated. Weekend rock music concerts at Lytton Plaza downtown attracted youths and radicals, often ending in broken store windows and rock-peltings of police in riot gear. After one such concert in 1970, the crowd refused to disperse at the 11 p.m. curfew and 200 people were arrested.

Development Foes Solidify

At the same time, new opposition to development began to jell. In 1970, the Palo Alto Medical Research Foundation proposed an 18-story hospital on a two-block site near the Palo Alto Medical Clinic. Nearby residents reacted by forming an organization that expanded citywide to fight for preservation of the Professorville neighborhood. The hospital proposal went on the ballot as Proposition L, and opponents attacked the location and size of the project, but not the hospital itself. Their bumper stickers reading "L No — The Site's Not Right" carried the day. Then, early in 1971, voters turned back a proposed two-block-wide, high-rise downtown office development nicknamed "Superblock."

Among the results of these defeats were the formation of a new citywide residentialist precinct organization named the Association for a Balanced Community and the election of three residentialists to the council. Voters were clearly

PALO ALTO HISTORICAL ASSOCIATION

"Superblock" was a proposal to build a two-block-wide high-rise office building in downtown Palo Alto, which the voters denied in 1971.

opting for less growth. At the end of the year, an establishment councilperson resigned, opening the door for a new residentialist majority. Unlike the situation in the mid-'60s, however, council members on both sides got along and kept their differences political rather than personal.

Spotlight on Social Programs

The rise of the new majority changed the city government dramatically. The council of the early 1970s took a more active part in policy-making, curtailing the role of the city manager. George Sipel replaced a battle-worn George Morgan as city manager in 1972, and began an evolution toward team management within the city staff. City services broadened into social programs including child care, drug abuse prevention and senior services. The Palo Alto Housing Corporation had been set up in 1969 to purchase land for low- to moderate-income housing, and the city assisted private developers in building senior housing as well, abetted by federal grants.

Palo Alto took a hard look at its vast, mostly undeveloped uplands in a two-year Foothills Environmental Design Study. The result: a minimum lot size of 10 acres. This zoning brought on numerous lawsuits, most of which the city won, except for Arastra Ltd.'s suit over 512 acres in the lower foothills it wanted to develop. Under court order, the city bought Arastra's land for $7.5 million to settle the case.

Ending decades of resistance, Barron Park was annexed to Palo Alto in 1975, after a promise from the council not to change the semi-rural character of the mainly west-of-El Camino Real area.

Also in 1975, the residentialist majority ended abruptly after a campaign driven by controversy over the radical political activities of the city-funded drug program's staff. However, the new majority had ridden in largely on protect-the-neighborhoods campaigns of a conservative hue. In fact, residentialism — at times liberal, at times more conservative — had become the dominant local philosophy by the end of the 1970s. Rival political slates or lists of candidates vanished from the election scene in 1981, as most of the council members agreed on major planning and zoning issues. Many goals of the early residentialists had been met, including a limit on industrial and residential growth, protection of the baylands and foothills and extension of city government into social services.

Slate campaigning had been a feature of Palo Alto city elections from the start. Among the campaign coalitions that wrote their rhetoric and advertising into local history were the Improvement Club (1894), Business Men and Tax-Payers' League (1913), Anti-Saloon League (1918), Palo Alto Progressive League (1927), the Better Government League and the Citizens Emergency Committee (1935), the Civic League of Palo Alto (1949), Citizens' Committee for Civic Improvements (1957) and numerous others, some flourishing for several elections. One vintage year was 1955, with Citizens for Representative Government, Committee for Good Government, Committee for Regional Planning and Committee Against

57

Dog Haters Ordinance. Another was 1967, with the Palo Alto Recall Committee, Committee for the Future of Palo Alto, United Palo Altans, Palo Alto Town Hall, Voters for Independent Councilmen, Committee Against Irresponsible Recall and Palo Alto Civic League (not to be confused with the old Civic League of Palo Alto).

Environmentalism at the Forefront

As the 1980s began, the issues became more subtle. William Zaner took over as the fourth city manager; in a commentary on the scarcity of affordable housing, the council wrote mortgage assistance into his employment contract.

One example of environmentalism's growing political clout came when citizens voted in 1980, and again in 1985, to close Palo Alto Yacht Harbor, which had been created in 1928. Dredging required to keep the harbor channel usable for watercraft of even moderate draft had become expensive, and dumping of spoils on the baylands had prevented their reclamation as marshlands. The electorate's decisions sent long-ensconced Sea Scouts and boat owners looking for new

moorings, and opened the way for the first Bay Area effort to restore a freshwater and saltwater marsh. Funded by a $1.2 million California Coastal Conservancy grant, the marsh restoration in 1992 was named for former Council Member Emily Renzel, its leading proponent.

Cable TV had been debated for years, and by the mid-'80s it became a reality, incidentally enabling politics watchers to keep an eye on the council from their homes. Cable Co-Op serves Stanford, Atherton, East Palo Alto and Menlo Park along with Palo Alto.

In 1985-86, the city took steps to reduce the potential of more downtown office growth, which had threatened more density and traffic congestion. Housing continued to be an issue, but many residents began to question whether increased density might not change the city's character while doing little to reduce the 3-to-1 jobs-housing imbalance. Midtown district residents fought with some success to retain their neighborhood businesses on Middlefield Road between Colorado and Loma Verde avenues in place of proposed new condominiums.

Palo Alto's yacht harbor, created in 1928 by City Engineer John F. Byxbee, finally closed in 1986 when the environmental problems associated with dredging and disposal of spoils were viewed as outweighing the recreational value of the harbor.

New Trends Surface

Increased election of women to government posts had become a marked trend. By the mid-'80s, four of Palo Alto's nine City Council members were women. Another trend was Palo Alto's more active participation in regional issues, a change from the days when the city, far from the county seat, exercised its independence in such ways as having its own health officer and tax assessor. No longer an isolated community, the city recognized its role as part of a larger region grappling with such urban devils as transportation, solid waste disposal and housing.

The city had also begun to look at ways to uphold Palo Alto's traditional identity as a fine place for families, despite data showing that average residents were older and more affluent, and that housing costs were too high for most young families to afford.

In 1980, at the urging of Gail Woolley, later a council member and mayor, an ordinance was enacted creating a Historic Resources Board and declaring an intent to promote preservation of the city's historic buildings and neighborhoods. Professorville, the Squire House, Hostess House (currently MacArthur Park restaurant) and other structures have been identified as treasures through this program.

During the mid-1980s, the city acted to save a formerly private ice skating rink in Midtown. Voters gave close to a 70% margin of approval in November 1985 to a measure to acquire the Winter Lodge in a trade for unused park land. The city-owned recreational facility now is operated and supported through a nonprofit corporation.

Early in 1986, the City Council enacted a pioneering Seismic Hazards Ordinance requiring owners of 99 potentially hazardous structures to have them inspected for earthquake safety. The ordinance did not mandate repairs, however.

The city and the Palo Alto Unified School District worked together to maintain an outstanding kindergarten-through-high school education system by encouraging city voters to pass a utility tax in November 1987. Proceeds of the tax are applied to lease surplus school plants for city recreational and cultural uses. In a related step in 1991, the City Council adopted a master plan for development of the former Cubberley High School site and buildings, but did not immediately fund it.

As the 1990s dawned, many of the challenges facing Palo Alto as a city stemmed from its own success. Palo Alto's high quality of life, its outstanding array of city services and its proximity to Stanford University all made it a most desirable place to live and work. One manifestation of this success was the citywide building of new and remodeled homes as large as the municipal codes would allow. Some irate residents contended that such houses were overbuilt and out of scale with the character of their neighborhoods. As a result, technically sophisticated building regulations were adopted.

In mid-1992, Bill Zaner, 55, announced his resignation as city manager, touching off a widespread search for a new manager. "The 1980s was the era of what seemed possible and the 1990s is the era of what seems impossible," commented Council Member Liz Kniss. "I think Bill's saying it's a new era, that it's time for a new leader."

Owen Whetzel, a *San Jose Mercury News* columnist with a bent for satire, on October 21, 1992, wrote a mock ad for the job.

WANTED: City manager for Palo Alto, Calif. Pop. 57,000. City motto: "Now that I've moved here, you shouldn't." World-class university is across the bay, Stanford is nearby. Manager works at the pleasure of a city council of nine. Successful applicant must be able to handle such critical disputes as speed bumps, a skateboard park, noisy volleyball players, leaf blowers, noise that bounces from a nearby outdoor arena and ongoing debate over outdoor sculptures. Must be physically fit and able to work a full day and attend city council meetings, recognized as the best theater in the area. Successful candidate must know how to provide a multitude of public services

June Fleming was appointed as Palo Alto's fifth city manager in 1993.

without a prayer of an idea of how the city can pay for them in the future...

In January, the council promoted June Fleming, former assistant city manager and earlier director of libraries. As the new city manager, she became the first woman and the first minority person to hold the municipality's top professional job.

Partisan Balance Shifts

For at least half its existence, Palo Alto was a safe Republican stronghold of a rather progressive stripe. Except for favoring Theodore Roosevelt's Bull Moose Progressive Republican insurgency in 1912 and Woodrow Wilson in 1916, it backed regular Republican presidential candidates from William McKinley (1896) through Richard Nixon (1960), staying loyal to Herbert Hoover in 1932 even in the early Depression's cruel grip. The GOP's outstanding precinct organization of the post-World War II years managed to turn out almost every potential vote for Dwight Eisenhower in 1952 and 1956 and for Nixon in 1960.

The balance tipped in the late '60s, when Democratic Party registration in Palo Alto passed the Republican total. Since Lyndon B. Johnson's campaign in 1964, the Democratic presidential nominee has run up a majority in the city every time but once. The exception was in 1980, when independent John Anderson ran, with *Peninsula Times Tribune* backing. Democrat Jimmy Carter still scored a Palo Alto plurality over Republican winner Ronald Reagan and Anderson.

Three Leaders in Congress

Several men who have served long stints in Congress launched their political careers in Palo Alto. Palo Alto-born Senator Alan Cranston worked at a downtown real estate firm while organizing the California Democratic Council. He became state controller before winning, in 1968, the first of four terms in the U.S. Senate — the most for any Californian since Hiram Johnson. At a title company a few doors from Cranston's Palo Alto office worked Don Edwards, a Democratic congressman from a San Jose district since 1963 — and at that time Edwards was state president of the Young Republicans! Paul N. "Pete" McCloskey, Jr. was a Palo Alto lawyer when, as a Republican, he won a special congressional election in 1967; he held the office for 17 years. Both McCloskey and Cranston made bold if brief runs for their party's presidential nod. McCloskey challenged his party's incumbent chief executive in the aftermath of Nixon's Cambodia incursion in 1970. Cranston made his bid on a peace platform in the early stages of the 1984 campaign.

Local politics has been a training ground for State Senate and Assembly members, too. Two 1980s graduates to Sacramento are State Senator Becky Morgan (1984-), a Republican who was first elected to the Palo Alto Board of Education (1973-78) and then county supervisor, and Assemblyman Byron Sher (1980-), a Democrat with a long record as mayor and city councilman. Earlier legislators from Palo Alto were Byrl Salsman (Assembly, 1939-43, Senate 1943-49); Assemblymen Raup Miller (1943-47), Adron Beene (1937-

PALO ALTO TIMES

Former Mayor Alan Henderson speaks to the City Council at one of the weekly Monday night meetings. Citizens may listen to the meetings on radio or view them on local cable television.

39) and Frank Crist (1931-35); Assemblyman and Senator Marshall Black (1903-1913) and Assemblyman Fayette Mitcheltree (1905-07). A number of other Palo Altans ran but lost, some, like Egerton Lakin, several times.

A Commitment to Reform

In county politics, Palo Alto has often played a leadership role in bringing about modernization and reform. Among the Palo Altans who filled the Fifth Supervisorial District chair in the recent past were Becky Morgan (1981-84), Wesley L. "Bud" Hubbard (1957-60) and Walter S. Gaspar (1953-56). When an incumbent sheriff was convicted and jailed in 1945, Gaspar, freshly retired from service as commandant of Marines at Moffett Field, plugged the gap as interim sheriff until 1947. As supervisor, Gaspar stoutly defended a new county charter providing for a county executive system. Hubbard's foremost accomplishment was securing agreement on bringing a state water project into the county. Morgan stood firmly for budget restraint.

Given the level of Palo Altans' involvement with their city and with politics, the prospect is that there will always be new problems to solve by lively debate and, perhaps, showdowns at the polls.

Joseph Hutchinson, the pioneer "mayor," once said in reflecting on his career in Palo Alto:

Above and beyond the political battles, and there were many, the shouting and yelling, and there was much, I shall never forget the selflessness of the Palo Alto people. The people of this town will not only build with their hands but with their brains as well.

Hutchinson also wrote, in a pamphlet issued a few months after incorporation, "Palo Alto resents outside interference. She is able to take care of herself." Whether this can remain so in the face of regional, state and federal pressures of myriad sorts may be a test for the community's future leaders.

The Alpine Inn (also known as Rossotti's) is the oldest tavern in continuous operation in California.

6

Liquor: A Potent Issue

*"In case you do have a depot, I wish you would provide that
no whiskey shall be sold within a certain distance."*
— *Senator Leland Stanford, in a letter to Timothy Hopkins, January 8, 1888*

L iquor was a defining issue — locally and nationally — at the time Stanford University was founded and Palo Alto was subdivided. It remained a politically potent subject for half a century, and continued to be of local import for more than 30 years after that.

Nationally, the Prohibition Party's strength peaked in the elections of 1888 and 1892, presidential years in which U.S. Senator Leland Stanford was a potential candidate. Locally, saloons in Mayfield and Menlo Park were exceptionally numerous in that era. Indeed, the "road to Mayfield" was soon to be celebrated in beery ballad by the less inhibited of the university's male students.

Senator and Mrs. Stanford were not teetotalers; neither were Timothy Hopkins and his wife. Guests at their households often were served alcoholic beverages, and Stanford owned extensive vineyards, wineries and brandy stills. However, both public men also had a strong sense of propriety. For business, social and political reasons, neither wanted his actions to constitute a public statement of support for vulgar village carousing or collegiate imbibing.

Setting an Example

Hopkins had all but completed his platting of University Park when Stanford wrote a letter to him, dated January 8, 1888, saying he found the proposed location of a railroad station for Palo Alto satisfactory, but was not sure one so near Menlo and Mayfield could be afforded by Southern Pacific. Stanford went on to say:

In case you do have a depot, I wish you would provide that no whiskey shall be sold within a certain distance. I think I should object to a depot of any kind if whiskey could be sold near it, as the location is so close to my University. As far as your lots are concerned I think they would more readily find purchasers if it were known that no saloons would be established near them.

The knowledge that no liquor could be sold in the place would, I think, have a very favorable influence upon people wishing for quiet homes where they could raise their children.

Hopkins' response was the deed restriction shown on the following page — a restriction that served its purpose for many years. Even so, it fell short of being ironclad in the eyes of pioneer Palo Altans. The *Palo Alto Times,* arguing for incorporation, pointed out that a city could set its own standard and not have to depend on the reversionary deed restriction outliving Hopkins. (Hopkins gave the reversionary rights to Stanford University long before his death in 1936.) On August 23, 1895, a *Times* editorial said, "Those who are made sick daily by running against drunken sots on the streets of their towns, don't know how pleasant it is to pass weeks and months without the sight of a fool drunkard." The editorial added that the prohibitory ordinance (quoted on the next page) made "sure and permanent the principles on which the town stands."

> *" ... this indenture is made upon conditions that the second parties, their heirs or assigns, shall not at any time manufacture or sell to be used as a beverage, any intoxicating liquor or permit the same to be done on the premises hereby conveyed."*
>
> *— Reversionary restriction placed by Timothy Hopkins in deeds to all lots in Palo Alto, 1889.*

> *"It shall be ... unlawful for any person or persons ... to establish, open, keep, maintain, or carry on, or assist in carrying on, within the corporate limits of the Town of Palo Alto, any tippling-house, dramshop, cellar, saloon, bar, bar-room, sample-room, or other place where spiritous, vinous, malt or mixed liquors are sold or given away ...."*
>
> *— Section 1 of Ordinance No. 2 adopted by the new town Board of Trustees, April 1894.*

Officeseekers Fall in Line

For decades, every officeseeker from town trustee to president of the United States had to cater to these sentiments. The Women's Christian Temperance Union (WCTU) was active locally, and from 1906 to 1913 the Anti-Saloon League led state prohibition drives.

Palo Alto businessman Marshall Black won election to the State Assembly in 1902 and two years later to the State Senate, being re-elected twice thereafter. Black, a Republican who on occasion also won the Prohibition Party nomination, sponsored the law passed in 1909 banning liquor sales within 1.5 miles of a university campus, with hearty backing from Stanford officials. (A savings and loan scandal later overtook Black and, in a special election in January 1913, he became the first officeholder ousted through a new California recall procedure he himself had sponsored. From his county jail cell, he pronounced the voters' recall decision proper.)

The 1.5-mile rule was written to apply only to Stanford University and was aimed straight at Menlo Park's 14 barrooms. Initially, the San Mateo County supervisors, who governed unincorporated Menlo Park, paid it no heed, and the saloonkeepers continued to sell alcoholic drinks. But the university won a court test of the law in March 1910, and then gained the decisive backing of the California Supreme Court in June 1911, with the result that the Menlo Park watering holes had to close.

Meanwhile, the 1909 Charter adopted in Palo Alto by a fairly close margin contained an article on alcoholic liquors styled after Ordinance No. 2 of 1894. With some added verbiage aimed at bottle clubs, its first section said:

> *It shall be unlawful for any person or persons, firm, corporation, club or association or member of such club or association to establish, carry on, keep or maintain a place where spiritous, vinous, malt or intoxicating liquors or any admixture thereof or any alcoholic drinks whatsoever are sold, kept*

for sale, offered for sale, furnished, distributed, divided, delivered or given away.

Two additional sections banned sales, deliveries, sales solicitations and order-taking within the city limits, and in any way maintaining a club room. The penalties, as before, were a fine of up to $300, jail for up to three months, or both. (In 1950, when a new charter was proposed and adopted, the six sections of this article were included word for word. By then, however, there had been vast state and national changes, and in 1958 City Attorney Robert Michalski pronounced the charter provisions unenforceable.)

Of course, not every Palo Altan agreed with the anti-booze majority. Early on, renegade beer wagons presented a challenge to lawmen. Smuggling of booze from nearby towns for private consumption was common, if illicit, and "wet" voices were heard now and then. When asked about running for the City Council in 1915, Richard Keatinge said: "I am not at all the kind of person for a town trustee. I drink beer with my dinner, and I would smoke tobacco if my stomach would let me. The holier-than-thou attitude makes me tired."

Timothy Hopkins liked to tell the story of the Palo Alto man who roused him from his bed late one night and, saying he had a sick wife, demanded a bottle of champagne (then often prescribed medicinally). When it was procured from Hopkins' private cellar, the caller took it as a matter of right rather than courtesy and went off saying: "If you had not founded your damned town with those liquor restrictions I could have got the champagne at home."

Waterworks Whistle Hails Prohibition

World War I spurred enactment of a temporary wartime prohibition act, and in 1917 the proposed 18th Amendment to the U.S. Constitution went to state legislatures for ratification after getting the necessary two-thirds vote in Congress. On January 16, 1919, the *Times* noted, "36 blasts of the waterworks whistle in Palo Alto this morning meant ratification of the prohibition amendment by 36 states. What more appropriate agent than the 'waterworks' of a dry town could be chosen to celebrate the downfall of John Barleycorn?" In early 1920, when Prohibition took nationwide effect, bans in 33 states already covered 63% of the populace.

In practice, enforcement intensity varied in

PALO ALTO HISTORICAL ASSOCIATION

Mayfield's notoriety as a "wet" town included the Mayfield Brewery.

keeping with local sentiments. In November 1921, Santa Clara County voters favored enforcing federal Prohibition by reinstating a county enforcement act; the Palo Alto vote was 1,299 for, 371 against.

The "noble experiment" ran into trouble, what with "Roaring '20s" speakeasies (covert night clubs serving booze), illegal stills and the participation of organized crime in bootleg liquor traffic. However, in 1926 when Santa Clara County voted on repeal of the Wright Act, the enforcement measure adopted by Congress, the Palo Alto area opposed repeal 2 to 1.

Prohibition Hurt Hoover

Hometown hero Herbert Hoover's insistence that he would enforce Prohibition as long as it was the law of the land helped get him elected in 1928. By 1932, public opinion had shifted but Hoover's position had not, and his refusal to make the slightest concession was almost as significant in his defeat as was the Depression. The Democratic Party platform had called for repeal, and the election sank Prohibition along with Hoover. Prohibition's drawbacks had shaken even Palo Altans. Although they still favored Hoover, they split 3,558 yes to 3,587 no on repealing the Wright Act. By June 1933, Palo Altans saw fit to give repeal a 2,972-1,570 majority.

3.2 Beer Flows — Except in Palo Alto

Congress amended the Volstead Act in March 1932 to exempt 3.2 percent beer, defining it as nonintoxicating. Throughout the nation near-beer flowed — except in Palo Alto. Court tests ensued, and finally on July 20, 1934, sale of "New Deal beer" began on University Avenue. Small cafes offering it had to serve it with meals, however.

In 1930 and 1932, Palo Alto attorney Frank Lee Crist, a Republican, was elected to an Assembly seat. In 1934, Crist was challenged in the Republican primary by H. Dewey Anderson of Cupertino, a Stanford researcher. Anderson's ads attacked Crist for (1) voting for bills to abolish the dry zone around universities, and (2) handling proceedings

seeking to measure the 1.5-mile dry zone not from campus boundaries but from the administration building. Crist denied being a "wet," but Anderson outpolled him on the Republican ticket. Crist won the Democratic nomination by cross-filing, but without his own party's nomination he was out of the race.

Two years later, Adron Beene, Crist's law partner, ran for the same seat and drew opposition fire for having represented beer-sale petitioners. In 1940, Beene yielded to another Republican, Byrl R. Salsman, who later stepped up to the State Senate and in 1949 resigned to become a Superior Court judge. By then, the booze issue in elections was lightening up as California moved toward a uniform, state-run alcoholic beverage control system.

The Front's Last Hurrah

Palo Alto's anti-liquor front made its last big united stand in October 1951. Rallying to protest beer sale licenses at two markets near a Midtown school were the Unified School District, Council of Parent-Teacher Associations, Stanford University, Citizens League for Liquor Law Enforcement, Ministerial Association, WCTU and Council of Churchwomen. It became something of a last hurrah.

Late in 1953, state authorities granted a license to a hard liquor store at Loma Verde Avenue and Middlefield Road, beyond the 1.5-mile limit. "We used to make protests," Mayor James Marshall said ruefully, "but the state authorities never paid any attention to them. They said we had no jurisdiction over liquor matters."

Yet the deed restrictions Timothy Hopkins had donated to Stanford remained in force. Then, in December 1970, a Superior Court ruled that the university could not prevent the owners of the President Hotel from serving alcoholic beverages in a restaurant. The victorious attorney? None other than Frank Crist, who in May 1971 lifted downtown's first legal cocktail at The Shutter, now Henry's. (Later Crist said the whiskey failed to arrive on time so the first drink pictured in the news photo was actually water.)

Jack Kava and Frank Crist celebrate the end of the restriction on serving alcoholic beverages in downtown Palo Alto in May 1971.

Judge Peter Anello, explaining the President Hotel decision, said that the automobile age had made liquor readily available to Stanford students. Stanford had approved a liquor license for its faculty club, and permitted students of age to drink in dormitories and eating clubs, he added. Lastly, 15 places downtown were selling beer. Conditions had so changed in 80 years, Anello concluded, "that it has become substantially impossible to secure the benefits intended by the original restrictive covenant in the Hopkins deed."

The decision threw light on the fact that, back in 1932, Crist had broken a similar deed restriction on University Avenue property across the creek in East Palo Alto, giving "Whiskey Gulch" its start. Bars such as Ethan's and liquor stores thrived there in the post-Prohibition years, while roadhouses and restaurants sprang up along El Camino Real south of the 1.5-mile limit — Dinah's Shack, L'Omelette, Longbarn and others, including, after a move, Ethan's.

In the aftermath of Judge Anello's decision, Nellie Broderson, a longtime anti-liquor crusader, told a reporter: "We can't do a thing, public opinion being what it is." The local WCTU had long since passed out of existence, she said.

Even so, the *Times* did not abandon its policy of refusing liquor advertising until after longtime editor Dallas Wood's death in 1974.

A "Dry" Town No Longer

Late in 1978, with the state ban on hard liquor sales within 1.5 miles of Stanford University about to expire, the City Council adopted a measure requiring liquor stores to get a conditional use permit in order to stay in neighborhood commercial zoning. Doing that needed the approval of three city boards. But even the institution of a complex process could not water down the fact: Palo Alto no longer was a "dry" town. When supermarkets finally put in full liquor lines, scarcely a ripple of protest broke the surface.

Today Palo Alto has numerous restaurants with liquor service, plus tippling-houses and tasting rooms and bottle clubs and bars. The city even has a winery, Sherrill Cellars, on Skyline Boulevard, along with two downtown breweries and an annual University Avenue "Palo Alto Celebrates the Arts" street fair with free-flowing beverage service. Still, relatively few off-sale stores exist downtown. Aside from such vestiges, and many memories of the strife of bygone years, the liquor issue is dead as an empty bottle.

The annual Art and Wine Festival on University Avenue has become popular with residents and visitors to Palo Alto.

The Children's Library with its storybook tile fireplace was another gift of Lucie Stern in 1940.

7

Cultural Cornerstones

*"New colleges in new territory are a standard part of
American history. ... Sectarian or not, those colleges were the
harbingers of civilization to new settlements preoccupied with survival.
In every locality where they were established, they preceded the arts,
literature and science, but they encouraged all three. ... At their best,
they helped to shape the new civilization that slowly grew up
in the new place out of the compost of the old. ... "*

— *Professor Emeritus Wallace Stegner*
1991 Founders' Day Address, Stanford University

In the pioneer years leading up to incorporation, Palo Altans indeed were preoccupied with survival in the form of getting settled. However, they also felt — and fed — a hunger for social and intellectual stimulation.

The tradition of a vigorous and innovative cultural life began as the town's first families gathered for picnics and potlucks, enlivened by spontaneous singing and dramatic skits. As the years passed, cultural endeavors became closely tied to Stanford campus activities, as so many townspeople were faculty and staff members.

Church life also afforded an early medium for cultural growth. Before any churches were built, townspeople organized union services, church schools and semisocial groups. Even when congregations formed and began to erect sanctuaries, members visited each other's doings a lot. After the Presbyterians built the first downtown church, it quickly became a town social center.

A reflection of the town's early social life and the churches' role is found in an incident related by Nellie May Smith, a Stanford physics student who came to Palo Alto with her father in 1898.

Father and I went to the Baptist Church services the first Sunday after our arrival. They were held in Nortree Hall. A tall young man graciously ushered us to a seat. In the evening we went to the Presbyterian Church, then on the corner of University and Waverley. The same young man met us with a gracious smile and ushered us to a seat. We began to wonder if he was a professional usher, but we were soon to discover that if the Baptists needed an organist they borrowed from the Episcopal Church, and the Baptists were simply helping someone else in return. The fellowship between the churches in those early days was very unusual for those times...

Nellie Smith's story had a sequel: In 1900, she married the tall usher, James Stroner. And at their golden wedding anniversary in 1950, she retold the tale.

Senator and Mrs. Stanford, Timothy Hopkins and the university faculty and students all had a hand in early church development. Although the Stanfords had established the university on a nonsectarian basis, they firmly believed in a Creator and wanted students exposed to the best in religious thinking. They made numerous gifts to churches. Hopkins gave $1,000 each to help two churches buy their sites, and according to some accounts, made the same offer to other new churches. Professors took prominent parts in the lay leadership of all the early churches, and students often attended, for there was only a small chapel on campus until the completion of Stanford Memorial Church in 1902.

Churches fostered the founding of many of the city's cultural and artistic organizations. One of the first was the Woman's Club of Palo Alto, which in 1894 grew out of the Mothers' Club organized at the Presbyterian Church by Mary Grafton Campbell. Mrs. Campbell presided over the Woman's Club in its first four years, during which its membership soared from the charter 25 to more than 100 who met its requisites: respectability and intelligence. At the club's second meeting, secretary Anna Zschokke recorded, Mrs. Campbell made "a stirring address, congratulating Palo Alto upon being no longer a sort of half-orphan but now having both city fathers and mothers, thus insuring a prosperous future, a nurturing of its spiritual and refining issues as well as its material welfare." Mrs. Campbell's use of the family simile came naturally, as her friend Julia Gilbert explained in a memorial tribute.

Losing her own baby, she gave love and care to many children — 13 girls and boys of other mothers she reared in part or fully. It was the attitude of motherhood that she unconsciously assumed toward every infant, enterprise or needy person that came within her influence...

Humble Beginnings

The Woman's Club soon began an organized effort to broaden the community cultural base by establishing a public library. In October 1895, the club took steps to raise funds and secure donations of books, and in August 1896 the library opened in Simkins stationery store at 166 University. Several hundred books were shelved in the store, but the public did not use them much. In February 1897, a reading room opened in a building at University and High Street; later that year it moved to a new location on Emerson Street between University and Hamilton. Anne Hadden was appointed librarian in 1899 with her sister Elizabeth as her assis-

Palo Alto's Carnegie library on Hamilton Avenue opened in 1904.

tant. In 1902, the city government took over support of the library. Julia Gilbert, a library board member, later was honored as "a constant source of inspiration" to the institution in its fledgling period. She not only raised $1,000 (a large amount then) to get the library going but also, in 1899, when it was decided to catalog the collection, did much of the work herself. As for her ideals for book selection, she wrote:

Our effort was to study the peculiar needs of this town and to meet those needs without reference to the stock plans of the usual library. No book has gone on our shelves until it has been investigated from this point of view after the literary quality and moral tone had been passed upon.

Setting a Pattern

This cycle — origination of a cultural group under the aegis of a church or some university influence, then provision of a base for the activity by voluntary subscription for rental or purchase, and ultimately municipal assumption of the function — was to be repeated often as Palo Alto grew. In many cases, the final step to full city sponsorship was not taken, as the cultural activity remained a voluntary, nonprofit operation. However, it has not been unusual for such operations to receive city encouragement in the form of low-cost space rentals, subsidies or other assistance. In lean times, when little or no funding could be committed, citizen volunteers have carried on or enhanced cultural enterprises by investing their personal energies and original ideas. Recognizing the special hospitality of the Palo Alto climate for cultural nurture, generous individuals or foundations have contributed major enabling gifts.

Convincing Carnegie

Soon after the city took control of the library, Town Trustee John F. Parkinson, on a trip to the East Coast, approached philanthropist Andrew Carnegie about funding help for a public library building. Carnegie's secretary told him the town was too small — its 1900 census count was 1,658. But Parkinson made such a convincing appeal that Palo Alto received notice March 4, 1903, that Carnegie had agreed to give $10,000. The cornerstone was laid November 17, 1903, at a site at Hamilton and Bryant (now part of the Civic Center) and the library opened November 1, 1904. In 1908 the basement was finished for use as a meeting room and for storage. New wings were added and opened for use in February 1923.

Merger Starts Branch Libraries

Mayfield's 1925 merger with Palo Alto led to the start of a branch library system, for the first branch was set up in the old Mayfield Town Hall on California Avenue near El Camino Real. (Mayfield had a small library in Roberts Drug Store.) In 1936, a new building, erected with federal Works Progress Administration (WPA) funds, opened in Mayfield Park at 2300 Wellesley Street in College Terrace.

The next branch set a precedent for the entire West. The Palo Alto Children's Library, built behind the Lucie Stern Community Center at 1276 Harriet Street with funds provided by Mrs. Stern in 1940, became the first new U.S. library built solely for children.

After City Hall was relocated at Newell and Embarcadero roads in the 1950s, a new Main Library was erected nearby, at 1213 Newell, in 1958. A downtown branch at 270 Forest Avenue across from the Civic Center opened in 1970. Other branches were established at Mitchell Park, 3700 Middlefield Road, in 1958 and at Terman Park (in the closed Terman Middle School) at 661 Arastradero Road in 1985.

In the 1970s a computer-based circulation system replaced the old manual checkout method, and in 1987 the system was upgraded with an online public access catalog replacing the card catalog. Usage of the libraries, traditionally high, was reported in 1991 at 18.5 items (books, records, tapes, etc.) per capita per year, about three times the state norm and close to the highest rate in California.

Book-centered groups have been an enduring

feature of town life, whether library-connected or independent. Around 1895, a group of young professors in Palo Alto — all pinched by Stanford University's financial bind — formed the Neighborhood Book Club at Augustus T. Murray's suggestion. Each bought a book to share; every two weeks the books rotated. A book auction at the end of each year helped raise funds to buy new volumes. The club has remained steadily in operation. John Waldo Mitchell served for 32 years as treasurer; his daughter, Sarah Clark, is a fourth-generation member.

In Search of Meeting Space

During the dawn years of Palo Alto cityhood, privately owned halls, usually occupying the upper floors over downtown stores, met the needs of various cultural organizations for meeting space. A good example is the First Church of Christ, Scientist, officially organized in 1899 after Christian Scientists had met for about two years in a private home. Until the church's own building at Bryant Street and Forest Avenue was finally ready late in 1916, services were held in at least nine different places. In the early years, Fraternal Hall, Nortree Hall, Parkinson's Hall, the Madison Thoits Building and Jordan's Hall were used. Later, services were held in Mullen's Hall, the Marquee Theatre, the Old Presbyterian Church at University and Waverley and the Masonic Hall.

Many other religious, cultural, fraternal and special-interest groups made similar odysseys in their quests for suitable meeting places. The Woman's Club of Palo Alto built a clubhouse in 1916 at Homer Avenue and Cowper Street where the club has carried on its fostering of cultural, civic and social life and where many other groups have rented space. The Armory, built in 1909-10 at 623 Alma Street, near Hamilton, for the use of Palo Alto's Company L of the California National Guard, accommodated mass meetings until the early 1920s.

Palo Alto's Own Community House

At the end of World War I, an opportunity arose for the city to own a building with substantial space

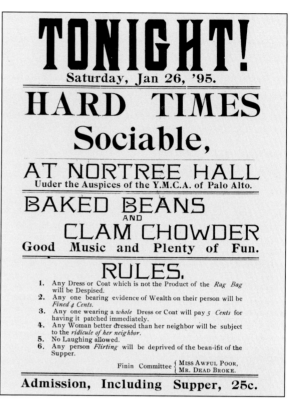

TONIGHT!

Saturday, Jan 26, '95.

HARD TIMES
Sociable,

AT NORTREE HALL
Uuder the Auspices of the Y.M.C.A. of Palo Alto.

BAKED BEANS
AND
CLAM CHOWDER

Good   Music   and   Plenty   of   Fun.

RULES.

1. Any Dress or Coat which is not the Product of the *Rag Bag* will be Despised.
2. Any one bearing evidence of Wealth on their person will be *Fined 4 Cents.*
3. Any one wearing a *whole* Dress or Coat will pay *5 Cents* for having it patched immediately.
4. Any Woman better dressed than her neighbor will be subject to the *ridicule of her neighbor.*
5. No Laughing allowed.
6. Any person *Flirting* will be deprived of the bean-ift of the Supper.

Finin Committee { Miss Awful Poor, Mr. Dead Broke.

Admission, Including Supper, 25c.

PALO ALTO HISTORICAL ASSOCIATION

The young town of Palo Alto entertained itself in the days before the cinema, radio or television.

allowing varied uses. The YWCA Hostess House, designed by architect Julia Morgan and located at Camp Fremont in Menlo Park, was moved across San Francisquito Creek and onto a site on The Circle, off University Avenue between the train station and El Camino Real. Its dedication as Community House on November 11, 1919, just one year after Armistice Day, was a gala occasion. An estimated 3,000 people marched from the Charter Oak at Waverley and University to the site, led by the Stanford Band, the Base Hospital Band, the Stanford ROTC, the Daughters of the American Revolution, the Native Sons of the Golden West and the High School Cadets.

Community House — one of the first such municipally operated centers in the United States — quickly became the place to go for Saturday night dances, Sunday musicales, weeknight classes, plays and other events. Josephine Duveneck, in her autobiography, *Life on Two Levels*, told how

Fraternal Hall on University Avenue is the last of the early meeting halls in Palo Alto. It was built in 1898.

The Hostess House, moved to Palo Alto at the end of World War I, was the town's first community center. It later served as a veterans hall and today is the home of MacArthur Park restaurant. Caretaker Charles Olaine poses proudly.

she set up an employment bureau there. "The Center could respond to expressed needs and, not being bound by any past tradition, could instigate new activities on a purely experimental basis," she observed. Night school classes started there grew rapidly and were taken over by the high school. Other activities initiated at Community House included a health center, the Girl Scouts and the Palo Alto Business and Professional Women's Club. When the building was enlarged in 1921, an outdoor theater was added at the rear.

The May Festival

The Children's May Festival, which is due to mark its 70th anniversary in 1994, dates its count from 1924, when the Community Center Commission based at Community House first sponsored it as a city event. However, there were at least four earlier observances. One, in 1913, drew about 500 people to the town's new playground at Webster Street and Addison Avenue on the then "new high school block." A second, in 1915, sponsored by a newly organized Civic Forum, combined a historical pageant and a Shakespeare festival, but was forced indoors by a three-day windstorm and chill weather, and lost $75. In 1921 the old Civic League put on the festival and raised $4,400 for a library addition. The Parent-Teacher Association took over in 1923, conducting a fete that earned several hundred dollars for the school dental clinic. For a few years beginning in 1924, the proceeds paid for Community House repairs.

The festival grew into an annual event of major moment in Palo Alto, featuring children parading

The May Festival parade celebrates the children and pets of Palo Alto, an annual tradition since 1924.

Lucie and Ruth Stern, Palo Alto's "fairy godmother" and her daughter, in Ruth's home at 1950 Cowper Street.

on University Avenue with their pets, tricycles, bicycles, wagons and homemade floats. A May queen and her court added to the colorful spectacle, as did Scout units in formation, marching bands, mayors and marshals, horseback groups, fancier floats, picturesque vehicles and other trimmings. A pageant and maypole dances have often been on the program. (In the 1990s, with the city involved in sponsorship of the Palo Alto Black and White Ball the night before the festival, the parades became more subdued. Proceeds of the ball help to fund recreation programs.)

In 1929, a Playgrounds and Community Recreation Department was founded, with offices at Community House.

Monthly little theater productions, using a portable stage and large screens over which scenery could be hung or tacked, evolved into something more formal in 1931. Local dramatists banded together as the Palo Alto Community Players with Community House as their base. In their premier season, the Players presented 10 full-length plays and three one-acts. The crowded and varied program activities soon outgrew the locale. Help of the most timely sort arrived in 1933. In July of that Depression year, the Palo Alto Community Theatre was presented to the city, the gift of a generous benefactor, Lucie Stern.

Palo Alto's "Fairy Godmother"

Lucie Stern, who came to be called "Palo Alto's fairy godmother," had inherited a portion of the Levi Strauss fortune through her late husband, Louis Stern. In addition to her many important and

Children's Theatre production of "James and the Giant Peach," held in the Secret Garden, June 1985.

generous gifts to the community, she showed great and kindly interest in its young people. She entertained youths often at her home at 1990 Cowper Street. There a closet with an ample stock of clothing was available to any youngster who might be in need. The theater became the first unit of the new Community Center in a corner of Rinconada Park, at Middlefield Road and Melville Avenue. Since the later development of other community centers, it has been designated the Lucie Stern Community Center.

On July 7, 1933, the curtain rose on the Players' first production in the new theater, "Grumpy," directed by Ralph Emerson Welles, who had become the group's leader six months earlier. Welles led the company for more than 40 years as it evolved into one of California's largest and most successful amateur theater groups. A wing added in 1934 provided space for a rehearsal hall and costume room. Improvements continued over the years. In the early 1980s the theater was renovated, and during the work, the Players performed in the Civic Center council chambers. The Players have continued to mount four to six productions a year at the Community Theatre, which seats 426 and has also housed many other sorts of gatherings.

A second unit of the Community Center, a gift from Lucie Stern's daughter Ruth, was dedicated in April 1935. It is a constantly used facility containing administrative offices, meeting rooms and a ballroom where dances, dance classes, meetings and parties are held.

Especially for Children

From the first days at Community House, children's dramatics ranked high among the activities, with plays performed on both indoor and outdoor stages. With the move to the new Community Theatre, one of the city's best-known cultural programs came into being. Hazel Glaister Robertson founded the Palo Alto Children's Theatre and served as its director from 1932 until 1953. "Beauty's Beast" was the first production, in January 1933.

Before long the Children's Theatre became a full-scale producing company, requiring its own facilities. Again Lucie Stern supplied a substantial gift, making possible construction of the Community Center's Children's Theatre Wing. Patricia Briggs has been the director of the theater since 1961. In 1987, the Children's Theatre marked its 50th anniversary with a repeat performance of "Snow White and the Seven Dwarfs," the inaugural show in the new 208-seat theater in January 1937.

Boy Scouting in Palo Alto dates from 1912, when the movement was very new. The present Stanford Area Council, Boy Scouts of America, was organized in 1940 with headquarters in a wing of the Community Center. Girl Scouting in Palo Alto began in 1922. The privately financed Girl Scout house, named for First Lady Lou Henry Hoover, was built in Rinconada Park in 1925; in 1936 it was moved to its present location behind the Community Theatre to make room for the Children's Theatre.

Another widely admired youth program, developed under the leadership of Josephine O'Hara, is the Palo Alto Junior Museum. It was founded in 1934 in a basement room of the old Sherman School, on the site of the present North County Courthouse. The museum moved in 1938 to the basement at the Community Theatre, and in 1941 into its own building nearby. The building, the first separate one in America to house such a museum, was the gift of Morris Frost in honor of his mother, Margaret Frost. In 1943, a science wing was added; other additions include a small outdoor zoo display of live animals.

TheatreWorks began in 1970 as a theater group for teenagers. Founder and artistic director Robert Kelley, a Palo Alto-born creative writing graduate of Stanford, led in establishing a company known for its innovative approach to producing plays. It has evolved from a semi-amateur community troupe into a professional company, one of the largest performing arts organizations

PALO ALTO COMMUNITY THEATRE/ANITA FOWLER

Theatergoers in the patio of the Lucie Stern Community Center. The theater was the first of several gifts to the community by Palo Alto's "fairy godmother," Lucie Stern.

The Lucy Evans Baylands Nature Interpretive Center is built on pilings at the edge of the salt marsh in Byxbee Park.

PALO ALTO WEEKLY/RENEE BURGARD

marked as a center for cultural activities. Renovated at a cost of $350,000, the Cultural Center opened in May 1971. The former council chamber and anterooms became a small auditorium for concerts, recitals, lectures and other public performances. An art gallery occupied former office space, and another wing was outfitted for art workshops and classes. Allan Longacre, its first director, promoted the Cultural Center as a home for both educational enrichment and hands-on participation in the arts.

Many private groups have rented municipal facilities, such as Cultural Center space. One with very long continuity is the Fortnightly Music Club, organized in 1908 by a number of Stanford faculty wives as a music study group that met on alternate Monday afternoons — that is, fortnightly. At first, a particular subject would be chosen for study, with one or more members giving an illustrative musical performance. Within a few years, the Fortnightly evolved into an evening performance club, accepting both men and women members. Gradually the membership expanded to incorporate nonperformers and music lovers from surrounding communities. In 1915, Fortnightly members were instrumental in sponsoring professional concerts at Stanford that paved the way for the later campus Concert Series and more recently the

Lively Arts at Stanford series.

The Fortnightly Club has remained active in advancing the standards of music in the community and sharing the talent for and enjoyment of music through performance. Active members are now chosen by audition.

The Morris Club, a men's singing group, formed in 1916 and remained active until the early 1940s. Originally a church unit, this club was but one element of the long and honored tradition of high-quality church music performance in Palo Alto. The First Congregational Church of Palo Alto, for example, began an arts program in the late 1970s that has become an ongoing concert series and annual October Festival.

The West Bay Opera Company originated from an adult education workshop conducted by Henry Holt and established itself as a Palo Alto institution with performances at the Lucie Stern Community Theatre beginning in the 1956-57 season. Since Holt's death in 1969, his wife, Maria, has guided the company, attracting performers and audiences for grand opera productions at the Community Theatre, typically three in a season.

Musical performances in the community, and drama, too, were stimulated for more than 50 years by the reviews of Dorothy Nichols. Paul Emerson, arts editor of the *Palo Alto Times*, also is remem-

Maria Holt, standing beside a photograph of founder Henry Holt, has guided the West Bay Opera since his death in 1969.

bered for his pioneering coverage and suggestions for tapping the Palo Alto area's full performing arts potential. CAPA (Council for the Arts — Palo Alto Area), William Whitson's Palo Alto Chamber Orchestra and other arts groups benefited from their appearances in Emerson's "Spotlight" column and feature spreads.

Popular Musicians

In addition to fostering a wide array of classical musicians, Palo Alto has made its mark in the popular music field. Among those who emerged from one of the city's high schools or became identified with Palo Alto in later life have been such stars as folk singer Joan Baez; Dave Guard of the Kingston Trio; rock musicians Jerry Garcia, Phil Lesh and Bill Kreutzmann of The Grateful Dead;

singer Grace Slick of the Jefferson Airplane; keyboardist Gregg Rolie of Santana, Journey and The Storm; guitarist Stanley Jordan; and jazz duo Tuck (Andress) and Patti (Cathcart). Anne Robinson and her then husband, acoustic guitarist Will Ackerman, established Windham Hill Record Builders with headquarters in Palo Alto. Stars of the '90s who rose locally are two mainstays of the acclaimed rock group Ugly Kid Joe, lead vocalist Whitfield Crane and guitarist Klaus Eichstadt.

Another local institution of many decades standing is the Pacific Art League, formerly called the Palo Alto Art Club, formed in 1921. Initially, the club maintained a studio at 340 Melville Avenue, where members attended classes in drawing and painting taught by instructors from the art faculties of Stanford and San Jose State University. Since the late 1950s the club has owned gallery and class space downtown at Forest Avenue and Ramona Street.

Growing a Garden Club

The Garden Club of Palo Alto formed in 1917 to help wartime residents obtain cheaper vegetables by growing crops in back yards and vacant lots. One of its early projects was a "Save the Oaks" campaign, waged to preserve the venerable trees scattered through the original townsite. The club staged its first annual garden show in 1935. Fifty years later, in 1985, the City Council accepted a proposal from the Garden Club and other interested citizens to preserve and maintain the Elizabeth F. Gamble house and gardens at 1431 Waverley Street. Miss Gamble had maintained the 2.3-acre property as a showplace, often sending cut flowers to delighted recipients around town. She deeded the house and yard to the city at her death. After long debate as to how to use the property, the Garden Club plan won out with the proviso that enough funds be raised to sustain the Gamble Garden Center far into the future.

The Red Cross

Although Red Cross activity in the Palo Alto-Stanford community began during the Spanish-

PALO ALTO WEEKLY/RENEE BURGARD

Elizabeth F. Gamble willed her home and gardens at 1431 Waverley Street to the City of Palo Alto. The Gamble Garden Center operates the facility.

American War, the Palo Alto Area Chapter of the American Red Cross was not formally chartered until October 1916. Dr. George J. Peirce and Lydia Mitchell were foremost leaders in its early years.

The chapter, which swelled from 155 to 4,550 volunteers during World War I, has always drawn members from nearby communities as well as Palo Alto. Its activities have varied with the needs of passing eras, ranging from rolling bandages and sewing hospital gowns for soldiers to operating a motor corps, mobilizing local flood relief, raising funds to aid disaster-stricken areas, sharing in the work of social and health agencies, arranging aid to prisoners of war, collecting blood donations and teaching such courses as water safety and first aid. Helping the homeless and having teens drive its cars in a program aimed to curb student drunk driving are recent additions.

In 1948 the chapter moved into its own building at 400 Mitchell Lane, opposite the downtown train depot, on a half-acre portion of El Camino Park leased from the city for $1 a year. It took elections in 1970 and 1976 to work out lease conflicts with the 1965 park initiative and extend the lease until 2013. The chapter now pays all taxes and assessments on the property. A new chapter building was erected in 1982.

The YMCA and YWCA

The city has active YMCA and YWCA organizations, serving both youths and adults. Each has its own building — the YMCA of the Mid-Peninsula maintains its Palo Alto Center, one of several, at 3412 Ross Road, and the Mid-Peninsula YWCA is at 4161 Alma Street. These agencies have reached out far beyond the roles their original names defined, and adapted their programs often to meet residents' changing needs, whether for classes, physical training, social interaction, camping experiences, crisis counseling, sports, child care or other purposes.

Four Sister Cities

A broadening of cultural interests to the international scene occurred in 1962, after the mayor of Palo Alto received a letter from the mayor of Palo, a tiny rural town in the Philippines, suggesting that the cities become sisters. The result was the formation of Neighbors Abroad, and the subsequent adoption of three more sister cities: Oaxaca, Mexico; Enschede, Netherlands and Linkoping, Sweden.

Palo Altans have made numerous trips to the four sisters, and have entertained their visiting

PALO ALTO WEEKLY/CAROLYN CLEBSCH

The "Foreign Friends" at Embarcadero Road and Waverley Street is one of many pieces of public art located throughout the city. It is a gift from Palo Alto's sister city in Sweden.

leaders. In Palo, the Palo Alto group built an educational resource center and sponsored a library. Sister Cities International honored Neighbors Abroad in 1989 with a "Best Overall Program" award sponsored by the Reader's Digest Association.

Support for Seniors

In the mid-1960s, the public began to be aware that the area's rapid growth and cost inflation was making life difficult for some of its seniors. A study of downtown census tract 5113, made through the Community Council of Northern Santa Clara County in 1964, identified special needs of seniors and began exploring ways to meet them. Among the results were a small seniors' information center at the new downtown library and stimulation of housing and bus services. Meanwhile, a seniors guild at the First Methodist Church began testing weekly low-cost lunches for persons residing nearby. In 1972 the Rotary Club of Palo Alto established La Comida de California, a hot-lunch program for seniors, initially at All Saints Church.

When the north county council lost its United Way funding and was phased out, its Senior Division voted in 1968 to continue under a new name: the Senior Coordinating Council of the Palo Alto Area, Inc. (SCC). Carol Bernhardt made the transition as executive director, and in 1973 directed a comprehensive study of Palo Alto area residents 60 years or older, with both foundation funding and city support. This study identified the need for a central senior center; a senior day care and health program, started in 1976 at the Palo Alto Baptist Church; and a home repair service, also set up in 1976 with strong municipal support.

After years of discussion with city officials, it was decided that SCC would be the primary provider of services for seniors and consultant for their needs in Palo Alto. The city made the old Police/Fire Station at 450 Bryant available, and SCC, in a campaign led by Wesley "Bud" Hubbard and Dr. Sidney Mitchell, raised more than $1.2 million to fund renovation of the building. The new Senior Center opened in September 1978,

PALO ALTO WEEKLY/CAROLYN CLEBSCH

A Senior Center audience listens as former Congressman Tom Campbell delivers a talk in the G. Derwood Baker Distinguished Lecture Series.

The Senior Center at 450 Bryant opened in 1978 after a $1.2 million renovation of the former police and fire headquarters.

bringing many services under one roof. These include information and referral, classes, lectures, cultural events, the expanded hot-meal program still called La Comida, tax counseling and legal assistance, the fix-it service, a home equity loan program and RSVP — the Retired Senior Volunteer Program, which helped to generate what is now known as the Executive Service Corps.

The SCC also sponsors annual Lifetimes of Achievement awards. The Downtown Farmers' Market is one of its fund-raising activities. City funding, 38% of SCC's outlays in 1978-79, was down to 20.7% in 1991-92 owing to growth of private giving sustaining the now almost $1.5 million expenditures.

Banned in Palo Alto!

Early residents strongly believed in the power of cultural events to influence local audiences. From 1921 until 1954, the city's Board of Commercial Amusements ruled on what movies Palo Altans could see. Although the board claimed its job was not to censor films, theater managers did not show any it found objectionable, such as *Flaming Youth* and movies featuring Fatty Arbuckle, after he gained "unsavory notoriety." In January 1954, the board attracted attention when it banned *Donovan's Brain* with Lew Ayres as "gruesome," *Man Crazy* as an "exposure without a remedy," and *The French Line* with Jane Russell as "too controversial" (Russell herself was dubious about the propriety of her dance). The next month the board rated *Miss Sadie Thompson* starring Rita Hayworth "adults only." Then a theater manager challenged the board's powers in court, and for a time after March 25, 1954, its pronouncements were advisory only. Then they stopped entirely.

A Limit to Public Tolerance

In the changing times of the 1960s and '70s, the local public's tolerance broadened, but an episode in late 1976 demonstrated that it could still be stretched to the snapping point. Massage parlors that were obvious fronts for prostitution had built up, particularly along southerly stretches of El Camino Real. Early one Friday, acting in tandem with the District Attorney's Office, the Palo Alto Police Department closed 17 massage and nude dance joints. The lawmen utilized a novel legal approach: action under the Red Light District Abatement Act, which put the onus on owners of the premises involved. The abatement foray caused so much trouble for the owners that massage never came back. The *Times* editorialized:

> ... *Palo Alto, whose people have never considered their hometown any sort of an "open city," finally has shed its unwanted reputation as the Peninsula's largest sex-shop center. It is poetic justice for a city of rather conservative social tastes not only to find the means of brushing off these leeches, but also to show the way to other cities that dislike being victimized...*

A more pleasant chapter in the city's entertainment annals opened in the late 1980s when David Woodley Packard undertook a costly restoration of the Stanford Theatre on University Avenue,

PENINSULA TIMES TRIBUNE/VERN FISHER

David Woodley Packard restored the Stanford Theatre and continues to screen films from the golden era of Hollywood.

backed by funds from his parents' family foundation. In 1990, Packard began presenting double bills of classic films from Hollywood's golden years, with theater organ music before most showings.

Despite all the pressures of mass culture toward nationwide homogeneity, it is difficult to read the record of Palo Alto's history without concluding that the penchant of its people and its local government for creating distinctive new cultural activities and sustaining the classic ones may last for at least another 100 years.

Butcher Patrick Lowery of the Midtown Safeway surveys the damage left by the October 1989 earthquake.

8

Shared Memories, Unforgettable Events

"It was like a terrier shaking a rat."
— *Professor Guido Marx on the 1906 earthquake*

As a community, Palo Alto has felt the heat of national attention and shared the suffering and sorrow of earthquakes, wars, depression, floods and droughts.

In one milestone event of the community's fledgling years, a hometown favorite son, Herbert Clark Hoover, was elected president of the United States. Lingering even longer in early residents' memories was the great earthquake of 1906. Also indelibly etched in the consciousness of those who endured them were two wartime eras, 1917-18 and 1941-45, and the austerity of the in-between period: the Depression of the 1930s. In 1955, San Francisquito Creek overflowed, flooding a large part of the city. And in 1989, another major earthquake struck. In the winter of 1990-91, a long string of freezing nights combined with a protracted drought to do unprecedented damage to Palo Alto trees and gardens.

Of all these episodes, the 1906 earthquake caused the greatest immediate disruption of townspeople's lives and routines.

Violent Shaking, and Then…

Just before dawn on April 18, 1906, the earth began to shake violently, rousing townspeople from their slumber. Engineering Professor Guido H. Marx, who lived off campus in Professorville, recalled that he and his wife, Gertrude, were "rudely awakened by the shaking of the house and the accompanying rumble, roar and crash."

Retelling the story later, Marx wrote:

"What is it?" said she.
"It's an earthquake — and it's a bad one,"
I replied.
"What shall we do?"
"Stay right here. This little house will last as long as anything."

I knew the sturdy construction of our bungalow… but in my secret heart I felt that nothing could survive such vicious shaking, that this was the end for us. It was like a terrier shaking a rat.

But the Marxes did survive; their children also were safe. Their four brick chimney tops came down, as if sliced off at the roof. A broken water line in the kitchen had to be shut off. Little else was damaged, however, and outside all looked peaceful; they even thought of going back to bed, but decided to stay up to restore order.

Marx, whose leg was in a cast due to a baseball injury, grew vexed when the busman did not arrive to take him to the campus. Then word of damage at Stanford began to drift in. He headed downtown on crutches, and was shocked to see buildings in ruins along University Avenue. Hobbling on to the university, he found students and faculty milling about "like disturbed cattle."

"No one at first was able to take in the magnitude of the disaster," Marx observed. It took time to comprehend that the university had to be shut down because so many buildings were unsafe.

Scientific instruments had recorded a long temblor, 48 seemingly interminable seconds, and the most intense on the San Andreas Fault in all California's years as a state, 8.3 on the Richter scale.

Palo Altans found that almost every brick chimney in town had fallen. Some chimneys had crashed through roofs; many houses were jarred off their foundations. For the most part, however, the wood-frame houses withstood the severe shaking fairly well, and fortunately, Palo Alto reported no serious injuries. Lack of reinforcement and faulty construction could be detected in the most heavily damaged business structures along University Avenue and on The Circle. Some with side walls ripped off and floors sagging to the ground had to be torn down; others were judged worth repairing. Business district losses approximated $140,000, while damage to residences totaled $25,000 (in 1906 dollars, with chimney repairs figured at $5 each). Water and power service were soon restored.

Tremendous damage occurred at Stanford University, where two lives were lost. Otto Gerdes of College Terrace, a fireman at the powerhouse, was crushed in the crash of its towering smokestack, but not until after he had bravely closed the master electric switch. J.R. Hanna, a student, was killed when one of Encina Hall's stone chimneys fell through the roof. Entrance gates at El Camino Real lay flattened, and up Palm Drive at the entry to the Quadrangle, the giant Memorial Arch sprawled in ruins. The clock tower atop Memorial Church had plummeted through the roof, wrecking the interior, blowing out the mosaic-faced front wall and destroying stained-glass windows. A number of arches on the Quad had shifted and were damaged. Near the Oval, the recently completed library and gymnasium were demolished. Many called it a blessing that Mrs. Stanford, who had died in 1905, just the year before, had not lived to suffer this devastating blow.

In the confusion caused by the quake and its aftershocks, many wild rumors circulated in Palo Alto and on campus, including one that San Francisco had been inundated by a great tidal wave. By noon, however, the truth could be seen in the smoke-filled sky to the north — San Francisco was burning, not drowning. As night fell on that terrible Wednesday, Palo Altans could read

Lirio Hall, an early meeting hall used for church and social affairs and private school classes, before and after the 1906 earthquake.

newspapers outdoors by the light of the flames 30 miles away.

By the next day, Palo Alto's problems looked puny in comparison with those of the metropolis. At first, expecting hordes of refugees, the town stationed deputized guards on its outskirts, with orders to watch for suspicious characters. Before long, it became clear that the influx would not be massive — that Palo Altans would have to take aid to stricken San Francisco, where the reported toll ran to more than 450 people killed, 1,500 injured and 250,000 left homeless, and where fires burned on relentlessly. Later research has pointed to as many as 3,000 deaths.

One messenger who brought word of San Francisco's plight was Paul C. Edwards, a Stanford senior who later became editor of the *San Fran-*

cisco News. Edwards had ridden north with three other collegians in a horse-drawn rig, intent on delivering the story of campus damage to the San Francisco newspapers — until he learned the papers were shut down. About dawn, he returned to Palo Alto by rail; the trains were running irregularly, their telegraph wires down.

The local press was spreading what news it could gather. Damages rendered the *Palo Alto Times* unable to publish in its offices on the second and third floors over H.W. Simkins' stationery store. But once the shaky building was braced, composing room superintendent W.F. Henry and linotypist E.B. "Ned" Young evaded police guards and got in to retrieve cases of pied type, which they took to F.A. Stuart's undamaged print shop on High Street. It was nighttime before they managed to run off about 200 copies of a special edition. The weekly *Palo Alto Tribune*, its shop still functional, got out an extra but for lack of electricity had to print it on a job press by foot power. The *Daily Palo*

Alto, forerunner of the *Stanford Daily*, put out several editions in each of the next two days.

John F. Parkinson, who had just taken over as president of the city's Board of Trustees, called a mass meeting for Thursday evening. Palo Altans, along with Stanford faculty and students, organized a food chain to help supply paralyzed San Francisco. Trustee George J. Carey, a butcher, gave several hundred pounds of meat for soup, outlying dairies promised milk and bakeries gave bread. Early Friday, a train from Palo Alto carried the first supplies from outside to San Francisco: 150 gallons of soup, 900 gallons of milk and 7,000 loaves of bread. Volunteers from the campus rode along to distribute food and help staff emergency hospitals. Medicines, clothing and cash donations soon followed. In Palo Alto, a camp for the homeless near the town plaza at University and The Circle sheltered 500 to 600 refugees.

The spacious Congregational Church, completed less than a year earlier, became the town's

Frazer & Company store on University Avenue at Emerson Street following the 1906 earthquake.

main relief station. F.E. Perham wrote that situations arose there that were almost beyond belief, and related this one:

> *A man left his wife on a downtown street corner of the stricken city [San Francisco] while he went to his office to see what he might save from the impending wreck. When he returned the fire had swept that district. His wife had fled, but whither? Wildly seeking her he was told that she had likely been swept along with the throngs going down the Peninsula. Footsore and desperate, he arrived at this shelter. He was set at table for food and rest. Lo! Opposite him sat his wife. A joyous meeting!*

Despite the trauma of the quake, Palo Altans began cleaning up and rebuilding damaged structures almost immediately. Within two weeks, nearly every merchant was doing business much as before the shaking, mindful of Parkinson's stern order forbidding any gouging of the unfortunate. Life soon returned to normal.

Homemade Holidays

In the early years of incorporation, entertainment in the form of movies, radio and television was yet unborn, so the community provided its own fun and uplift. The Fourth of July, in particular, was celebrated with fervor. In 1895, for example, ceremonies began with Old Glory being hoisted to the top of a 100-foot flagpole at The Circle. Then came a parade four blocks long, with floats, cyclists and equestrians. After that, celebrants progressed to a clambake, a concert and a grand ball at Nortree Hall (on University Avenue opposite Florence Street) attended by 40 couples.

In 1901, live oaks on The Circle were decked with red, white and blue bunting and American flags for the Glorious Fourth. Two hose companies staged a fire drill race, and businessmen from the south side of University Avenue outpulled the north-side team in a tug-of-war. J.F. Parkinson, merchant and town trustee, won the fat men's

50-yard dash and took home a box of cigars.

By 1904, Palo Alto was inviting visitors from throughout the region for its Independence Day wingding. Paraders formed up that year in seven large divisions; their march began with a bang from no fewer than 10,000 firecrackers. Lunch tables under a big tent near Ramona Street and University accommodated 5,000 people. Then the action shifted to a baseball game at the field at Hamilton Avenue and Middlefield Road. Evening brought another ear-splitting bang, this time from 35,000 firecrackers.

Chautauquas and Circuses

Less noisy but still crowded and popular were the annual Chautauquas that began a decade later. These traveling performances, named for the New York state town where they originated, merged culture with showmanship. A big tent at University and Bryant Street sheltered Palo Alto's initial Chautauqua (July 16-21, 1914). The program included a lyric glee club; Bronte, "the smartest dog in the world"; Ciricillo's Italian band; singers from the Taviu Grand Opera Company and, of course, lectures.

Subsequent Chautauqua locations reflected the town's growth. In 1923, the tent was pitched at Lytton Avenue and Ramona. A year later, the site was University and Middlefield on the edge of town.

Circuses came to Palo Alto often. The one oldtimers remembered best was the Palmer Brothers' Wild Animal Circus that first performed on November 5, 1921, on grounds between the railroad and the state highway (El Camino Real). When the time came to pack the wagons a few days later, part-owner W.F. Palmer, the man with the payroll, had vanished — and with him most of the sideshow: the fat girl, the midget maiden, the pigmy boy and the bushman.

So the circus with 190 employees was stranded. Before long, neighbors began complaining about lions roaring, elephants trumpeting and smells multiplying. The city, which controlled the grounds, tried raising the rent from $10 to $100 a

A poster announcing a Chautauqua meeting in Palo Alto.

The United States Army operated Camp Fremont, a training facility, during World War I in Menlo Park.

day. That got the site cleared — the ponies and horses went to the Stanford stock farm, the wild animals to the Army remount station opposite the base hospital (later the Menlo Park VA Hospital). The train stood for a while on a spur track at Runnymede, near Ravenswood. Finally a veteran showman rescued the circus and rehabilitated it for the next season.

Entertaining the Troops

After the United States entered World War I in 1917, the U.S. Army built Camp Fremont in a sector of Menlo Park extending from San Francisquito Creek to Santa Cruz Avenue, between El Camino Real and University Drive. Because the camp was so close to Palo Alto (indeed, Mayor C.P. Cooley boasted of his part in attracting the Army's interest), residents pitched in to help make its officers and enlisted men feel at home. The National Defenders Club — a forerunner of the World War II USOs — opened in Palo Alto on April 3, 1918, managed for the War Camp Community Service

by the National League for Women's Service and based in two large rooms above the Post Office. In May, the City Council voted to pay for the utilities. More than 400 volunteers enrolled, operating the canteen as well as scheduling band concerts, songfests, plays and other entertainment. There were plenty of troops to work with — at its peak, Camp Fremont's muster ran to 42,000. Said the *Times*:

> *The khaki chaps truly appreciate the hearty welcome of Palo Alto. They appreciate it because it seemed to break the spell that becomes so tiresome especially in time of war, and at the same time it aroused a keener appreciation of the principle for which our country is now fighting.*

Before the United States entered the war, Palo Altans rallied to aid Herbert Hoover's relief efforts for Belgium, a country devastated in the war's early stages. Beginning in 1915, they put on several Belgian Relief street fairs and raised money to aid the victims of battle and economic dislocation. These events preceded organization of the Palo Alto Red Cross chapter in 1916.

After America had become a combatant, the town took part in meatless Tuesdays, wheatless Wednesdays and even an ice cream-less day. Two war casualties that hit Palo Altans hard were the deaths of Lt. Alan Nichols, the high school principal's son, and Lt. Arthur Clifford Kimber, both of whom had gone overseas with the Red Cross ambulance service and then had become aviators for France with the Lafayette Esquadrille. Six others among the 432 men who enlisted locally in the American Expeditionary Force lost their lives.

Bringing the World Home

During the 1920s, events and personalities of international stature began to touch the Palo Alto-Stanford community. These centered around Herbert Hoover ("Bert," to old friends), a member of Stanford's pioneer class who once was photographed as a member of a University Avenue surveying crew. Hoover had earned world renown and a fortune as a mining engineer, returning to Stanford at intervals to serve as a trustee, teach and finally build a campus home. During World War I he became national food administrator, and afterward oversaw the relief of starving Europeans. Then he became secretary of commerce under Presidents Harding and Coolidge.

Crowds celebrating Herbert Hoover's election as president of the United States at his Stanford campus home November 6, 1928.

93

Nominated for president by the Republican Party after Coolidge chose not to run again, Hoover delivered his acceptance speech August 22, 1928, in Stanford Stadium before a vast throng of admirers. His fall campaign concluded in Palo Alto, and on the night of November 6, Herbert and Lou Henry Hoover listened to radio returns at their home. Famed bandmaster John Philip Sousa was conducting a concert that evening at the Stanford basketball pavilion, and when word came that Hoover had bested Al Smith for the presidency, Sousa's musicians rode up San Juan Hill to the Hoover house in hastily arranged buses. There the band serenaded the Hoovers with "Hail to the Chief" and other rousing selections as townspeople and campus figures crowded around.

Four years later an exhausted President Hoover received a loyal welcome at the Palo Alto depot as he ended his re-election campaign. But events had turned against him. The Great Depression was on, and Franklin D. Roosevelt had defeated him.

Extending a Helping Hand

Arriving on the heels of the booming 1920s, the Depression spurred a community effort to help those who were without homes, money, food or hope. In 1931, Captain Jesse Glover and his wife, Mary Belle, established The Shelter to assist the droves of unemployed men passing through the area in search of jobs. The Shelter was nicknamed "Hotel de Zink" after Palo Alto Police Chief Howard Zink, whose department handled all donations and bookkeeping. In 2 1/2 years of operation, The Shelter housed and fed 50,000 transients for up to three days, let them chop wood or do other work and then sent them on their way.

As problems of the homeless again came to the fore early in the 1990s, a new Hotel de Zink materialized. The name was given to a rotating shelter for the homeless, hosted by 12 Palo Alto churches and the Urban Ministry led by the Rev. Jim Burklo. Shelter guests could stay for up to two months while seeking work and acquiring means for independent living.

"A Day That Will Live in Infamy"

Shattering the quiet of a Palo Alto Sunday on December 7, 1941, radio stations broadcast the news that Japan had launched a sneak air attack on Pearl Harbor and other U.S. and British bases in the Pacific and Far East. Suddenly, preparedness steps — notably the prewar draft registration, in which Stanford graduate student John F. Kennedy had drawn his number in Palo Alto — made more sense.

As the United States shifted to a full war footing, civil defense forces hastily organized lest Japanese pilots or submariners attack coastal targets. Through blacked-out Palo Alto, troop trains and motorized troop convoys moved up the Peninsula to debarkation points in the upper bay. Some were bound for the Pacific, others for North Africa or the European Theater of Operations.

Army bombers and fighter planes based at Moffett Field flew over the Santa Clara Valley until the Navy regained use of the former dirigible station as an anti-submarine blimp base. During the jittery days after Pearl Harbor, an anti-aircraft battery stood watch on a hill near Page Mill Road and what is now Foothill Expressway. In May 1942, Palo Alto's Japanese-American residents, whether citizens or not, were unceremoniously shipped off to inland internment centers.

The war also brought food and fuel rationing, victory gardens, scrap collections and war bond drives. Townspeople operated a USO hospitality house for visiting servicemen at the home of Mrs. Walter Rodgers on University Avenue at Webster Street. In hundreds of Palo Alto homes, a red-bordered flag hung in a front window. A blue star inside the border meant a son or daughter in the armed forces; a gold star stood for a soldier, airman, sailor or marine who would not be returning. Each passing year multiplied the number of stars — of both colors. (Seventy-four former Palo Alto High School students gave their lives, including two women, Virginia Ruth Mayer and Margaret Neubauer, and they were by no means all the community's war dead.)

Depression Era unemployed men awaiting temporary room and board at The Shelter.

In the 1980s the Urban Ministry provided assistance to the area's homeless at its "Rolling Estates,"
which rotated among sites around Palo Alto.

Palo Alto children participate in one of the World War II scrap drives by collecting old tires for the war effort.

Palo Altans did their part for the World War II bond drives. This scene is at the University Avenue train station.

By D-Day, June 6, 1944, when the Allies landed in Normandy, it clearly was only a matter of time — and of grim fighting and long homefront production shifts — before the Axis was defeated. Palo Altans celebrated Germany's surrender on May 8, 1945, V-E Day, with solemn church services; not until Japan gave up on V-J Day, August 14, 1945, did townspeople raise a din of blaring auto horns, clanging garbage-can lids and hoarded fireworks. The town was still very dry; many celebrants spurned gasoline rationing and drove to restaurants south of Palo Alto, buying out their liquor and food stocks. Many a roadhouse had to close early that night.

Conversion to peacetime life ran a rough road for a time, but everyone yearned for it so ardently as to take the bumps with few complaints. Mustered-out veterans soon flocked to Peninsula colleges to start or complete their educations with GI Bill of Rights financing. As soon as housing was

available, veterans bought, using low-interest GI Bill or Cal-Vet guaranteed loans. This push to become educated and settled, sometimes both at once, spurred the creation of housing tracts. In turn, the surge of subdivisions eventually pushed the city south from Oregon Avenue to San Antonio Road and east to Bayshore Highway.

Nature's Challenges

As work progressed on new streets south of Oregon, flooding became a wet-weather problem in the late 1940s, but it was nothing like the Christmas flood of 1955. In that year, a tropical storm blew in to cap several wet days. Heavy rain soaked the city for hours on the night of December 22 while extremely high tides slowed the flow of runoff water into the bay. When debris clogged San Francisquito Creek at the Bayshore Highway bridge, backed-up torrents broke through the creek's south bank behind Edgewood Drive

PALO ALTO TIMES/GENE TUPPER

Winter floods were common in the 1950s, the most serious being the December 1955 flood.

shortly after midnight. Water several feet deep poured down Greer Road and flooded scores of homes in low-lying areas. Families waded to safety or in some cases had to be evacuated by boat. Matadero Creek also topped its banks, and underpasses were inundated. This flood, and one of less severity in April 1958, led to major creek channel improvements along San Francisquito, Matadero, Adobe and other creeks, and better tide gates in the baylands flood basin.

More of nature's 100-year tests lay ahead. Still to come were four years of drought in the late 1970s, a Mediterranean fruit fly infestation in 1981 and a second protracted dry spell bridging over from the 1980s into the 1990s. Moreover, the second drought was punctuated by a major earthquake, and then by a freezing spell which, while not extraordinary for colder U.S. regions, was the worst an urban Palo Alto with its usually mild climate had ever experienced.

A Pesky Problem Hatches

The Medfly problem hatched with the discovery of the destructive pests in San Jose and Mountain View neighborhoods. State officials at first attempted to eradicate the Medflies with ground spraying, quarantines, biological tricks and orders to strip the home-grown fruits and vegetables that many Peninsula people delight in raising. When that failed to end the infestation, aerial spraying of malathion, a pesticide, was ordered by Govenor Edmund G. "Jerry" Brown Jr. under pressure from federal agriculture officials.

Nighttime helicopter runs commenced July 14, 1981, in Zone 1, comprised of the portion of Palo Alto between Oregon Avenue and San Antonio Road and adjoining sectors of Mountain View and Los Altos. It was the first such pesticide drop over an urban region, and drew long, angry protests and claims for damages to car finishes. Night spraying continued over the region intermittently for about four months, then resumed in 1982 until June in some Peninsula zones. California finally was pronounced Medfly-free in September 1982. Later on, Medflies were found in

other parts of California, but state officials were cautious about invoking new aerial spraying.

The Mosquito Menace

Although the Medfly campaign was the most dramatic pest suppression battle to affect Palo Altans, it was not the only one. In the city's early days, clouds of marsh mosquitoes taking wing near the bay made residents' evenings miserable for 10 months every year. In 1918, the Matadero Mosquito Abatement District was formed to control the insects. By the time the district was dissolved in 1961 and the Santa Clara County Health Department took over, it extended over almost all the land from Stevens Creek to the north county line, including Palo Alto, Mountain View and the Los Altos area.

"The mosquitoes were so terrible we couldn't enjoy our residences or yards in the summer," Frank Hoge, a founder and longtime board member, said of why the district was first organized. "Outdoor living was pretty much of a dream." To gain control, district crews sprayed oils or larvicides on pools where the skeeters bred and gave free mosquito fish to owners of outdoor fish ponds. One board member, Donald Steel, devised a drainage system to keep stagnant water from puddling on the bay flats. Even so, heavy spring rains, notably in 1932, 1949 and 1957, hatched problem years. The dissolution of the Matadero district — because the problem was deemed under control and the county could take over — marked the first abolition of a Palo Alto area taxing agency by a public vote.

Another Hard Shaking

Almost exactly 83 1/2 years after the great earthquake of 1906, a major quake struck at 5:04 p.m. on October 17, 1989. Palo Alto again felt a violent bucking of the ground — and again was spared the deadly damage that befell San Francisco and other areas. At 7.1 on the Richter scale, the '89 temblor was no match for "The Big One" in force, yet it initiated new generations of residents to earthquake survival and tested the quality of

PENINSULA TIMES TRIBUNE/JOE MELENA

A time-lapse photograph of helicopters sweeping over Palo Alto in the Medfly war in the spring and summer of 1981.

many decades of construction.

During the Loma Prieta quake, as it was named, chimneys toppled again. Locally, the heaviest damage occurred along the easterly base of the foothills, with the hard-hit Veterans Administration Hospital in Palo Alto requiring $56 million in emergency repairs and sustaining doubled per-patient costs until 1995. Windows shattered in downtown businesses, and power went out, but there were no grave injuries. One landmark tower, the 70-year-old Campanile at Palo Alto High School, was damaged, but in the end escaped being razed.

As in 1906, Stanford University took a sledge-hammer blow in '89. Once again, Stanford Memo-

rial Church incurred heavy damage, along with parts of the Main Quad and some of the older residence halls. The damage bill on campus settled at $110 million.

The greatest casualties were recorded in Santa Cruz County, Oakland and San Francisco. Overall, Northern California's loss totaled 67 lives and an estimated $10 billion in damage.

Apart from the VA hospital, damage to private buildings in Palo Alto ran roughly $20 million, and that to public buildings, $200,000. Damages in the 11-story Channing House, and the risk of worse in a bigger quake, prompted its retiree residents to agree to retrofit the building with huge underground shock absorbers — a mitigating technique known as base isolation — at a cost of $7 million.

A Long Dry Spell

Although a dry year or two in Central California is commonplace, the low-rainfall years beginning with 1986-87 not only lasted unusually long but also forced breaks from past public and private practice. Rationing of water purchased from the San Francisco-owned Hetch Hetchy system or pumped from Palo Alto wells grew stringent, and many residents let lawns die or replaced them with drought-tolerant landscaping.

In December 1990, just when residents hoped rains would break the dry cycle, a string of icy Arctic air masses brought in California's worst winter cold in more than half a century. During a dozen nights leading up to New Year's Eve, Palo Alto's low temperatures fell below the freezing point, mostly in the mid-20s and in some locations in the teens. Daytime warming often was too slight to thaw the stone-cold ground.

Frozen pipes burst, swamping local plumbers with repair work. The public was asked not to try to protect pipes by keeping water trickling because of the water shortage. Subtropical trees, already stressed by the drought, perished or were set back severely. In a climate and location that normally supports as wide a variety of trees as can be found anywhere, carobs, geijeras, Brazilian peppers, black acacias, eucalyptus, myoporums and sweet shades, among other trees, were decimated or worse. Succulents went limp, and tender garden plants succumbed by the thousands.

A drop saved is. . .

To paraphrase Ben Franklin's sage advice, water saved now helps preserve our precious and limited future supply. So far this winter, city-wide water conservation has dropped significantly. Despite cooler weather and some rainfall, water shortage conditions continue. Palo Alto still needs to meet its monthly water allocations from San Francisco Water Department. **Everyone must cut water use this winter to minimize use of wells and to avoid steep penalties.**

We all need to use water wisely, especially during the current drought conditions. Since the rainy season doesn't end until April, we won't know until then whether our water restrictions from San Francisco will ease or tighten. In the meantime, the City is preparing for different scenarios and will continue to update you on the water situation.

If you haven't cut your water use yet, you need to start today. Call Utilities Energy Services at 329-2241 if you need ideas on reducing water use.

. . .a drop earned!

The Palo Alto Utilities promoted water conservation during the drought years of the late 1980s and early 1990s.

Before letting up, the big freeze continued a day or so into 1991, which became the year the jacarandas didn't bloom in Palo Alto. Throughout California, crops and often the groves where they grew were lost in the freeze — the third most costly natural disaster in state history, after the 1906 and 1989 earthquakes.

For all the calamities encountered in a century — onslaughts of nature with its terrifying temblors, parching, flooding and icing, and dangers humans have a hand in creating — Palo Altans have been exceptionally fortunate. No catastrophe in the city has exacted a massive toll in lives, and no setback has left such grave wounds that they could not be remedied or outgrown rather rapidly. Civic forehandedness may have played a small part in this — the body politic has learned and applied lessons from each earthquake, each drought, each new kind of disaster. Nevertheless, active preparedness for what have come to be known as worst-case scenarios continues to be seen as clearly warranted. Palo Alto's luck might some day fail.

The architecture of the new Plaza Ramona blends with its historic Ramona Street neighbors.

9

Architecture and Annexations

*From 1970 to 1987, the Palo Alto Board of
Realtors calculated, the average value of houses
in the city increased by more than $40 a day.*

P alo Alto is a city known for rich architectural variety. This diversity derived in part from the city's long build-out period — the eight decades it took to use up most available building sites — and in part from the extensive remodelings of the 1980s and early 1990s, which transformed the appearance of many tract homes.

Eye-catching styles range from venerable Victorians to Classical Revivals and Colonials, and from early Spanish Colonial Revivals to California Ranch Houses. More than a few designs evident in this mix were pioneered locally.

Visitors driving through established neighborhoods often find pleasure in the houses and landscaping they see, and residents visiting a street like "Christmas Tree Lane" (the 1700 and 1800 blocks of Fulton Street) in season witness not only dazzling holiday displays but also an underlying neighborliness at work.

It was not always thus. Neighborliness existed from the start, but otherwise the town was anything but an impressive sight in its first few years of existence. An early resident described it as "one immense stubble waste with huge oak trees," and added, "There was no discernable road but by observing the stakes one could find what might be a path or trail."

The story begins with the purchase of 697.5 acres by Timothy Hopkins, with the blessing of Leland Stanford, on February 28, 1887, a matter of weeks before ground was broken for the new university on Stanford's farm. Later Hopkins added 40 acres. The platting of the town, first called

University Park, was delayed, apparently because Hopkins initially assigned the job to Southern Pacific draftsmen and then decided to have it redone.

Not until June 7, 1890, as the haying season ended, did lots go on public sale. Various real estate agents combined forces and ran an excursion train from San Francisco to the new town site. Investors visited in record numbers and bought whole blocks for future sale. Other people came from all over California to look over the area and to buy property for future homes. They were followed in 1891-92 by residents of neighboring Mayfield who wanted to start businesses, by faculty members of the newly opened university and by families from far and wide who sought to buy land to provide housing for themselves and their children, many of them now students at the university.

The first home built in the Hopkins tract was Anna Zschokke's. She and her husband, living in Santa Clara, had bought a site intending to build when their oldest son was ready to enter Stanford. Her husband's death speeded the move; the widow and her children rode north in a wagon in 1890 and camped under a tree for weeks while their house was being built on Homer Avenue near High Street.

Queen Anne Victorians

Because Palo Alto was founded so late in the 19th century, many architectural styles popular earlier in the 1800s were not widely used in the city,

103

notably Gothic Revival and Italianate and Eastlake Victorian. Many of the town's first houses were of the Queen Anne Victorian style, a design marked by corner towers, numerous gables, porches and balconies and a variety of siding materials, with predominantly classical details.

In 1894, crews built a large Queen Anne Victorian for dentist Charles Decker at Waverley Street and University Avenue, costing $6,000. This residence, known as the Decker House, was moved from the corner to *510 Waverley Street* when the Decker Oaks Building was erected. There it still stands, now devoted to business uses.

In the same year, T.B. Downing, later a member of the first City Council, selected builder W. Matlock Campbell to design what many regard as Palo Alto's finest example of a Queen Anne Victorian. Located at *706 Cowper Street*, at Forest, this house features a corner tower, numerous gables, varied shingle patterns, a round window and a porch abounding with gingerbread. Due to extensive renovation in the 1970s, it has been saved as one of the city's most venerable buildings, and is listed on the National Register of Historic Places. (A listing of all Palo Alto structures listed on the National Register of Historic Places appears in Appendix A. In the remainder of this chapter, buildings so honored are designated

The Downing House at 706 Cowper Street was built in 1894.

The Sunbonnet House at 1061 Bryant Street was designed by Bernard Maybeck in 1899.

with a star.)

The flamboyant Queen Anne style was not limited to the downtown district. A subdued Victorian erected in 1889 at *2310 Yale Street**★** is the oldest surviving house in College Terrace. It was built for Robert Norton Kee, and has been maintained as first built. Another Queen Anne was built in 1889 at *1021 College Avenue* for Christopher Ducker. In 1893, Walter Miller, one of Stanford's first faculty members, had a two-story Victorian built at *2275 Amherst Street* where it still stands.

Shingle Style

The Shingle style was also popular in Palo Alto's first decade. A large cluster of homes of this design is found in Professorville, a historic district listed on the National Register and bounded approximately by Ramona and Waverley streets and Addison and Kingsley avenues. The best known is the "Sunbonnet" house at *1061 Bryant Street,* designed by the major Bay Area architect Bernard

Maybeck for Emma Kellogg in 1899. An earlier example of the style is *1005 Bryant,* built in 1893 for Professor Frank Angell.

Although the houses in the 1100 block of Ramona were built a decade later, they form the most cohesive Shingle style group in the district. In contrast to the Victorian Queen Anne style, which emphasized structural details, Shingle style walls and roofs enclose the interior space with a continuous skin. Colonial elements are often used, but they are integrated into the overall design by the all-encompassing shingles.

The Shingle style also embraces the Craftsman movement in which natural materials and continuity between indoors and out are emphasized. Interior redwood paneling, living and sleeping porches, trellises and groupings of windows are Craftsman features. The residence built for Professor Leander Hoskins at *365 Lincoln Avenue* in 1896 is an excellent example. Prominent exposed timbers support the roof and eaves; heavy unadorned porch columns and groupings of windows are also characteristic features. Other examples of this style are the cottage at *132 Lincoln* and the large residence at *601 Melville Avenue.*

Stanford University fraternities influenced the town's early styles, as they built or leased several of the largest residences. In 1895, Sigma Alpha Epsilon fraternity spent $10,000 to erect a 25-room house on Emerson between Forest and Homer. At 707 Bryant, construction crews completed work in 1897 on what became known as the Delta Tau Delta house — a Queen Anne that stood until 1976, when it was demolished to make way for condominium units. But the boom in such roomy residences did not last, because in 1906 Stanford University required fraternities to locate

their living and meeting places on campus. However, many a Palo Alto house was built with an extra room or two to accommodate Stanford student renters.

A Barn-like Meeting Hall

Palo Alto's first commercial structures were known more for function than for grace. Most were simple wooden buildings. Among them was Nortree Hall, a rather homely two-story building erected in 1892 on University Avenue opposite Florence Street, where Liddicoat's is today. What it lacked in architectural style it made up in purpose. The building had stores on the first floor and a hall for public meetings on the second. Religious services, public assemblies, concerts, dramatic productions,

PALO ALTO HISTORICAL ASSOCIATION

This roomy building at 707 Bryant Street was built for a Stanford fraternity in 1897. It was demolished in 1976 to make way for condominiums.

PALO ALTO HISTORICAL ASSOCIATION/HILL & YARD

University Avenue at The Circle in 1895.

dances, socials and political meetings all found shelter in its barn-like enclosure. Nortree Hall was razed in 1923 and replaced by Liddicoat's.

One hall was not enough to meet every need. When it became apparent that various fraternal organizations needed a suitable gathering place, several early residents formed a private stock company to build it. In 1898, the group brought together architect Samuel Newson and contractor M.P. Madison and commissioned them to erect a two-story structure at *University and High*. Fraternal Hall★ (sometimes referred to as Fraternity Hall) was built at a cost of $9,736 with stores on the first floor and meeting space above. Although the structure has undergone several remodelings, it still stands.

Frank Davis is credited with building some of the important early buildings on The Circle, as well as two once familiar landmarks that are long gone now: the Bank of Palo Alto at The Circle and University and the Palo Alto Hotel at Alma and Lytton.

To get from building to building in pioneer days, residents had to walk through dust or mud,

or on crude wooden walkways made of planks 12 feet long. Near the turn of the century, the first permanent sidewalk, constructed of bituminous rock, was put down in front of Nortree Hall. By 1912, the town could boast nearly a mile of concrete sidewalks.

The First Subdivisions

Sales of the Timothy Hopkins properties continued for decades, directly and indirectly. Even so, the first addition occurred in 1894 when J.F. Parkinson, businessman of many interests, bought Alba Park, near today's Rinconada Park, and subdivided its 15 acres into lots.

A more major subdivision occurred in 1898, when the Seale tract south of Embarcadero Road was cut into blocks. Its streets were broad — 60 feet wide —and their names extended the practice Hopkins had established of naming streets for authors, so that the succession of Kingsley, Melville and Kellogg continued with Churchill, Coleridge, Lowell, Tennyson and Milton (later renamed Seale).

Toward the end of the 1890s, Palo Alto had

107

The Squire House at 900 University Avenue cost approximately $15,000 to build in 1904.

begun to show signs of maturing. From 1894 to 1899, a total of 261 structures had been built. In 1896 alone, the town grew by 31 residences, eight stores, two barns, one school and one stable.

In the early 1900s, some new Palo Alto homes were built in the Classical Revival style with symmetrical facades, classical detailing and Palladian windows. A textbook example is found in Professorville at *334 Kingsley Avenue*, which was built in 1903 for Professor James Rollin Slonaker. The centered door and symmetrical arrangement of the windows, bays and dormers are key elements as well as the corner pilasters and dentil cornice.

Palo Alto's best-known mansion of the early 20th century appeared in 1904 at *900 University Avenue*⋆, across from the Dayan mansion at *449 Seneca Street*, a Colonial built in 1895. The house at 900 University was the home of John A. Squire, built at a cost of about $15,000. The work of architect T. Patterson Ross and builder George W. Mosher, the Greco-Roman or Neo-Classical Revival house stands today as a state historic landmark. Two years after the Squire house was erected, the Peck-Wilson house was built at *860 University*⋆ in the Colonial Revival style.

Another early residence by a recognized master is the Thomas Williams house at *351 Homer*

LELAND the Pioneer Ideal City

FOUNDED UPON THE PROFIT SHARING PLAN

HOTEL LELAND TO BE COMPLETED NOVEMBER, 1908

Adjacent to the Leland Stanford Jr., University. First excursion a great success. **Another excursion Sunday, July 14,** 9:30, a. m., Third and Townsend; 9:40 a. m., Valencia station.

Lot purchasers to become members of the **LELAND IMPROVEMENT CO.** owners and builders of Leland. Lots $300 and upward **with every improvement** before every lot. Stock $50 per share. **$5,000,000 to be expended for utilities and improvements** which are being rapidly built. **Be a pioneer investor and profit sharer. Don't fail to attend next excursion.** Write for booklet. Call at office, which will be open until 8 p. m. and until 9 a. m. Sunday. Tickets for sale only at Leland Company's office.

Leland Improvement Company

19 Seventh St., Grant Building   San Francisco, California

Developers promoted new cities wherever there was the promise of money to be made. The city of Leland was promoted beginning in 1907, but never materialized.

Avenue, designed in 1907 by Ernest Coxhead in the Tudor Revival style. The recessed loggia marks the separation of the two functions of the structure: residence and medical office. Dr. Williams began his medical practice in Palo Alto in 1904 and later served on the City Council.

Apartment Construction

Colonial Revival was the style chosen for one of Palo Alto's first apartment buildings, built at *626-631 Emerson Street* in 1903 by J.B. Daley, pioneer businessman and real estate developer. The two-story building had four six-room flats, which continued to be occupied for about eight decades. In 1987, the structure was renovated for office uses.

The "Ideal City" That Never Was

Just to the southeast of the Seale property, on 888 acres of the old Clarke, Curtner and Emmett ranches, running about a mile along the railroad line from Colorado Avenue to present-day East Meadow Drive, a syndicate of San Francisco businessmen in 1907 projected Leland, "the ideal city." It was to have a five-story, $500,000 hotel of Moorish architecture; a cannery, a shoe factory and other enterprises along the bay front; water transportation and a Methodist college. Local businessmen also were among the organizers: Alfred Seale, J.F. Parkinson, real estate man C.M. Wooster and builders John Dudfield and William Dean. Lots sold for $300 with a share of Leland Improvement Co. stock thrown in.

Leland never got past the planning and promotion stage. The bubble burst when the Market Street Bank of San Francisco failed; its cashier and Leland's leading organizer, W.B. Nash, later was convicted of falsifying bank statements and died in jail in 1912. The property was sold several times, and in 1912 a group of Spokane capitalists offered 5-acre farm parcels under the name Stanford

Irrigated Acres. A few "city farmers" planted berries and vegetables.

Old Seale Ranch Activity

In 1917, the 1898 subdivision of the Seale tract, by then known as the South Palo Alto tract, was annexed to Palo Alto. In that same year, another portion of the old Seale Ranch was subdivided. Alfred Seale and Gus Laumeister spent thousands of dollars grading and surfacing the streets. Along Oregon Avenue, three-acre parcels were offered as "little farms" where buyers could grow corn, tomatoes, alfalfa and pears. Farming was destined not to last, although Oregon Avenue remained on the edge of town for many more years.

Jane Stanford's Southgate Sold

Southgate, between the Palo Alto High School site and Mayfield, was subdivided in 1923. Its name alluded to its location on the then southern edge of Palo Alto and the Stanford campus. This property was the only piece of university-owned land in Palo Alto ever released for purely residential use; Jane Stanford, who had owned it, willed it to the university when she died.

Two hundred Southgate lots 50 to 60 feet wide and 100 to 116 feet deep were advertised. All carried deed restrictions specifying that no house could cost less than $4,000; no cattle, horses, hogs or poultry could be kept on the property and no persons of African, Japanese, Chinese or Mongolian descent were to use or occupy the houses. (Decades later a U.S. Supreme Court decision voided the racial restrictions.)

Similar restrictions existed in a posh 1920s subdivision, Crescent Park, except that houses there could cost no less than $10,000. The tract was bounded by Hamilton Avenue, Southwood Drive, San Francisquito Creek and Chaucer Street. To ensure high neighborhood standards, the architectural style of each house had to be approved by the homeowners association.

The Italianate house at *423 Chaucer*, built in 1923, was the work of prominent Bay Area architect Julia Morgan. Several houses by a second

major Bay Area architect, Gardner Dailey, can also be found in this subdivision. Dailey designed *1800 University Avenue* in 1930 and *27 Crescent Drive* in 1934, both in Spanish Colonial Revival Style.

Charles Sumner, who worked locally, also designed several Palo Alto houses in the Spanish Colonial Revival Style. A particularly fine example of his work is at *1370 Lincoln Avenue.*

In Mayfield, too, real estate agents were taking new interest in laying out and adding new subdivisions. The Curtner, Evergreen and Sunnyside tracts between El Camino Real and the railroad line north and south of the old town limits were annexed to Mayfield. In 1923, 500 lots were offered on terms as low as $1 a week, yet buyers were often slow in putting up houses. All Mayfield areas, new and old, were annexed to Palo Alto in 1925.

Early California Style

As Palo Alto grew in the 1920s and '30s, an important architectural style came upon the scene: the Spanish Colonial Revival design. This style has been cited frequently as having helped to establish the image of the community.

PALO ALTO HISTORICAL ASSOCIATION/ CAROLYN CADDES

Birge Clark designed more than 200 buildings in Palo Alto and on the Stanford campus.

Lucie Stern commissioned Birge Clark to design this home at 1950 Cowper Street for her daughter Ruth.

The first Spanish Colonial Revival house in Palo Alto, designed by Santa Barbara architect George Washington Smith, was built in 1924 at *1336 Cowper Street★*. A nearly blank front facade and windows opening onto an internal patio distinguished it from other houses of the era.

Soon afterward, a home-grown architect, Birge Clark, emerged as the foremost exponent of this style, which he called Early California. Indeed, Birge Clark's work over half a century on both local homes and commercial buildings established him, more than anyone else, as the chief architect and shaper of the community.

The son of Arthur B. Clark, Stanford professor of art and architecture and Mayfield's first "mayor," Birge Clark assisted his father as "clerk of the works" for the Lou Henry Hoover house on the Stanford campus. Former President Herbert Hoover gave the home to Stanford after his wife's death for use as the university president's residence.

Clark, the only architect with an office in Palo Alto between 1922 and 1930, went on to design a total of 98 Palo Alto residences, including all of the homes on Coleridge Avenue between Cowper and Webster streets, and 39 Stanford campus homes. Three residences of which he was most proud were the Dunker House at *420 Maple Street★* and the Charles and Kathleen Norris House at *1247 Cowper Street★,* plus the Lucie Stern residence at *1990 Cowper.* The latter led to a long and productive association with the charitable Mrs. Stern that resulted in several buildings of the Community Center at *1305 Middlefield Road* as well as the Children's Library nearby and the Sea Scout base at the harbor.

Other well-known civic buildings by Clark include the the former police-fire station at *450 Bryant*, now the Palo Alto Senior Center, and the U.S. Post Office, now called the Hamilton branch, at *380 Hamilton Avenue★*. (The Hoovers, whom

The Ramona Street Historic District recognizes the designs of Birge Clark, Pedro de Lemos and others.

he had known since boyhood, gave Clark vital White House help in rescuing his graceful post office design from conformity-minded federal bureaucrats.)

The 500 Ramona Block

Architect Clark also had a hand in designing a highly distinctive business block in downtown Palo Alto: Ramona Street between University and Hamilton. With gentle archways, wrought iron work, tile roofs of varying heights, and courtyards, this block showcases the Spanish and Early California styles.

The first to go up, in 1925, was the Gotham Shop at *520 Ramona*, built by artist-craftsman Pedro de Lemos, curator of the Stanford Museum. De Lemos had bought the property to preserve the old oak tree (finally removed in the 1980s). He designed the structure around the venerable oak and created shops with rustic benches, ceramic tiles and stucco walls. In 1938, de Lemos built another Spanish Colonial Revival commercial office building across the street at *533-539 Ramona*, with a recessed arched entrance, an interior patio, wrought iron and more tiles.

Birge Clark, William Weeks and other architects added to the Spanish flavor of what de Lemos started. In 1928, Clark designed the multistory *Medico-Dental Building* at Hamilton and Ramona, which now has the University Art Center on the ground floor. Across Ramona, Weeks designed the *Cardinal Hotel*, Palo Alto's first non-wood hotel. Excitement attended the Cardinal's debut, for it became the scene of tea dances and balls. The hotel had another purpose: It was intended to help make Hamilton a commercial street.

The unified aspect of the 500 Ramona Street block was recognized by its designation in 1985 as a Historic Architectural District on the National Register of Historic Places. Since then, Jim Baer's *Plaza Ramona* and other remodelings at the University Avenue end of the block have enhanced the theme.

San Franciscans Escape Fog

The flush era of the late '20s spurred apartment construction. William Staller built the Laning Chateau, also known as Staller Court, at *345 Forest Avenue* in 1927, and Casa Real, across the street at *360 Forest*, in 1930, retaining ownership of

The Laning Chateau at 345 Forest Avenue was built in 1927.

both. Laning Chateau, a five-story structure in Spanish Colonial Revival style, contains 85 three-room apartments. Its L-shape allowed its corner site to become a miniature plaza garden with a fountain. Casa Real, built in the same style, contains 40 apartments. During the 1930s, Palo Alto became an informal resort for San Franciscans who rented apartments to escape their city's fog and enjoy the sunshine and the swimming pool behind Casa Real.

During the 1920s and '30s, a number of other styles gained representation among Palo Alto residences, including the Tudor Revival, for example residences at *1445 Bryant* and *345 Coleridge;* the Monterey Revival, such as the residence at *1870 University;* and the Medieval Revival, notably the de Lemos House at *100 Waverley Oaks.**

The Depression years halted most Palo Alto construction. When new building resumed in the late 1930s, the Moderne style was introduced. Moderne buildings were primarily functional with smooth walls, corner windows, rounded corners and a horizontal emphasis. The University Avenue railroad depot is Palo Alto's major streamlined Moderne structure.

The Ranch House Appears

About 1935 the California Ranch style house appeared, combining features of the Craftsman bungalow and the period bungalow of the 1920s. Houses of this style were on one level, with a low-pitched hip or gable roof. They were usually sheathed in stucco, shingles or clapboard, with glass sliding doors leading to covered porches.

Early Ranch style houses dating from the 1930s were the work of an internationally known architect, William W. Wurster. Their hallmark was a glazed gallery serving as a multipurpose living space joining the interior with the exterior. The Le Hane House (1937) at *1935 Webster Street* and the Raas House (1939) at *2240 Cowper Street* are examples.

Much later "Ranch style" came to be an imprecise, catch-all phrase used much like the labels Victorian and bungalow. Nonetheless, the term implies a house having a simplified horizontal profile with a liberal use of glass to integrate outdoor living spaces.

The Leland Manor subdivision opened in 1939 as Palo Alto's first with underground utility lines, hence no overhead telephone or power wires. It is located between Seale and California avenues

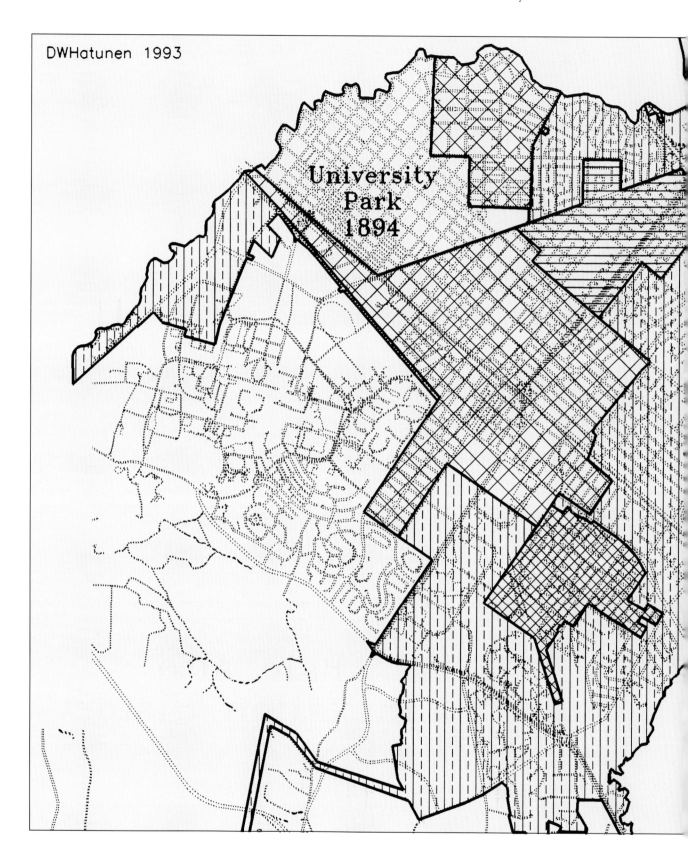

DWHatunen 1993

University
Park
1894

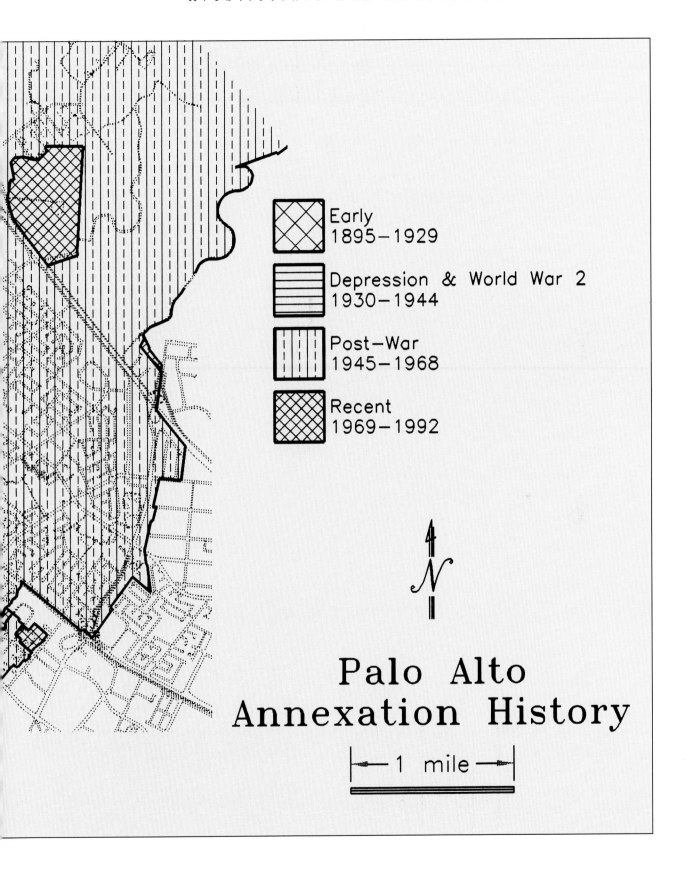

Early
1895–1929

Depression & World War 2
1930–1944

Post–War
1945–1968

Recent
1969–1992

N

Palo Alto
Annexation History

├─── 1 mile ───┤

and between Middlefield and Newell roads. No "designed for living" Leland Manor home was to cost less than $6,500.

Wartime Housing Crisis

World War II shortages of manpower and material brought residential building virtually to a standstill. At the same time, families of defense workers and members of the armed services and refugees from Pacific outposts moved into Palo Alto, creating a severe housing shortage. By 1943, new families were estimated to be arriving at a rate of five to ten a day. "Share the home" became a popular slogan, and many residents answered the call.

The war's end did nothing to alleviate the housing crisis — instead, the crisis worsened for a time. In December 1945, the city building inspector reported a need for at least 1,000 new homes. Newcomers were sleeping in garages, basements, attics, woodsheds and even remodeled chicken coops.

Builders and developers trooped to Palo Alto to attack the postwar shortage. From 1944 through 1958, they opened more than 30 new housing tracts within the city, and many more in Barron Park and other unincorporated sectors under county government administration. The tracts sported names ranging from Camelot Gardens and Cardinal Manor to Palo Alto Orchards. Gradually the dairies and farms south of Oregon Avenue vanished, to be replaced by more subdivisions. At a pace slackened mainly by the scarcity of available land, subdivision building went on through the 1960s and into the '70s.

A closer look at wholesale homebuilding shows that a fast pace was set from the start. For the first six months of 1946, city officials approved 689 residential building permits and gave six subdividers the go-ahead to build 630 more new homes. Between 1947 and 1949, the population increased 14 percent, to 26,000.

In 1949, before the U.S. Supreme Court had finished striking down racial restrictions in real estate covenants, the Palo Alto Fair Play Council bought six acres of land in South Palo Alto to set up a "laboratory of interracial living." This tract, on Lawrence Lane and adjoining lots on Colorado Avenue and Greer Road, was named for its organizer, black educator Paul Lawrence, then a student at Stanford University. Families of black, Asian and white heritage bought homes, priced about $9,000 in 1950, and enjoyed neighborhood harmony.

When Acquiring a House Was Easy

Acquiring a new house in Palo Alto may never have been easier than at the most opportune times during this period of great expansion. War veterans and others eager to buy had ready financing aid in the form of several types of low-interest government loans. Developers managed to produce a large supply of single-family, detached houses priced to suit the great influx of families.

PALO ALTO HISTORICAL ASSOCIATION

The postwar housing boom attracted thousands of war veterans with offers of no down payments.

Builders Stern and Price offered houses for sale by 1948. During 1950, Barrett and Hilp began marketing the first units of the 70-acre Boulware tract, bounded by Newell Road and Channing Avenue. Coastwise and Oddstad were other active builders. Seven other tracts opened in Palo Alto that same year, including one whose new form of home packaging had great impact on Palo Alto's later development: the Eichler Home.

Actually, the first Eichlers had appeared outside Palo Alto's then city limits in 1949, in the Bol tract in Barron Park and in another enclave along Park Boulevard off Charleston Road. In 1951, a few Eichlers were built in the Green Gables subdivision. In 1952, they sprouted in droves with construction of the Fairmeadow tract off Alma Street between East Meadow Drive and Charleston Road. A dairy still operated on Charleston, and ranch land lay nearby.

A Handy Mortgage Package

Joseph Eichler was not an architect, but he thought he knew what Peninsulans wanted in their homes. His houses were, first of all, handy mortgage packages, for they typically came equipped with the standard household appliances all covered in the monthly payment. Their contemporary style departed from any housing Palo Altans had seen before. Eichler houses had flat or slightly pitched tar-and-gravel roofs, wood exteriors and interiors based on a concrete slab, radiant heating, open kitchens, dining and living areas, and large floor-to-ceiling windows looking out on private gardens or patios. Veneer-paneled interior walls opened at the top to partition but not fully close off some rooms.

Another touch was design of the Eichler Homes by architects — a rarity in tract housing. Two firms, Anshen and Allen of San Francisco and Jones and Emmons of Los Angeles, were employed. At prices ranging from $11,000 to $14,000, buyers eagerly snapped up the houses, and Eichler welcomed customers of any race, color or creed. Of the 2,380 dwellings built in Palo Alto in 1952, most were Eichler homes.

Ground was broken for the Greenmeadow tract in 1953, not far from Fairmeadow, off Alma Street by Adobe Creek. Streets there, although sometimes irregular in form, did not repeat the circle patterns used in Fairmeadow as a means of separating homes from main traffic arteries. Greenmeadow was said to have been Joe Eichler's

PALO ALTO HISTORICAL ASSOCIATION/
CAROLYN CADDES

Joseph Eichler's subdivisions sprouted throughout south Palo Alto as the housing boom of the 1950s brought in thousands of new Palo Altans.

PALO ALTO HISTORICAL ASSOCIATION/ GLORIA BROWN

117

personal favorite because of its central recreation complex and private park maintained by the community. The active homeowners association Greenmeadow residents established is the city's largest.

In the mid-1950s, entrances through atrium courtyards became an Eichler Homes trademark, and builders far and wide copied this innovation by architect S. Robert Anshen. The last large-scale residential subdivision within the city limits was the Royal Manor tract, located along Louis Road between Loma Verde Avenue and East Meadow Drive. When Eichler began building there in 1957, it was the largest still undeveloped property in Palo Alto. Three- and four-bedroom homes there sold initially for $21,000 to $24,000.

Taking a Stand

Eichler was the first local builder to proclaim boldly that he favored selling houses to minorities. He derided the notion that minority owners reduced property values. When the Associated Home Builders, Inc., a regional trade group, refused to support his position of selling to everyone in 1958, he quit the organization.

By 1957, as lots grew more and more scarce, architects and builders realized that Palo Alto's homebuilding boom was dying. With a push from high construction costs, new housing starts were declining. By the early 1960s, an ebbing became evident in the high birth rate that had fueled the postwar baby boom.

In 1972, some two-story Eichlers were offered in Los Arboles, a small tract off Middlefield Road at Ames Avenue, at $74,000 to $83,500. New tract building was virtually over, but prices were yet to hitch onto the gross inflation of the late 1970s and early '80s.

A Six-Figure Home Sale!

One milepost of rising home prices was the sale in 1972 of the Pedro de Lemos hacienda for more than $100,000 — the first Palo Alto home sale in the six-figure class. In 1987, insurers valued the same dwelling at $1.6 million. At the same time, the Palo

Alto Board of Realtors calculated that, since 1970, house values in the city had increased by more than $40 a day. Tract houses originally priced at $20,000 or less were selling in the $300,000 to $500,000 range.

By 1961, apartments had become a way of life in Palo Alto as an alternative to single-family home ownership. The annual rate of apartment building had jumped from 78 units in 1950 to 671 in 1959. Factors spurring apartment construction included the dwindling stock of home sites, a growing population of young workers filling jobs in electronics plants and the inability of some to finance house purchases.

Highly visible apartment units built in the 1960s and '70s included two *S.T. Tan apartment complexes* on Arastradero Road and *Forest Towers*, at Forest Avenue and Cowper Street downtown. Meanwhile, the *Hotel President*, Palo Alto's leading hotel for several decades, was converted to an apartment house in 1968.

Conversions Rouse Controversy

In the 1970s, a housing trend emerged that upset some apartment tenants and pleased others: the conversion of apartments to individually owned condominiums. By a vote of its tenants, the apartment complex at *101 Alma Street* became a condo cluster, ending 13 years of renting. At the *Oak Creek Apartments* on Sand Hill Road, renters rejected a proposal for a similar conversion.

During the late 1970s and early '80s, many condominium units were built in Palo Alto. In 1982, at a time when the market was beset by high interest rates, 160 downtown units were put on sale. Investors bought many of them and put them to initial use as rentals, while others remained empty. As the prices of single-family homes continued to increase, the condominium market revived as a local source of lower-cost home ownership, but even the price of condos edged up. In 1991, the average single-family home sold for $465,901, the average condominium and town house for $284,793.

Some of the condominium complexes were

Palo Alto Central opened in 1986 offering retail and office space, as well as condominiums.

built in the Midtown area. In 1985, the classrooms and offices of the former Hoover School off Middlefield near Colorado Avenue were razed for a 99-unit condominium layout. For the first seven years, it was to be rentals with five separate buildings and a park. In 1986, ground in the Midtown area formerly occupied by Carpenters Hall and the Chinese Community Center was used for 24 condominiums. In 1984, during the early processing of these projects, a rebellion by some residents broke out against tearing down businesses for more condominiums. The result was to save the Arco station at 2995 Middlefield and the All Peninsula Veterinary Emergency Clinic at 3045 Middlefield.

Downtown, the *Abitare* complex units on The Circle were sold at prices ranging from $169,000 to $199,000. Late in 1986, *Palo Alto Central* was built near the California Avenue train depot —

and, as a rarity in city history, had a geographically correct name. Later came the *Mayfield Condominiums*, on Page Mill Road between Birch and Ash streets, designed for a difficult location by Archon Architects.

New Challenges Face Architects

From the architect's standpoint, the new challenge was to work within Palo Alto's exacting requirements on confined lot sizes. Innovative solutions became visible, especially downtown. Architect George "Tad" Cody designed *365 Forest Avenue* as a large condominium including both residences and commercial spaces — a mix Cody had championed earlier during a general plan revision. It won plaudits for blending well with two older apartment buildings nearby, the Laning Chateau and Casa Real. Across the street at *653-685 Waverley*, architect John Brooks Boyd designed

The upscale Garden Court
Hotel on Cowper Street
opened in the late 1980s.

COURTESY OF GARDEN COURT HOTEL

another large condominium. Boyd, once coordinator for Eichler Homes' two architectural firms, had also designed hundreds of town houses and duplexes on limited lot sizes.

Another architect, Tony Carrasco, showed what can be done with in-fill projects on Ramona between Homer and Forest, creating new housing that sometimes retained the old street front look. Carrasco also did the *Whole Foods* grocery at Homer and Emerson in association with designer Richard Elmore. Elmore had a hand in the *Garden Court Hotel* design, working with Spencer Associates architects. The latter, whose staff revered founder Ted Spencer as the man who turned Stanford away from building in the foothills, did the Downtown Library and both Palo Alto's nature interpretive centers, Baylands and Foothills. *The Redwoods*, across El Camino Real from Dinah's Shack, designed by Fisher Freedman, has been cited as perhaps the city's most successful large condo project.

Architects John C. Northway and Robert H. Stoecker have done numerous residential remodelings but no multiple housing. Their firm planned the *Stanford Book Store* building at High and University, and was selected by the city to design the addition of library and stage facilities to the Children's Theatre, a 1992-93 project.

Where the city once had but one architect, it now has scores, operating under very different conditions from those Birge Clark faced when he started.

A New Building Tide
As the 1980s dissolved into the 1990s, Palo Alto's neighborhoods were in the midst of a rebuilding boom. Soaring land prices combined with demand for larger and more efficient homes had put a premium on Palo Alto property. In some cases, homeowners built second stories or other large additions; in other locations, developers found it economically feasible to tear down existing resi-

dences and build larger ones. The number of single-family residences demolished rose from 14 in 1987 to 50 in 1989.

Critics asserted that some houses were being built or remodeled with little sensitivity to the aesthetics of surrounding neighborhoods, or were out of scale with adjacent houses. To some observers, this became evident when homes were built on two former school sites, Crescent Park and Ross Road. As a result, the City Council enacted an ordinance allowing only about half as much structure in relation to lot size in order to preserve the general compatibility of buildings that has existed for a century.

Although some of the houses built during the great post-World War II spurt were small and lightly constructed, neither they nor other modest homes built at any time in the hundred years have ever become blighted zones that invited massive redevelopment. To the contrary, owners facing family space crunches have often found remodeling a preferred choice to moving, especially after passage of Proposition 13 in 1978 stiffened the tax costs of "buying up."

In general, development of the city has not caused residential districts to be plowed under or suffer loss of essential character. In many cases, improvements have led to a district's enhanced appearance; the boulevardizing of El Camino Real, which had the effect of cleaning up some shoddy commercial strips, is a case in point. All in all, residents and their dwellings — whether one-family homes, duplexes, condominiums, or apartments — have held their own in ongoing contests with the forces of business expansion. Near the one-century mark, that tradition showed no signs of eroding.

Rising property values in the late 1980s prompted the construction of houses maximizing square footage.

The 1951 graduation ceremony at Palo Alto High School.

10

Schools: Palo Alto's "Main Business"

"Of course in time the University will be complete from the kindergarten to the post-graduate course, but that can only be after a village has grown up around the University."
— *Senator Leland Stanford, as quoted in the* San Francisco Examiner, *March 31, 1891*

Education has been a central interest in Palo Alto from the start. Indeed, until the electronics industry emerged and "Silicon Valley" began to flourish, many people considered Palo Alto's main business to be education. Although Stanford University stood foremost in this "business," the townspeople were clearly committed to good elementary and secondary education as well. Many of them had come so their children could attend Stanford, and those children needed a good preparatory system in order to qualify. A strong public education program has been an ongoing source of Palo Alto pride, and fine private schools have complemented the public schools.

Senator Stanford's dream of an entire educational complex may have attracted some of the early settlers of University Park. The university, visibly rising from "the plain of Menlo" from late 1887 on, encouraged belief in his lower-school promises. Jane Stanford's sponsorship of the free kindergartens in Mayfield and Menlo Park, and of a school for young workers at the horse farm, attested to the couple's good intentions. In 1890, in a letter he wrote to his wife, the senator came close to deciding to build the secondary schools between today's El Camino Real and the Quad. A week before his death in 1893, he again wrote of his vision of "a complete system of education from the kindergarten school up." His death ended any dream of the Stanfords providing the schools themselves — although Mrs. Stanford later built the campus grammar school. But it can be argued that in a broader sense the community carried the dream on to fulfillment, though very slowly.

First, however, the pioneer settlers, many of whom had children, had to face reality. The school for Palo Alto was in Mayfield, a long wagon ride away. It was not a bad school as schools then went, and a tradition of almost 40 years stood behind it. As for a high school, none existed anywhere nearby.

The Mayfield School District had been formed in 1855. Its first school, described as a log cabin-like "herring box," stood on Birch Street between Sherman and Grant avenues (now the North County Courthouse site). In 1867, a two-story schoolhouse was built on the same site to better serve Mayfield and its surrounding farm families. This second building was sold and moved off the site in 1898, when the third Mayfield school was erected there. Sherman School, a six-room wooden building, cost $14,000 and proved to have a useful life of more than 40 years. The superintendent of schools ordered it torn down in 1940, but the old building received a harvest reprieve because bees nesting over the front columns were producing 10 gallons of honey a year.

The Two-Mile Rule

A painful schism in the school district began early in 1892. Anna Zschokke related it in her pioneer history:

This Mayfield school housed students for more than thirty years, from 1867 until 1898.

Mothers had often sighed over the drawback of having to send the little ones so far to school as Mayfield (two miles). The county superintendent, being interviewed, favored our having a school, declaring we had plenty of children, and directed that we take the necessary steps. . . . This was done, but Mayfield so emphatically rebelled at having our end of her district cut off, insisting that we were not the required two miles from her schoolhouse, that we dropped the matter until we had a set of men here who could push the project through in spite of all opposition. . . .

[Early in 1893 the Improvement Club appointed a school committee, which insisted the measurement must be of the walking route, not the rail line.]

Feb. 3 the school committee, by official survey, proved that we were two miles from the Mayfield schoolhouse. They had ascertained that we had 54 children of school age. These facts made us feel sure of a school here by fall.

And so it happened. On March 20, 1893, County Superintendent of Schools L.J. Chipman established the Palo Alto district and appointed the Improvement Club's nominees — H.G. Wilson, Frank Cramer and W.E. Norris — as trustees. On May 20, the community cast 45 unanimous votes for a $15,000 school bond measure, despite the national financial panic that year. About 10 weeks later, electors again voted unanimously for a

This two-room school on Bryant Street, Palo Alto's first, was built in four days in 1893.

school tax — and unmistakably had begun a tradition of strong community support of schools. All available able-bodied men were summoned to build a temporary two-room schoolhouse on Bryant Street between University and Hamilton avenues. Completed in four days, it opened September 5 with nearly 80 pupils and two teachers, Mayme J. Bass, who had taught at Mayfield, and Mrs. E.L. Rich. Miss Bass acted as principal.

Permanent School Readied

School trustees next acquired a site at the corner of Webster Street and Channing Avenue for a permanent school, and then approved plans for a two-story, six-room schoolhouse there, designed for 240 pupils. Grammar school children began classes there in 1894. Meanwhile, Mrs. Zschokke and others organized a private high school. It began classes in September in the two upstairs rooms of Channing School with 20 students, each paying tuition of $6 a month. The Palo Alto High

School District was formed in 1898 as a separate legal entity, but with the elementary district trustees doubling as high school trustees. Minutes of those meetings frequently read, "The elementary district is now adjourned. The high school district meeting is now called to order."

Attendance rolls kept growing, and soon the elementary district needed its upstairs rooms. There were no immediate plans for a high school building. So, in 1897, Anna Zschokke mortgaged her house, bought a lot, hired an able contractor and built a three-room high school with good plumbing. (Her grandson later revealed that she had financial support from a Zschokke family revolving fund established in Switzerland years before.) Her building, including a science wing added later, housed high school students until 1901, when a larger high school was built on Channing Avenue across the street from the grammar school (Channing House now stands on this site), financed by a $20,000 bond measure voters

At the turn of the century Channing Avenue was the center of education in Palo Alto. The high school, on the left, was located across the street from the elementary school.

Mrs. Zschokke made no money, neither did she lose any, as the rent paid for the cost of installing and of removing the temporary woodwork.

The new high school was a square, two-story frame building with nine classrooms, an assembly hall and an ample basement devoted to a woodworking shop, dressing rooms and storage. Just before it opened, A. Morris Fosdick was appointed Palo Alto's first superintendent of schools with responsibility for both elementary and high schools.

Graduates Welcomed at Stanford

Birge Clark, a 1910 graduate of Palo Alto High School, later recalled that 38 of his class of 42 went on to enter Stanford, where there was then no tuition and where Palo Alto graduates — many of them professors' sons and daughters — were welcomed. The on-to-college average was high because compulsory attendance then ended at age 16, so most of the non-college-bound had left before becoming high school seniors.

Rapid growth in Palo Alto school enrollment resulted in the Homer Avenue School being built adjacent to the high school in 1902 at a cost of $7,475. In 1905, Lytton School, built during the superintendency of Charles C. Hill (1903-07) at a cost of $21,648, opened with 10 classrooms and a large assembly hall. Miss Elizabeth Van Auken began her teaching career at Lytton in 1912, became its principal in 1917 and served 36 years in all. Lytton School closed in 1964 and was torn down so the site could be used for the Lytton Gardens senior residence units.

During his eight-year term, Superintendent Joseph Crittenden Templeton played a significant part in securing a freeholders' city charter for Palo Alto, enabling the school board to replace the limited county school curriculum with its own progressive course of study. He can also be credited with planning for a state teachers' retirement fund and creating the California Interscholastic Federation, the statewide body governing high school sports.

The active interest of parents in school affairs took formal shape late in 1909 when, the *Palo Alto Times* reported, "A movement was in progress among the mothers of children in the grammar school and the teachers to form an organization which had as its objective the furthering of the best interests of the school." Mrs. E.G. Greene, president of the Woman's Club of Palo Alto, led in fostering Parent-Teacher associations at the Lytton and Homer Avenue schools and, in 1913, at the high school. The latter unit soon merged with those of the grammar schools with 33 charter members and Mrs. Greene as president. By 1915, a single overall PTA for Palo Alto was in place.

PALO ALTO HIGH SCHOOL—THE MADRONO, 1934

Walter Nichols served as the principal of Palo Alto High School from 1915 until 1935.

Combining Forces

In 1912, the idea of a union high school district including Palo Alto, Mayfield and Stanford was considered. It became a reality in 1916, bringing the advantages of a larger territory, new leadership and more assessed wealth. Superintendent Templeton had taken the lead in securing passage of a $200,000 bond issue for a new high school, and his successor, Walter H. Nichols, negotiated a $1-an-acre ($30-a-year), 99-year lease for the site at Embarcadero Road and El Camino Real with the Stanford University Board of Trustees and President Ray Lyman Wilbur. The deed restricted its use to educational purposes only. Years later the school district exercised an option included in this agreement and purchased the site for $1,000 an acre. The lease and purchase amounted to the Stanford promise of a secondary school — the site, at least — being made good at last.

The switch to Mediterranean-style architecture for the new high school, designed by the Los Angeles firm of Alison & Alison, resulted from Nichols' advocacy. He also saw to it that the school had an ample auditorium with a full stage, making it a community resource for drama and other performing arts.

A Christmas Eve March

Nichols, his faculty and the entire student body marched on December 24, 1918, from the Channing Avenue building to the new Palo Alto Union High School, and ceremonially occupied it. (The Christmas Eve timing resulted because schools had been closed in October due to the Spanish flu epidemic, so the holidays were cut short to meet minimal school year requirements.) The old high school building became an intermediate school. The 1894 Channing Avenue School was razed a few years later.

When the superintendency and principalship were split in 1919, in response to feelings that schools other than "Paly" High might be getting too little attention, Nichols chose to remain where his heart was, serving as Paly's principal until his death in 1935.

ELECTION FOR HIGH SCHOOL SITE
Saturday, Oct. 21

YOUR VOTE IS NEEDED

Polling Place, Present High School

The "Central" Site is the only Stanford land offered for sale or that can be leased with option to purchase, or portion purchased and balance leased.

Any amount of land wanted is offered at $1.00 per acre per year. No higher rent is asked.

The "Central" Site is the most convenient to Palo Alto and equally central for the other districts. No legal complications threatened.

PHONE 115 FOR FREE AUTO TO TAKE YOU TO THE POLLS

PALO ALTO HISTORICAL ASSOCIATION

Poster advocating the approval of the proposed new high school site on Embarcadero Road, 1916.

Albert C. Barker (accompanied by his dog, nicknamed "Barker" by the students) became superintendent in 1920 and served until 1936, presiding over the final years of consolidation and then unification. Why these merger steps? After the union high school district was formed in 1916, a later survey report pointed out, "There was now within the boundaries of the original Mayfield elementary school district one high school with a board of trustees, and four elementary districts, each with its own board — 17 board members, in charge of five schools... ." The numbers clearly depicted the problem of articulating the academic preparation of students entering the high school.

Bold Consolidation Plan Fails

In 1922, a bold plan to consolidate the Palo Alto and West Side union high school districts (the latter, now Fremont UHSD, serving Sunnyvale and Cupertino) went to an election, but was rejected. A *Times* editorial post mortem declared that "the people of Sunnyvale, fooled by misrepresentations, defeated their own interests." An eleventh-hour handbill had warned West Side, "Don't be stampeded into Palo Alto." The *Times* added: " ... the only stampeding into Palo Alto that has been done in the past has been by the outside districts themselves in sending their children to Palo Alto's school, already crowded by our own children, and insisting upon their attendance here on a 'representation without taxation' basis." Mountain View, which at one time aspired to become the area's sole union high school and junior college district, stood aloof.

Long after all neighboring areas had their own high schools, certain prominent families along the swath from Cupertino to Woodside continued to wangle permission for their children to attend Palo Alto High School — a foretaste of the "sneak-ins" that occurred in a new period of educational ferment in the 1960s.

The quickened growth of the '20s produced both new elementary school plants and moves toward consolidation. A second ceremonial procession occurred in 1924 when upper-grade students at the Mayfield district's Sherman School moved to the new Mayfield School on Stanford-owned property on El Camino Real between Page Mill Road and California Avenue. In Palo Alto, Walter Hays School (named for a beloved school board president and Presbyterian minister who had died suddenly) opened in 1923, Addison School in 1925 and the two-room South Palo Alto School in 1926. In 1950, the latter school was retitled Herbert Hoover in the first of a spate of renamings that were to go on for decades.

Public School Kindergartens Open

At the time Walter Hays School opened in 1923, one of the Palo Alto district's first two kindergartens began operating there — the other was at Lytton School. Until then, a number of private kindergartens had served local families. In 1919, the Board of Education had rejected petitions to establish two kindergartens because it was felt that making suitable provisions for the eight grades should be given first priority.

The Stanford Elementary School District, created in 1899, agreed to annexation to the Palo Alto system in 1923. Mayfield's district followed in 1925 when Palo Alto annexed the Town of Mayfield. The little Purissima Elementary School District in the Los Altos hills remained separate until 1931. Its annexation at last gave the elementary and high school districts identical boundaries. That turned public attention to the goal of unifying them.

Assemblyman Frank Crist of Palo Alto sponsored legislation permitting unification. A state-led survey of the local schools followed. Several months of discussion ensued, and on December 4, 1931, the citizens of Palo Alto voted in favor of consolidation, which ultimately resulted in total unification in July 1936.

Meanwhile, Palo Alto Union High School was enlarged in 1927, completing the original design, which had been cut back in 1918 due to World War I shortages. The high school's enrollment doubled between 1920 and 1930. Another remodeling, for safety, occurred after the 1933 Long Beach earthquake and subsequent passage of the state Field Act; structural corrections also were made at Addison and Mayfield schools. This work was financed by passage of a bond issue, which — despite the Depression — earmarked $15,000 for purchase of a junior high school site.

A Showplace Junior High

The newly unified district purchased 16 acres at Middlefield Road and Santa Rita (now California) Avenue from Mrs. Alfred Seale. With funds from a $360,000 bond measure, passed by a 6-to-1 margin, the district built the junior high and named it for Dr. David Starr Jordan, Stanford's first president. In 1937, Principal Glenn Goddard opened this "showpiece of the Palo Alto school system," an expansive one-story layout with amazing window lighting and walls of glass, designed by Birge Clark and his brother David. Jordan served seventh, eighth and ninth graders, and Paly High became a three-year school. At that time Jordan stood at the edge of town; with the great post-World War II

By the 1950s the school district was building schools rapidly from the same or slightly modified blueprints.

surge in homebuilding and school registration, its location became ideally central for about a dozen years.

In May 1938, women for the first time made up a majority of the Board of Education, but they used their husbands' names in public life: Mrs. W.O. Shreve, Mrs. Charles J. Crary and Mrs. Calvin P. Stone. The balance soon tipped back to a male majority; when it shifted again in 1978, customs had changed and the three women appeared in minutes as Jean Amick, Joan Johnston and Becky Morgan.

New subdivisions built south of Embarcadero Road in the late '40s and '50s brought in thousands of new students. Between 1941 and 1951, Palo Alto school attendance jumped 223 percent, and that was just the start. In 1947, David Packard, head of a then-small electronics firm, was elected to the Board of Education, representing a new generation of parents. Packard championed a program of planning for growth that, by the '50s, had the district building from one to three new schools each year — and keeping ahead of the demand.

He later dismissed this feat as a matter of applying "third-grade arithmetic," but Palo Alto was almost alone on the Peninsula in not having to resort to state aid financing for school construction, with its attendant strings of state control from Sacramento.

A "Lighthouse District"

The board raided an Oregon college of education to bring in an experienced school superintendent, Dr. Henry M. Gunn, who led the system from 1950 to 1961 in a climb to distinction as a "lighthouse district." In that time the district not only kept ahead of the tidal wave of additional students in providing space but also in recruiting teachers and attaining new levels of curricular excellence.

Barron Park and Crescent Park schools opened in 1948, and Barron Park was quickly enlarged to double its size — it also served as an informal community center for the unincorporated neighborhood around it. Elizabeth Van Auken School opened in 1950. Hard-pressed, the district resorted to building schools from the same or slightly modified blueprints. Green Gables and Fairmeadow

Superintendent Henry Gunn and Principal Elizabeth Van Auken celebrated fifty years of Lytton School in 1955.

PALO ALTO HISTORICAL ASSOCIATION

Gunn High School opened in 1964 on Arastradero Road.

opened in 1951, Garland and Loma Vista in 1952, Ventura, Ohlone and Palo Verde in 1953, El Carmelo in 1955, Ortega in 1956, De Anza and Greendell in 1957, Fremont Hills in 1959 and Ross Road and Escondido in 1960.

Obviously, the secondary system also had to proliferate. In 1953, Ray Lyman Wilbur Junior High School was built on East Meadow Drive between Alma Street and Middlefield Road. After Wilbur became the second junior high school, Cubberley High School was opened at 4000 Middlefield Road in 1956 as the district's second high school. It was named for Ellwood Patterson Cubberley, longtime dean of the Stanford School of Education.

Voters Back School Bonds Strongly

Confident in the system and thoroughly indoctrinated in the need to keep abreast of rising enrollment, district voters gave overwhelming margins of support in passing bond issues in 1945, '49, '51 and '54 totaling more than $11 million. Between 1948 and 1956, a senior high school, a junior high school and 13 elementary schools were built. As growth accelerated, student enrollment more than doubled between 1950 and 1956.

The last round of secondary school construction saw a third junior high school, Terman, open in 1958 on Arastradero Road. It was named for famed Stanford psychologist Lewis M. Terman, who had used many Palo Alto students, among others, as subjects in his gifted child studies. Henry M. Gunn Senior High School, also on Arastradero, was ready for students in 1964. Its design reflected new departures in campus planning, and included the 989-seat Spangenberg Theatre, the district's largest, named for a dedicated trustee who died in office, Stanford electrical engineering Professor Karl Spangenberg.

Although building and growth created mile-

The Music For Minors program is one of the arts experiences available to Palo Alto students such as these at Palo Verde School in 1987.

posts, other factors such as trustees, superintendents, administrators and staff, parental involvement and the students themselves contributed heavily to the Palo Alto schools' flavor and standing. During the first 50 years, a solid academic curriculum mirrored the expectations of a community that included both well-educated professionals and middle-class families determined to see their children receive a better education than their own. With the wave of population growth arose a demand for educational vision, which Dr. Gunn supplied for a decade. His style was to grant a large amount of autonomy to each school principal and staff. Following Robert Johnson's controversial nine-month tenure, the pendulum then swung, under Harold Santee, to a more cen-

tralized approach. (Under James Brown, in the 1990s, the pendulum swung back to make school-based management the operating theory.)

From Sputnik to New Math

The Soviet Union's 1957 launching of Sputnik, the first Earth-orbiting satellite, caused a deep reappraisal of the schools' effectiveness and American education in general. Science, from biology to chemistry to physics, changed totally. Special new curricula developed by nationwide commissions, in which Dr. Gunn participated, were introduced. Even elementary science changed to a hands-on approach. Various university-spawned efforts to improve curricula, such as the School Mathematics Study Group program developed by Stanford

Professors Edward Begle and Patrick Suppes, were tested within the district. This led to the "New Math," which radically changed the teaching of mathematics and resulted in some areas, such as algebra, being taught in lower grades.

The '60s also saw rapid advances in the use of technology in education — language laboratories, projects in the new field of computer science, use of educational television and videotaped lessons, microfilm research and the like. Advanced students who mastered subjects quickly and in depth were given the opportunity to take college-level courses in high school, for college credit. Historically, Palo Alto students have led California in the number of Advanced Placement tests they have taken. (When Vietnam War era tensions wracked the high schools, students showed they were also adept at argumentation and hassling. Indeed, the latter term became the title of a book by a Cubberley teacher about the struggles.)

Why the high AP test participation? As Palo Alto students generally came from educated families, the schools concentrated on providing high-quality teachers to children already well endowed. Parents, for their part, put pressure on the school district to enrich the educational lives of their children.

Alternative Schools Blossom

One outgrowth of accommodating parental concerns was the establishment of two very different alternative schools in the '70s. Hoover School was first with a back-to-basics curriculum, homework every night and no parents in the classroom. At the other end of the spectrum, Ohlone School was set up to provide a deliberately open, friendly environment with a special focus on self-esteem.

Curriculum changes have also reflected changes in the United States and in the fields of learning theory and child development. From the late 1960s through the mid-'70s, the country was concerned with civil rights, cultural differences and educating children of low-income parents. A number of Palo Alto families cooperated with East Palo Alto families in a "sneak-in" program to provide so-called

foster homes for black children from the Ravenswood School District. In Palo Alto, with fewer low-income children, efforts were made to use special federal and state funds in innovative ways, such as experimental prekindergarten classes mixing children from low-income and middle-income families. Efforts also focused on multicultural education and encouraging activities that exposed children to the many valuable differences existing in varied cultures.

Child development research blossomed in the 1960s. Under Adult Education, Palo Alto had two thriving preschool parent education programs, Pre-School Family and the Parents Nursery Cooperative. In 1968, after a survey of the need, a state-subsidized child care center was established, named after Besse Bolton, who with the backing of Adult Education head Ray Ruppel pioneered preschool programs. In the '70s state funds became available to qualifying elementary schools under Early Childhood Education, and almost all elementary schools participated in that program.

A Tradition Falters

In 1967, Palo Alto's long record of school bond approvals came a cropper on the issue of whether to rebuild completely or simply renovate Palo Alto High. (One other bond measure had been rejected in 1939 when, the *Times* explained, voters were jittery about war fears and the "Ham and Eggs menace" — a radical state $30-every-Thursday welfare proposal.) First, in February 1967, an $11 million bond measure including $6,150,000 for a new Paly, polled only 64.4% favor — several points less than the two-thirds support needed. When a second try was made in October, voters approved Measure A, $7.5 million to expand and improve schools throughout the district, including repairs at Paly, but turned back Measure B, $2.6 million more to build a new Palo Alto High School, although 64.59% of those voting favored B. After agonizing over the intent of the voters, the school board went ahead with repairs, improvements and demolition of some of the old buildings. In March 1972, Paly improvements costing $4.2 million were dedicated, including a library resource center, English building, performing arts center, social science center, foreign language center, girls' gymnasium, swimming pool and a science, business and technology building. The latter included a science resource center named after former PTA Council President Marian Bloom.

By 1970, the unified district's postwar construction record read: 18 new elementary schools, two new junior high schools and two new high schools. Student enrollment had peaked in 1968 at almost 16,000. The district had more than 1,200 faculty and staff members, and after Harold Santee became superintendent in 1962, had developed a cabinet system of running the district.

The last new school built was named for Lucille M. Nixon, a teacher and curriculum consultant killed in a tragic accident, and the first American not of Japanese ancestry whose haiku won an invitation to the Japanese emperor's annual poetry party. Nixon School opened in 1970 as a replacement for the old Stanford Elementary School, which had been built near the campus in 1919. But there was already talk of the need to begin closing lower schools soon because of declining enrollment. Available land for residential development was vanishing, and school attendance was leveling off. With the populace aging and fewer young families moving in, school enrollment began to fall — markedly in the elementary schools.

Enrollment Plummets

By 1975, when Newman Walker became superintendent, enrollment was down to 12,800 and closures were inevitable. State-mandated equalization of per-pupil expenditures was being established through the *Serrano v. Priest* court decision and its legislative follow-ons, upsetting Palo Alto's familiar underpinning of high property values and voter-supported high tax rates. Passage of Proposition 13 in 1978 pinched school finances even more, capping the ability of school districts and other local agencies to raise taxes without a two-thirds majority vote.

A long series of belt-tightenings began as control shifted to the state. During the 1974-75 school year, 85.4% of the Palo Alto schools budget had been generated by local property taxes, while the state contributed 11.3%. By 1979-80, the state was providing 60.6% and local taxes 33.5%.

In 1976 the junior high schools became middle schools with grades 7 and 8, while the 9th grades shifted to high schools. Then in 1978 Terman was closed.

School Closings Strain Tempers

The school closings touched off stormy debates as parents fought to keep their neighborhood schools. Argument about which of the three high schools to close generated the most rancor; Cubberley, having the least extensive plant, was selected and was shut down in 1979, leaving slow-to-heal emotional wounds and a new chapter in inflamed north-south relations in Palo Alto.

One technique to relax neighborhood tensions as schools merged was to change the name of the surviving school. For instance, Barron Park School became Creekside School in 1979 when students from the closed Ventura School transferred there. In 1982, Green Gables School was rechristened Duveneck School as students who had been at Crescent Park School moved there.

In 1985, the year Jordan Middle School closed, Julian Crocker succeeded Walker as superintendent and found himself dealing with the last phases of the student population decline. By 1987, only 7,920 youngsters were attending schools in the district — the peak enrollment had been cut in half. Eleven elementary schools, two middle schools and one high school had been closed, and the school board was planning to close a second high school.

At this point a voter rebellion put a new trustee majority in control. The scheduled second high school closure was called off, and a decision was taken to reopen Jordan Middle School in 1991 and relieve crowded conditions at Jane Lathrop Stanford Middle School (formerly Wilbur), with grades 6, 7 and 8 at both schools. To ease the financial

Palo Alto High School's academic decathlon team returns as state champions, 1983.

bind, the Palo Alto Unified School District and the city worked together to win voter approval of a utilities tax and a program of leasing unneeded school plants and playfields to the city to manage.

Under Crocker's leadership, Palo Alto and seven southern San Mateo County school districts settled a long-running lawsuit charging the districts with racial discrimination. The Tinsley case settlement allowed minority students to transfer across county and school district lines to attend Palo Alto and other schools. Sneak-ins were no longer needed.

"How Well Our Kids Achieve"

When he departed in 1989, Crocker called attention to the unified district's breadth. "It's a great district," he said. "I guess we've come to accept how well our kids achieve here. Our kids have been amazingly successful, and not just in academics. We have amazing artists, musicians, athletes, writers." A few years earlier, Palo Alto's art and music programs had won special national honors. Meanwhile, its academic decathlon teams continued to win or place very high in regional, state and national competition.

James R. Brown, who replaced Crocker, led the district into calmer waters, symbolized initially by the return of students and teachers to a refurbished Jordan plant in 1991.

Public participation in school studies and planning became a hallmark of the Palo Alto district long ago. Through PTAs, citizen advisory committees and other study groups, residents supplemented efforts of professional employees and elected officials. In 1987, the Palo Alto Foundation for Education began sponsoring fundraising activities in order to award grants to teachers for small, creative projects of the sort that are cut back as school funds tighten. In its first year, the foundation encouraged citizens to donate their state tax rebate checks to the district general fund, the foundation or a PTA. The general fund received about $30,000 from the campaign.

After changes in state law ushered in collective bargaining in 1976, the Palo Alto Educators Association, a unit of the California Teachers Association, represented teachers in contract negotiations. In 1978, the association began sponsoring annual Sally Siegel Friend of Education awards, named for an educational activist and school board watcher, honoring staunch supporters of public schools from both the staff and the community.

"Night Life That Pays"

Although K-12 education has been its main concern, the unified district has done yeoman work in meeting demands for adult education over the years since 1922, when it began offering English for the foreign-born and citizenship training. During World War II, the program was utilized to train defense industry workers in machine shop, welding and aircraft sheet metal skills. A primary aviation ground course also was offered and attracted learners from far and wide, as there was no residence requirement.

In the postwar years, a great surge of enrollment led to day as well as "night life that pays" classes in a vast array of subjects. In 1948, for example, 150 persons were on a waiting list for an upholstery course! Nearby districts copied the preschool and family life education courses for parents. In the mid-1960s, before the full buildup of community college course offerings was in place, Palo Alto's Adult School was serving about 10,000 persons in four quarters each year.

A Junior College?

Local interest in a junior college began in earnest in the mid-1920s when Stanford University President Wilbur enunciated a policy of reducing Stanford's lower-division enrollment in order to put more emphasis on professional and graduate studies. He sought to shift freshmen and sophomores to junior colleges.

Peninsula high school districts from Sequoia (Redwood City) to Los Gatos expressed interest in creating one or more junior colleges at meetings instigated, in part, by Professor Sidney Townley, who became a member and then president of the Palo Alto Board of Education after the annexation of the Stanford elementary district. Expecting that an election to form a junior college district would be scheduled in a year or so, the Palo Alto Union High School District board created a junior college division in 1927, and placed 60 JC students in the high school's newly enlarged facilities with selected Paly faculty members as their professors. Meanwhile, the university trustees had indicated that a site of about 100 acres would be made available east of Page Mill Road in what is now Stanford Research Park, and Dr. Townley had suggested having Stanford faculty share the teaching load at the junior college.

The First and Last Class

In March 1928, the Palo Alto board voted to discontinue the junior college — still in its first academic year — because the district had run out of funds. Another reason was doubt about the legality of a junior college district that might bridge the county line, or an operation subsidized by City of Palo Alto funds that would serve areas outside the city. Thus, Elinor Cogswell later wrote, "The first graduating class became the last graduating class. Commencement was a doleful affair, for the 'pioneers' had been full of zest and hope and plans."

In 1945, the junior college issue, brewing in the previous nine years, came to a boil again. After sampling opinions, the Palo Alto Board of Education found strong opposition and postponed the project indefinitely. A decade later, the proposal was taken off the table and in October 1956, Palo Alto joined with the Mountain View and Fremont Union (Sunnyvale and Cupertino) high school districts in asking the state Board of Education to set an election. The vote, in January 1957, resulted in approval by a 5 2/3-to-1 margin, and two weeks later an interim board picked the name "Foothill"

Palo Alto Unified School District

DEPARTMENT OF ADULT EDUCATION

SUMMER QUARTER -- July 1 through August 16, 1968

REGISTRATION STARTS JUNE 19

Announcement of Classes for Adults

"Night Life That Pays"

• Palo Alto Adult School

50 Embarcadero Rd., 325-4473

BUSINESS AND COMMERCIAL

COURSE	INSTRUCTOR	DAY	HOUR	ROOM	FEE
Bus. Machines and Data Processing Introduction	Mr. Langdon	M	7:00-10:00	116	$2.00
Typewriting	Mr. Collins	MW	7:30- 9:30	112	2.00

CITIZENSHIP, SOCIAL SCIENCE

Citizenship Preparation	Mr. Jorgenson	MW	7:30- 9:30	39	—

FAMILY LIFE EDUCATION

(Under the supervision of Mrs. Betty Rogaway, Consultant)

*Education for Childbirth	Mrs. Coward	W	7:30- 9:30	Girls Gym Rules Rm.	1.00
**Education for Childbirth *Note from physician required	Mrs. Palmer	Th	9:30-11:30 AM	Girls Gym Rules Rm.	1.00
**Starts July 11					
+The Pre-First Grade Child	Mrs. Keneshea	Daily W	9:00-12:00 8:00-10:00	Fairm'dow Fairm'dow	1.00 1.00

+Pre-registration through Kindergarten teacher—classes coincide

PRE-SCHOOL FAMILY

Note: Mothers and children attend class together. Class will start June 17. Fees listed are Adult Education tuition only. Lab fee additional.

**Observation	Mrs. Debs	TF T	9:00-11:30 7:30-10:00	1st B. Chch. 1st B. Church	1.00
**Observation	Mrs. Rognas	W W	9:00-11:30 7:30-10:00	1st B. Chch. 1st B. Church	1.00
**Observation	Mrs. Mather	Th Th	9:00-11:30 7:30-10:00	1st B. Chch. 1st B. Church	1.00
**Participation	Mrs. Neall	M-F M	9:00-11:30 8:00-10:00	2328 Louis 2328 Louis	1.00

**Pre-registration required.

FINE ARTS AND CRAFTS

Ceramics	Mr. Jang	W	9 a.m.-12:00	115	4.00*
Ceramics	Mr. Jang	M	7:00-10:00	115	4.00*
Ceramics	Mr. Owen	W	7:00-10:00	115	4.00*
Landscape Painting	Mrs. Siegel	T	9 a.m.-12:00	111	2.00

*Includes supplies other than clay.

HOMEMAKING

Clothing Workshop	Mrs. Greenwood	W	7:00-10:00	106	2.00
Pattern Drafting & Dress Design	Mrs. Greenwood	M	7:00-10:00	106	2.00
Pattern Drafting & Dress Design	Mrs. Greenwood	W	9:00-12:00 AM	106	2.00
Upholstering	Mrs. Brown Mrs. Ronner Mrs. Campagne	TTh	9:15- 3:45	2081 Bayshore Frontage Rd.	15.00
Home Decorative Arts	Mrs. Hunt	M	9:30-11:30 AM	14	1.50
Home Decorative Arts	Mrs. Hunt	W	7:30- 9:30	14	1.50

(Use of plant material and other media)

• Cubberley Adult School

4000 Middlefield Rd., 321-0888

BUSINESS AND COMMERCIAL

COURSE	INSTRUCTOR	DAY	HOUR	ROOM	FEE
Shorthand Review (Gregg)	Mr. Collins	Th	7:30- 9:30	U-7	$2.00
Typewriting, Beginning	Mr. Lehner	TTh	7:30- 9:30	U-5	2.00
Typewriting, Review	Mr. Collins	T	7:30- 9:30	U-7	2.00
(Brush-up course using electric machines)					

SOCIAL SCIENCE

The Negro in America	Mr. Fleming	T	7:00-10:00	H-8	2.00

FAMILY LIFE EDUCATION

Education for Childbirth	Mrs. Luenberger	T	7:30- 9:30	G-19	1.00
(Note from physician required for enrollment)					

FINE ARTS AND CRAFTS

Ceramics	Mr. Rogers	T	7:00-10:00	K-5	4.00
Ceramics	Mr. Rogers	Th	7:00-10:00	K-5	4.00
Ceramics	Mr. Rogers	T	1:30- 4:30	K-5	4.00
Ceramics	Mr. Rogers	Th	1:30- 4:30	K-5	4.00
Japanese Brush Painting	Mr. Oda	T	7:00-10:00	K-3	2.00
Japanese Brush Painting	Mr. Oda	Th	9:00-12:00	418 Ramona	2.00
Acrylic Painting	Mr. Barrio	W	1:00- 4:00	K-4	2.00
Acrylic Painting	Mr. Barrio	T	7:00-10:00	K-4	2.00
Painting, Intermed. Oils	Mrs. Anshen	Th	7:00-10:00	K-4	2.00

Preregistration recommended for above classes.

HEALTH AND PHYSICAL EDUCATION

Swimming, Beginning	Staff	TTh	7:30- 8:30	Pool	4.00
Swimming, Intermediate	Staff	TTh	8:30- 9:30	Pool	4.00

(Instruction only—not recreational. Students furnish own suits and towns.)

HOMEMAKING

Clothing Workshop, Beg.	Mrs. Peterson	T	7:00-10:00	J-2	2.00
Clothing Workshop, Intermed.	Mrs. Peterson	Th	7:00-10:00	J-2	2.00

LANGUAGE, READING, WRITING

English, H.S. Review	Mrs. Kickbusch	TTh	7:00-10:00	B-4	3.00
French Review	Mr. Norton	Th	7:30-10:00	D-6	2.00
Italian Review	Mr. Calma	T	7:30-10:00	D-3	2.00
Spanish Intermediate	Mr. Bernal	Th	7:30- 9:30	B-3	2.00
Spanish Review	Mr. Bernal	T	7:30- 9:30	B-3	2.00
Writers Wrkshp	Mrs. Mudra	T	7:00-10:00	H-1	2.00

"Night Life That Pays" was the slogan of the adult education program in the Palo Alto schools for years.

for the junior college district. In May 1958, a $10.4 million bond issue to build a campus in the Los Altos hills passed; meanwhile, classes began at the old Highway Grammar School in Mountain View, the campus until September 1961.

A Community College District Soars

Two veteran Palo Alto school trustees, Merrill Vanderpool and Nathan Finch, served on the interim board, and Palo Altans Mary Levine and Robert Peckham won terms in the first board election. After building the Foothill College campus, and completing the De Anza College campus in Cupertino in 1967, the district renamed itself the Foothill-De Anza Community College District. It soon rose to the top rank of California community colleges. Foothill College set up a major branch at what was Cubberley High School, now

termed Foothill's Middlefield campus, and offered courses at 60 off-campus locations. Prior to fee increases instituted in 1992 and 1993, more than 20,000 students attended Foothill each quarter during the day, evening and on Saturday, taking college-credit courses or community services fee courses for personal growth.

Together with still-busy Adult Education, and with Stanford, which began offering continuing education courses in the late 1980s, Foothill has played a large part in feeding the enormous educational appetites of mature Palo Altans and their neighbors.

Meeting Special Needs

From early on, Palo Alto had endeavored to monitor the health of its pupils and do what it could to remedy learning problems. For many

PALO ALTO WEEKLY/CAROLYN CLEBSCH

The orthopedic unit at Juana Briones School is one of the programs developed for students with special needs.

years, the district employed physician E.J. Strick and dentist E. Pearl Hannah to check students' health. Later growing numbers made it possible to develop specialized facilities, such as the Juana Briones School orthopedic unit and the Ruth Jackson Hearing Center, both serving an area extending beyond the district's limits.

Other special schools serving youths from a wider area also have made Palo Alto their home. Martin J. Spangler School for the Mentally Retarded and Physically Handicapped, operated by the Santa Clara County Education Department, was built at Middlefield and Charleston roads in 1967. Two other institutions fronting on Middlefield between Charleston and the Mitchell Park Community Center — Community Association for the Retarded Inc. (C.A.R.) and PCC Children and Youth Services Inc. (PCC is from the old name, Peninsula Children's Services) — formed an affinity group with the school.

Spangler School typically has had about 60 students, each with an individually designed educational program. C.A.R. doesn't have a school, but has served Spangler, PCC and the Juana Briones orthopedic unit by providing after-school recreation including swimming. PCC routinely has drawn more than 50 children whose emotional disabilities render them unable to attend regular school; it has been run as a private nonprofit operation, although the 23 school districts in Santa Clara and San Mateo counties from which the children come contribute some funding.

The Children's Health Council School, with about 50 students divided between its headquarters site on Sand Hill Road and the old Fremont School in Menlo Park, was set up for attendance on the same basis described for PCC. Palo Alto Unified has operated the school at Lucile Salter Packard Children's Hospital at Stanford for about 30 K-12 children at a time. Long ago, it was known as the Stanford Convalescent Home School.

Private Schools Sprout; a Few Take Root

Although private schools are not as prominent in California as on the East Coast, dozens of them have taken root in and around Palo Alto in the century since Stanford University opened in 1891. Most of them have sprouted, flourished for a time and then declined or moved away. A few of these independent experimental laboratories of education, giving high priority to each student's individuality and self-discovery, have lived on as hardy perennials.

Initially, the private schools were linked to Stanford in one or more ways. Dr. David Starr Jordan, the pioneer president, personally encouraged the founding of several. The founders often were freshly graduated from Stanford, or had come to the area hoping to combine teaching with graduate study. Also, some early patrons of the private schools were parents ambitious to have their offspring attend the university and unsure, for one reason or another, that the embryonic public schools could fill the bill.

Castilleja Hall began under the name Adelante Villa in a quaint frame house in the foothills behind Stanford. Its founders, Lucy Fletcher and Eleanor Brooks Pearson, had been encouraged by biologist-administrator Jordan, and he suggested the name "Castilleja," Spanish for the native wildflower Indian paint brush. After operating for one year tucked away off Alpine Road, the girls school moved to Bryant and Lincoln, and later to 1121 Bryant. In its second year, Castilleja Hall had 26 students in two divisions — a preparatory school for girls and a primary section for children under the age of 12. In 1901, the *Palo Alto Times* reported that Mrs. Louise Bayard Angell had purchased Castilleja Hall and that Mrs. Annie E. Peck, who had run the preparatory division for two years, had "concluded not to open it this year." It never reopened.

Castilleja School for Girls

Castilleja School for Girls, one of the earlier private schools, has proven the most long-lived of those still remaining. Castilleja opened in 1907 at 1121 Bryant Street, the fruit of Dr. Jordan's urging of Mary Ishbel Lockey, a 1902 Stanford graduate, to start a girls school. Confusingly, to history readers,

Academy in 1925, and its uniformed cadets became a familiar sight in town. Major Nichols, a graduate of the academy, purchased it in 1950 when Colonel Kelly retired. About 100 students were enrolled in 1960 when it merged with Miss Harker's to become the Harker Academy. For another 12 years, the Harker Academy operated successfully in Palo Alto. Then, in 1972, the school moved to San Jose. The two sites in Palo Alto were sold, and 30 Eichler Homes were built there.

Many other private schools operated for a time in Palo Alto. Maynard Shipley, a Stanford graduate, opened the Palo Alto Academy in 1904. By 1906, the academy and its 50 students were based in Lirio Hall on Waverley near Lytton Avenue. Its founder abandoned it for financial reasons — luckily, for the 1906 earthquake shook Lirio Hall flat.

Dr. Grenville Emery, who had come to Palo Alto with Colonel Kelly to purchase Manzanita Hall, ranked as a leading private school educator. In 1920, he began his own high school for boys. Seale Academy, located in the old Seale residence at the corner of California Avenue and Byron Street, ran for five years before ill health forced Dr. Emery to retire and close the school in 1925.

Another military school was based in Barron Park during the 1920s. Col. Sebastian Jones began the California Military Academy after moving from New York to the old Barron mansion on Military Way. The mansion sheltered the classrooms, meeting rooms and mess hall, while the remodeled stables housed the dormitory. The school, opened in 1923, operated until Colonel Jones' death forced its closure.

Col. William G. Muldoon, a renowned World War I Army officer, had come to Palo Alto to work with Colonel Jones. After closing the academy at the end of 1929, he established his own school, the Muldoon Academy, at the old Seale residence, where the Seale Academy had been a few years earlier. Colonel Muldoon's cherished hope of making the operation a success foundered, after four years, on the financial shoals of the Depression.

Interdale School for Boys, founded by E. Allen

Roseboom, opened in September 1936 on the Barron estate. Less than three months later, on November 29, 1936, the mansion burned to the ground, leaving the school homeless. During the Christmas holidays, Interdale moved to Drexler Hall in what is now Ladera. Its enrollment peaked at 60 students before bankruptcy forced it to close after 10 years of operation.

Parochial and Other Private Schools

Palo Alto's first Roman Catholic parochial school, St. Thomas Aquinas School, opened its doors on Channing Avenue to 250 students in 1950. With the creation of a new parish, the school was renamed St. Albert the Great. It served grades one through eight. A second Catholic parochial school, St. Aloysius, opened in 1954 on Middlefield Road. Its name was changed later to Our Lady of the Rosary, reflecting another parish division.

During the 1970s, declining student populations created financial difficulties that threatened to shut both schools. In 1978, they merged to form one school with two campuses, named St. Elizabeth Seton School. The operation at two locations continued until fall 1986 when operations were consolidated at the Channing Avenue site. By 1991 enrollment in the K-8 school had settled at about 250 students, mainly minority youngsters from East Palo Alto.

Although not located in Palo Alto, Peninsula School has had many ties to the city. Peninsula School opened in September 1925 with 42 children and Josephine Duveneck as the first principal and leader of a group of parents who operated this progressive education experiment in the old Coleman mansion in Menlo Oaks, east of Menlo Park. The parent cooperative school, affording an alternative to the structure of the public schools and other local private schools, has thrived. During the early 1990s, its enrollment ran about 245.

Mid-Peninsula High School in Palo Alto was established by Philip Bliss, a former Cubberley High School teacher, and others in 1978 as an independent, nonsecular school designed for high-potential, low-performance students. It occupied the former Garland School plant and enrolled about 150 teenagers. The Peninsula French-American School, taking prekindergarten through sixth grade students, is at the same site.

Keys School at 2890 Middlefield Road, partially in a unit of the First Christian Church, started in 1977 with Mrs. Elizabeth Danon, a former Harker Academy teacher, as principal. Her successors were Barbara Butterworth and Tim Willoughby. The school, featuring small classes, sought to balance individual creativity and academic proficiency in its 196 K-8 students. Keys School was named for Mrs. Alice Keys and her son, Noel Keys, both educators.

The Mid-Peninsula Jewish Community Day School was founded in 1990 at the Jewish Community Center, formerly Terman Middle School, as Palo Alto's only Jewish private school. It had 70 children in the K-4 grades in 1992-93, with the announced intention of adding one grade a year until it reaches K-12 status.

Numerous other private elementary schools with no more than a dozen students have operated in Palo Alto from time to time, and nursery and preschools abound. Together with the public schools, all these private educational enterprises have explored varied ways of teaching children and meeting any special needs they may have.

Were Senator Stanford to return for an inspection, one might think he would find his vision of a complete educational system at Palo Alto — even if it is a system perpetually in flux — fulfilled in large measure.

St. Elizabeth Seton School continues the Catholic parochial tradition in Palo Alto.

Out for a ride in a horse-drawn surrey on Sand Hill Road.

11

Getting Around

Until the first Spanish explorers rode in on horseback, walking was the main means of travel in the San Francisco Bay Area. True, the Ohlone Indians did venture into sloughs and bay inlets in canoe-shaped rafts made of tightly lashed bundles of tule rushes. Although unsinkable, these vessels became waterlogged, limiting how far they could go. Even during the rancho era and the days of early American settlement, walking remained a common means of getting around.

The "Middle Road" and Other Routes

Paths and trails through the willow thickets near the bay and the dense chaparral growth near the foothills gradually developed into the first roads. In summer, the "middle road," meandering roughly along today's Middlefield Road route, tended to be favored, for it was shorter and had an easy ford at San Francisquito Creek. But owing to its proximity to the bay flood plain, it sometimes became too marshy for rainy-season traffic, and then higher ground was preferred. This route, the one the padres trod, lay west of what travel promoters in the early 20th century titled El Camino Real, "The King's Highway," to commemorate the Spanish expeditions.

After surveyors laid out what is now El Camino in the 1850s, it bore a more prosaic name: the San Francisco-San Jose road. It afforded the first four-wheel vehicles — stagecoaches and wagons — a fairly direct route. Later, people in Mayfield and Palo Alto called it the county road because Santa Clara County maintained it, and still later, the state highway. For decades before Bayshore Highway and its improved version, Bayshore Freeway, were built, El Camino bore the main stream of traffic up and down the Peninsula.

Other early routes include Arastradero Road, originally a timber-drag road from the redwoods to Santa Clara and San Jose, and parts of Embarcadero and Newell roads that crossed the Seale and Greer properties to bay landings on San Francisquito Creek. Page Mill Road connected Mayfield and its lumberyard with the forested lands of William Page to the west; beginning in the 1860s, wagons hauled timber down steep slopes and around tight curves on its narrow track.

Californios of the rancho era, among them many mission-trained Indians, were renowned horsemen, masters of skills vital in moving open-range cattle to other pastures or to slaughter for their meat and leather hides. The rancho period also saw heavy use of *carretas* — two-wheel carts with solid wooden wheels, drawn by a yoke of oxen. These carts — introduced by the Spanish — carried families, supplies, tanbark and piles of hides to market. But they were slow and uncomfortable, so that in the 1840s a trip from the northwestern Santa Clara Valley to San Francisco might take three days.

Ships, Wagons and Stagecoaches

Then the 1849 gold rush cast a backwash of new

Teams of oxen were used to haul logs from the hills to the numerous sawmills located in the area.

settlers over the Peninsula, and with them came both ships and four-wheel vehicles. Lumbermen cut redwood trees in the vast mountain forests to the west, and at first teams of oxen dragged the huge logs downhill over dusty trails to sawmills. Crews then loaded the milled lumber onto large wagons, which oxen, horses or mules pulled to wharves on the bay. From there, shallow-draft schooners, and later steam-powered side-wheelers and stern-wheelers, carried the cargo to booming San Francisco. The city had burned down several times in the 1850s and 1860s, and its appetite for building materials seemed insatiable.

Meanwhile, the pace of passenger travel picked up. Horse-drawn buggies and wagons replaced the clumsy carretas. John W. Whisman started a

stagecoach line between San Jose and San Francisco in September 1849 — a trip through dust or mud that cost $32 per passenger. Competition soon emerged, and before long better coaches, more horses, improved roads and heavier traffic cut the fares in half, then reduced them again. By 1853, Hall & Crandall's one-way fare had dropped to $10.

The Railroad Reaches Mayfield

When California became a state in 1850, its land-transportation vehicles and roads could only be rated primitive in comparison to those of the eastern United States. But the timing of statehood proved propitious for one form of transportation then maturing: railroads. A railroad line from San

A steam locomotive crosses San Francisquito Creek into Santa Clara County sometime between 1864 and the early 1880s.

Francisco down the Peninsula to San Jose was first suggested in 1849, but not until 1860 did firm plans to build one develop. What with shortages of manpower and capital and the impact of the Civil War, the project took a long time to complete. The San Francisco and San Jose Railroad at last reached Mayfield on October 17, 1863, providing the occasion for a grand celebration. The three railroad promoters, foundryman Peter Donahue, Judge Timothy Dame and auctioneer Henry M. Newhall, staged a picnic excursion for 400 invited guests, including two governors — Leland Stanford of California and Addison Crandall Gibbs of Oregon. After making a maiden run to Mayfield, the train stopped briefly, then backed up to the San Francisquito Creek bridge by the tall tree for a "bounteous collation" of "fowl, ice cream, and unlimited champagne." On the morn-

ing after, regular two-trains-a-day service between Mayfield and San Francisco began.

Trains Doom Competitors

Extension of the line to San Jose was completed on January 16, 1864. The days of the stagecoach as a main-route carrier were numbered. So was transportation of passengers on steamboats plying the South Bay. The steamboats' reputation already had been wounded when the side-wheeler Jenny Lind exploded and sank off Las Pulgas Ranch (Menlo Park area) in April 1853, with the loss of 31 lives.

The railroad ultimately figured in the doom of another mode of South Bay transportation: scow schooners. These shallow-draft ships continued to carry bulk cargoes for decades, however. When low water grounded a scow schooner, its flat bottom rested stably on the bay mud until a rising tide floated the boat again. At high tide, they sailed up to wharves — at Cooley's Landing at the Ravenswood Port or Wilson's Landing (originally Clarke's) on Mayfield Slough near its juncture with San Francisquito Creek — and loaded hides, lumber, grain, hay, oyster shells and produce such as strawberries to deliver to San Francisco. According to John Lucas Greer, Captain Wilson's boat carried local ranchers' grain from the warehouse at his landing to San Francisco for $1 a ton, much to the vexation of the railroad company. Cooley's Landing extended its pier 1,500 yards into the bay to facilitate the loading of bricks.

"Next Stop: Mayfield"

Soon the railroad, which in 1870 became the Southern Pacific Company (SP, for short), ran two trains each way daily. Commuter service had arrived and continues to this day, and the gaps from one town to the next had shrunk. Peninsula rail service had beaten transcontinental train travel by a good five years. Well-to-do San Franciscans found new reason to look for country estates or summer retreats in the warmer climate an easy ride "down the Peninsula." Trains from San Francisco chugged through such larger centers as San Mateo and Redwood City and also served small communities like Millbrae, Belmont and Menlo Park. "Next stop: Mayfield," the conductors called. Palo Alto was still decades in the future.

Trains set a new standard of swift, dependable service, and led in intercity transportation for many years. Townsfolk guarded their railroad access jealously, so station location emerged as a factor.

It upset early Mayfield residents when they discovered that the station named for their town was being located about a half-mile northwest, near Churchill Avenue. Sarah Wallis led a movement to relocate the depot to a site handier for Mayfield's people, and William Paul gave the lots. The campaign took two years, but finally SP moved the building to the present California Avenue station site. The depot established there

in 1869 served until 1954, when a more modern building replaced it. In the 1980s the present California Avenue station was built in conjunction with the shops and housing of the adjoining Palo Alto Central real estate development.

A Shed-like Station but No Town

At University Avenue and the railroad tracks, the first station was a small open shed facing The Circle. Real estate concerns built it to serve an excursion train from San Francisco for an auction sale of town lots on June 7, 1890. This facility alleviated the need to transport the crowd of several thousand in horse-drawn conveyances from either Menlo Park or Mayfield. After the sale, trains occasionally stopped at the shelter on signal. Even so, whistlestop debarkers found few landmarks at first.

Susan K. Branner, wife of Professor John Casper Branner, wrote of their arrival by train in Palo Alto in 1891:

> ...When we finally stepped off at Palo Alto, we found a small platform for a station. Not a house or building of any kind was in sight. What is now Palo Alto was an open field apparently stretching away for miles...

Landscape architect Frederick L. Olmsted recorded in April 1888 that Senator Stanford had revised campus plans so as to provide "an avenue [Palm Drive] to a proposed railway station." However, perhaps because Stanford was deposed as SP president in 1890, the travail of the station's birth was protracted.

At last the railroad announced that after December 12, 1892, its local trains to San Francisco would start from Palo Alto instead of Menlo Park. At about the same time, surveyors were reported arranging the site for a new stone station — which was never built. Instead, in 1893 the open shed was enclosed and finished as a waiting room, with welcome heating. A boxcar was positioned near the waiting room, and between the two, a small temporary structure was placed. It served as an office for Robert Danneberg, express and baggage agent, ticket seller and telegraph operator, all rolled into one.

Eight Trains a Day Each Way

The shift of the local terminus from Menlo Park to Palo Alto, effective February 7, 1893, immediately impacted the local liverymen — Jasper Paulsen, Dan Smith and Victor Yesle; they had to reconfigure their services. On the new timetable, eight trains each way served Palo Alto daily.

Exactly where the permanent station should be located was an issue that split the newborn town's businessmen. In written appeals to Senator Stanford they gave arguments for leaving it on the side toward the town rather than moving it to the university side, and for and against placing it north or south of University Avenue. Stanford refused to help finance a station styled after the university buildings. So, in 1896, a wood-frame station was built on the campus side of the tracks. It served for nearly 45 years, despite several attempts after the turn of the century to have a new and larger station erected on the town side. In 1910, Southern Pacific announced plans for a new station and a subway under the tracks, but the town opposed the subway, so nothing was built.

An Undercrossing — and a New Station!

For decades the need for an undercrossing at University Avenue grew more urgent as trains stopped traffic. The opposing interests finally came to an agreement, resulting in an underpass project completed in March 1941. At the same time, SP built a new station in a streamlined *moderne* style, with the main depot still on the campus side and a small shelter on the downtown side. The *Palo Alto Times* reported:

> *Palo Alto staged one of its biggest celebrations ever to mark completion of the new train station and the two underpasses: one taking University Avenue under the SP tracks, the other routing El Camino Real under University Avenue.*
>
> *Governor Culbert Olson cut an inch-thick garland of marigolds and then hopped aboard the first official car to ride through the two underpasses. Then came a parade of 2,000 people, 400 horses and a variety of vehicles hewing to a transportation theme. Nearly a dozen bands tootled, and seven Army planes from Moffett Field roared over. Girls in kimonos preceded 38 Japanese-American Association members carrying a huge American flag, 40 by 75 feet, and applause greeted this patriotic display all along the parade route.*
>
> *The occasion coincided with the start of Stanford University's 50th anniversary commemoration, and the sharing of Palo Alto and Stanford interests was duly noted in oratory lauding the $700,000 project.*
>
> *A transportation exhibit stood by Alma Street near Hamilton Avenue, including Southern Pacific's new Daylight engine, dining car, chair car and lounge; an 1875 wood-burning Virginia & Truckee Railroad engine; a new Pacific Greyhound Luxury Super-Cruiser bus; and a replica of Boxcar No. 1725, which was Palo Alto's makeshift ticket office when liveryman Jasper Paulsen bought the first ticket from agent R.L. Danneberg.*
>
> *The crowd filling the reviewing stands and adjoining areas was estimated at 15,000.*

Refurbished in the early 1980s, the Palo Alto station became a regional transit center serving Santa Clara County and San Mateo County transit bus passengers as well as CalTrain commuters.

Commuter service continued to grow as Peninsula communities expanded. By 1940, about 8,000 commuters rode the weekday trains. Early wood-burning locomotives had been replaced by steam locomotives fueled by oil, and in the '40s diesel engines took over. In 1954, commute service reached a peak of 16,000 commuters car-

This train depot served the town and university from 1896 until it was replaced by the present station.

Construction of the University Avenue underpass coincided with the building of the new train station.
They opened with great fanfare in 1941.

ried daily by Southern Pacific trains. After that, completion of new freeways lured many passengers away from rail service and into automobiles. Patronage had dropped to 11,500 daily commuters by 1964.

Southern Pacific spoke plainly about its desire to get out of the local passenger business. Citing growing deficits and shrinking patronage, the company sought permission from the Public Utilities Commission (successor to the once mighty Railroad Commission) to end commuter service. In 1980, an agreement by Peninsula transit districts with support from the state's California Transportation Agency created CalTrain to operate the commuter line, initially using SP equipment and personnel. Housing scarcities and reverse commutes to Peninsula and Silicon Valley jobs helped to boost CalTrain ridership to more than 23,000 a day in the early 1990s, yet save-the-train crises replayed year after year like a "Perils of Pauline" serial.

The Era of Genuine Horsepower

Although Palo Alto's beginning in the early 1890s coincided with the age of the "iron horse," or railroad, the earlier age of the four-legged horse galloped on for a time. Yet even by the time of Senator Stanford's death in mid-1893, his stables of trotters and race horses had passed their zenith. Barely two months later, Stanford's valet, Edward Largely, told a newspaper reporter, "There isn't one man on the place now where there used to be ten." In the town, however, the need for more ordinary horsepower boomed. Several livery stables and blacksmith shops sprang up. Faculty, students, visitors and their bags had to be driven from the train to the campus, and drayage required many horses.

PALO ALTO HISTORICAL ASSOCIATION

Horse-drawn vehicles carried students and visitors from the rairoad depot to the campus.

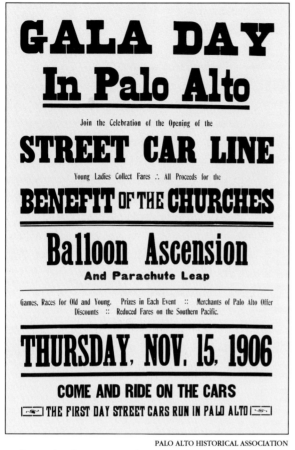

GALA DAY
In Palo Alto

Join the Celebration of the Opening of the

STREET CAR LINE

Young Ladies Collect Fares ∴ All Proceeds for the

BENEFIT OF THE CHURCHES

Balloon Ascension
And Parachute Leap

Games, Races for Old and Young.   Prizes in Each Event   ::   Merchants of Palo Alto Offer
Discounts   ::   Reduced Fares on the Southern Pacific.

THURSDAY, NOV. 15, 1906

COME AND RIDE ON THE CARS
THE FIRST DAY STREET CARS RUN IN PALO ALTO

PALO ALTO HISTORICAL ASSOCIATION

When Palo Alto's streetcar line opened in 1906 it was a big day for celebration. Even the schools closed.

Jasper Paulsen's livery stable on Alma Street put a memorable conveyance on the roads. Paulsen acquired a 32-passenger wagonette, painted maroon except for its yellow wheels, to haul passengers to and from the campus. Once the train station was built, it became common to see one or more buggies, hacks, surreys or horse-drawn buses waiting to take train riders to their final destination. A driver named Asa Andrews, widely known as "Uncle John" and famed for his tall tales (such as that Senator Stanford had imported the campus ground squirrels at great cost), had a faithful horse named Marguerite. In the 1980s, harking back to the livery days, Stanford University began operating small red buses called Marguerites around the campus and to and from the train station.

Sparks Fly Over Electric Streetcars

Shadow competition for the livery stables had been present since before the university opened, for electric streetcars were proving their feasibility in many localities. There was talk of an electric line to Stanford from Palo Alto and another from Mayfield. Indeed, Mayfield made a definite proposal that was given to a professor to study in the summer of 1891, and he reported favorably to Senator Stanford. Franchises for a line from the Palo Alto station were sought in 1891 and again in 1892. But Stanford did not approve these ideas, nor was he ready to build his own electric lines. So for light rail, a long ripening period ensued, with exceptional political infighting.

Electric railroads got started in booming San Jose in the late 1880s, and expanded in the 1890s. By 1900, syndicate promoters were talking big about running lines down both sides of the South Bay, and Southern Pacific officials were quietly watching. Owners began to consolidate local lines, and the first interurban service in Santa Clara County began in 1904. A few months earlier, John F. Parkinson and a group of associates formed the Palo Alto and Suburban Railway Company to build a streetcar system in Palo Alto. They had in hand a local franchise for a line up El Camino Real from the Mayfield town limit to University Avenue, east on University through the business district, and south on Waverley Street to Embarcadero Road. Their capitalization was only $100,000, but it was rumored that Parkinson had rich and influential backers and intended to build a line all the way from San Mateo to San Jose.

Parkinson's group lined up support in San Mateo County and acquired an option to buy the San Jose and Santa Clara electric line. Meanwhile, the Southern Pacific had struck back, gobbling up the new San Jose-Los Gatos interurban and announcing it would build electric roads down both sides of the bay. One of its managers, Oliver Hale, spoke of building a Palo Alto line.

Gathering more backers, Parkinson incorporated the Santa Clara Interurban Railroad and unveiled plans for a steam train line from San

Mateo through San Jose to Gilroy, with a Stanford University branch. However, he lacked both the university's assent and a franchise through Mayfield.

Hale and Parkinson and their allies clashed at two epic meetings of the Mayfield Board of Trustees. In the end, the board refused Parkinson a franchise despite his threat to bypass Mayfield by going through the Seale tract. When he departed for New York to firm up his financing, Southern Pacific officials managed to undercut him. Discouraged, Parkinson sold his franchise in October 1905 to a Santa Clara County syndicate headed by Lewis Hanchett of San Jose and utilities promoter John Martin of San Francisco. A few months later, Southern Pacific created the Peninsular Railroad Company. Before long, SP began work on its Mayfield-Los Altos cutoff, designed to enable steam trains to meet interurbans at several points.

A Gala Celebration

Meanwhile, Hanchett, using Parkinson's franchises, started work on the Palo Alto streetcar lines in 1906. The system called for the main line to run down University Avenue and out to Marlowe Street, just west of San Francisquito Creek and the Woodland Acres tract. A second line branched off at Waverley Street and ran south to the end of town at Embarcadero Road. A short branch from University ran along Emerson Street to Hawthorne Avenue and accessed a car barn and transformer station at Hawthorne and High Street.

November 15, 1906, was a gala day in Palo Alto. The new streetcar lines opened that day, and the whole town celebrated. School children enjoyed a holiday and 30 of the community's young ladies acted as streetcar conductors, collecting fares as a benefit for the town's churches. Field events such as a "fat gents" race and tugs of

PALO ALTO HISTORICAL ASSOCIATION/FRANK DAVEY

Town leaders pose in front of one of the streetcars on opening day, November 5, 1906.

155

war between schools marked the occasion, as did the thrills of a balloon ascension and a parachute jump. Rain delayed the aerial circus but by no means dampened the enthusiasm.

Hanchett and Martin, proprietors of the Palo Alto streetcars, continued in hot competition with Southern Pacific. They secured permission for the University Avenue double tracks to cross the main rail line, and then laid track south along El Camino Real toward Mayfield. But in 1907, their hope of linking up a rival interurban loop was dashed by local problems and the onset of a depression. Isolated in Palo Alto with a small system, Hanchett and Martin accepted a buy-out offer from SP in August 1908.

A Five-Cent Ride from Town to Campus

From then on, things fell into place. Peninsular announced plans to electrify one set of tracks on the Mayfield cutoff, and Stanford trustees finally granted a lease for campus service. In mid-1909, SP consolidated its operations under a slightly altered name, Peninsular Railway Company, and in October 1909 opened service to Stanford.

The Stanford line ran out Galvez Street to Panama Street, behind the Quad. Extensions in Palo Alto lengthened the University Avenue line to a creek crossing, and the Waverley Street line to Oregon Avenue. Five-cent rides between town and campus proved very popular. In winter, when muddy streets bogged down pedestrians and bicycle riders, trolleys were a perfect solution.

In 1910, the Peninsular Railway's interurban loop reached Palo Alto. From San Jose, the line ran to Cupertino and turned north through Los Altos along what is now Foothill Expressway to Mayfield. Then it ran alongside El Camino Real, joining the Palo Alto-Stanford line at University Junction, between Embarcadero Road and University Avenue. The 80.5-mile interurban also connected to Saratoga, Los Gatos, Campbell and Alum Rock Park, and outings such as the $1 "Blossom Valley Trip" packed the big red cars frequently. But no electric rail links with San Francisco or Oakland were ever forged.

By the 1920s, the Stanford-Palo Alto line had been dubbed the "Toonerville Trolley," after a popular comic strip of the day. Elinor V. Cogswell, editor of the *Palo Alto Times*, fondly recalled her days riding the trolley as a Stanford student and then as a reporter. She said the trolleys served as a social and cultural center for faculty and students, who "rode back and forth between town and Quad, studying, making dates, carrying on political campaigns, chatting with friends, weaving plots and plans."

"If regulars failed to board the trolley at the usual corners," she wrote, "the motorman would wait for a few minutes while ears strained to hear hurrying footsteps." She noted, too, that people crowded the trolleys, especially in rainy weather, to attend concerts at the old Stanford Assembly Hall.

Autos and Buses Roust the Trolleys

Trolleys thrived locally for more than 15 years. But the automobile came of age, honking for paved streets and the right of way, and bus manufacturers connived to have light rail ousted, finally winning out. Pressed by local officials to pave main routes between the rails at high cost, as their franchises required, the electric rail companies began closing marginal routes in the 1920s.

In 1925 the streetcar rails on University Avenue were pulled up and motorbus service began. Interurban and Palo Alto depot-to-Stanford trolley service survived for a while, with car storage relocated to the university corporation yard. To reach the campus, a Palo Alto resident had to pay a 10-cent fare for the motor bus, walk a way to the Stanford trolley and pay another 6-cent fare. In the first year of bus operations, operating costs rose while patronage fell 16% — a little-noted portent of problems to come.

Interurban revenues kept declining. Good times in the late '20s had boosted automobile ownership to a South Bay figure of one car for every 2.92 residents. A crisis came in 1929 when state authorities decided automobiles and trucks must have more room on Highway 101 (then El

Camino Real) between California Avenue and downtown Palo Alto. Peninsular either had to move the interurban tracks — at a cost it couldn't afford — or abandon them. The interurban's closing forced the shutdown of Stanford's Toonerville, with students, who for years had played trolley pranks, providing semi-mock mourning. Buses to the campus replaced the electric car, and SP's Mayfield station became the transfer point from heavy rail to interurban. The Depression added its weight to auto traffic's impact, and Peninsular gradually shut down its interurban service, closing the Mayfield-San Jose line last, on October 1, 1934.

Bus Service Barely Survives

In Palo Alto, one of the first cities to switch completely from streetcars to motor buses, Peninsular found the bus system a drag. The Southern Pacific subsidiary had no interest in this new form of transportation, even when the Railroad Commission ordered it to replace the interurban with bus service from the Palo Alto SP station to downtown San Jose. When Peninsular prepared to abandon city bus service in Palo Alto, as it had a legal right to do, Floyd Pearson's new Palo Alto Transit Company came forward to rescue the city lines in 1933, and a year later to take over the Palo Alto-San Jose run.

In 1941, two taxi service operators formed Palo Alto City Lines and bought the Palo Alto local routes; in 1949 the company was reorganized as Palo Alto Transit. Because of World War II shortages, the early '40s had been boon years for bus operators, but after gasoline rationing ended and autos could be obtained, patronage declined. By the mid-1950s, Peninsula Transit began asking for direct subsidies from Palo Alto and other cities it served. In 1962 Palo Alto's city government agreed to subsidize the service and a year later bought nine new olive-and-yellow buses. But subsidy costs kept on mounting until Palo Alto, eager to get out of the business, sold its buses to the new Santa Clara County Transit District in 1972.

For many decades, the terminal for Pacific Greyhound and Peerless Stages buses stood at Alma Street and Lytton Avenue, across from the train depot. When the San Mateo County Transit District took over Greyhound's Peninsula commuter bus service, the Palo Alto terminal was no longer used. It closed in October 1980. Santa Clara County Transit's early history included experiments with Dial-a-Ride and propane-powered buses, both instituted by a Palo Altan, James T. Pott. Pott was also the main architect of the expressway system, an effort to serve burgeoning automotive traffic without all the expense and land consumption of a full freeway system.

The Auto Grows Up with Palo Alto

The automobile grew up with Palo Alto. Ray Lyman Wilbur, a busy medical practitioner during the 1901-1910 years, recounted his transition from horse-and-buggy times this way:

> *I can see myself… pedaling about Palo Alto and the Stanford campus on my bicycle or using livery horses, trying to keep up with my rapidly growing practice, until I was able to get my fine carriage horse Bob, and then my first automobile, an Autocar runabout with a straight bar instead of a steering wheel, which was to be succeeded at intervals by automobiles of more modern design.*

As Palo Alto developed, so did the community's dependence on the automobile. The first cars, like Fred Smith's horseless buggy, were novelties. They caused problems, but townspeople usually tolerated their presence. Mrs. Stanford banned automobiles on the campus because they scared the horses, but most people found the early cars magnetic in their attraction. As their numbers grew, autos changed the appearance of Palo Alto — as was the case, sooner or later, almost everywhere in the nation.

Palo Alto still was dotted with oak trees, many growing in the middle or at the edge of its streets. These trees had been no great obstacle for horses and wagons, but automobiles traveling over the

Three bicyclists pedaling through Mayfield on Main Street (now El Camino Real), circa 1888.

cycling as a sport. The Palo Alto Bicycle Club, organized in 1894, engaged in Sunday rides to and from San Jose, where expert cyclists raced at a velodrome.

Difficulties involving bicycles developed early. Thefts were already a problem in 1901 when the *Palo Alto Times* noted, "One cannot safely leave a wheel on the sidewalk for a few minutes

... lest someone may ride it away." Bicycle riding on sidewalks was of greater concern. In winter months, unpaved streets became seas of adobe mud, bogging down bicycles; riders preferred the hard, clean wooden sidewalks. After several bicycle-pedestrian incidents, town officials acted to ban bicycling on the sidewalks, but the new law was only partially successful.

PALO ALTO HISTORICAL ASSOCIATION

Signs such as this one at Newell and Embarcadero roads mark the system of bicycle lanes throughout Palo Alto.

In the 1920s, the police began enforcing an ordinance requiring lamps on bicycles ridden at night. Licensing began in 1936 with a fee of 25 cents per year. Between 1936 and 1948, records show, 13,236 bicycles were registered in Palo Alto.

Concern arose in the 1940s and 1950s over juvenile bicyclists' problems. Cycling safety was stressed at Bicycle Days at Rinconada Park. When a 1945 ordinance banning the obstruction of sidewalks by parked bicycles took effect, 14 offenders were caught on the first day. The first-offense penalty was two days without one's bike.

Bicycling's popularity surged anew in the late 1960s and, as in the 1890s, adults shared this interest. In 1967, the City Council approved bicycle-route streets through Palo Alto marked by signs, but the poorly planned routes were not popular with cyclists or the community. In 1972, a new 74-mile system of bike lanes was created, causing some conflicts with advocates of street parking. In the mid-'70s, bike bridges were built across San Francisquito Creek at San Mateo Drive in Menlo Park and at Waverley Street, and across Adobe Creek at Wilkie Way and other points.

Safety amid automobile traffic became a growing concern as more and more multigear bikes and mountain bikes appeared on city streets. Bicycle commuting became part of the city's transportation planning in the 1980s, championed by City Council Member Ellen Fletcher. The Bryant Street "bike boulevard" opened in 1982 to provide a safe, direct cross-town corridor for these commuters.

Palo Altans Take to the Sky

World War I created avid public interest in aviation. Palo Alto area people eager to try flying went up for rides in 1919 with Valdo H. Brazil from the Stanford flying field, and in the early 1920s with Ray Sullivan, whose aeroplane flights from a field on Embarcadero Road near the city waterworks (just east of Rinconada Park) cost $2.50 each.

Lt. Norman Goddard opened the Palo Alto School of Aviation in 1928 on Stanford land near the corner of Stanford Avenue and El Camino Real. The field, with two hangars, a ground school, a small office and a strip of grass for a runway, was used by the U.S. Department of Agriculture's division of forestry as its flight center from 1929-34. One of the school's first graduates, Paul Mantz, won the world championship in 1929 for flying the difficult outside loop, and went on to become a stunt pilot in Hollywood. Goddard was killed at an Alameda County air show when the wings fell off a glider he was exhibiting. Mantz, too, ultimately died in a crash.

In the early 1930s, Palo Alto officials moved to establish a municipal airport on the bayfront. While that work was in progress, the air school decamped from Stanford, chased by a lawsuit filed by College Terrace residents who attacked it as a public nuisance and menace. Among the School of Aviation personnel making the move in 1935 was Jack Nystrom, who, together with his son, Jim, went on to log more than 50 years of family

The original Palo Alto Airport was on Stanford land near the intersection of El Camino Real and Stanford Avenue.
It was relocated to the baylands in 1935.

Air traffic controllers at Palo Alto Airport serve the general aviation needs of northern Santa Clara County.

association with airport operations.

Shortly before World War II broke out, scores of Stanford students learned to fly at the baylands airport. It closed during the war, but Palo Alto Airport Inc. contributed to the war effort by setting up flying schools at King City and Dos Palos.

Shifting the County Line

Open again in 1946 with two all-weather strips, Palo Alto Airport gained flight students and aircraft rapidly, passing the 100 tie-downs mark and receiving a top rating from the Aircraft Owners and Pilots Association in 1947. In the early 1950s, one runway was relocated to make room for the Palo Alto Municipal Golf Course. Part of the airport lay in San Mateo County, which for a time shared in operating the field. In 1963, after complex legislative action, the county boundary was adjusted to move about 400 acres at the airport into Santa Clara Clara County, in exchange for a Skyline swap benefiting San Mateo County. Since then, Santa Clara County has operated the airport under lease from the city. For a time, scheduled flights served its heliport.

Federal air controllers have operated its tower since 1967. In 1980, the city negotiated a deal to allow 510 tie-downs but no second runway. In fiscal 1990, the general aviation airport, 67th busiest in the nation, at times recorded 100 takeoffs and landings on its 2,500-foot runway in a peak hour, and an annual average of 234,000.

Noise problems prompted city officials to oppose a second runway. The problems continue, but efforts to curb them, mounted by the Palo Alto Airport Joint Community Relations Committee, have been cited by the Federal Aviation Administration as an example of good airport/community relations. In addition to use by its resident fleet of business and recreational craft, the airport accommodates emergency transportation of medical patients and equipment to Stanford University Hospital.

Around the World in 84 Days — Submerged

One Palo Alto native son, Navy Capt. Edward L. "Ned" Beach, wrote a singular chapter in transportation history in 1960. Beach skippered the nuclear-powered submarine USS Triton as it circumnavigated the world submerged, a 36,000-mile voyage lasting 84 days and following approximately the course charted by Ferdinand Magellan's expedition of 1519-21, which first circled the globe. Beach, a World War II naval hero, also wrote several best-selling novels about submarine duty. His father, a Navy captain too, held office as Palo Alto city clerk after retiring from federal service.

Palo Alto-Stanford Astronauts

To date, no spacecraft has been launched successfully from Palo Alto. However, two U.S. astronauts have carried the city's name into space. The first, Owen K. Garriott, a Stanford electrical engineering professor, made two flights, the 60-day Skylab III mission in 1963 and the 10-day Spacelab I mission in 1983. The second, Loren Acton, a solar physicist at the Lockheed Palo Alto Research Laboratory, flew on the midsummer 1985 Spacelab 2 mission, one of the last Challenger flights before a launch disaster destroyed that space shuttle. Acton returned home from his experience as the scientific payload specialist convinced that Earth must not only keep its own affairs in order but must deal in the next 1,000 years with what he called "planetary issues" — what happens to the oceans, the land mass and the atmosphere. A number of other astronauts have taken part in local activities while training at the National Aeronautics & Space Administration's Ames Research Center in Mountain View or at Stanford University, where Sally K. Ride, the first U.S. woman in space in 1983 and a repeat crewperson in 1984, received degrees through her doctorate in physics, and later taught.

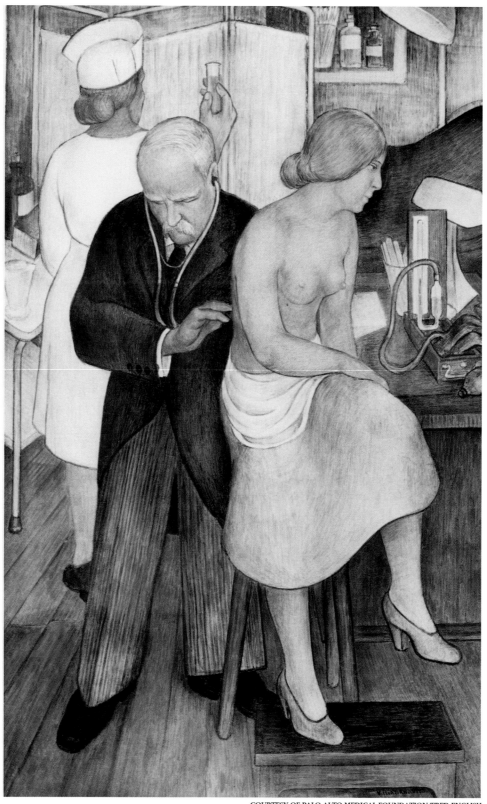

*Victor Arnautoff's murals created a mini-scandal when the new
Palo Alto Medical Clinic building opened in 1930.*

12

"Say Ahh"—The Community's Health

*" … the people by reason of their costly experience are awake to
the value of knowledge, alertness and cooperation in sanitary
matters… the public health of the community of Palo Alto and
Stanford University is safeguarded to a marked degree."*

— *Professor J.C.L. Fish, President, Palo Alto Board of Health*
Report in 1905 on 1903 Typhoid Fever Epidemic

The most menacing threat to public health in Palo Alto occurred in the spring of 1903, when a typhoid fever epidemic broke out in and near the town, and at Stanford University. Only a handful of physicians practiced locally then — a far cry from the thousands within the medical community today. But they were competent and conscientious, and aided by the public health steps taken in Palo Alto's first decade as a municipality, they coped with the crisis, though it took a dozen lives. The cause of the epidemic was assiduously ferreted out, and from then on, Palo Alto's raised public-health consciousness remained at a remarkably high level.

Health ranked as a prime concern of citizens who voted the town into being in 1894. They wanted a pure water supply and proper sanitation. So in August, four months after incorporation, the Board of Health set up by the town trustees named Dr. E.W. Charles the first health officer. He focused attention on the need for untainted water, adequate sewage disposal, safe plumbing and milk inspection.

After bringing deep water wells into a city system in 1897, the town passed a bond issue to install the first underground sewer line in 1899. An ordinance directed residents to connect with the sewer, fill cesspools and remove privies. (Because most Palo Alto houses had been built with modern plumbing, outhouses were less common than in the typical 1900s town, although some existed.) Early in 1903, a Board of Health inspector arrested more than 50 property owners for failing to comply with the law. The shock treatment worked: Practically all privies and cesspools soon vanished.

A Frightening Epidemic

There had been almost no typhoid in Palo Alto and little at Stanford before 1903. However, the community knew that its "floating population" — students who came and went, train commuters, tourists and vacationers — posed a higher risk of importing infectious or contagious diseases than would a static population.

A few cases of typhoid fever (an acute infectious disease caused by bacteria that enter the body via contaminated food or water) appeared before the epidemic struck in March 1903 but were not reported to the Board of Health until later. The epidemic reached full force in April, and then slackened through May. In all there were 236 known cases, 60 of them outside the town limits, in a community population estimated at 3,500. Twelve of the persons infected died; eight of them were Stanford students.

Since 1895, a Students' Guild had been providing sickroom and nursing services at Stanford, supported by students who each contributed 50

The Students' Guild operated the first hospital in Palo Alto, on Lytton Avenue at Cowper Street.

cents a semester. It was an early form of prepaid health care. The typhoid outbreak spurred the guild, working with the university hygiene department, to rent a building in Palo Alto and make it a hospital. A second temporary hospital was set up later, and on campus some infected students were quartered in Encina Hall.

"... but for the Students' Guild and its instant activity there would have been four times the actual number of deaths," wrote Stanford President David Starr Jordan, who held a medical degree but had never practiced. Jordan praised the night-and-day labors of two professor-physicians, William F. Snow and Ray Lyman Wilbur. Palo Alto's lone doctor, Howard Black, had also toiled valiantly.

Pinpointing the Source

Scientific detective work traced the source of the virulent fever. Clues led to the Parreiro dairy farm

on Los Trancos Creek about five miles from town. Milk from the dairy was bought by a Palo Alto dairyman who had delivery routes in the town and supplied two fraternity houses on campus and a restaurant patronized by Stanford students. Dr. Snow and Dr. Clelia D. Mosher of the Stanford hygiene faculty assisted Fish in preparing the Board of Health report, which, Orrin Elliott noted, read "like the plot of a tragedy."

Care in the crisis took on odd aspects. "One of the methods to control the epidemic," Dr. Wilbur wrote in his memoirs, "was for me to turn out at half-past four in the morning and go down with a shotgun to the dairy to make sure that no milk left it (the dairyman had tried to bribe me with three $5 gold pieces)." Wilbur added:

... I still remember the mother (incidentally the wife of a professor) who thought that I as deputy health officer had been absolutely

unfair in stopping the milkman from delivering milk that contained typhoid organisms. She said the dairyman was a good church member and certainly would do nothing of that kind to hurt little children. In order to show her faith in him she went out to his dairy, got some milk and brought it home. The result was that she had to care for three members of her family with rather severe typhoid fever.

Reflecting in the 1940s on the typhoid ordeal, Wilbur commented, "... one finds in the Stanford-Palo Alto community today one of the best local public health services anywhere." No epidemic borne by milk or water ever broke out in Palo Alto again.

Students Establish First Hospital

After the calamity passed, the Students' Guild purchased the hospital on Lytton Avenue at Cowper

PALO ALTO HISTORICAL ASSOCIATION

Louis Olsen was Palo Alto's health officer for 35 years.

Street. It was equipped with an operating room — the only one on the Peninsula — and enlarged to serve 20 patients. Student fees were raised and made compulsory. Townspeople also were admitted; however, not until 1906 did the hospital stay in operation during the university's summer vacation.

Meanwhile, Palo Alto became the third city in the state, after San Francisco and Los Angeles, to employ a full-time health officer, Hubert Jenkins. In 1914 the city established compulsory garbage collection; not long afterward, Louis Olsen, a student of civil and sanitary engineering at Stanford, became a city sanitary inspector and wrote a thesis on refuse disposal, describing Palo Alto's system.

Olsen's job turned full-time in 1917 when the Board of Public Safety promoted him to city health officer. In 1918 he hired the first county public health nurse, Rachel Miller, just at the time Palo Altans discovered that the dreaded Spanish influenza epidemic was not going to miss them after all. (The epidemic caused an estimated 850,000 deaths in America — roughly 16 times the toll of U.S. battle deaths in World War I.)

A Second Epidemic

The flu came on in October and spread with frightening speed. Olsen himself fell ill, as did the sanitary inspector. Even so, city leaders responded sensibly. They ordered the schools closed, and appealed to children not to play in groups. Churches, theaters, the library and pool parlors all shut down; meanwhile, the U.S. Army's Camp Fremont in Menlo Park was quarantined. The Board of Public Safety (now exercising the old health board's functions) decreed that all persons dealing with the public — merchants, bankers, barbers, butchers, city workers — must wear a gauze mask over the nose and mouth. Postal deliveries all but stopped. Little knots of people meeting on the street to chat might be asked by a law officer to disperse lest their socializing spread the germ.

Physicians appealed daily for nurses and

To ensure the public's health, the city employed dairy inspectors to check the dairy herds.

nurses' aides to help them render care around the clock. Despite their labors and all the precautions, the flu took its toll. Within the space of two days, Palo Alto and Mayfield had eight deaths; Camp Fremont had more than 30. Then, in November, the epidemic disappeared rapidly. By mid-month, few new cases were reported, and they were mild. The gauze mask order was lifted on November 17, days after a flu-muffled celebration of the end of World War I.

Building a Health Department

Louis Olsen remained as health officer for 35 years, building his department to state and national prominence. Among its mileposts were: milk grading beginning in 1914; compulsory tuberculin testing of dairy cattle, 1916; diptheria immunization, 1924 and construction of a sewage treatment plant (to "establish a precedent for other cities which must use the San Francisco Bay for disposal"), 1933. By 1934, the state Depart-

ment of Public Health praised Palo Alto's record, achieved at a cost of 83 cents per capita per year, as "not excelled or equalled by any other city in California."

In the early days, Olsen doubled as city hall majordomo — an informal city manager. By the 1940s, he headed a health staff of 12. In 1952 the county government assumed responsibility for public health from the city, and Olsen retired. After that, he put in seven years as Stanford's health officer.

Hospital involvement was part of what boosted Palo Alto's program to top national honors. The Guild Hospital that grew out of the typhoid calamity was supplanted in 1910 when Peninsula Hospital opened. This second hospital, considered modern and well-equipped, was built by a private association owned mainly by local physicians. The three-story, wood-frame structure occupied part of the triangle of land bounded by Embarcadero Road, Cowper Street and Churchill

Soldiers from Camp Fremont march down University Avenue wearing gauze masks to guard against the flu epidemic in 1918.

The Peninsula Hospital, built in 1910, operated until 1931 on the present site of the city's lawn bowling green.

Avenue. Its initial capacity, 35 to 40 beds, was later expanded to 48.

For the next decade Peninsula Hospital served the community well, earning a total gross profit of $40,000 in its first eight years but never paying dividends to shareholders. Then World War I inflated costs and took away staff. The standard of care suffered and the hospital lost $12,000 between 1918 and 1920. New funds were needed to rebuild the staff and buy new equipment, but based on their sour experience, stockholders were reluctant to inject fresh capital. In 1921, the association announced that it wanted to dispose of the hospital or convert it to an apartment house. The group approached the city as a possible purchaser.

A City-Owned Hospital

With population rising and concern growing about losing the hospital, city officials put before voters in June 1921 a proposal to buy Peninsula

Hospital from its owners. A spirited campaign ensued. Opponents sniped at the physicians for pleading poverty. Proponents claimed that the hospital, to be managed by Stanford, could employ student nurses at $5 a month whereas professional nurses earned $90 a month. Yes votes prevailed, 779 to 137, and Palo Alto became a rarity: a city that owned a hospital.

Renamed Palo Alto Hospital, the facility was turned over to the Stanford Medical School to manage under a 20-year agreement. In 1921, the city health laboratory was combined with the hospital lab, and the city's baby welfare and child health programs were moved into the new health center. Explaining the unique arrangement, Louis Olsen said, "the hospital is not a free institution, such as a county hospital… all patients pay the regular charges. The hospital is, in fact, a municipal hospital functioning as a voluntary or private hospital."

Dr. Russel V.A. Lee later wrote:

The new city-financed Palo Alto Hospital opened in 1931, and reopened in 1965 as the Herbert Hoover Pavilion.

PALO ALTO HISTORICAL ASSOCIATION/DAN BAKER

In the first few years of this arrangement, the city barely made expenses... but in a few years in spite of the inadequacy of the facilities and the uneconomical size of the old plant, the hospital was making money for the city. It became increasingly apparent, however, as the town grew that the old hospital could not serve any longer and this was given more point by the occurrence of three fires which escaped being disastrous by a rather narrow margin.

In the mid-1920s the Palo Alto Medical Association (later Society) began pursuing a plan for a new hospital. In March 1927, the association proposed that Stanford offer university land as the site for a new hospital, including an isolation wing for student patients (who by law could not be brought into the city with infectious diseases).

The association proposed also that Santa Clara County set aside certain beds for nonpaying county patients.

An investigating committee of local doctors then formed to look into building and operating a new hospital. Among its members were Drs. Josiah H. Kirk, Jerome Thomas, Robert Reynolds, Granville Wood and Russel V.A. Lee. Speaking for the Medical Association, Dr. Lee said the new hospital should have at least 100 beds. City Council members took initial fright at the cost, but relented after a group of private citizens contributed $150,000 in cash — with no strings attached.

Stanford agreed to lease a 10-acre site in the arboretum near El Camino Real and Palm Drive. The terms, outlined by University President Ray Lyman Wilbur in a letter to the City Council, provided for a continued operating agreement and a new 99-year site lease.

Bonds for a Hospital on Campus

A $250,000 bond issue was put before voters in June 1929, and carried 2,378 to 386. The bonds, plus donations and gifts, financed a new five-story, fireproof, reinforced concrete hospital, completed in May 1931. Including equipment, the cost came to $480,000. The old hospital was razed in 1931; the city paid the hospital fund $30,000 to retain its site, which later became the lawn bowling green.

The Palo Alto Hospital Auxiliary formed in 1929, long before the new hospital was ready, and quickly gained several hundred members. These women were dedicated to providing financial aid for needy patients and furnishing flowers, books, magazines and miniature Christmas trees to "humanize" the hospital.

In 1931, the auxiliary committee composed of Mesdames Edwin J. Thomas, T. A. Storey, James G. Sharp and Jerome B. Thomas launched a study of hospitalization insurance for Palo Alto. Increasingly grim Depression years sparked interest in finding ways to increase occupancy and make the hospital more available to residents of moderate means. In November 1934, the City Council voted to appropriate general-fund money to pay up to $2.50 a day of the bill of any resident occupying a bed for which the daily rate was less than $8. As a deluxe room with private bath and phone was $14 a day and a single room $8 a day, that meant subsidies for beds in double rooms ($6.50) or wards ($5), or infants' cribs ($1 a day). From November 1, 1934, through June 30, 1935, subsidy payments totaling $8,521 went to 556 bona fide residents. The subsidy — remaining at $2.50 and becoming "merely a gesture," as Dr. Dell Lundquist put it — continued until 1964.

Once again community growth began to overtax the hospital's capacity, and the Medical Association proposed expansion. In February 1938, Palo Alto voters approved a $175,000 bond issue to finance an 80-bed addition, 1,402 to 308. One foe of the measure argued to no avail that during the previous fiscal year, hospital occupancy had been 73.7%, and a mere 36.1% of the patients were residents, while 40.9% were nonresidents and 23% students.

Because an expected grant from the federal Public Works Administration was delayed until 1939 and then fell through, original plans were scaled back. Even so, the City Council had to close the gap between the bonds plus interest and the $212,960 construction contract. The addition was finally completed in 1940, boosting the hospital's capacity to 163 beds.

"Then came the war," *Times* Editor Elinor Cogswell recounted later, "and grim years when the manager cleaned the surgery and the dietitian washed the dishes and well-to-do Palo Alto women in nurses' aides uniforms scrubbed floors."

After World War II, the well-established cycles of demand eating up new hospital capacity recurred, resulting in ever more elaborate solutions. Knowing how physicians evolved local patterns of individual and group practice helps in understanding these events.

Pioneer Physicians Hang Out Shingles

In the pioneer years, physicians set up offices in hotels or downtown buildings, often dividing their practices between Palo Alto and one or more other cities, and sending patients who required hospital care to San Francisco. Later, individual practitioners broadened the geographical locations of various offices as better transportation alleviated the need to be close to a hospital. Some doctors managed to continue solo practices for a whole career, arranging substitutes through informal alliances. Among the widely known physicians who did this were Edith Eugenie Johnson, the "White Angel" who delivered more than 3,500 Palo Alto area babies, Harold Beaver, Granville Wood, William Lewis and David I. Hull.

Others built more formal associations. One early physician was Dr. Thomas Williams, a legendary football star at Stanford. Williams began his Palo Alto practice in 1904, and Dr. George Barnett later became his partner. Barnett left in 1924 to join the Stanford Medical School faculty in San Francisco, and subsequently Dr. Russel V.A. Lee joined

Dr. Russel V. A. Lee, founder of the Palo Alto Clinic, was outspoken in his progressive views on health issues.

Dr. Esther Clark, an early partner in the Palo Alto Medical Clinic, founded the Children's Health Council.

Dr. Edith Eugenie Johnson delivered more than 3,500 Palo Alto babies in her career.

Williams in practice at Hamilton Avenue and Bryant Street. Out of this association grew the Palo Alto Clinic, which was formally founded in 1929 after Dr. Williams had retired. (In the 1950s, to conform to a new state law, its name became the Palo Alto Medical Clinic.)

Early partners included Drs. Lee, E.F. "Fritz" Roth, Esther Clark, Blake Wilbur, Milton Saier, Harold Sox, H.L. Niebel and Robert Dunn. Each was hired as the patient load grew and the partners felt justified in employing an additional specialist.

The Clinic Builds

In 1930 the Clinic built a Spanish-style structure at Homer Avenue and Bryant, two blocks from the original office. Its opening created a mini-scandal, for murals by the old entrance on Homer, commissioned by Dr. Lee, depicted some partial nudes, and townspeople jammed traffic on that avenue hoping to get a peek at them.

Locally and nationally, solo physicians greeted group practice — a radical innovation then —

173

design was faulted almost from the start for operational inefficiencies; for instance, doors opening onto patios from ground-floor rooms were too narrow for beds to be wheeled through. Mere months after the opening, a surge of patients admitted by the two medical staffs filled the "house," and friction between community and faculty physicians grew.

The old Palo Alto Hospital had been closed when the new one was opened; now plans were made to refurbish it. The Palo Alto-Stanford Hospital board approved a $1.1 million renovation project, but it took until May 15, 1965, to complete the work and reopen the facility under a new name: Herbert Hoover Pavilion. Even with the added beds, a shortage continued.

Filing for "Divorce"

In 1967, the breach worsened. Medical School Dean Robert J. Glaser and Stanford President Sterling proposed that the university buy out the city's share in the hospital. They said the unwieldy setup was hampering the medical school's teaching and research programs. After a prolonged community debate, the City Council agreed to the sale, and Stanford became sole owner of the hospital and its 663 beds. Stanford paid the city $1 million cash, assumed payments on $3.5 million worth of hospital construction bonds over a 20-year period, and guaranteed certain specified community hospital services for 40 years, or until 2008. Community physicians on the medical staff kept their affiliations, and retained the right to admission of Palo Alto residents on a priority basis for 370 beds.

While the drama of what some feature writers called the Palo Alto-Stanford hospital "divorce" was being played out, the new $20 million Veterans Administration (now Veterans Affairs) Hospital on 92 acres of Stanford land on Miranda Avenue had opened in 1960, supplementing the Menlo Park VA branch established in 1924. The VA Medical Center (VAMC) afforded veterans access to over 50 clinical specialties, including open-heart surgery. There researchers have studied

such medical problems as Alzheimer's disease, cancer, schizophrenia and nerve regeneration. VAMC is closely affiliated with Stanford Medical School; it trains hundreds of medical students and resident physicians each year, and more than 70 of its staff members hold full-time Stanford faculty appointments.

Another local factor on the hospital front was the opening of El Camino Hospital in Mountain View in 1961, serving residents of Mountain View, Los Altos, Los Altos Hills and Sunnyvale. Its main initial impact was to reduce the Palo Alto-Stanford load of obstetrics cases near the end of the baby boom era. (Another district hospital, Sequoia Hospital in Redwood City, had been serving south San Mateo County residents since 1950.)

Clinic Hospital Plan Runs Aground

Frustrated by difficulties in getting patients admitted to the renamed Stanford University Hospital, Clinic physicians and community leaders began to think fondly of the days when the city had its own hospital. The Palo Alto Medical Research Foundation Board of Trustees began exploring the idea of developing a "hospital of the future." Dr. Russel Lee made the concept public in 1967, and in February 1968 the research foundation received a $257,519 grant from the U.S. Public Health Service for initial study. Plans were developed for a $21 million, 300-bed building on a two-block site between Bryant and Waverley streets just south of the Clinic. At first it was to rise 18 stories; later the height was scaled back.

Intense opposition to this plan arose, primarily from a group of residents of nearby Professorville who feared that the neighborhood would be forever changed. The city approved the rezoning for the hospital, but residents succeeded in putting the proposal to a hotly contested citywide election, and it was narrowly defeated.

During the 1970s a new health-care trend developed: more outpatient medicine. This trend began to ease the demand for hospital beds, and had a massive impact on Stanford Hospital and hospitals everywhere. Suddenly hospitals had sur-

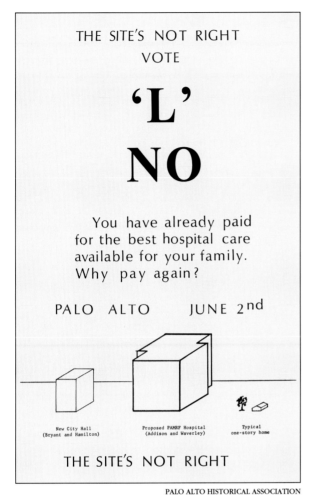

THE SITE'S NOT RIGHT
VOTE

'L'
NO

You have already paid for the best hospital care available for your family. Why pay again?

PALO ALTO   JUNE 2nd

New City Hall
(Bryant and Hamilton)   Proposed PAMRF Hospital
(Addison and Waverley)   Typical
one-story home

THE SITE'S NOT RIGHT

PALO ALTO HISTORICAL ASSOCIATION

The proposed Palo Alto Medical Clinic hospital was defeated by the voters in a 1970 election.

plus beds available. Community physicians, particularly at the Clinic, soon saw the defeat of the new downtown hospital in 1970 as a blessing in disguise.

An outpatient surgery facility called Surgecenter, part of an Arizona firm's chain, opened in 1974 at Waverley and Forest Avenue. Community physicians began to use it for minor surgical procedures, enabling their patients to go home without an overnight hospital stay. In 1986, for example, more than half the Clinic's 5,000 surgeries were performed on patients who went home after a few hours.

Solo practice became rare. Douglas N. Jenks, who practiced 18 years on his own and then joined the Clinic for 18 more, explained that the

growth of health maintenance organizations swamped independents with paperwork and overhead. Moreover, as Palo Alto reached a medical saturation point, no new doctors were coming in and there were few he felt comfortable "signing out to" for a weekend off. On the other hand, Dr. Jenks said, he regretted losing the solo general practitioner's freedom to make his own schedule and be more available to patients — access he was sorry to see patients lose.

In 1980, the Palo Alto Medical Clinic, which is the physicians' for-profit partnership, contracted to staff the health care division of the nonprofit Palo Alto Medical Foundation (successor to the old Medical Research Foundation). The Palo Alto Medical Foundation for Health, Research and Education, to use its full name, was created under new state legislation to streamline administration and expand programs to educate patients, medical professionals and the public.

By 1991, Clinic facilities had sprawled over parts of nine blocks. A proposal to consolidate and rebuild them on 2 1/4 blocks in a $100 million project that would add 45,000 square feet won approval from city authorities, but was challenged in a June 1992 referendum. Voters gave the plan a go-ahead. Soon afterward, however, the Clinic announced that it had agreed to affiliate with Sutter Health of Sacramento, and planned to move all its operations to a site including the former Hubbard & Johnson lumberyard between El Camino and the rail line, north of Town & Country Village shopping center.

As of 1993, the Clinic had about 160 physicians in Palo Alto and a branch in Fremont. Its records listed 110,000 patients and an annual total of nearly 500,000 patient visits for appointments with medical personnel or for laboratory services.

Stanford Center Grows by Leaps and Bounds
During the early 1970s, area growth and rising demand for health services prompted Stanford to launch the first of several major expansions of its hospital. What started as a $9 million project swelled to an $18 million addition, which resulted

in much improved operation despite some design and construction flaws — a level bridge had to be built between the original building's operating rooms and the new wing's post-anesthesia recovery area to end wheeling patients on gurneys uphill and down.

A decade later, Stanford announced plans to expand the medical center again to improve and broaden its offering of services. The $153 million project was completed in mid-1988 and dedicated that September. The new 276-bed wing provided much-needed operating rooms and intensive care units, more private and semi-private rooms, and consolidated clinical laboratories. With these new facilities in service, in-patient care was concentrated at the medical center and suspended at Hoover Pavilion, which thereafter was devoted to outpatient care. The hospital medical staff had increased to 1,357, including full-time medical school faculty members and physicians in private practice. Along nearby Welch Road had grown a concentration of doctors' and dentists' offices and ancillary medical services.

Stanford Medical Center enjoys a worldwide reputation for its lifesaving heart and heart-lung transplant operations, developed by Dr. Norman Shumway, and for its treatment of Hodgkins disease with radiology, perfected by Dr. Henry Kaplan. In addition, it has been the crucible for a host of other medical breakthroughs.

Special Care for Children

A major expansion of the medical center, completed in 1991, brought the 142-bed Lucile Salter Packard Children's Hospital into service. Its name commemorated "Lu" Packard, long a supporter of children's medical care and a hospital auxiliary leader. She and her husband, David Packard, gave $40 million of the $100 million cost through their family foundation. The Children's Hospital is an outgrowth of one of Stanford University's traditional charities, the Stanford Convalescent Home.

In 1917, Stanford Lane Hospital in San Francisco began providing summer outings in sunny

COURTESY OF PACKARD CHILDREN'S HOSPITAL
Lucile Salter Packard

climates for young patients with rheumatic fever and other long-term illnesses. In 1920, the Convalescent Home became a permanent establishment on the site of Leland and Jane Stanford's residence alongside San Francisquito Creek, near where the Stanford Shopping Center was built decades later. Strong ties grew with the university and Palo Alto. Convalescent Home auxiliaries supported varied activities for the children, and "Con Home Day" became a campus tradition. With classes dismissed, Stanford students spent a day each May sprucing up the grounds and entertaining the young patients. Sam McDonald, already a Stanford institution as superintendent of athletic buildings and grounds, cooked a tasty barbecue for student workers. (During World War II, McDonald cultivated a vast victory garden to supply the Con Home kitchen.)

Through the years, and particularly after the medical school moved to the campus, the Convalescent Home expanded its role to include treatment and research; meanwhile, its focus changed

*Opening day in 1991 at the Lucile Salter Packard Children's Hospital. The facility honors a longtime
supporter of children's health care.*

as antibiotics tamed the worst effects of rheumatic fever. In 1964 its name became the Stanford Children's Convalescent Home. In 1969, a new building was dedicated, and in 1970 came another name change to Children's Hospital at Stanford. In 1982, directors of the Children's Hospital and Stanford University Hospital agreed to consolidate all pediatric services and build the new Packard Children's Hospital.

The Children's Health Council (CHC), a non-profit center established in 1953 under Dr. Esther Clark's leadership, provides outpatient rehabilitative services and other services for children with disabilities. At its headquarters near the old Children's Hospital, the CHC shelters a school for children with emotional and mental disturbances, with a branch in Menlo Park. Nearby Ronald McDonald House operates in conjunction with the Children's Hospital and CHC, providing tempo-

rary housing for child patients and their families.

Innovative Health Enterprises

Palo Alto is home to numerous other innovative medical and health enterprises. Channing House, with apartments for persons 62 and older, opened at Channing Avenue and Webster Street in 1964 as a pioneering experiment in lifetime medical care. Lytton Gardens III, opened in 1983 as an adjunct to Lytton Gardens senior residential center, provides skilled nursing care for its residents and others. Among those served by the 120-bed facility are patients from the adjoining Webster House, completed in 1985 as a residence for seniors, offering comprehensive lifetime health care.

The Flora Lawson Hewlett Apartments on Welch Road first were occupied in 1987. Also called HOME as an acronym for Housing for Medical Emergencies, the 42 one-room apart-

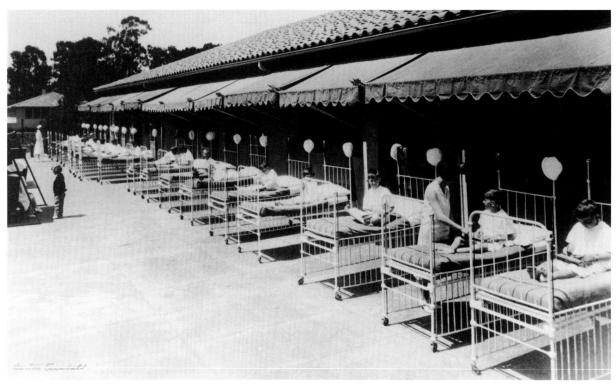

Young patients show off their al fresco school setup at the Stanford Convalescent Home (later Hospital), established in 1920 on the site of the Stanford family residence.

ments provide low-cost, short-term housing for outpatients and the families of inpatients at Stanford Medical Center. The William and Flora Hewlett Foundation financed the construction. Stanford University provided the land on a $1-a-year lease.

The Community Association for the Retarded, popularly called C.A.R., provides programs and services for children and adults with developmental and other disabilities. Its structure at 3864 Middlefield Road opened in 1963; the Betty Wright Swim Center was added later. Next door to C.A.R., the Peninsula Children's Center, founded in 1960, provides an alternative to institutionalizing children with severe emotional and behavioral problems.

The Peninsula Center for the Blind had its beginning in 1936 as the Palo Alto Society for the Blind. Responding to needs for housing for low-income blind people, the society opened its first unit of residential home care in Palo Alto. Eventually property at Addison Avenue and Cowper

Street was acquired to house 14 people. In the early 1960s the society began to expand its services to meet the needs of all blind people in the community. In 1971 the residential program was phased out in favor of rehabilitative services for blind children as well as adults, and the name was changed to the Peninsula Center for the Blind and Visually Impaired. All programs and services operate out of the former home at 948 Cowper.

The Mental Research Institute (MRI) began in 1958 under the Medical Research Foundation's wing, aiming to give behavioral scientists a facility for research into the causes, treatment and prevention of mental illness. Psychiatrists Don D. Jackson and Jules Riskin were leading figures in its founding, and their associate Virginia Satir became widely known for her books and teaching. Family therapy has been the focus; MRI set up the first U.S. clinic to deal with dysfunctional families as a whole, rather than single afflicted family members.

The Sensory Access Foundation, also based in

Palo Alto, applies high technology to the creation of special equipment so that persons with impaired vision or hearing can perform in a work environment.

Locally Developed Care Travels

Although the Palo Alto-Stanford medical community routinely draws in patients from points near and far, programs have developed that convey care in one form or another to faraway places. Hesperian Foundation brings small numbers of Mexican children to Palo Alto for corrective surgery, and is widely known for a book written by its executive director, David Werner, titled *Where There Is No Doctor: A Village Health Care Handbook*. This practical compendium of basic medical information is in print in more than 60 languages; about 2 million copies of the first edition are in circulation around the world. In a revised edition published in 1992, Werner addressed a section to village health workers, saying at the end:

The key to good health lies within you and your people, in the care, the concern, and appreciation you have for each other. If you want to see your community be healthy, build on these.

Interplast, Inc., is another Palo Alto-based group. Its members make trips to provide free reconstructive surgery to persons in developing countries with cleft palates, burns or other disfiguring conditions. Dr. Donald R. Laub, then Palo Alto-Stanford Hospital chief of plastic and reconstructive surgery, founded Interplast in the late 1960s; it attained nonprofit status in 1973. Nationwide in scope, Interplast has affiliates in Australia, Germany, Italy, Turkey, the United Kingdom and Chile. Its U.S. teams of plastic surgeons, anesthesiologists, operating and recovery room nurses and sometimes pediatricians have logged more than 22,000 surgeries over the years; about 300 medical personnel participate each year. In addition to arranging its teams' trips abroad, Interplast brings some patients to the United States for care and, in addition, brings nurses and doctors as visiting scholars. Dr. Laub has said:

The wonderful thing about Interplast is that it transforms lives for the better, and not only the lives of the people we treat. Providing transformative, reconstructive treatment to people who would not otherwise receive it also changes us. It happened to me and I have seen it happen again and again to others on our medical missions.

Thus Palo Alto and Stanford people, who began with a keen concern for their own health, have in the course of a century created a large, productive and innovative medical community. Next to electronics, it has been the second-leading aspect of the area's economic base for decades. The high-quality care local residents sought for themselves has been extended, with their strong backing, to other cities, other states, indeed, other continents. Palo Alto has made itself not only a healthy place but a health-giving place of global scope.

PALO ALTO WEEKLY/CAROLYN CLEBSCH
Promotion of AIDS awareness in Palo Alto included Roxy's store-window message in 1987.

The University Avenue business district in the late 1930s.

13

Open for Business

*"I don't think Palo Alto residents are aware of
the area's position as a first-rate educational,
commercial, cultural and scientific area."*

— Real estate developer Ryland Kelley, 1965

Although the older town of Mayfield had a well-developed business district along Main Street (now El Camino Real), Palo Alto's settlers of the early 1890s wanted a marketplace of their own. They soon got one.

Merchants began opening commercial establishments on The Circle, which scribed an arc near University Avenue's intersection with the railroad tracks. Businesses sprouted on the town side like wildflowers in the open fields nearby. Some Mayfield merchants decamped to Palo Alto or opened branch stores there.

The inner part of The Circle enclosed a public plaza shaded by oaks; the outer rim was the new town's prime business address for several decades. However, the tide of commerce gradually spread east along University and just off the avenue to both sides on High and Emerson streets.

The Bank of Palo Alto occupied a small but imposing building at the corner of The Circle and University. A few doors away, at The Circle and Alma, Fred H. Smith opened his cyclery, selling bicycles, sporting goods and even motor cars for a time. Smith's On The Circle was to last for 70 years. The Palo Alto Hotel, a big, barn-like structure at Alma and Lytton Avenue, accommodated visitors arriving by train at the nearby depot. Later the bus station replaced it.

J.J. Morris, a real estate agent who sold lots and whole blocks of the new town, had his office on the first block of University. Parkinson Lumber Co. sprawled out nearby with materials for the new houses being built. The Oak Billiard Parlor, plumber Louis Dahl (whose son John later succeeded him), Slades's Barber Shop and Meany the Tailor all opened for business.

Wooden sidewalks provided an escape from the dust of summer and the mud of winter on the newly graded streets. Between High and Emerson, shoppers bought groceries at Earle and Suiter's, footwear at Thoits Shoe Store and sundries at Simkins stationery store.

At Emerson, businesses began to thin out. On the corner of University and Emerson stood The Fair, a general store that called itself "the place of a thousand bargains" in the 1895-96 City Directory. It stocked woodenware, crockery, stoneware, tinware, fresh fruits, cutlery, toys and groceries. "Terms: Always cash," the ad said sternly. On side streets were located Harms' Blacksmith Shop, the Worrell Wood Yard, several livery stables and Luscher's carriage-painting shop.

The Merchants Organize

In 1895, the Retail Merchants' Protective Association organized as the first of a succession of active mercantile groups that boosted town improvements and gave voice to commercial concerns. Through this association, store owners kept a watchful eye on student trade, and urged residents to shop only at hometown stores.

By the early 1900s, the business district had pushed up University and out along side streets — on High, Emerson and Ramona.

G. W. La Peire and Son Grocery at 521 Ramona Street remained in business until 1918.

Frazer & Co. billed itself in 1908 as "Palo Alto's Big Store" with two corner locations on University, at High and at Emerson. The store advertised Carter underwear, Phoenix silk sox, Best Ever boys suits, Buster Brown hose and *Ladies Home Journal* patterns.

Other popular stores were Fuller & Co. groceries at 161 University; G.W. La Peire groceries on Ramona Street; Congdon & Crome, news dealers and stationers, at University and Ramona and Mendenhall's dry goods store at University and Bryant. La Peire was revered by Stanford faculty wives for his easy credit policies during the university's bitterly lean years after Senator Stanford's death.

A New Chamber of Commerce

In 1902, the Palo Alto Board of Trade formed. A schism occurred in 1909 when the board supported the proposed city charter and leading businessman J. F. Parkinson fought it. In 1910, the Palo Alto Chamber of Commerce was organized, with J.F. Parkinson — not surprisingly, for he was into almost everything — as president. The chamber, launching an effort that continues in the 1990s, stirred up support for community projects and diligently promoted the town.

New business places reflected the changing interests of residents.

The Varsity and Stanford motion picture theaters, not far apart, competed near the end of the silent films era and on into talkies in the 1930s. Ostrander's music store carried instruments and sheet music. Dodson's, at 340 University, sold the popular Victrola windup record player and phonograph records. A roller skating rink in the 400 block of Bryant Street, opposite today's Senior Center, was trendy for a time; bowling alleys came later. Smith's On The Circle cyclery added a new line: the Stanley Steamer automobile.

An Auto District Builds Up

Walter G. Bernthal was the authorized Model T Ford dealer at 525 Alma beginning in 1920. Other automobile dealers opened salesrooms and garages along Alma, High and Emerson. Robert F. Benson sold Studebakers at Alma and Forest, and Durlin B. Hackett ran the Hupmobile agency at 619 Forest — later he sold Pontiacs. The new Ford

PALO ALTO HISTORICAL ASSOCIATION

The Hackett Pontiac dealership at High Street and Homer Avenue opened in 1936.

dealer, Shaw Motor Co., moved to a new building on Forest at Emerson; there in 1928 the Model A Ford was put on public view in Palo Alto for the first time. Stanford Auto later displayed Packards at the former Ford agency showroom on Alma. Paddleford's Chevrolet (later Cadillac and Oldsmobile) was on Emerson at Homer, where George Paddleford remained the dealer for 51 years.

In the years before World War II, other well-known downtown businesses included Ben Allen's Palo Alto Hardware on University at Bryant; the First National Bank of Palo Alto, at University and Ramona and Mills the Florist, originally on The Circle. Favorite gathering places for lunch or for sweets after a movie were University Creamery at 209 University, Peninsula Creamery at Hamilton and Emerson ("the home of the famous milkshake") and "Sticky" Wilson's Confectioners at University and High, which could also seat banquet crowds. (The candy business Ernest Wilson originated while in the Stanford class of 1899 later had branches in Stockton, San Jose, Sacramento, San Francisco and Oakland.)

Downtown Grocery Stores Abound

By the '20s and '30s, other fixtures of the downtown business landscape included Weingartner Co., druggists; Werry Electric; Mac's Smoke Shop and J.F. Hink & Son, a department store that succeeded Mendenhall's. Among the grocery stores were two Piggly Wigglies on University; Purity Market, first on University and then just off the avenue on Waverley; Liddicoat's and Saunders' Cash and Carry, 322 University. Also popular were Kenyon's Pharmacy and Young Drug Co., The Clothes Closet at 520 Ramona, Walster's department store, the Palo Alto Sport Shop, T.C. Christy Co., where high school athletes bought their block-letter sweaters, and bakeries such as the Golden Poppy and Golden Crescent.

The Chamber of Commerce and Civic Association, to give its full name, spoke with growing leadership on civic enterprises, backing bond issues for a new Palo Alto Hospital, new schools, underpasses at the Embarcadero Road and

The Peninsula Creamery, long a popular eatery for Palo Altans, as it appeared before remodeling in 1993.

"Sticky" Wilson's on University Avenue, shown in 1925, was popular for its confections.

PALO ALTO HISTORICAL ASSOCIATION/GLORIA BROWN

Mac's Smoke Shop on Emerson Street is known for its wide assortment of periodicals.

University Avenue rail crossings, a new Palo Alto airport in the baylands and better city parks and playgrounds.

A New Business Boom

Business boomed in the years after World War II, as Palo Alto grew in its new status as a light industrial site and a center for construction of suburban homes. Initially, downtown firms thrived in this era, and California Avenue gained patronage as a shopping area. Stores selling homeowners do-it-yourself supplies seemed to take root everywhere, such as California Paint and Wallpaper, opened in 1946.

Plant nurseries also were busy providing homeowners with landscaping and garden materials. The Home Garden Nursery, a prewar favorite

PALO ALTO HISTORICAL ASSOCIATION

Pharmacist Stanley Bishop stands in front of his California Avenue Pharmacy in 1930.

PALO ALTO HISTORICAL ASSOCIATION

This 1933 ad in the Palo Alto Times lists meats and produce at Depression era prices.

in the Seale addition, gave way to housing, but was replaced by others around the city's perimeter. Schmidt Nursery on Lambert Street, where William Schmidt became noted for hybridizing fuchsias, geraniums and pelargoniums, finally closed after 30 years. Later, establishments such as Woolworth Garden Center took hold.

While the boom was still new, Stanford University announced plans to develop a shopping center near the old Stanford Barn, and to annex the site to Palo Alto. Thus began local experience with the decentralization of retail activities, which before long was a national phenomenon.

"An Ambiance... Second to None"

When the Stanford Shopping Center opened in 1956, it had 45 stores, including The Emporium, and some shops that had long been University Avenue fixtures, such as Roos Bros. and Gleim Jewelers. It was successful from the start, and grew even more so after Macy's opened in 1961, Saks Fifth Avenue in 1963 and Bullock's in 1972. Nordstrom replaced Bullock's in 1984. Year after year the shopping center has remained in the top ranks of Bay Area suburban malls, earning rich revenues for the university and fat sales tax income for Palo Alto.

By August 1991, as the center marked its 35th anniversary, director David Longbine could claim with little fear of dispute that its mix of architecture, location and stores give it "an ambiance ... second to none." By then, the roster ran to 138 stores and shops and 12 restaurants, and the center was famed for its progressive fashion statements and the varied entertainments on its plazas.

As the baby boom of the 1950s and '60s crescendoed, other outlying shopping centers were built: Town & Country Village at Embarcadero Road and El Camino Real, on the historic Greer property, once the town's circus grounds; the California Avenue district; and Midtown, centered at Middlefield Road and Colorado Avenue. Along El Camino Real's course from the south end of the campus to the city limits at Adobe Creek, strip development brought many small businesses into

Lytton Avenue side of the block, but El Dorado Insurance Co., which owned the office center for a time, dropped plans for the twin tower in 1969. Instead, a low-rise Bank of America office was built later on the site at the Cowper-Lytton corner.

Building Up and Out

Meanwhile, Alhouse, who had opened his own firm, began in 1960 to develop Stanford-owned lands fronting the west side of El Camino Real between California Avenue and Page Mill Road. A six-story building at 2600 El Camino was completed in 1967, increasing Stanford Financial Square's total office space to 100,000 square feet.

Another mid-'60s project was the California Lands Building on Sheridan Avenue near the North County Courthouse. It was to be 10 stories ultimately, but the upper six floors never were added.

In 1968, Alhouse and Thomas Ford, former Stanford land development officer, announced their intent to build a "one-stop financial shopping center" on Stanford lands at Page Mill and El Camino, then a horse pasture. Initially, a large hotel was to be part of the complex, but the hotel

idea soon died. (In 1992, it revived.)

In 1970, 800 opponents of the plan petitioned Stanford University development officials, to no avail. Dillingham Development Co. came into the project and in 1972 completed two 10-story towers designed by Albert A. Hoover and Associates, Palo Alto architects. The complex, known as Palo Alto Square, included two movie theaters and a two-acre park between the towers. With about 300,000 square feet of office space, its capacity rivaled the downtown center.

The site of the abandoned Mayfield Elementary School on El Camino Real near Page Mill Road — property that had been leased by the school district from Stanford University — remained vacant. A proposal to build a large office building on this site failed as a result of protests by activist Stanford students.

Attempts to proclaim "the sky's the limit" for Palo Alto development ran into a major roadblock in 1971 when a proposal for "Superblock," a high-rise downtown office project two blocks wide, was rejected by voters. Within a few years, the city had clapped a 50-foot limit on building heights,

Palo Alto Square, distinguished by its two ten-story towers, was completed in 1972.

COURTESY OF HOOVER ASSOCIATES/JON BRENNEIS

The general contracting firm of Wells P. Goodenough played a leading part in Palo Alto construction for decades.

so structures built in the next two decades went no higher than five stories. Notwithstanding the height limit, business in commercial real estate thrived until a downturn dating from about the time of the Loma Prieta earthquake in October 1989. Nearly four years later, doubt persisted as to whether the old momentum would be regained.

Building Becomes Big Business

Building contractors have been a part of Palo Alto commerce since hammer blows began to sound in the 1890s. Until after World War II, most construction jobs within the city were relatively small. Out-of-town firms as well as locally based ones have always competed for the choicer contracts.

The New Cardinal Hotel, for instance, was built in 1924 by John Madsen and the President Hotel in 1929 by Minton Construction Co., then of Palo Alto. In 1932's tough times, Minton closed its building arm and retreated to its Mountain View lumber and milling business.

Wells P. Goodenough was a leading general contractor from the booming 1920s on, and bridged over to the post-World War II years. In the 1930s, his firm built the Lucie Stern Community Center and the first Palo Alto Clinic unit. Other contractors active in the '30s and '40s included Schmaling & Stenbit, Aro & Okerman and Jim Stedman.

After the war Howard J. White emerged as a leading Palo Alto commercial and industrial builder. (White's base ultimately moved to Mountain View.) The company built the *Palo Alto Times* plant, the Clinic expansion, and many stores and industrial structures. Other locally based general contractors prominent in the booming 1950s and '60s included E.A. Hathaway, Leon and Jack Wheatley, Barrett & Hilp and Carl Holvick (originally Carl-Ray Co.).

The Wheatley firm built Escondido Village at

Stanford, Lytton Gardens and Forest Towers. Holvick erected the first tilt-up structure in the area, and 101 Alma with the first slip-form elevator core. Haas & Haynie put up Channing House.

By 1993, Vance M. Brown & Sons was the oldest large general contractor still based in the city. Vance Brown began in 1932 with remodelings and other small jobs. During World War II he closed his business and worked for the U.S. Army Corps of Engineers. After the war, he built theaters and stores. By 1949, his elder sons, Robert V. and Allan F. Brown, had joined him, and the firm successfully bid many school projects until 1962. Consciously trying to lower its portion of public work, the company by 1970 had dropped school jobs and was doing all private negotiated contracts, the largest being Hewlett-Packard's Building 11. The original YMCA, Unitarian Church and Palo Alto Commons were other contracts the firm had.

Aggressive out-of-town rivals (often with a Palo Alto resident as a partner or executive) included Carl Swenson, San Jose; Williams & Burroughs, Belmont; and Ralph Larson & Sons, San Francisco.

Construction techniques changed radically in the decades after 1950. By the 1990s subcontractors were being used more than ever, as well as architects and specialized engineers. Know-how gained in distinctive local projects often was exported; for example, architect Joseph Ehrlich of Palo Alto, after executing plans for the *Wall Street Journal's* Stanford Research Park facility, was tapped by the company to do satellite publishing plants in other U.S. regions. Ehrlich, a protege of Birge Clark, also designed Hewlett-Packard's first sawtooth-roofline building in Palo Alto, and after that, many more HP structures in Palo Alto and elsewhere.

A Prestigious Address

The Chamber of Commerce stated in a 1990 directory, "Palo Alto enjoys prominence and visibility as a regional and international professional and financial center. Its many law, accounting and investment advisory firms provide critical support services for Silicon Valley."

Some of the city's long-established law firms, such as Thoits, Love, Hershberger & McLean, Ware & Freidenrich, and Crist, Griffiths, Schulz & Biorn, adapted their capabilities well to the new opportunities offered by the surge in high technology and the jump by Palo Alto-based corporations to the international level. Meanwhile, newer firms have carved niches for themselves, notably Wilson, Sonsini, Goodrich & Rosati in such facets of corporate law as securities, mergers and acquisitions, technology licensing, taxes and intellectual properties. Started in 1966, Wilson, Sonsini

PENINSULA LIVING/ROBERT H. COX
Restaurateur John Rickey, shown with chef Fred Aebelhard, developed the garden motel concept.

has grown to more than 180 lawyers. Limbach, Limbach & Sutton, Townsend and Townsend, and Flehr, Hohbach, Test, Albritton, & Herbert also have made their marks in patent, trademark and copyright law.

The area's renown as a technical law center has prompted large Eastern firms to establish branches in Palo Alto. When Fish & Neave, a New York firm specializing in intellectual property law, did so in 1992, partner Edward J. Mullowney said a consultant had reported that Palo Alto, rather than San Jose, would be the premier Silicon Valley location.

A number of venture capitalists set up shop in Palo Alto, but they operated in scattered locations rather than in a cluster like the one land developer Tom Ford, formerly of Palo Alto, established in Menlo Park at 3000 Sand Hill Road. Among many management consultants based in the city, one of the most widely known is Tom Peters, author of a syndicated newspaper column. Another famed local innovator is Regis McKenna, known for public relations and marketing strategy coups. Earlier, after World War I, Rex F. Harlow had settled in Palo Alto, taught at Stanford and founded the American Council on Public Relations. W.T. Davis started a Palo Alto PR firm in 1922.

Until the late 1940s, investment houses in Palo Alto were local independents or branches of small regional firms. J. Earle May, who set up his firm in 1944, became the grand old man of the industry, still active in the 1990s. Dean Witter & Co.'s Palo Alto office handled the area's first initial public offering of common stock for Varian Associates in 1956.

New Accommodations

Construction of hotels and motels in the post-World War II surge gave the city sufficient room capacity to host small to medium-size conventions and business meetings. One of the first to be built on the southerly portion of El Camino Real, where the hostelries tended to cluster, was Rickey's Studio Inn. John Rickey, its proprietor, used lawns and shrubbery, pools and statues, even swans, to

PENINSULA TIMES TRIBUNE

Whole Foods, the only supermarket in downtown Palo Alto in the early 1990s, caters to Palo Altans' health-conscious tastes.

create a novel trend in 1952: the garden motel. Before long, it was being imitated wherever the climate permitted. Rickey decorated his restaurants, too, with art works from Europe. At the height of his career he was operating Dinah's Shack and Rick's Little Corner in addition to the Studio Inn.

The Hyatt chain in 1962 bought what became Hyatt Rickeys and after 1969 ran it in tandem with the Hyatt Palo Alto across El Camino, an eight-story hotel with elaborate fountains, which entertainer Doris Day had opened in 1962 as the Cabaña. In June 1993, Hyatt Corp. shut the aging 200-room Hyatt Palo Alto because of declining business. Hotel experts said that its small rooms

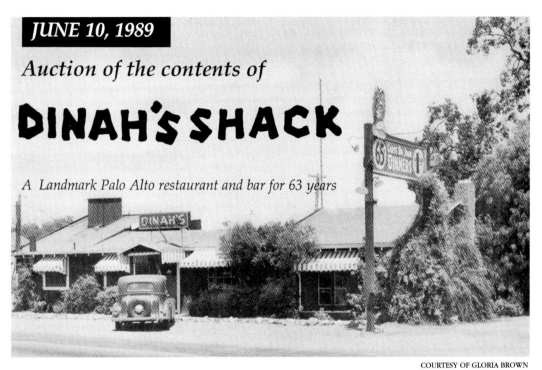

COURTESY OF GLORIA BROWN

The contents of Dinah's Shack went on auction in 1989 after the restaurant closed following 63 years in business.

PALO ALTO WEEKLY/CAROLYN CLEBSCH

Bergmann's Department Store, the last of the old-time department stores, closed in 1992 after serving shoppers in the Midtown business district for 36 years.

and lack of sprinklers prevented its economical adaptation to modern trends.

Another accommodation for visitors was created in 1973 after voters approved Clement Chen's plan to build the Holiday Inn Palo Alto/ Stanford at 625 El Camino Real, near University Avenue, a site the municipality had used for a corporation yard and animal shelter. The inn was equipped to render special services to Stanford University Hospital outpatients and their families.

In 1986, the city gained one more commodious hostelry with meeting and banquet rooms when the luxurious Garden Court Hotel opened at 520 Cowper Street, near University and the Palo Alto Office Center.

Redevelopment Follows Downsizing

In 1986 the City Council adopted an ordinance downzoning business properties by limiting additional commercial development downtown but offering an incentive for any project that added space to provide public benefits. Subsequently, redevelopers such as Charles J. "Chop" Keenan and Jim Baer began to buy up and redevelop various properties.

Keenan's buys included theaters, the former auto row district and leased buildings in Stanford Research Park. The Wells Fargo Bank building at Hamilton and Waverley and Whole Foods Market at 774 Emerson Street are among the products of his efforts.

Baer and his partner, Chuck King, have rebuilt or renovated about half of the 30 downtown buildings they own or manage. Baer made a showpiece of the Plaza Ramona at University and Ramona, a Spanish-style structure in harmony with the Ramona Street historic district. It was the first project allowed to break the 50-foot downtown height limit, a tradeoff for the upgrading of a public alleyway at the rear of the building.

Officials pleased by Baer's work cited its quality and elegant touches as promising steps toward transforming the downtown. This most recent transformation, begun in the '80s and including the renovations of the Stanford and

Varsity theaters and the opening of other night spots, appears to have greatly strengthened the University Avenue district's lease on business life.

Hardy Perennials Survive

The changes that are a constant in business march on, razing or transforming familiar landmarks. F.W. Woolworth Co. at 352 University Avenue has given way to Longs Drug Store. Dinah's Shack, closed, awaits probable demolition by new owners. J. Magnin and Roos Bros., later Roos-Atkins, are nowhere to be found, although they once were prominent both on University Avenue and at Stanford Shopping Center. Rapp's Shoes, an aggressive downtown retailer for decades, has departed. Bergmann's, an old-style department store in Midtown, has folded, along with all but one Co-op Market. The collapse of the *Peninsula Times Tribune* — born the *Palo Alto Times* — took the city's first century-old business off the head of the longevity list.

Still, some hardy perennials survive. Dahl Plumbing, founded in 1897, continues. Thoits Insurance has a lineage going back to the J.J. Morris real estate agency in 1890, although insurance sales did not begin until later. Roller & Hapgood (now "& Tinney") began directing funerals in 1899. Mills the Florist dates from 1903. Congdon & Crome stationers was founded in 1904, as was Alta Mesa Memorial Park. Wiedeman's menswear began in 1906, carried on in a tent when it lost its lease, and later occupied several locations, as well as having done business under two different spellings of the founder's name.

Stanford Electric Works began selling lighting equipment in 1914. Peninsula Creamery and Douglas Fabrics both were founded in 1926. Depression era start-ups that survive include the Palo Alto Sport Shop (1930), Gleim Jewelers (1931), Cornish & Carey (1935), Peninsula Plating Works (1937) and the most successful of them all, Hewlett-Packard Company (1939), whose story is told in the next chapter.

The marketplace the pioneers wanted has multiplied manyfold.

Artist Greg Brown poses with his burglars atop Wiedeman's on University Avenue — one of his whimsical wall paintings.

The garage at 367 Addison Avenue where William Hewlett and David Packard began their company.

14

Innovation in Industry

*"I thought when the original company [Federal Telegraph]
closed its doors in 1932 and moved to New Jersey that
electronics in Palo Alto was finished. Now they've come
back because this is where the electronics industry is."*
— Lee de Forest, revisiting Palo Alto in 1956

Before Palo Alto became an incorporated city and during its early days, lumbering and farming were the main Peninsula industries. Redwoods cut in the mountains to the west were carted or dragged to towns and ports near the bay for milling and shipping. Grains, hay, fruit and vegetables grown in the vicinity, along with some livestock, were consumed locally or gravitated to San Francisco markets as fresh or processed foods. Sawmills, breweries and canneries employed scores of Mayfield and Palo Alto residents.

Other industries producing goods by manufacturing or processing did not immediately gain a foothold in the little college town. When one — electronics — finally did, the area's goose that would lay the golden eggs proved to be science-based and closely linked to Stanford University teaching and research. Its precursors, however, dated from 1853, when wires were hung from a line of scrawny poles passing north and south through the future city. The California State Telegraph — Western Union's ancestor — ran from San Francisco to San Jose, then east to Stockton, Sacramento and Marysville.

Ten years later, the telegraph line flanking Southern Pacific's newly laid railroad tracks became the best local communication channel, and youngsters hung around depots to watch operators keying Morse code messages. SP's system handled Western Union traffic for way points like Mayfield and Menlo Park — plus the latest news.

Then in 1882 a single telephone line connected San Francisco and San Jose, passing through Palo Alto-to-be. With that, the portents of the future lay in place, awaiting epic developments in the new century.

An Amateur Radio Hotbed

In 1902, Italian physicist Guglielmo Marconi crowned his studies of radio waves by receiving in Newfoundland signals transmitted from England. His feat created a worldwide sensation. Stanford professors shared the excitement with students and their own sons, and soon Palo Alto became a hotbed of amateur radio experiments.

Cyril F. Elwell, who had been born in Australia of American parents, worked his way over on a ship in 1902 and studied at Manzanita Hall in Palo Alto. Then he entered Stanford in engineering. After the 1906 earthquake, Elwell tested a radio theory by stringing an antenna from the dome of the heavily damaged library — a caper that got him ordered off the campus by Trustee Timothy Hopkins.

Another 1902 newcomer to Palo Alto, Douglas Perham, also was mastering electrical apparatus, but from the mechanic's viewpoint. Perham set up the first X-ray equipment used by a local dentist, and in 1906 installed a spark-set radio transmitter in his quarters on Alma Street between Lytton and Everett avenues. He exchanged Morse code messages with another "ham" transmitting from a few blocks away. In 1908, Perham moved his radio

Early radio broadcasting research was conducted at 913 Emerson Street.

set to a house he bought for $1,500 at 913 Emerson Street, where he equipped a machine shop out in back.

Meanwhile James Arthur Miller had moved to Palo Alto with his mother in 1907 to prepare to attend Stanford. By that fall, Miller had built atop their house at 580 Addison Avenue a 75-foot antenna for what he described as the first radio station in town. Perham's was the first radio spark transmitter, and Elwell later developed one of the first West Coast radiotelephone broadcasting stations. Miller's amateur cronies were Roland Marx, son of Professor C.D. "Daddy" Marx, and George Branner, son of Professor John Casper Branner. Young Marx erected an antenna over the barn behind the family home at 357 Kingsley Avenue, while young Branner joined Miller in the California National Guard to establish a signal corps. Miller also organized a Coast Radio Company of other hams from the region, and in 1908 built and sold to a San Franciscan the first piece

of electronic equipment made in Palo Alto.

Elwell had taken a well-paid job developing electric smelting in 1908. But electrical engineering Professor Harris J. "Paddy" Ryan persuaded him to quit and, on behalf of two Oakland investors, the Henshaw brothers, to investigate a wireless telephone system utilizing the McCarty damped wave, whose developer had died suddenly. Elwell bought a house at 1451 Cowper Street, on the Embarcadero Road corner, and put up two 75-foot wooden masts. Turning the bungalow into a wireless telephone station, he worked it with a station five miles away in Los Altos.

Elwell Broadcasts a Waltz

When Elwell broadcast a wavering version of "The Blue Danube" to stations in Mountain View and Los Altos, he proved that five-mile voice radio communication was possible — although static and transmission breaks left listeners to fill in the missing measures from memory. That, said Elwell, was why he chose the familiar waltz.

After trying the McCarty and other damped-wave systems for about a year, Elwell concluded that only continuous waves (C.W.) would allow good quality wireless telephony. Knowing that Valdemar Poulsen had developed an arc converter in Denmark, Elwell telegraphed Poulsen asking his price for U.S. patent rights. The price proved too steep for the Henshaw brothers, who dropped out. Elwell went to Denmark anyway in May 1909 and, backed by President David Starr Jordan, who put up $500, Dr. Marx and others on the Stanford faculty, made a deal with Poulsen for U.S. development rights and brought back a sample 100-watt arc generator. With it, C.W. broadcasting was initially demonstrated between the Miller and Marx stations.

Elwell, a capable organizer, founded the Poulsen Wireless Telephone and Telegraph Company in October 1909, selling shares in Palo Alto. In 1910 Elwell bought Perham's house and steel shed at 913 Emerson and moved his wireless station and workshop into it. Later he added an adjoining bungalow at 218 Channing Avenue.

Left: Cyril Elwell, radio pioneer, came to Palo Alto in 1902.

Right: Lee de Forest and Elwell's radio research team made important discoveries during de Forest's stay in Palo Alto.

In 1911, Elwell's pioneer company was reorganized into the Poulsen Wireless Corporation as a holding company and the Federal Telegraph Company as the operating company, a wholly-owned subsidiary, for tax purposes. Elwell, as chief engineer, demonstrated 50-mile, two-way, continuous wave transmission between Sacramento and Stockton. Then, to silence critics, he set up a third station near Ocean Beach in San Francisco, with 300-foot wooden masts designed by Professor C.B. Wing. After that, Federal developed a chain of 16 high-power wireless stations in the United States, fabricating equipment for them at the 913 Emerson shop, where Perham worked as a mechanic until 1912. In 1912 Elwell opened commercial communication between San Francisco and Honolulu, then the world's longest such circuit (2,100 nautical miles).

De Forest Joins Elwell's Team

Despite these successes, a glaring need for technical advances in signal quality was evident. Elwell knew of the work done in the East by Dr. Lee de Forest, who in 1906 had invented a thermionic, three-electrode vacuum tube he called the audion. By adding a wire grid between the heated filament

and a plate, de Forest had amplified weak incoming signals. But development had been slow. De Forest's New York company was near ruin, and he was enduring "days of poverty," as he put it, in San Francisco when he and Elwell met. Elwell offered de Forest a job in July 1911 and set up a radio research team including technician Charles V. Logwood and telephone company engineer Herbert Van Etten. Van Etten's parents lived in Palo Alto, and his brother and sister attended Stanford; de Forest soon moved his widowed mother to town.

Intensive experiments by the team during 1912 produced two epochal breakthroughs. First, by "cascading" a series of audions they developed the first genuine amplifier. To test it, they played records out the window through a small loudspeaker, measuring progress by how many blocks and half blocks away it could be heard. After obtaining a two-block gain, de Forest satisfied himself that enormous amplification could be demonstrated. The amplifier was an essential part for both radio and telephonic long-distance communication.

A Powerful Discovery

During the same summer, the team accidentally hit

Federal Telegraph Company's manufacturing plant on El Camino Real operated from 1917 to 1932.

upon the feedback principle — that by feeding back part of the audion's output into its grid, a self-regenerating oscillation (or reversal of current flow) could be caused in the circuit. This single invention, suitably modified, was capable of either transmitting, receiving, acting as an oscillator or amplifying radio signals. As developed in Palo Alto in 1912 and subsequently improved elsewhere, the audion tube made possible live radio broadcasting and became the key component of all radio, telephone, radar, television and computer systems until the transistor was invented in 1947. California Historical Landmark No. 836 at Channing and Emerson describes the birthplace of modern radio electronics.

Diagrams and notes Van Etten jotted in a dime notebook were decisive supporting evidence later when the U.S. Supreme Court finally awarded the feedback oscillator patent to de Forest in a case hotly contested through the federal courts by Edwin Armstrong, who also invented the superheterodyne receiver and FM broadcasting.

Since de Forest had acquired a series of audion patents beginning in 1907, he was able to sell certain rights to American Telephone and Telegraph Co., which had long sought a repeater to boost long-distance telephone calls past a limit of 900 miles. Federal Telegraph retained only "shop rights," and it went on developing wireless radio using the Poulsen arcs. Both Elwell and de Forest left the company and Palo Alto in 1913, and Leonard F. Fuller became Federal's chief engineer. Fuller, Roland Marx and Ralph Beal worked out the theory of the great arcs that Federal Telegraph subsequently built to become the backbone of U.S. Navy communication during World War I.

Training Distinguished Engineers

Inundated with orders, Federal built a manufacturing plant facing El Camino Real and backing on the railroad tracks, near the present Holiday Inn site. Operations there from 1917 to 1932 peaked with war production in 1918 when 300 workers were employed. The company also served as a training ground for many engineers — most of them Stanford graduates — who went on to distinguished careers in radio and electronics. Among the foremost were Harold F. Elliott, who later developed a radio broadcast receiver for mass production, and many radio pushbutton tuning devices; and Charles V. Litton, a key man in Federal's transition in the 1927-34 period from the arc generators to vacuum tubes. Litton later set up his own company in Redwood City to fabricate glass-blowing tube lathes and other components vitally needed as Bay Area electronics production grew.

Another was James Arthur Miller, who became a recording pioneer. (Curiously, when Miller received his first patent in 1912, together with Oliver S. Hoover, it was not for an electronic device but for a mechanical one: an automatic hammer.) Aside from Federal Telegraph, Palo Alto's most successful industry during the 1920s was the Boden Automatic Hammer Company, which could hardly meet demand. During the Depression, however, homebuilding all but stopped and automatic hammer production had to be shut down.)

Three engineers were brought over from Denmark by Elwell to help manufacture the first Poulsen arc generators. One of them, Peter V. Jensen, later devised the first moving-coil loudspeaker, and started a company called Magnavox. Frederick Kolster, who had invented the radio direction-finder in 1913, worked with Federal Telegraph as its chief research engineer in Palo Alto from 1921 to 1931 while the firm produced the radio compass and, later, radio broadcast receivers he designed. In 1928, Kolster did directional antenna experiments using the first big parabolic reflectors seen in town.

COURTESY OF PERHAM FOUNDATION ARCHIVES

Douglas Perham, C. Albertus and Peter Jensen, left to right, pose with a Federal-Poulsen arc generator.

The Mackay Radio and Telegraph Company's Palo Alto baylands transmitting station was used for ship-to-shore communications.

A Mast in the Marsh

Federal Telegraph built a transmitting station in the Palo Alto baylands in 1921. Known as the Marsh Station, and by radio call letters KWT (later adopting the San Francisco call KFS), it lay amid ponds south of where Embarcadero Road now crosses Bayshore Freeway. A 626-foot antenna mast towered over the station, secured by numerous cables and guy wires and surrounded by a forest of smaller antennas. Professor Wing and his former student, Federal Telegraph employee Ralph A. Beebe, designed the mast.

Mackay Radio and Telegraph Company bought the Marsh Station in 1927 to use for point-to-point and ship-to-shore communications. Soon afterward, on March 21, 1928, Mackay became a unit of International Telephone and Telegraph Company. Mackay enlarged the station in 1928 and again in 1935. By '35, vacuum tube oscillators had replaced the less efficient Poulsen arcs for generating high frequency transmissions — a conversion marking the start of shortwave radio. The tall mast stood as a landmark until 1960, when it was removed as obsolete. By then, Mackay, renamed American Radio and Cable Company, was leasing modern submarine cables and later communications satellites. KFS (under a later corporate name, ITT World Communications) still handles ship-to-shore traffic, leasing a small station site from the City of Palo Alto, which now owns the marsh.

Manufacturing operations of Federal Telegraph were relocated to Newark, New Jersey, in 1931, when company officials decided that Palo Alto was too isolated from sources of supply, skilled workers and major markets.

Revisiting Palo Alto in 1956, Dr. de Forest told a reporter, "I thought when the original company closed its doors in 1932 and moved to New Jersey that electronics in Palo Alto was finished. Now they've come back [as Federal Telecommunication Laboratories, an ITT unit] because this is where the electronics industry is."

Indeed, despite Federal Telegraph's Depression-era exodus, seeds planted by the early experimenters and by the firm's operations had

Stanford Professor Frederick E. Terman, the intellectual father of Silicon Valley.

PALO ALTO HISTORICAL ASSOCIATION

continued to bear fruit in Palo Alto and many other places. The far-flung nature of Federal's operations, reaching across the Pacific and Atlantic oceans and later extending to Latin America, gave Palo Alto industry an international focus early in its annals. So did interchanges with scientists trained in Europe.

Fuller, Federal's chief engineer, later became head of the University of California electrical engineering department. He arranged for Federal to give UC a leftover 80-ton, 1000-kilowatt arc converter, which Dr. Ernest O. Lawrence used to construct his first successful atom-smashing cyclotron at Berkeley. Another converter gathered dust until the City of Palo Alto, which had taken over the plant for a corporation yard, sold it to unsuspecting agents of Japan buying scrap metal before World War II.

Garage Industries

One of a second wave of Stanford faculty sons who steeped themselves in radio, Frederick E. Terman, served as a lab assistant at Federal and later rose to head Stanford's electrical engineering department and finally the School of Engineering. Terman wrote the leading textbook on radio engineering, and became the founding father of a Palo Alto electronics surge after the Second World War — the true start of "Silicon Valley."

Mention electronics firms founded in a Palo Alto garage and most local residents think of Hewlett-Packard Co. But HP wasn't first. Elwell's shop on Emerson might be considered. In addition, Johnson-Williams, Inc., was started in Oliver Johnson's small garage at 430 Tennyson Avenue in 1927. Johnson and Philip S. Williams, Stanford graduate engineers working for Standard Oil Company, in their spare time developed a "gas sniffer" to detect leaks in big tanks holding combustible or noxious gases. Their sons later carried on the business in Palo Alto and Mountain View until the 1970s.

In another garage shop, at 1505 Byron Street, Gerhard R. Fisher invented the M-Scope, a device for detecting metal and water as deep as 20 feet underground. He operated Fisher Research Laboratories on University Avenue just across San Francisquito Creek from 1936 until 1967, when he retired; later a firm that bought the business moved it to Hanford in California's San Joaquin Valley. Fisher had originally come to Palo Alto to work for Federal Telegraph.

John M. Kaar's garage was in Menlo Park, but he soon moved his business of developing two-way mobile radio telephones to Palo Alto, occupying a number of locations from 1936 to 1965. Kaar's first order was to install a receiver in poundmaster Gerald Dalmadge's dog wagon, connecting it to the police network. In 1947, Kaar Engineering took over a plant at 2995 Middlefield Road that the Jack-Heintz Company had partially built in 1940 to produce aviation electronics. Jack-Heintz abandoned the site because of a labor dispute and moved to Cleveland, Ohio, where the firm made big profits during the war.

Not the First But the Most Famous

A one-car garage at 376 Addison Avenue is justly the most famous of them all, for there in 1938 William Hewlett and David Packard, two Stanford graduate engineers encouraged by Dean Terman, began working toward what today ranks among the top 30 U.S. manufacturing firms.

As a graduate student in Dr. Terman's com-

Young William Hewlett and David Packard formally began their partnership on January 1, 1939.

munications laboratory, Hewlett had developed a resistance-tuned oscillator. When he and Packard carried out their dream of starting a company on January 1, 1939, it was their initial product. Walt Disney Studios gave them their first big order: nine oscillators for sound production of the movie *Fantasia.*

By the time World War II began, the partners had developed a line of electronic measuring devices, operating in leased space. Then Hewlett was called to Army Signal Corps duty, and Packard managed production of components used in secret devices such as proximity fuzes that helped the Allies win the war. In 1942, HP built its own plant with a distinctive sawtooth roofline on Page Mill Road near the railroad tracks.

After a brief but rocky postwar readjustment, HP expanded its line of measuring instruments and was ready when electronics demands soared in 1950 with the Korean War's onset. For several years the company's output and work force doubled annually.

Packard pioneered new management concepts, too. His belief that a company's responsibility extended not only to shareholders but also to its employees, customers and community found expression in varied ways: profit-sharing; a willingness in tough times to furlough the whole work force rather than lay anyone off; a tradition of close cooperation with customers, even competing firms started by ex-employees; and extraordinary participation by top executives, including the partners, in civic leadership, on the theory that "the environment in which our people work has a good deal to do with the success of the company," as Packard put it.

Packard served on the Palo Alto Board of Education and later as a Stanford University trustee. Hewlett was on the hospital board. Among other HP officials active in public life were Noel Porter, mayor of Palo Alto during part of the booming '50s, and Bernard Oliver and Don Hammond, school board members.

Going Global

HP became one of the pioneer settlers of Stanford Industrial (now Research) Park, where its world headquarters remains. The company — always focused on the scientific and technical market — expanded into medical test equipment, hand-held calculators designed for engineers and ultimately computers, printers and accessories. In 1957, HP — incorporated by the partners in 1947 — put stock on public sale, began to acquire smaller companies and moved some production to other U.S. areas. By 1959 the company had subsidiaries in Switzerland, Germany and England; Japan came a few years later.

By 1992 Hewlett-Packard had 89,000 employees worldwide, about 4,300 of them in Palo Alto; 1992 sales were $16.4 billion.

The Brothers Varian

Another giant company sprouted from a basement laboratory at Stanford's Physics Corner. Professor William W. Hansen, who later developed the linear accelerator, aided brothers Russell and Sigurd Varian in their joint research aimed at developing a system for locating airplanes with a radio beam. This teamwork yielded the klystron tube, in which Russell Varian's idea for bunching electrons in waves is embodied. It was typical of how they worked together: Sigurd, a former airline pilot, projected the need, Russell figured out how it could be met and Sigurd built the device. The

COURTESY OF VARIAN ASSOCIATES

Russell and Sigurd Varian's development of the klystron tube led to their company being the first tenant of the Stanford Industrial Park.

invention made microwave radar possible and is considered a turning point for the Allies in World War II.

Klystron production began in a Sperry Gyroscope plant on Long Island, N.Y., but after the war ended, the brothers — who had lived in Palo Alto as boys — returned west with colleagues to found Varian Associates in 1948. Initially located in San Carlos, the firm in 1950 took Stanford Industrial Park's first lease, moving in 1952.

Beside the Varians, the founders included Stanford Professors Hansen, Edward L. Ginzton and Leonard I. Schiff, and H. Myrl Stearns, a skilled manager. Hansen died in 1949, soon after mortgaging his home to give Varian Associates a just-in-time loan. Discoveries he had made together with another Stanford physicist, Nobel Prize winner Felix Bloch, in the field of nuclear magnetic resonance laid the basis for applications by

Russell Varian in such analytical instruments as spectroscopes and magnetometers. Hansen's linear accelerator found uses in cancer therapy and industrial X-rays.

After Russell Varian's death in 1959 and Sigurd's in 1961, Ginzton emerged as the firm's guiding scientific figure. As of the early 1990s, Varian Associates stood as a worldwide company with annual sales far exceeding $1 billion. Its medical and instrument units accounted for nearly half of total sales, slightly ahead of electron tube devices used in communications, radar and defense. Semiconductor manufacturing equipment was a growing segment.

Although Varian had manufacturing plants in four U.S. states and seven foreign countries, the Palo Alto campus remained a significant manufacturing site as well as the headquarters and research center. The firm employs about 9,100 persons, 2,700 of them in Palo Alto.

Industry in the Air

The community's involvement in the air age became more direct shortly after World War II. In 1930-31, Palo Alto had joined other Bay Region cities in luring military aviation to what became Moffett Field. Later it vested local pride in research at Ames Laboratory, Mountain View, for the National Advisory Committee for Aeronautics — later the National Aeronautics and Space Administration (NASA).

In June 1946, the young Stanley Hiller, already a famed helicopter pioneer, moved production of his model MH44 into the city's Warehouse No. 2, Federal Telegraph's old haunt. Nearly two years later, the plant was relocated on Willow Road east of Bayshore. Although outside Palo Alto proper, the operation had support from the Chamber of Commerce and local businessmen, many of them stockholders in United Helicopters (later renamed Hiller Helicopters).

PALO ALTO HISTORICAL ASSOCIATION

Stanley Hiller, with support from local investors, was producing three helicopters per week in his local plant by 1949.

By 1949, "the world's largest manufacturer of commercial rotary-wing aircraft" was producing three helicopters per week. Several early '50s models were touted as the commuter vehicle of the future, such as the Hiller Hornet, which sold for $5,000, weighed 356 pounds and could be parked in the family garage. For publicity, a Hornet helped dry a sodden Stanford Stadium field before a Saturday football game by hovering for three hours six feet above the turf. But in 1965, Hiller lost a key Army contract and the plant closed.

By then, Palo Alto had landed a lasting role in aerospace. Lockheed Missiles & Space Division's move north from Van Nuys in September 1956 became the marker event. LMSC (the division was later renamed Company) established its research laboratory in Stanford Industrial Park, and its headquarters and main production facility in Sunnyvale, adjoining Moffett Naval Air Station.

The unit's well-planned move set the stage for rapid growth, especially after the Soviet Union's Sputnik II flight in 1957 spurred U.S. fleet ballistic missile and satellite programs to wartime speed. Lockheed's laboratory, enclosing about 250,000 square feet on a 22-acre site, has taken on a wide variety of research projects. LMSC and the lab are striving to remain an integral part of the projected space station and Mars missions, and of U.S. strategic defense.

Lockheed was one of the first big companies whose top leaders had no strong affinity with Stanford to select the industrial park. They were much attracted by Terman's plan of letting companies there work closely with the university on technical matters. It enabled some Lockheed scientists and engineers to take part in an honors degree program on campus, while Stanford professors could serve as Lockheed consultants.

Industrial parks later dotted the entire Peninsula, but the 655-acre Stanford Industrial Park — renamed Stanford Research Park in 1982 — has played a unique role as the font of Silicon Valley ideas and a model of university-industry cooperation.

"Clean Light Industry" Reveals a Dark Side

A dirty side of the park's "clean light industry" surfaced in the 1980s when various inorganic chemicals were found to be leaking from company sites into groundwater and fanning out under the nearby Barron Park residential area. The state ordered companies involved to band together in monitoring and cleaning up the contamination. Some federal Superfund money was committed locally.

Still, the 26,000-employee research park continued to flourish. In 1983, a federal report hailed it as the first and "widely considered the most successful" facility of its kind. Along with electronics firms, it is home to high technology companies engaged in medical research, specialty publishing and numerous other fields.

Syntex Settles in Palo Alto

Syntex Corporation, founded in Mexico in 1944, won fame for its discoveries and production of oral contraceptives in 1964 — a breakthrough attributed largely to Carl Djerassi, later a Stanford chemistry professor. That same year Syntex established its U.S. administrative and research headquarters in Palo Alto. By 1990, its annual sales had grown to $1.5 billion and the company was best known for its development of Naprosyn and related nonsteroidal anti-inflamatory drugs for arthritis, pain and inflammation. Of Syntex's global corps of more than 10,000 employees, approximately 1,800 were engaged in 1992 in research and administration on the 106-acre Palo Alto campus.

Syntex won renown for encouraging its employees to volunteer for community academic, cultural and environmental activities, and for its high percentage (46.3) of women in professional and managerial jobs. Syva Company, a Syntex medical diagnostics subsidiary, markets tests to detect alcohol and all commonly abused drugs. Alza Corp., a Syntex spinoff also located in the research park, has developed skin patches and other drug delivery systems.

Another research park tenant with about 1,000 local workers is Watkins-Johnson Company, established in 1957. The firm is named for its cofounders, Dean A. Watkins, a Stanford electrical engineering professor who invented the helitron tube, and H. Richard Johnson, who had directed microwave tube research at Hughes Aircraft Company. Their business has centered on defense electronics and semiconductor manufacturing equipment. A traveling-wave tube fabricated by Watkins-Johnson, an 8-watt amplifier, powered communications from Pioneer 10, the first satellite to escape the solar system. Designed to last 27,000 hours, or three-plus years, the tube had, as of 1992, continued to function for more than 20 years.

Shockley Returns to Develop Transistor

A big change in electronics followed the invention of the transistor at Bell Laboratories in New Jersey in 1947. The tiny device replaced bulky tubes in many products and spurred the use of printed circuits. William Shockley, who won the 1956 Nobel Prize in physics as the transistor's co-inventor, had lived in Palo Alto from 1913 to 1922 while his father taught at Stanford. He decided to return to Palo Alto to develop the device under the aegis of Beckman Instruments, Inc., which set up the Shockley Semiconductor Laboratory and also located its medically oriented Spinco Division in the industrial park in 1956-57.

Eight young research scientists working with Shockley grew dissatisfied with his management style and broke away, carrying on development work in their own Palo Alto garages and living rooms until they secured cash backing and formed Fairchild Semiconductor Corporation. In 1959, in an unimposing Charleston Road building, Robert Noyce led this group in scoring a signal technological breakthrough by inventing the first commercially practicable integrated circuit. This complete electronic circuit within a small silicon chip revolutionized Silicon Valley's semiconductor industry.

Noyce and Gordon Moore later founded Intel Corporation, while others of the "Fairchild Eight" — Julian Blank, Eugene Kleiner, Vic Grinich, Jean Hoerni, Jay Last and Sheldon Roberts — played

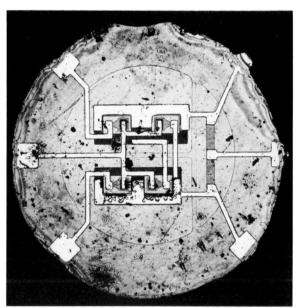

The integrated circuit symbolizes the development of Silicon Valley and its effect on the lives of people throughout the world.

key roles in other facets of semiconductor development.

Landmark Discoveries

The site at 844 E. Charleston Road is memorialized as California Registered Historical Landmark No. 1000; a plaque says the integrated circuit "brought profound change to the lives of people everywhere." In reporting the dedication in August 1991, the *Peninsula Times Tribune* contrasted the new landmark with Landmark No. 976, which marks the garage where Hewlett-Packard began as "The Birthplace of Silicon Valley." As noted earlier, another landmark, No. 836, identifies the radio research lab site at Emerson and Channing.

In addition to Alza and Beckman, a tier of research park employers with between 500 and 1,000 employees includes the Electric Power Research Institute and IBM Scientific Center.

Among other research park firms, one of the best-known is the Xerox Palo Alto Research Center. PARC, established in 1970, had the mission of expanding Xerox Corporation's role beyond reprographics into information handling and communications. In the process, researchers de-

Development of the Stanford Industrial Park, renamed Stanford Research Park, resulted from the cooperative efforts of the city, Stanford University and the industrial tenants.

veloped a dozen breakthrough computer technologies, most of which were later exploited by other regional firms. Among the best known are portable computing, the laser printer, the first easy-to-use word processing program and the Postscript language used in desktop publishing.

In the 1990s PARC pursued a vision of the "ubiquitous computing environment," an office of the future embedded with computers "transparent" to their users.

The research park also is home to a satellite printing plant of *The Wall Street Journal* and to Dialog, a massive computer data base developed by Lockheed and now owned by Knight Ridder Inc. Ex-tenants include Eastman Kodak and General Electric Microwave Laboratory.

Other Industrial Clusters

Another sector of the city became an industrial location in 1958 when Philco Corporation moved its Western Development Laboratory to a site at West Bayshore Frontage Road and San Antonio Road. At Philco, a radio maker that expanded into high tech communications, giant parabolic antennas designed to warn of missile attacks or transmit commercial satellite signals became a familiar sight. The facility later took the name Philco Ford and then Ford Aerospace while it was owned by Ford Motor Co., which ultimately sold the unit in 1989 to a French-Italian combine called Space Systems/Loral. The firm now builds communications, meteorological and other satellites; its 2,200 Palo Alto employees occupy 30 buildings along Fabian Way.

Sun Microsystems Inc., another company that owes its origin to the collaboration of a Stanford professor, Forest Baskett, and his talented students, is based nearby. Sun, a computer work stations manufacturer with annual sales of over $2 billion, bought and renovated Ford Aerospace's five-story building and in 1990 moved President Scott McNealy and 1,050 headquarters employees there from Mountain View.

Other computer and software companies and components suppliers occupy spaces on San Antonio Road and both Bayshore frontage roads.

Manufacturing Goes South but Research Remains

Palo Alto for years was the heart of Northern California's electronics industry. Gradually the center shifted south. By 1978 HP President John A. Young forecast the end of Silicon Valley's manufacturing heyday. Instead, Young said, there would be greater emphasis on headquarters operations, research centers, pilot production lines and prototyping operations requiring highly skilled people. By the mid-1980s, the accuracy of his prophecy was evident.

Industry in Palo Alto remains closely allied with Stanford and three nearby research complexes: the Stanford Linear Accelerator Center and SRI International (originally Stanford Research Institute), both in Menlo Park, and NASA's Ames Research Center in Mountain View. Particle physics research at SLAC, a broad range of applied research projects at SRI and aerospace experimentation at Ames, with its arrays of supercomputers and wind tunnels, all employ Palo Alto residents and resonate throughout the city and Stanford.

The DAvenport Exchange

Near the beginning of this chapter, a single long-distance telephone line that ran through the future Palo Alto was mentioned. In 1892, as the population reached 300, J.F. Parkinson was appointed the local agent for Sunset Telephone and Telegraph Company, and a public telephone was installed in his lumber yard office. In 1896, B.F. Hall took over the agency in his drug store, and there were three Palo Alto listings in the state directory — a number that jumped to 70 by 1899.

As Pacific Telephone & Telegraph Company developed, with much of its business necessarily conducted town by town, Palo Alto became a favored exchange, one that got innovations early. By 1910, with the population 4,486, Palo Alto had 1,282 phones; by 1929, at the end of a booming decade, the 15,000 residents shared 6,508 phones.

Dial installation for the DAvenport exchange was completed in 1948. In 1951, *Business Week* reported more than 300 telephones a week were being installed in the area. As of 1975, Palo Alto with 102.2 telephones per 100 residents had topped the 1:1 ratio and ranked fifth nationally.

Today a raging river of voice and data transmissions flows to and from Palo Alto's industries, businesses and homes. Activities clustered here form part of one of the world's most intensively used communications centers, a center likely in years to come to be even more plugged in globally, in earth orbit and in outer space.

Fresh Ideas and Future Dreams

A glimpse of future patterns may be seen in some of the team research efforts bringing modern computer power to bear in applying scientific discoveries in many fields. The computer's ability to search vast data bases rapidly and to simulate everything from spacecraft designs to pharmaceutical effects is speeding up processes that formerly took long years.

A prime example is the entrepreneurial activity of Alejandro Zaffaroni, chairman of Alza Corp. and progenitor of several specialized research park endeavors. One, DNAX Research Institute, applies genetic engineering in studies of allergies, inflammation and infectious diseases. In 1982 DNAX was acquired by Schering-Plough Corp. of New Jersey. Another, Affymax Research Institute, formed in 1989, is designed to speed the identification of promising drugs through systematic search processes. Zaffaroni was joined in setting up this institute (a subsidiary of a Netherlands corporation) by three Stanford faculty superstars: Carl Djerassi, chemistry; Avram Goldstein, pharmacology; and Joshua Lederberg, 1958 Nobelist in medicine, later president of Rockefeller University in New York.

Other omens point to an ongoing place for

Palo Alto in the evolution of new technologies. In 1993, Paramount Communications Inc., the giant movie studio and book publisher, chose Palo Alto as the place for a research center devoted to "the new Hollywood" — a multimedia combination of traditional books, movies and television with new electronic technology. Sueann R. Ambron, a former Stanford professor chosen to head the new Paramount Technology Group, said the company decided to locate its "media kitchen" in Palo Alto because "the technology is hanging off the trees here."

Another futuristic activity with a local foothold is the "technology of the tiny," or nanotechnology, which involves creating structures atom by atom and molecule by molecule. Its leading theorist, K. Eric Drexler, is based in Palo Alto, as is the Institute for Molecular Manufacturing.

Although much of the Palo Alto work force (roughly three times the resident population) is engaged in the affairs of large national and international concerns, garage invention is far from outmoded. Offspring of high technologists, Stanford graduate students schooled in an ever-expanding spectrum of disciplines and skilled technicians in the tradition of Douglas Perham still toil night and day in home workshops to hone innovations they hope will launch entrepreneurial careers. For example, in 1992, in a Palo Alto garage, brothers John and Jim Slater and their partner David Zhu — organized as Nomadic Technologies Inc. — were perfecting software to direct user-friendly robots that might soon do housework.

Whether from amply financed and elaborately equipped research teams, or from individuals with little but a dream, fresh ideas and a shoestring budget, more breakthroughs appear likely to lie ahead.

Recycling has become part of the lifestyle of Palo Altans.

15

Utilities: A City Monopoly

As of 1992, consumers in Palo Alto — the only city west of the Rockies operating its own gas and electric utilities — enjoyed the lowest gas rates and the lowest electricity rates in California.

In its first 25 years of incorporation, the City of Palo Alto took control of all three major utilities serving its residents — water, electricity and gas — as well as a fourth, sewers. In doing so, it established a rare degree of municipal ownership of services.

Getting water was a primary purpose for making the village of 1894 a city, and consolidating various private sources of water supply was a first order of business, as related in Chapter 4.

Sewers came next — the townspeople voted almost unanimously for them. Then, with surplus funds left from the sewer bonds, City Engineer E.C. Moore rigged up a power generator to supply residents with electricity in the evening hours at a rate lower than a competing private company charged, as several professors in the town leadership had predicted could be done.

Around the turn of the century, rival companies vying with one another in new utility fields sometimes engaged in tricky schemes to get ahead. The private Redwood City firm that had found it could not best Palo Alto in a price war decided to try to steal a march on the city. The company, which had grown into the Pacific Gas & Electric Co., wanted to extend its lines through Palo Alto in order to serve a zinc processing plant near the bay. So, on a February holiday in 1912, PG&E crews strung lines through the town without getting a franchise.

Holiday or no, Palo Alto's men weren't caught napping. Getting wind of the PG&E caper, the city

engineer and the chief electrician gave up their day off and rounded up a city crew to tear out the unauthorized poles. PG&E bosses didn't know what had become of their poles and wires until they spotted a small newspaper ad telling where the material could be reclaimed — after payment of costs.

Adding natural gas took longer, because of opposition from local investors who hoped to participate in the profits and from PG&E, which had every intention of remaining the supplier and perhaps a secret hope of buying the distribution system eventually. The forces for municipal ownership suffered a setback at the polls when three city trustees were unseated. The new board franchised the private Palo Alto Gas Company, controlled by L.C. Low of Santa Clara, to lay a piping system and deliver gas purchased from PG&E.

After winning back control in the 1909 charter election, the council members favoring municipal ownership tried first to control gas rates and then to condemn the private gas system. The Railroad Commission — the forerunner of today's Public Utilities Commission — set the value of the gas installations at $65,500. Low's firm appealed, asking for $15,000 more. The Railroad Commission president invited Palo Alto officials to randomly examine the condition of the pipes. Searching out surface signs of soil decay and tree damage, canny city engineers contrived to find only leaky and rusty pipes buried beneath. Palo Alto Gas then

PALO ALTO HISTORICAL ASSOCIATION   STANFORD UNIVERSITY ARCHIVES   PALO ALTO HISTORICAL ASSOCIATION

Stanford Professors Charles D. Marx, left, and Charles B. Wing, center, took an active role in the development of the utility service in the young town of Palo Alto. John F. Byxbee, right, served as city engineer for 35 years.

abandoned its appeal. In 1917 a new municipal gas plant was dedicated, and the City of Palo Alto owned its three key utility systems outright.

Once the gas system was added to city-owned distribution of water and electricity, utilities faded from the forefront of municipal politics. There were still sources to procure, lines to build or rebuild and bond financing to approve, and later on, rising environmental consciousness led to changes. However, the main focus remained fixed on quality service and low rates — and earning a profit, a "must" the pioneering academics demanded from the first.

Along with Professors Charles D. "Daddy" Marx and Charles B. Wing, City Engineer John F. Byxbee, who served 35 years, did much to lay the foundation for the modern utilities. Marx and Wing were engineering department mainstays of the "Old Guard" — the pioneer Stanford University faculty. Both were civic-minded Professorville residents, and gave generously of their counsel in local, regional and state affairs; they often assigned their students to local research tasks.

Marx served as an early town trustee and councilman and then put in 30 years on the Board of Public Works. In a tribute to him in 1927, E.A.

Cottrell, another professor who served on the council, said, "Marx alone has contributed over $500,000 worth of expert service free of charge to the city."

Wing served on the council for 20 years and on the state Parks Commission for 22 years. He was a consultant on the construction of the Hetch Hetchy Dam, a milestone project in bringing Sierra Nevada water to San Francisco — and Palo Alto and other Peninsula cities.

Byxbee became the city engineer in 1906 and served until 1941. A baylands park dedicated in 1991 honors Byxbee, who with foresight bought baylands acreage for the city from 1921 on.

From "Coal Tar" to Natural Gas

Gas needed early attention, for the system Palo Alto had bought piped oil gas manufactured from "coal tar" — actually, residual oil. It was a messy process. In 1930, the city shifted to natural gas, which proved a better fuel. For a time, butane tanks placed near Rinconada Park helped meet peak demands.

In 1929, Palo Alto and PG&E litigated what constituted a fair and reasonable wholesale gas rate before the California Railroad Commission —

an issue they revisited regularly for the next 62 years. When the city began distributing natural gas piped by PG&E from the lower San Joaquin Valley oil fields, domestic usage started to rise considerably because of its cleaner-burning quality.

As a matter of policy, Palo Alto for decades charged gas rates equivalent to PG&E rates in surrounding areas. This pattern buckled for a brief period in 1975 when Palo Alto had higher rates, a reversal that prompted alarmed talk of selling the gas utility. Then events began to turn in Palo Alto's favor. In 1988, the city vacated its historic policy and dropped its gas rates below PG&E's.

The long period with PG&E as the city's major wholesale gas supplier ended in 1991 when Palo Alto entered a year-to-year contract with Shell Canada Ltd. Since then, gas from Canadian fields in Alberta has moved through the Pacific Gas Transmission pipeline, owned and operated by a PG&E subsidiary. The savings from this change of supplier enabled Palo Alto to set the lowest gas rates in California, and in 1992 the American Public Gas Association honored the city as America's No. 1 gas utility. Other suppliers compete annually with Shell Canada for Palo Alto's business.

From Well Water to Imported Water

Deep wells supplied Palo Alto with water — "hard" water, at that — for about half a century. Then in the mid-1930s worry arose about the falling of the Santa Clara Valley ground water table, in effect a vast underground reservoir. So in 1938 Palo Alto began to buy supplementary water from San Francisco, delivered through a 36-inch pipeline known as the Palo Alto pipeline. In ensuing years, increasing amounts were purchased

PALO ALTO HISTORICAL ASSOCIATION

This city powerhouse held a large diesel engine that provided electric power for the community.

The Mayfield Reservoir above College Terrace, shown drained for cleaning, continues to store water for the community.

to mix with well water.

In 1962, with some of its wells pumping more sand and less water, Palo Alto switched to 100% San Francisco water — mostly much softer water from Hetch Hetchy, a twin valley of Yosemite, plus a small portion of rain runoff captured in the Coast Range. The San Francisco Water Department's construction of additional pipelines enhanced the reliability of the Sierra Nevada source.

Only four city wells have been kept operable — Hale, Rinconada, Peers and Meadows — and they are for emergency use only. All water distributed is treated with chlorine, to kill any bacteria, and with fluorine, to control tooth decay.

The city receives Hetch Hetchy water at four connections, and maintains 4 million gallons of storage in the Corte Madera Reservoir for Stanford Research Park and 5 million gallons of storage in the foothills to equalize the supply and afford fire protection. Mayfield Reservoir, built in 1928, remains in use. Distribution is through 220 miles of water mains.

When a prolonged drought began in the late 1980s, Palo Alto water users extended the city's supply by cutting back their usage. By 1992, conservation had reduced water consumption to 35% below that of 1987, well below the 28% cutback mandated by the supplier. However, the reduced use led to a rate increase imposed by the city so as to bolster sagging water revenues.

The Utilities Department has used reclaimed water as Greer Park's entire supply since October 1991, and more recently has begun to use it to irrigate the Palo Alto Municipal Golf Course.

From Local to Imported Power

Although the Corliss steam engine installed in 1900 proved that the city could generate its own power economically, it could not meet growing demand for long. At first, Palo Alto purchased supplemental electrical power at wholesale rates from the competing private utility, United Gas and Electric (later absorbed by PG&E).

The first of several diesel engines was installed in 1914 at the city powerhouse in what is now Rinconada Park. Before the city bought the engine, Professors Marx and Wing had a barrel of California crude oil sent to Belgium, where the engines were manufactured, to see if they would run on it. When the fuel proved satisfactory, they persuaded the city to buy the engine. Utilities people from all over the country came to Palo Alto to see it generate power for the town.

PALO ALTO HISTORICAL ASSOCIATION

Beginning in 1914, city diesel engines supplied the electrical needs of Palo Alto. Later they were used only to meet peak loads.

Population growth and rising electrical loads prompted the city to connect to PG&E's system in 1923. From then on, use of the diesels was more and more limited to meeting peak demand. In 1948, manufacturers could no longer supply parts, so the city sold the old diesel engines for scrap.

In 1964, Palo Alto was able to buy into the federal government's Central Valley Project (CVP) power supply on "sweetheart" terms, so wholesale purchases from PG&E ceased. But they had to be resumed 20 years later when the city's electrical need exceeded its contracted level with Western Area Power Administration, the CVP agency.

The contract with Western expires in 2004 and Palo Alto has laid plans to renew it as the city's primary power supply. Meanwhile, steps to secure additional sources have been taken through the Northern California Power Agency (NCPA), a group of publicly owned electrical utilities in which Palo Alto is a leading member. Through the agency, the city has bought a 22.92% share of a 230-megawatt hydroelectric plant in Calaveras County that came on line in 1990, and a share of surplus Northwest power after a transmission line has been built. Palo Alto once owned geyser power through NCPA, but sold its share to Turlock because geothermal energy did not match local needs. The city has also invested in a 50-megawatt steam-injected gas turbine being developed in Lodi, scheduled to be in service by 1995.

In keeping with a philosophy of investing only in technologies that present minimal risk to the city and society, Palo Alto by policy has avoided direct participation in nuclear power.

Palo Alto's love-hate symbiosis with PG&E has continued, in a sense, because PG&E "wheels" bulk power over its lines to the city. Necessary negotiations have been done recently at arm's length, through NCPA and the federal Department of Energy. Palo Alto customers have often escaped PG&E outages because of the operational options open to city engineers. However, in a major transmission failure the city is vulnerable to blackout because it has no independent power source. (Some major users own standby generators.) For that reason, fuel cell technology has come under close city study through the Palo Alto-based Electric Power Research Institute and national and state associations. Fuel cells convert hydrogen fuel to electricity and heat, without combustion. Relatively small fuel cell units could be installed in Palo Alto to boost localized power reliability, perhaps by the year 2000.

Since underground cables were installed in the 1960s, about one-third of Palo Alto's electrical power has been distributed through them, the other two-thirds on overhead lines. The buried cables have had a remarkably low failure rate.

Through management efforts to control demand since 1985, the city has reduced peak demand significantly and lowered its energy need somewhat. One program, called Partners, encouraged industrial and commercial customers (together accounting for 87% of the consumption) to install energy-efficient devices that clipped peak demand. In another program, customers agreed to lower their load on request, thereby reducing their own bills and enabling the city to do the same by avoiding very expensive extra power purchases.

Refining Wastewater Disposal

Early residents were proud of the sewer system built beginning in 1896 with bond funds they voted. But flaws in the design surfaced much later, and led to a major development of regional cooperation.

The first 12-inch gravity outfall pipe dumped untreated wastewater right into Mayfield Slough. When the line became overloaded in 1919, the city built a second parallel line. Meanwhile Stanford University and Mayfield also laid lines emptying into the slough. At high tides, manhole overflows occurred in the lowlands.

To alleviate this nuisance and public health hazard, Palo Alto built a primary sewage treatment plant in 1934, with a 4,700-foot outfall extending 700 feet offshore. It was one of the first sewage treatment plants on San Francisco Bay, financed by a $90,000 bond issue and a $29,000 federal grant. Mayfield was part of Palo Alto by then, and Stanford agreed to pay the city to treat its sewage.

In the plant's early years, there were two special industrial waste problems — cannery solids from Sutter Packing Company and sewer-clogging chicken feathers from a poultry processing

Palo Alto's Advanced Wastewater Treatment Facility expanded its capacity in 1987.

PENINSULA TIMES TRIBUNE/BOB ANDRES

plant on El Camino Real. The problems weren't solved until both food processors left town.

The sewage treatment capacity, originally 3 million gallons a day, was increased two-thirds by a plant enlargement in 1948 and then doubled by another in 1956. Even so, it became apparent by the latter '60s that the plant would soon be overloaded again.

At about the same time, the state stepped up efforts to improve water quality in the shallow South Bay. Palo Alto, Los Altos and Mountain View soon faced "cease and desist" orders prohibiting the discharge of wastewater not purified by secondary treatment. So in October 1968, the three cities agreed to build a new plant to process their wastewater plus that of Stanford, Los Altos Hills, the East Palo Alto Sanitary District and a small district, Las Encinas, then serving Barron Park. A federal grant covered 55% of the $11 million construction cost. The plant was named the Harold L. "Doc" May Regional Water Quality Control Plant to honor the Palo Alto chief utility system engineer who championed the regional approach.

By the late 1970s, tightening regional standards necessitated an addition, the $8.8 million Advanced Wastewater Treatment Facility, with state and federal grants funding 87.5%. The aim was to provide full tertiary treatment, but during periods of heavy rain runoff in 1980, 1982, 1983 and 1986, the inflow exceeded the plant's capacity to meet the standard fully. So a project to increase capacity was completed in 1987, this time with no state or federal aid.

Palo Alto owns and administers the state-of-the-art plant; the 1968 tri-city pact, now effective until July 1, 2035, calls for proportionately shared upkeep and use.

A problem heavier than chicken feathers cropped up in the 1950s when it was found that chemicals such as silver and copper compounds flushed away by electronics firms were throwing bacterial sludge digesters at the treatment plant off their feed. The secondary treatment plant used an incinerator to dispose of sludge, eliminating the digester failures; however, the bay still needed to be protected from chemical wastes. So a control program was begun in 1971 and all the agencies adopted a new ordinance. It has been widely emulated around the San Francisco Bay.

When the tertiary treatment plant opened, a pretreatment program was launched and extended to cover hazardous materials. Plant processes, culminating in sludge incineration, proved to concentrate metals effectively. For a time a private service processed the incinerator ash to recover gold, silver and other precious metals. This contract rewarded the partner cities with revenue — more than $100,000 a year for Palo Alto at the zenith. Then tighter state standards forced industries to recover more of the metals at their plant sites and changed the city's recovery contract from a revenue to a cost.

Upgrading the Dump

In the early 1900s, most refuse from Palo Alto was burned in an incinerator located at Newell and Embarcadero roads. Excess wastes and residues were used as fill for extension of Embarcadero Road into the baylands. Then in the early 1930s the incinerator burned down, so disposal operations were moved to a site behind the sewage treatment plant. Dumping there was haphazard, and fires often burned for days, wafting up thick black smoke from automobile tires.

Despite its noxious side, the dump was a social center of sorts. Friends and neighbors hailed one another there, and children who rode with their parents found it a treasure-hunting ground. So did residents rummaging for just the right piece of wood or metal. For some years the dump was the launch site for municipal fireworks.

More sophisticated landfill operations began in 1954. Kids lost the run of the place and scrounging was halted. Various tactics have extended the landfill's once-projected 1994-96 closing date to a new estimate of 2021. These have included moving cut-and-cover work to new areas often and separating wastes into recyclables, compostable plant materials and garbage and trash. Yet the volume of 250 to 300 tons a day has

Before the days of the Palo Alto Sanitation Company (PASCO) Palo Alto's trash was hauled by horse-drawn wagons.

PALO ALTO HISTORICAL ASSOCIATION

The baylands dump is slowly filling up with the garbage of Palo Altans despite efforts to extend its closing date.

PENINSULA TIMES TRIBUNE/SAM FORENCICH

kept coming. In 1992, Palo Alto, Mountain View and Sunnyvale combined to arrange use of a new, long-term landfill site in Kirby Canyon, south San Jose. As of mid-1993, Palo Alto began to haul two-thirds of its solid waste there, via a transfer station in Sunnyvale, thereby lengthening the life of the baylands landfill.

Palo Alto's garbage collection is performed by the Palo Alto Sanitation Company, known for its spiffy vehicles and neatly uniformed crews. Recycling began in the early 1970s with the laborious efforts of volunteers who flattened one tin or aluminum can at a time. Before long the city inaugurated curbside recycling; Palo Alto's program, featuring a vehicle called a "goat" that eats cans, bottles and newspapers, has won many plaudits.

Renewing the Infrastructure

Public investment in Palo Alto's utilities systems is extensive: net fixed assets of $50 million in the electrical system, $13 million in gas and $11.6 million in water, for a 1991-92 total of nearly $75 million — projected to rise to almost $90 million in 1994-95.

Most of the systems, built in the 1950s or 1960s, or earlier, are gradually wearing out. The Utilities Department began an infrastructure project in 1993-94 that is designed to replace and upgrade the facilities on an ongoing basis. It is being financed from current rates and reserves, and is planned to consume less than 10% of the operating budget.

In a related step, the storm drain system was placed under utilities management in 1990. User fees have been levied to finance remedial work.

Among the equipment to be replaced is the 20-year-old billing system, which cannot apply the full capabilities of modern computers. Even so, Palo Alto residents who have compared their rates and consumption data with those of friends living elsewhere have often marveled at receiving such complete usage information.

Unusual Features

In California and other states west of the Rockies, Palo Alto was the only city operating both the gas and electric utilities as of 1992. Scores of other California cities own their electric systems; only two others, Long Beach and Coalinga, have municipally owned gas.

Palo Alto consumers had California's lowest gas rates *and* lowest electric rates in 1992. Gas rates were about 36% lower than PG&E's, electric rates 60% lower. Water rates about equalled those in comparable Bay Area communities. The 1992 situation has been described as a turnabout from 1939, when Palo Alto's water rates were the most favorable and gas rates the least advantageous.

Utilities staffers — some highly trained in electrical or mechanical engineering — are on call to an unusual extent to help customers find leaks or select energy-saving new equipment.

In 1991, the City Council — over the objections of City Manager Bill Zaner — set up a five-member Utilities Advisory Commission to review city utility rates and budgets. The idea behind the commission was that the city-owned utilities have grown so large and play such an important role in the city's financial health that they would benefit from some oversight by residents. Zaner and several council members expressed apprehension that a strong commission could gain control over the utilities, their budgets and the amount of their earnings transferred to the general fund. One champion of the advisory commission and critic of Utilities Department practices, former Council Member Emily Renzel, has said, "Palo Alto has been exporting huge environmental problems for years." She cited "slashing through forests" to build transmission lines, sharing in a dam project and exporting garbage.

Randy Baldschun, assistant director of utilities for administrative services, has listed four positive attributes of Palo Alto utilities: (1) low rates, which the city has always had; (2) excellent management and oversight by both staff and public; (3) willingness to take risks and (4) a high service level.

Although the city's future utilities may be beyond detailed imagining today, the first century's record has provided grounds for believing that these desirable qualities have become ingrained.

Palo Altans are leaders in recycling efforts.

The Police/Fire Building at 450 Bryant Street, circa 1940.

16

Justice and Public Safety

*"With little fear for their own safety, police officers, firefighters
and park rangers... rescued people, horses and livestock. Many times
public safety personnel risked their lives to escort residents down
fire-engulfed streets, only to return again to bring more people out."*

— Bruce C. Cumming, assistant Palo Alto police chief,
regarding the foothills fire of July 1, 1985

Becoming a city in the spring of 1894 entitled Palo Alto to have its own Recorder's Court, with jurisdiction over town ordinances and minor criminal matters. In the same balloting that decided incorporation, W.W. Truesdale, 60, a former gold miner, was elected town marshal, polling 64 votes, more than his three rivals combined. His duties included collecting taxes and license fees.

The legal system of that era had dual tracks: city and township. When Santa Clara County was created in 1850, the northwestern tip of the county was put in Fremont Township, whose justice of the peace sat in Mountain View. Then in 1889 the Board of Supervisors created Mayfield Township, including what became the City of Palo Alto five years later. The township justice of the peace presided over preliminary felony proceedings and minor civil and criminal cases.

After incorporation the township began to gall Palo Altans. In 1896 they petitioned the supervisors for a division into their own township. Mayfield, already stung by the separation of the Palo Alto School District from theirs, reacted angrily, especially because the petition trumpeted Palo Alto's claims of temperance and good morals. Gordon Wigle, father of Mayfield Justice of the Peace Gilbert Wigle, accused the new town's people of trying to legislate his son out of office.

One of the county supervisors had assured Palo Altans that their petition would be granted quietly, saying a large delegation need not go to San Jose. Appearing for the hearing, two town representatives were shocked to find 110 citizens of Mayfield present. The supervisors bowed to Mayfield. They approved the new township, but limited it to Palo Alto's city boundaries, leaving the Seale ranch and Stanford University in Mayfield Township. "Treachery," cried the *Palo Alto Times*, echoing the fury of scorned Palo Altans.

The Palo Alto Justice Court did not hear its first case until December 29, 1898, after E.G. Dyer had been elected justice, defeating Gilbert Wigle 251 to 6. The township also had a constable, Roger Spaulding — the "Old Sleuth," to readers of his exploits.

Two Courts for One Small Community

Thus the little community had two courts, each with its own magistrate, unlike other places where the same individual usually served as jurist in both courts. This situation prevailed for more than half a century, although the Recorder's Court was renamed the Police Court after Palo Altans adopted charter government in 1909. In 1922, the county supervisors abolished the Mayfield justice of the peace office, transferring jurisdiction to Palo Alto. When Mayfield was annexed in 1925, its police court was merged with Palo Alto's.

In Palo Alto's infancy, Marshal Truesdale, who

served three two-year terms, made two noteworthy arrests. J.E. Spencer was nabbed for selling intoxicating liquors and fined $100, which he was to pay or work off at $1 a day. Spencer got off on a technicality. The town trustees, in drafting the liquor ordinance, had failed to designate the jail where a sentence was to be served. (At one time the town had a tiny jail near Lytton Avenue and High Street, occupied mostly by tramps who were told to move on as soon as legal process permitted.)

A few months later in 1894, Truesdale, acting on a tip, led a raid on poker players at the rear of a pool room opposite the bank. One of the six card players was fined $40, the others $20 each, with 60 days to pay up.

While Truesdale's debut was placid, Justice Dyer soon ran into trouble — a public furor over a Chinese slave girl case (see Toward Integration chapter). He was indicted for allegedly releasing young Kum Quai to her abductors in the middle of the night. Townspeople irately protested Dyer's conduct, but the charges were ultimately dismissed.

Samuel W. Charles succeeded to the office when Dyer, only 35, died in 1901. An attorney and Stanford Law School instructor, Charles served until 1916 when he was killed in an auto-train accident at San Bruno. His wife, Isabel Peck Charles, was appointed to fill the office, becoming the county's first female judge. She immediately began law study, and later passed the bar and entered law practice. Mrs. Charles retired as justice of the peace in May 1929 shortly before she married Eliot F. Jones, a Stanford professor of economics.

Newspapers found novelty in her tenure. One photo caption writer called her "Mrs. Judge Isabel L. Charles." A headline said: "Making Ladies' Husbands Behave Only One of Many Extra-Official Duties of Woman Justice of the Peace."

The fourth and last Palo Alto justice of the peace was Edward E. Hardy, appointed just out of Stanford Law School. Well liked by both bar and public, Hardy served until 1953, when a new

Justice of the Peace Isabel Peck Charles became Santa Clara County's first female judge in 1916.

PALO ALTO HISTORICAL ASSOCIATION

Palo Alto-Mountain View Municipal Court created by the Legislature took over. Confined to a wheelchair from age 13 on, Hardy displayed artistic, musical and literary talents along with legal skill. He declined to seek the new judgeship, saying "streamlined justice" would spoil the personal contact with people he felt was most effective.

Policing in the Early Years

In its first 10 years as a city, Palo Alto had only two policemen: the marshal, initially paid $146 a month, and a night watchman. The latter, hired by merchants, also lighted the kerosene street lamps of the "9 o'clock town," an early-to-bed place then. In 1902, Marshal H.A. Ramsay managed to arrest 10 bicyclists before 7 a.m. for prohibited riding on the sidewalk (rather than on muddy University Avenue). Each offender was fined $2.50. Late in 1904, Ramsay at last was given the help of a day policeman, Billy Hill. For reasons unknown now, Hill was called "chief of police" — a position not formally filled until after adoption of the 1909 charter.

Town Trustee David Curry, founder of the Yosemite Park and Curry Co., launched a campaign against slot machines in 1905. At several stores, machines dispensed cigars for a nickel, spinning symbols that could win the buyer a prize. Curry branded them gambling devices and obtained warrants for their removal. When Marshal Ramsay tried to confiscate one, the merchant asked why he didn't "fix up the warrant so you can take my cash register too?" Another merchant put a sign saying "Not a gambling device" on his cigar machine, and refused to let it be removed. The district attorney pressed one case but the court ruled that the prosecutor had failed to show a crime because the ordinance was meant to ban machines used to gamble for money. Then two machine owners accused Curry of taking property without due process of law. With that, the anti-slots drive ebbed.

In April 1905, the region's law enforcers recorded an example of good teamwork. Palo Alto's entire police force — the marshal, constable, day policeman and night watchman — joined with the county sheriff, two deputies and Mayfield's constable to nab a pickpocket gang. After a chase involving southbound and northbound trains, lawmen caught the thieves' leader with the loot in a women's restroom. When he told the sheriff he had business that couldn't wait and thought the sheriff could use $200 or $300 to "call the matter off," he incurred an additional charge of bribery.

An episode foreshadowing future problems with politically aroused students occurred in 1905. A performance of "Uncle Tom's Cabin" was on at Mullen's Hall on High Street near Lytton Avenue. About 200 Stanford students subjected the show to a "rough-house," a college custom of the day involving boisterous joshing of the actors. Outside the hall, Hill and six deputies tried to quiet the students and isolate the ringleaders, but when one was taken into custody, others rushed to his rescue. A free-for-all broke out. Several outsiders were swept into the fray and suffered black eyes and bruises, and one student needed stitches. The chief culprits were arrested the next day, and Stanford President David Starr Jordan promised that any student positively identified as taking part in the fracas "would be dropped from the campus." One man was later put on trial, but a jury returned a "not guilty" finding.

E.F. Weisshaar, elected marshal in 1906, served as poundmaster, sanitary inspector and tax collector as well as policeman. When he put a list of delinquent taxpayers in the newspaper, attorney Joseph Hutchinson, a former town trustee, sued on grounds that the listing was libelous. The practice promptly stopped.

In 1907 the marshal and other city officers moved into a "temporary" city hall in the 400 block of Ramona Street, pending erection of permanent quarters later at University and Waverley, which were never built. Fifteen years later, in 1922, a second story was added to the facility on Ramona.

Creating a Public Safety Board

Despite the threat that a proposed charter might eliminate the marshal's office, four men sought the post in 1908, with incumbent Weisshaar running far ahead of ex-Marshal Ramsay. Early in 1909, the charter was voted in. It created a Board of Public Safety, which selected the night watchman, Joseph Mathison, as Palo Alto's first chief of police. The first policeman assigned to assist Mathison, Chester F. Noble, was elevated to chief in 1911.

The charter substituted the Police Court for the Recorder's Court, whose judges had almost all had brief terms except for Monroe H. Thomas (1904-09). Thomas was police judge from 1911-15, and then yielded to Egerton D. Lakin, the first of two attorneys who did long stints in the part-time office. Lakin, founder of the firm now called Lakin-Spears, ran the court from 1915 to 1929 while doubling as a city councilman and volunteer Chamber of Commerce secretary.

John E. Springer was next, presiding from 1929 to 1948. Springer, an extra large man, usually did not sit on the high bench, preferring a place at the counsel table. He was widely known for a sign displayed to alleged traffic offenders. It said:

THINGS WE KNOW WITHOUT BEING TOLD:
 1. *You were not going that fast.*
 2. *You are a careful driver.*

3. The cop did not pace you.
4. The fast ones got away.
5. You favor law enforcement, but...
(So tell us again. We love it.)

As that sign suggested, heavier vehicular traffic and improved roads had changed Palo Alto's police problems. Indeed, that traced back to 1911 when Noble became chief. The town was no longer so isolated, and automobiles were reported "going at least 30 miles per hour on city streets." Such speed violated regulations stemming from the charter saying no vehicle was to exceed one mile in six minutes, or 10 mph. One Saturday in 1913 Noble used his personal car to catch a speeding motorcyclist — a student doing 30 mph on Waverley Street — and then nabbed a speeding driver on Lytton Avenue.

Three years later parent groups voiced concern about children obtaining cigarettes. Noble concluded an investigation by arresting Kohachi Sato at his grocery store at 733 Ramona Street just after he sold a quantity of cigarettes to a 17-year-old youth.

Even with the rapid World War I buildup of Camp Fremont in Menlo Park (where military police were among the troops trained), Palo Alto experienced only a few minor rumbles involving the doughboys. In 1918 several women's organizations prompted Mayor C.P. Cooley to name a committee to consider appointing a police matron. As a result, on May 7, 1918, Nellie F. Goodspeed was appointed matron with orders to look after the welfare of young girls in the community and pay particular attention to "strangers" arriving in town. At year's end, with the war over and Camp Fremont due to close, the Board of Public Safety decided the police no longer needed a matron. Mrs. Goodspeed resumed her post with the Travelers' Aid Society.

By 1922, police officers began to use automobiles occasionally to patrol streets and chase speeders. But they had to borrow cars from other city departments, and often none was available, so the nine officers continued to patrol on bicycle or foot. Until that time, there had been no formal reports or recordkeeping. Chief Noble studied the system of renowned Berkeley Chief August Vollmer and installed one like it. In 1922, he informed the public safety board, 2,101 reports were filed and 503 arrests made, including two for burglary, six for embezzlement, five for cigarette sales to minors, two for vulgar speech and 230 for speeding or illegal parking.

Around-the-clock police service began in Palo Alto on September 1, 1923. It required the addition of a night desk officer. Residents could contact the police at any hour by telephoning "Palo Alto 8."

Officers still wore no uniform — only a badge on the shirt or coat. Then a Redwood City policeman stopped a speeder on El Camino Real and got beaten up because the speeder took him for a bandit. That triggered a move toward uniforms. Chief Noble told the council he favored them, if two officers could work in plain clothes. As 1923 ended, four Palo Alto officers began wearing uniforms.

The Police Department Upheaval of 1924

In 1924, a citizens' committee aimed 25 charges at Chief Noble and sought his removal. One allegation was that he had skimmed money from police bicycle auctions and used the cash for personal purposes. Noble, who kept the accounts in his head, denied the accusations leveled against him and branded them the nefarious work of the Ku Klux Klan.

The Board of Public Safety investigated the charges and initially exonerated the chief, who then resigned. But after Mayor A.M. Cathcart gave the board a stinging public scolding for disregarding clear evidence, the board rescinded Noble's resignation and dismissed him for insubordination. The City Council split 6-5 against a motion expressing confidence in the public safety board, with Councilwoman Josephine Duveneck forcing the roll-call vote. The board soon resigned, as did most of the police force.

When accused of using the bicycle funds, Noble had handed over $308 to the city attorney.

*Howard Zink was Palo Alto's police chief
from 1924 to 1952.*

After his removal as chief, Noble was cleared of criminal charges, sued to get the $308 back, and won.

Howard Zink Takes Command

Howard A. Zink, a college graduate who had joined the force in 1922, replaced Noble as police chief and served with distinction for 28 years. He began by winning approval for stepping up patrols, expanding the force from 9 to 12 men, buying two cars for police use only and raising officers' salaries to $150 a month. The new Board of Public Safety agreed, and also proposed hiring a woman welfare officer to deal with troubled women and youths. Miss Rilla Wycoff became the pioneer welfare officer.

Zink also tangled with the Klan, but fought and won against accusations like those made against his predecessor. He upgraded the Police Department by setting up the first training courses and fitness standards for officers, bringing in new equipment and tightening traffic controls. In October 1924, the new official police uniform made its debut: a wool navy blue coat and matching pants with sky blue trim. The city provided sterling silver badges, but the officers had to purchase their own uniforms, .38 caliber revolvers and any other personal equipment. Officers whose uniforms were torn in the line of duty had to replace them at their own cost.

One request Zink made was denied. He had enthusiastically proposed adding one police dog for each officer "to double the size of the force." The public safety board turned him down, and dogs were not used by the department until 1982.

Wanted!

One more notorious "first" befell the Palo Alto police in 1924: a deadly shootout marking the arrival in town of dangerous professional criminals. Two officers stopped a car after midnight to check out two men who, as it turned out, had just burglarized the Sunshine Store on University Avenue. One suspect thrust a gun at one approaching officer, who had to raise his hands while the second burglar took his service revolver. Just then the second officer came up behind and used his service revolver to hit the gunman on the head. The man turned and fired, but missed; the officer shot him in the chest, inflicting a fatal wound. Running, the disarmed officer was shot in the leg by the second burglar, who then exchanged wild shots with the other officer and at length escaped. The dead burglar later was identified as a Kansas felon wanted for a parole violation.

Chief Zink expanded the use of fingerprinting and photography, and instituted training on the penal code, city ordinances, criminal investigation, target practice, jujitsu, collection of evidence and

Members of Palo Alto's Police Department pose in back of their headquarters in 1938.

first aid. With Mayfield added to the policed area, the department needed to communicate quickly over greater distances. A searchlight installed atop City Hall was used to signal officers in Mayfield to call in; red lights and buzzers mounted on downtown buildings alerted patrolmen on that beat. Not until the advent of portable radios in the 1960s were these signals fully outmoded.

Palo Alto's "Fire Laddies"

Although pleas for municipal help in fighting fires began a few months after incorporation, it took two total-loss fires in 1895 to get Palo Alto Volunteer Fire Company No. 1 organized and equipped.

In petitions to the Board of Trustees, a dozen signers in July 1894 and 24 businessmen a year later (after a house burned down) offered to organize a volunteer fire company if the town would buy apparatus and supply water. Delayed in acquiring the waterworks, the trustees buried the petitions, despite editors' jibes urging them to

act even if they had to sell the street scraper to pay the cost.

On December 14, 1895, two buildings at 210-216 University Avenue burned to the ground. Dr. F.H. Moss, a surgeon who lost his upstairs offices, took the lead in forming a fire association. It started three days later at a large and enthusiastic meeting. On December 20, 25 members signed its constitution and bylaws and paid initiation fees and first-month dues. Longtime civic leaders among the charter members were C.J. Brown, J.F. Parkinson, E.C. Thoits and J.E. Vandervoort. The next night the company petitioned the trustees asking for apparatus and a place to keep it.

The trustees responded on January 4, 1896, authorizing purchase of the apparatus. The *Times* said Joseph Hutchinson, the board chairman, personally guaranteed payment of the $350 cost. As for a place to put it, Southern Pacific had completed a new train station and donated the old structure, provided the town would move it and

PALO ALTO HISTORICAL ASSOCIATION

An early Mayfield fire wagon.

PALO ALTO HISTORICAL ASSOCIATION

Human-powered hose cart races by Mayfield volunteer firemen were a popular entertainment in the late 1890s.

clear the land. M.P. Madison won a $45 contract to move the building to 441 High Street, a lot the town rented for $1 a month. The volunteers first met in the "Truck House" on February 6, 1896. In March they ordered a 131-pound bell, and raised $24.89 to buy it.

While an out-of-town vendor cast the bell,

local blacksmith C.E. Gilcrest fabricated the first two hose carts in the summer of '97 for $163 each. That set the stage for competition by two hose teams that raced to the Truck House when the fire bell rang. The first team ready to haul its cart to a fire won a $2 reward while the rival squad got $1. Before long, intercity hose races became featured

233

Fourth of July events.

By December 1898, the inventory read one hook and ladder rig (horse-drawn), two hose wagons, 1,500 feet of hose and three small houses, one a 20 by 30 clubhouse built by the volunteers — total value $2,341.28. There had been four alarms in the past year with a loss of $1,300, which might have been $9,100 but for the "fire laddies," as the paper called them. Proud as they were of their work, they were not without critics. In April 1898, the *Times* commented:

> *In Sunday night's fire the so-called Palo Alto Fire Department succeeded in saving the most valuable part of the property — they saved the lot. Of course, the house burned*

up, but then a house will burn and a fire in a small town affords a recreation that goes a long way toward dispelling the ennui incidental to living in a village.

A few years later, the volunteers refuted those aspersions in action. They doused a fire in the second-story darkroom of Professor R.A. Swain's home at 454 Hamilton Avenue, saving a future mayor's house.

Gaining Official Status

In 1903, the company moved to 167 Hamilton Avenue. Then in 1907 headquarters occupied City Hall on Ramona between University and Lytton, with apparatus cached in five places around town

Would-be firemen sit proudly in a shiny Seagrave fire engine, pride of the Palo Alto department.

until 1912. In that year the department's first motor-propelled vehicle reached town at 4 p.m. after a drive from Oakland that began at 9 a.m. The combined chemical and hose wagon, one of the first bought by a West Coast town from the specialized Seagrave Co. of Columbus, Ohio, cost $5,450.

Several fires in the first quarter-century stood out in residents' memories. In October 1915, flames consumed the uninsured J.F. Parkinson lumber yard and planing mill — a $25,000 loss. Two months later the Ernest Wilson candy factory on High Street burned, a total loss except to kids who salvaged some scorched chocolate and gum. Another fire destroyed a threshing machine and field of grain in what is now Crescent Park. Lost in the Brackey barn fire at Hawthorne Avenue and Cowper Street were buggies, an automobile, a quantity of hay and two fine horses practiced in drawing ambulances.

In 1920, the volunteers reorganized, reducing their active list to 30 men who would be paid for monthly drills plus $1 to $2.50 each per fire. The City Council recognized them as the city's official fire department, led by a paid chief. Two years later the first modern pumper was acquired, and in 1924 the department was put under the Board of Public Safety. Soon after that the firemen took sharp issue with a proposal to move them out of City Hall and into a temporary shack; they insisted they'd been promised a permanent place since 1907. C.H. Jordan, their spokesman, said:

The Palo Alto fire department is saving the city of Palo Alto from $12,000 to $15,000 a year by giving fire protection equal to any city of this size in the state. We feel that for what we are doing for the city and public safety, some consideration should be given us in return.

Mayfield also had had a volunteer fire department. The annexation of Mayfield in 1925 added a second Palo Alto station, and in 1927, the city bought a second pumper and a city service truck.

In September 1926, the Masonic Temple interior burned. November 1927 was a bad month: On November 6, Mullen's Hall burned; the next day, fire razed the De Luxe Dance Hall. But a new era was about to begin.

New Headquarters

The City Hall on Ramona Street was becoming overcrowded, and the jail built behind it in 1916 was small, poorly vented and dangerous. After a study, officials decided to build a new police and fire building on city property facing Bryant Street, at the rear of the City Hall. Voters approved a $74,000 bond issue early in 1927 and by that December both forces occupied their new headquarters at 450 Bryant. It housed the police department, jail and fire trucks on the first floor, and the fire department offices and dormitory, the police squad room and the police court upstairs. A small pistol range and storage space were in the basement. This facility, much admired when built, and still in use as the Senior Center, served the fire command until 1966 and the police until 1970.

Volunteers had done the firefighting from the start, although from 1912 on one driver was paid, and in the 1920s the chief and a few others became salaried. Once in the new headquarters, however, full-time firemen bore the brunt of service, so volunteers, though still enrolled as callmen, gradually had less and less to do. The 1929 muster was 11 full-time firemen, led by Chief William Clemo, and 38 volunteers. About ten years later, it stood 14 paid, 18 volunteer.

At the department's 50th anniversary dinner early in 1946, there were other big blazes to recall. Eight buildings on The Circle had gone up in flames in March 1932; in 1936, Thoits Shoe Store on University Avenue burned.

The "War Against Speed"

As the 1920s' boom years gave way to slow growth in the Depression-gripped 1930s, the Board of Public Safety ordered a rigorous traffic safety campaign. With Judge Springer's cooperation, this "war against speed" made Palo Alto known as a city where speeding would not be tolerated, especially after Bayshore Highway reached University Avenue in 1932.

New stop signs roused protests by residents and merchants, and the City Council voted to remove many signs. Accidents again increased, and debate over what to do raged until a *Palo Alto Times* poll showed 804 for strict traffic enforcement and 60 against.

Recognizing hard economic times, the judge gave minor traffic offenders the choice of a fine and license suspension or execution of small jobs for the city. Men became skilled wood choppers; women sewed at the community center or the transients' hostel.

A Respite for Transients

Jobless transients appeared in town in growing numbers, sleeping under trees near San Francisquito Creek and seeking handouts on downtown streets. The beggar problem and the pathetic death of an old itinerant from spider bites drove citizens into action. With full public support, the police

department took over an abandoned factory and converted it to The Shelter, a dormitory for transients. Captain and Mrs. J.W. Glover played leading roles in setting up the bunkhouse housing 60 men at a time but didn't want to handle the money, so Chief Zink did that, and the place was nicknamed "Hotel de Zink." Each man was given free meals and a bed in return for work for the city. As "roadsters" were directed to the hostel, panhandling dwindled. Between 75 and 125 vagrants were fed each day. A man could stay three days and three nights, but then had to move on. After the times grew better and the hostel closed, the police provided this service directly. Many a vagabond accepted "bed and breakfast" in the jail in return for one hour's work cleaning the police station.

Modern Methods

When Allene Thorpe Lamson was found lying in a bathtub at her Stanford campus home on Memorial Day, 1933, dead of a skull fracture, Chief Zink and Officer John Gilkey were the first lawmen to

Haircuts were provided to vagrants during their limited stay at The Shelter, nicknamed "Hotel de Zink."

reach the scene. Two women who had come to visit had been greeted at the door by the victim's husband, David A. Lamson, distraught and clad in bloody clothing. Zink took steps to preserve the crime scene, ordering friends of Mrs. Lamson to stop cleaning up spattered blood. He questioned Lamson, sales agent for the Stanford University Press, allegedly obtaining incriminating statements before the Stanford police chief and county undersheriff arrived. A length of pipe was found in a fire in the garden. The undersheriff arrested Lamson — who attributed the bludgeoning to intruders (although his defense later claimed it was a bathtub accident) — for first-degree murder. Zink summoned a lieutenant to photograph the crime scene.

Although the crime had occurred outside his jurisdiction, Zink gave expert testimony at the trial. Lamson was convicted and sentenced to hang, but after 13 months on San Quentin's Death Row won a new trial. The second trial ended in a jury deadlock, as did a third. A fourth trial was ordered in 1936, but the district attorney moved for dismissal on grounds that it would be impossible to get a unanimous jury verdict.

Lamson went free. His trials, through intense newspaper publicity, had focused national attention on the community, Chief Zink and modern police photography and evidence collection.

In 1934, the Palo Alto police became one of only a few forces in the nation with an operating police radio setup. The one-way, headquarters-to-field system was built under the direction of Stanford electrical engineering Professor Frederick Terman. Large radio receivers, taking up most of a patrol car's back seat, also were mounted in Stanford, Atherton and Redwood City police cars and in Palo Alto and Menlo Park fire chiefs' cars. Two-way radio communications began in 1939, and Palo Alto continued to handle radio traffic to and from 25 emergency vehicles of other jurisdictions.

Civil Defense

When news came of the Japanese attack on Pearl Harbor, the city immediately mobilized a civil defense organization set up previously. Chief Zink posted guards around reservoirs, the airport and other critical facilities. Sabotage or enemy attack was feared.

On December 8, 1941, the mayor's office asked for hand guns and for volunteers, promising training. Thus was born the Palo Alto Auxiliary Police, which at its wartime peak had 103 members. Two of the first volunteers, Marion Jewell and Milton Bevilockway, stayed active in the postwar police reserves until 1971.

Native-born U.S. citizens and resident aliens of Japanese descent were the subjects of police and FBI scrutiny. Several of their homes were raided. No "enemy agents" were arrested and only a handful of weapons or suspicious material was seized. When the Palo Alto area's 308 Japanese Americans were bused off to relocation centers in May 1942, their personal belongings smaller than cars and furniture were stored in the police station basement. Each marked item's owner received a receipt. Of the several thousand stored items, only one, a portable radio, was not reclaimed after the war.

Rebuilding in the Postwar Years

By 1945, with the home front stretched thin, the war had reduced the regular police force to 11 officers. Subsequent peacetime years brought rebuilding, reorganization and growth. In a 1947 report Zink noted that the department had only three men who had served steadily for more than six years. By 1948, however, personnel shortages had been overcome and the force was up to 32. In that year, on March 17, Zink fired five officers for taking candy from a store while on a stakeout near the Stanford Theatre.

World War II caused a big turnover in the Fire Department too. By 1947, Fire Chief Louis Ledford's crew numbered 23, full-time. A decade later, there were 56. Postwar firemen worked long hours for modest pay and ran up an enviable loss record: only 67 cents per capita as against the national average of $4. They ate well: In 1947, each

Palo Alto firefighters battle a blaze on Hamilton Avenue in 1950.

man contributed $4 a month for lunches and $1 for reading material and woodworking shop supplies. That year the Widows and Orphans Aid Association, active since 1930, drew more than 2,500 guests at $1 a ticket to its 17th annual Fireman's Ball in the high school boys gymnasium.

One last vestige of the old era faded out in 1948 when the audible fire alarm signals — a code known to many residents — were stilled. Mutual aid programs first adopted in 1951 linked Palo Alto and other departments in pacts aimed to negate perennial disputes about not venturing outside city limits.

Stretching to Form a Bar Association

The city had fewer than 20 practicing attorneys at the time the Palo Alto Area Bar Association was founded in 1934, so Stanford Law School professors were recruited to meet a requirement that a local bar association have at least 25 active members to be represented at the State Bar's Conference of Bar Association Delegates.

After operating through 1941, the association became inactive during World War II and for years thereafter. Activities were resumed in 1951. Both before and since then, many of the community's best known attorneys have served stints as president of the association. In the 1990s, with membership exceeding 400, the bar maintained an office and sponsored a nonprofit lawyer referral service.

The Surge of the '50s

As the great growth surge of the '50s built up, adoption of a new city charter eliminated the

Board of Public Safety and made new City Manager Jerry Keithley the boss of the police and fire chiefs. Very soon Keithley told the press, "Palo Alto has one of the five best police departments in the state." He praised its tough examinations, training course, high salaries and its chief.

The onset of the Korean War cost the force nine officers, setting back its traffic safety campaigns and pleas for more adequate roads. In 1952, Chief Zink retired and former Merced Police Chief William A. Hydie was hired. Hydie instituted daylight car patrolling, set up formal recruit training and sought to handle most juvenile problems using only local resources.

Establishing a Municipal Court

Californians voted in 1950 to adopt a court reorganization. Thus, the Palo Alto-Mountain View Municipal Court was born on January 5, 1953, replacing the police and justice courts. Its first jurist, former Mountain View Police Judge Alfred W. Bowen, sat both in Palo Alto and in Mountain View, where trial space was more adequate. When a second judge, Paul I. Myers Sr., was appointed in 1955, the two jurists rotated between the cities every six months.

Growth of the Palo Alto police force cramped its Bryant Street quarters. After a new City Hall at Embarcadero and Newell roads opened in 1953, the idea of building a police station and jail nearby was aired — and the neighborhood shouted it down. A few years later a proposal of a North County Courthouse offered a more integrated solution, with a jail near the courtrooms, but it had to go through a long "not in my backyard" outcry before a site at 270 Grant Avenue in the California Avenue district was selected. In May 1962, the new justice center opened with branch Superior Court facilities, the Palo Alto-Mountain View Municipal Court (at last centralized) and a jail holding up to 50 prisoners. Stanley R. Evans had just taken office as the third Municipal Court jurist; Bowen and Myers, whose rapport was minimal, soon made Evans the presiding judge.

Late in 1963 Evans was elevated to the Superior

Federal Judge Robert F. Peckham, left, swears in Judge William A. Ingram in 1956.

Court and Sidney Feinberg appointed to his place on the lower court. A fourth judgeship created by the Legislature was filled in 1968 by John M. Brenner. Others who served subsequently on the Municipal Court were Edward C. Scoyen, sworn in 1965 (replacing Bowen); William A. Ingram, 1969; J. Barton Phelps, 1970; James B. O'Grady, 1971; Timothy J. Hanifin, 1972; and Elva B. Soper, 1976.

The Municipal Court became known as one of the best, if not the best, in the state, and many of its jurists won renown in higher office. Feinberg stepped up to the Superior Court in 1975 and the State Court of Appeal in 1977. Ingram, who in 1957 was the first deputy district attorney assigned permanently to the north county, became a Superior Court judge in 1971 and a United States District Court judge in 1976. Both Brenner (1969) and Phelps (1972) were appointed to the Superior Court, and Brenner liked trial work there so well he declined elevation to the appellate bench. After retiring, Phelps became widely known as a "rent-a-judge" handling complex private litigation such as a major Advanced Micro Devices-Intel case.

The distinction of the crop of Municipal Court judges from the Palo Alto area matched that of earlier jurists from the city. Among them were Byrl R. Salsman, who left the Legislature for a Superior Court seat in 1949 and moved on to the Court of Appeal in 1961; Leonard Avilla, district attorney for 18 months before being named to the Superior Court in 1947; Homer Thompson, appointed to the Superior Court in 1961; Robert F. Peckham, named to the Superior Court in 1959 and sworn in as a U.S. District Court judge — the first assigned to San Jose — in 1966; and James Ware, seated as a Superior Court judge in 1988 and as a U.S. District Court judge in 1990. Before attaining senior judge status, both Peckham and Ingram did stints as chief judge of the Northern District of California. The two were prime movers in the 1985 publication of a history of the San Jose Federal Court.

Consolidation Ends Separate Court

On July 1, 1979, the Board of Supervisors consolidated all of Santa Clara County's Municipal Courts into one huge judicial district, ending the separate Palo Alto-Mountain View court. After that, many of the expanding county corps of judges rotated through periods of service in the North County Courthouse.

Among the attorneys practicing or living in Palo Alto who mounted to the bench after the mid-1970s were James W. Stewart, appointed to the Municipal Court in 1979 and elected to the Superior Court in 1984; David Leahy, appointed to the Superior Court in 1977 along with Peter G. Stone, who had been city attorney for Palo Alto and then for San Jose; Frank B. Cliff, appointed to the Superior Court in 1978; LaDoris H. Cordell, appointed to the Municipal Court in 1982 and elected to the Superior Court in 1988; and Diane Northway, Palo Alto city attorney for most of the '80s, appointed a Superior Court judge in 1990.

A Time of Turmoil

In the 1960s the social problems spawned by rapid expansion during the 1950s came home to roost. The Palo Alto police found themselves dealing with vastly higher numbers of burglaries, including daylight attacks on homes. Rapes, robberies and auto thefts increased. Narcotics violations, rare in the past, jumped from three in 1963 and 12 the next year to more than 100 a year by the decade's end. Juvenile officers were sent to delinquency control training.

At the same time, law governing police work grew more complex. In 1965, Judge Scoyen dismissed a case against a man who had been stopped for a broken taillight and, in a warrantless car search, was found to possess stolen groceries, still frozen. From then on, police realized, new search and seizure rules prevailed.

War raging in Southeast Asia and civil rights struggles at home prompted police to tone down their military image and try to improve community relations through youth citizen training programs. Civil rights demonstrations and antiwar protests began in 1965 and mounted ominously in 1967 with weekend gatherings in Lytton Plaza at University and Emerson where crowds of 400 or more spilled over onto the streets. Militant organizers gradually stepped up their goading of police and disruption of the downtown area.

On the night of Richard Nixon's election as president in 1968, more than 1,000 persons marched in an "electoral wake." Three dozen officers assigned to crowd control could not clear University Avenue until reinforcements arrived. Property damage ran to $2,000; eight arrests were made. Demonstrators had come from all over the Bay Area. It was evident that lawmen on duty could be swamped by such tactics.

Next came a series of small-scale bombings of antiwar establishments. The arrest of eight neo-Nazis in Menlo Park early in 1969 halted the bombings.

A Palo Alto police reorganization included creation of a new community relations division. However, protests against the war in Vietnam grew more and more violent. Targeting war research work in Stanford Industrial Park, 400

Anti-war protests in the 1960s created confrontations between protesters and the police.

rioters brought Page Mill Road traffic to a stand-still in May 1969. They abandoned cars in the road, flattened commuters' tires, set fires, broke windows and took press photographers' film. With the situation out of control, 150 officers from Palo Alto and three other jurisdictions moved in and a melee resulted at Hanover Street. When it ended, 93 persons had been arrested, $20,000 damage done, and two dozen police canisters of tear gas used. When a second attempt to disrupt work in the industrial park was made a few days later, police were ready. They moved in early and dispersed the demonstrators.

More Rising Tensions

In a portent of better days to come, 110 police employees moved in March 1970 from the department's long overcrowded base to spacious new quarters in the Civic Center on Forest Avenue between Ramona and Bryant streets. But the trial by protest was still on.

On July 4, after a day-long rock concert at El Camino Park, militants moved to Lytton Plaza and attacked police trying to enforce a new sound control ordinance. Four officers were injured. A week later, police moved swiftly to hem in a crowd of 500, and made 263 arrests for refusal to disperse.

Two days later, screaming members of the White Panthers and Mid-Peninsula Free University disrupted a City Council meeting — the first one in Palo Alto ever halted by violence. Four persons were arrested and dozens ejected.

To break the rising tension, City Manager George Morgan named an advisory committee to study police procedures and recommend ways to better police-community relations. Exhaustion sent Police Chief Hydie to the hospital, and a few months later he decided to retire, ending an 18-year stint in which he guided tripling of the force and many innovations. As parting gestures, he initiated citizen "ride-alongs," reactivated downtown foot patrols and tested team policing.

Meanwhile the manager's advisory panel recommended turning the department into a conflict-resolving agency rather than one of confrontation, toning down symbols of authority and resolving disputes "at the table" in advance rather than in the streets.

James C. Zurcher, previously chief at Sierra Madre, near Pasadena, became the new chief early in 1971. He emphasized the team management approach, eliminated the motorcycle squad (a longtime hazard to officers) and sought good rapport with council members, merchants and residents.

Sit-ins and Searches

This forward progress stalled on April 9, 1971, Good Friday. A violent sit-in at the Stanford Medical Center caused hospital administrators to call police to remove the demonstrators, who had barricaded themselves indoors. Police battered down the doors and in the ensuing melee two officers were seriously hurt and eleven, along with six protesters, suffered cuts and bruises. Twenty-three rioters were arrested; $100,000 damage was done to the building.

After *The Stanford Daily* published photos of the clash, police who hoped to obtain more evidence secured a search warrant from Judge Phelps and searched the student newspaper's office, but found no more pertinent pictures.

Because a newspaper was the object, the search roused furious protests. James Wolpman, the *Daily's* counsel, called it "a wholesale violation of constitutional rights," and filed a federal lawsuit against Zurcher.

Judge Peckham ruled in favor of the *Daily*, but finally, in 1978, the United States Supreme Court agreed by a 5-to-3 vote with Zurcher's claim that the warranted search was "appropriate."

Although the police had previously had women welfare officers and matrons, not until 1971 was the first woman police officer, Lynda Pritchett, hired. She was assigned to the juvenile and missing persons sections of investigative services. In mid-1974, a class of four women joined the force as patrol officers.

Intensified efforts to nab drug dealers led to the tragic death of 27-year-old Officer Gene Clifton in 1971. He died weeks after being wounded in a shootout at a suspected methamphetamine laboratory — the first Palo Alto officer to lose his life in the line of duty. Two years earlier, Reserve Officer Lester Cole had been killed by a drunken driver while directing traffic at an Alma Street crash site.

Chief "Super-Pig"

Trying new tactics to combat police-taunting demonstrators, Chief Zurcher labeled himself "Super-Pig" in leaflets appealing for peace at a 1972 demonstration. Objections from the newly formed Peace Officers Association, whose leader called it unprofessional, prompted a less dramatic approach the next time, though Zurcher went on using leaflets with good effect. But in April 1972, marches between Palo Alto High School and Stanford University — with talk of "taking" El Camino Real — led to road blockage for three hours and 205 arrests.

Under pressure, the City Council named a six-person panel to assess police tactics during four April days of strife. The committee reported that it "could find no evidence of misconduct on the part of a Palo Alto police officer," but questioned the necessity for arrests. It added that sheriff's

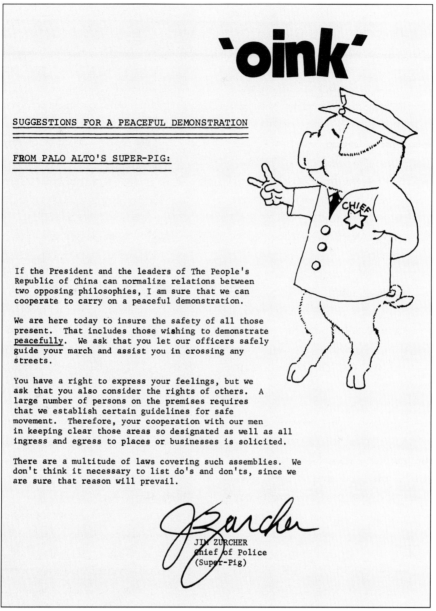

'oink'

SUGGESTIONS FOR A PEACEFUL DEMONSTRATION

FROM PALO ALTO'S SUPER-PIG:

If the President and the leaders of The People's
Republic of China can normalize relations between
two opposing philosophies, I am sure that we can
cooperate to carry on a peaceful demonstration.

We are here today to insure the safety of all those
present. That includes those wishing to demonstrate
peacefully. We ask that you let our officers safely
guide your march and assist you in crossing any
streets.

You have a right to express your feelings, but we
ask that you also consider the rights of others. A
large number of persons on the premises requires
that we establish certain guidelines for safe
movement. Therefore, your cooperation with our men
in keeping clear those areas so designated as well as all
ingress and egress to places or businesses is solicited.

There are a multitude of laws covering such assemblies. We
don't think it necessary to list do's and don'ts, since we
are sure that reason will prevail.

JIM ZURCHER
Chief of Police
(Super-Pig)

PALO ALTO HISTORICAL ASSOCIATION

Police Chief Jim Zurcher attempted to defuse possible confrontations with humor.

deputies had used excessive force in several instances. The demonstrators were told: Organize
better and maintain restraint. Then, with the Vietnam War winding down, a quiet summer on the
protest front ensued. Peace gradually settled in.

Starting in 1973, so many Palo Alto officers left
to head other jurisdictions in California and the
West that an ace police reporter labeled the city
the "cradle of police chiefs." Meanwhile, in addition to the first female patrol officers, the department was recruiting black, Hispanic and Asian
candidates. Before long, an emphasis on crime
prevention began to pay off in fewer burglaries
and higher homeowner awareness.

Prostitution in the form of massage parlors had
infested Palo Alto; by 1976 more than 20 such
places were operating. After trying various suppression methods to little avail, police and the

district attorney's office joined in applying an old red light district abatement law under which businesses allowing prostitution could be closed and their doors barred for a year. After a carefully planned crackdown, not one illicit massage parlor in Palo Alto ever reopened.

Police Neighborhood Watch Groups

Rebounding from a brief respite late in the 1970s, Palo Alto crime rose anew in the 1980s. Reduced police staffing in the wake of Proposition 13 had increased the public's vulnerability. In College Terrace, a sadistic rapist had made a series of attacks on single women for nine years. In 1979, complex surveillance and special investigative techniques were applied with no immediate result; they had been called off when, in 1980, a resident spotted and reported a prowler. A clever officer climbed a tree, waited and caught a suspect. Initial evidence was too scant to hold him, but weeks of intensive investigation led to an arrest, and a conviction followed.

Police derived the lesson that only if the entire community was involved could their work succeed. The council beefed up the budget for community crime prevention, and 37 neighborhood watch groups formed. Home burglaries dropped by more than one-third. Using police dogs at last, and employing computers and special software programs, police applied crime analyses to good effect.

At a crime prevention meeting in 1985, a citizen gave a possible clue to a community service officer. Within hours, it led to the arrest of a dangerous sex offender who had terrorized the Midtown area. By 1992, there were 400 neighborhood watch groups in the city, and nearly 100 volunteers were devoting many hours to police department tasks. A career criminal apprehension program was being applied to identify and isolate crime.

Christopher T. Durkin, up from the ranks, succeeded Zurcher as chief in August 1987. After Assistant Chief Bruce Cumming took the post of Menlo Park police chief in 1988, Captain Lynne

PENINSULA TIMES TRIBUNE/BOB ANDRES

Police officer Dave Hennessy puts his partner Alf through his training routine.

PALO ALTO WEEKLY/JOHN DUUS

A few police officers began pedaling beats in the late 1980s.

Ellen Johnson won promotion to assistant chief, the first woman to be Palo Alto's second in command.

An Ounce of Prevention...

Palo Alto's growth surge soon made itself felt by firefighters. By 1956, three Eichler Homes in Palo Alto and one Stern & Price house had been destroyed by fast-spreading fires. A group of Peninsula fire chiefs voted to act promptly to eliminate or minimize the cause of blazes in houses with wood-paneled interiors. Joseph Eichler immediately promised to use fire-retardant paint in his future models. Nevertheless, in 1957 Palo Alto adopted a pioneer fire hazard ordinance relating to private homes. It set flame-spread standards and banned use of highly combustible interior materials.

More than half the city's firefighters voted to join a union in 1958, and their struggle for official recognition took many turbulent months. Contract demands of what became Palo Alto Professional Firefighters Union Local 1319, such as merging with Mountain View and Los Altos fire forces, had some impact on city policy.

A minor fire on the 10th floor of Channing House in 1964 brought realization that an 85-foot aerial ladder rig acquired in 1955 was too short for upper-story rescues in high-rise buildings. So in 1974 the city bought a 100-foot Seagrave aerial ladder truck for $83,416. By Fire Chief William Korff's count, the city then had 40 high-rises.

Downtown Palo Alto's biggest fire did $500,000 damage to the 61-year-old Masonic Temple at Florence Street and University on January 29, 1971. Sixty firefighters with two ladder trucks and seven pumpers contained the stubborn fire in 90 minutes but had to spend seven hours to put it entirely out. Afterward, the Masons rebuilt the hall.

The mid-'70s brought several major changes. Palo Alto's first female firefighter was hired in 1974, though not until 1990 did station remodelings to create separate dormitory and locker room facilities begin. The annexation of Barron Park in 1975 wrote an end to its volunteer fire department; beside adding that territory, the Palo Alto Fire Department merged with Stanford University's private fire department in 1976.

New Paramedic Service

Most significantly, Palo Alto in the mid-1970s became the only city in northwest Santa Clara County to serve the public with fire department paramedics and transportation of emergency patients to a hospital. As of 1993, the paramedic function — enhanced by the provision since 1991 of a defibrillator to every engine company — accounted for a majority of the department's calls.

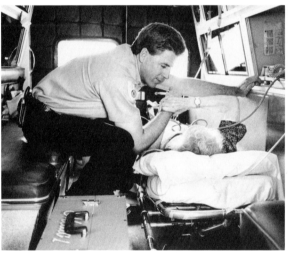

PALO ALTO WEEKLY/CAROLYN CLEBSCH

Palo Alto's Fire Department paramedics provide the community with emergency medical aid and hospital transportation.

Early in the 1980s a new fire threat emerged: potent, esoteric chemicals used in industrial high technology. Actually, it had been presaged in 1975 when a lithium explosion burned up $1 million in research at Lockheed's laboratory. To meet the new need, the fire department trained hazardous materials response teams clad in fully encapsulated suits to deal with toxic spills and fires. Off the emergency front, Palo Alto played a leading role in designing model Silicon Valley storage ordinances relating to toxic gases.

The spire of St. Thomas Aquinas Catholic Church rises amid the urban forest.

17

Keeping the Faith: Religious Life

"Overall, I think Palo Alto is a quiet, high middle class neighborhood that produces people who are aware and who seek balance. This city seems to have insight that material wealth is not the only way to live."
— *The Rev. Hiroshi Abiko, Resident Minister, Palo Alto Buddhist Temple*

"The demands on people's energies are endless, and one must deal with one's spiritual needs first. This offers liberation that comes when your life is in order."
— *The Rev. Dr. G. Clyde Dodder, Senior Minister, First Congregational Church*
Both quoted in the Palo Alto Weekly, *November 21, 1990*

In the beginning, residents of Mayfield and what was to become Palo Alto traveled to attend church — Catholics to Mission Santa Clara or St. Dennis Church at Searsville, Protestants to Cumberland Presbyterian in Mountain View or, to the north, Menlo Park Presbyterian or Holy Trinity Episcopal Church.

Soon they began to establish churches in their own towns. The earliest, built on donated land, were modest structures that proved movable, housing congregations that proved enduring.

In Mayfield, **St. Aloysius Catholic Church** was first; Jeremiah Clarke gave land on Page Mill Road west of El Camino Real in 1867 as a mission site. With funds collected by a priest, a simple frame structure with canvas windows, coal oil lamps, a bare wooden floor and seats for 148 was built and dedicated November 15, 1868, as Mayfield Catholic Church. After being under San Mateo Parish, then Menlo Park and after 1901, Mountain View, St. Aloysius became an independent parish in 1919. In 1920 the old church was moved to a College Avenue plot given by the Weisshaar family. A site at College Avenue and El Camino Real was acquired in 1923 but construc-

PALO ALTO HISTORICAL ASSOCIATION
Mayfield Catholic Church stood on Page Mill Road from 1867 until 1920. It was moved to College Avenue, then taken down in 1941 after today's St. Aloysius Church was built.

tion was delayed — the new church was not dedicated until 1940.

What is known today as **Wesley United Methodist Church** was dedicated as the New Mayfield Methodist Episcopal Church on August 10, 1873, at Sherman and Birch streets. William Paul gave the lot; the building cost $2,450. The Rev. W.W.

Thoburn, the pastor and an early Stanford faculty member, was instrumental in starting Protestant worship and the Methodist Church in Palo Alto.

In 1905, the renamed Methodist Episcopal Church of Mayfield occupied a new edifice at 459 College Avenue. More name changes ensued: to Mayfield Community Church (1924) and to College Avenue Methodist Church (1941). In 1959 a new sanctuary at 470 Cambridge Avenue was dedicated under the present name. The Rev. Amelia Chua succeeded the Rev. Kristin Sachen as pastor of the Tongan-American congregation in 1993.

Early Downtown Services

Settlers building homes in Palo Alto first rode to Mayfield or Menlo Park for services. Soon these pioneers — people well-versed in organizing churches — arranged open-air, all-faiths services in Palo Alto, and started a Union Sunday School

The Rev. Walter Hays preaches at the First Presbyterian Church, under construction in 1907 at Waverley and Forest.

The congregation of the First Presbyterian Church, which was at University and Waverley from 1896 until 1907.

and a Christian Endeavor Society. This ecumenical tinge persisted long after various denominations built their spiritual homes.

An excellent detailed description of the founding of Palo Alto churches during the city's first half-century appears in Guy Miller's *Palo Alto Community Book*. This chapter singles out examples of how early-day churches struggled to put down roots and grow.

After Lirio Hall was built, denominational services began there, gradually supplanting outdoor worship under oak trees near the lumber yard, with borrowed planks as seats. Episcopal Sunday morning services at Lirio began September 25, 1892, followed later that fall by Baptist evening worship and Methodist afternoon services.

Meanwhile, the Presbytery of San Jose adopted a plan for a Palo Alto church. Potential members endorsed it in November and bought a key lot on Hamilton Avenue between Bryant and Waverley streets for $1,150. Professor A.B. Clark drew plans and erection of a $2,600 sanctuary seating 200 began early in 1893.

In June, the Palo Alto Presbyterian Church (later renamed the **First Presbyterian Church of Palo Alto**) became the first to hold services in its own building downtown. But the site proved deficient — it was deemed "likely to be fringed on the west by barns, pigpens and henhouses." So the building was moved in 1896 to a $1,500 plot at University and Waverley, and became the young town's social center.

A decade later expansion prompted purchase of a new site farther from the heart of town, at Waverley and Forest. There a $37,000 structure was dedicated in 1908. After 50 more years of growth, First Presbyterian moved to its present home at Cowper and Lincoln.

In recent decades the congregation has been known for giving sanctuary to conscientious objectors during the Vietnam and Persian Gulf wars and to Central American refugees, and for helping found Lytton Gardens for seniors. Its historic Westminster House affords low-rent space for nonprofits such as Midpeninsula Citi-

zens for Fair Housing. Robert McAfee Brown, author and scholar of liberation theology, often preaches as an associate of the Rev. Diana Gibson, pastor since 1984.

All Saints' Episcopal Church became a mission in January 1893. A few months later, the priest-in-charge was informed that Timothy Hopkins had given $1,000 toward a site at Waverley and Hamilton. (Years later, Hopkins told an interviewer All Saints received the funds because his wife was an Episcopalian, whereas he had made an equal gift to the Presbyterian Church, his denomination.)

COURTESY OF ALL SAINTS' EPISCOPAL CHURCH

All Saints' Episcopal Church has been at Waverley and Hamilton since 1895. This church in the round replaced the original structure in 1968.

The mission struggled until the Rev. Robert Peet, former rector of a wealthy Newport, Rhode Island, parish, arrived in 1894. He solicited funds from friends "back East," enabling the doors of a simple, brown-shingle church to open in 1895. Still, it took until 1898 for All Saints to reach independent parish status under the Rev. D. Charles Gardner, later the first chaplain of Stanford Memorial Church.

As decades passed, the church added land and enlarged its buildings. All Saints had two rectors whose tenures spanned half a century: the Revs. David Evans (1910-25), founder of the Waverley Club, an ecumenical men's group that argued public issues, and Oscar F. Green (1925-61), who took a great interest in Stanford students.

After World War II, All Saints thought of moving south but ended staying downtown as the church longest in its original location. During the Rev. Richard Byfield's 1961-70 term, the parish converted to a new emphasis on the social gospel and replaced the old shingled structure with a radical concrete church in the round, dedicated in 1968. The Rev. James W. McLeod, rector from 1970 to 1993, invited La Comida to use the parish hall, which the senior luncheon group did for six years. All Saints gave space for the Palo Alto Child Care Center in 1974, and in 1976, in association with six other churches, became home to the Food Closet.

The **First United Methodist Church of Palo Alto** grew out of Dr. Thoburn's Lirio Hall services, and organized in January 1894 when 12 persons signed as intending to be members. Ultimately, the charter group grew to 24. In a leap of faith,

considering limited finances and numbers, the congregation initiated work on a $3,200 church at Hamilton and Webster, where corner lots had been given by Dr. Nelson J. Bird of San Francisco. The Presbyterians adjourned their own services to join in the dedication on February 2, 1896.

For years First Methodist was thought to be on the outer edge of town. At the time members decided to build, the pastor's wife recalled, there were no graded streets, no street lights, no sewer system, and "we waded through dust in summer and deeper mud in winter." But the town grew to meet the church, and by 1914 a new $36,000 edifice was built. More than 900 crowded its consecration.

Dr. R. Marvin Stuart, senior minister from 1942 to 1964, recorded increases in the size of the local congregation for 22 years before becoming bishop first in Denver and later San Francisco. In 1980,

PALO ALTO TIMES/KEN YIMM

The soaring First United Methodist Church, completed in 1963, occupies the site where two earlier sanctuaries stood. R. Marvin Stuart, above, its minister for 22 years, later became a bishop.

PALO ALTO HISTORICAL ASSOCIATION

252

Bishop Stuart retired to Palo Alto and became chaplain of Lytton Gardens.

Rapid expansion after World War II led to a $55,000 remodeling of the church in 1950 and a $300,000 expansion of the social-educational building in 1952. The city's largest congregation worshipped at the Varsity Theatre in 1961-63 during erection of a soaring new sanctuary seating 600. It was dedicated, free and clear, in 1989. The Rev. Douglas I. Norris, associate minister from 1969-74, has served as senior minister since 1983.

The **First Baptist Church of Palo Alto** had a colorful start. In 1891, the year Stanford University began classes, a small group of Baptists finished the day's work, ate dinner and "all went to the saloon" — a former Mayfield barroom they converted to a chapel where Mountain View's Baptist minister could preach. "We had one happy year there," wrote Mrs. Edward Loder, "then, the work being finished at Stanford, these families moved elsewhere, and the church disbanded."

On June 9, 1893, Baptists and other town folk thronged to the rail depot to see a "rolling tabernacle." After worship in Chapel Car Emmanuel, complete with pulpit, organ and seating for 140, nine charter members organized Emmanuel Baptist Church on June 18, 1893. The rail car rolled away, and for several years, halls provided locations for worship and members' homes sheltered prayer meetings.

In May 1897, the congregation changed its name to the First Baptist Church, and on July 15, 1900, laid the cornerstone of a new $7,000 church located at Bryant and Hamilton.

Late in 1943, a campaign to fund a new church at Bryant and California Avenue began. Sale of the old church in November 1945 added $45,000 toward the goal of $200,000. The colonial-style church was dedicated debt-free with ceremonies May 25-29, 1949. The Rev. Harold Bjornson served as pastor from 1967-81. Dr. Charles F. Syverson took the pulpit in 1989.

Four additional congregations — Unitarians, Disciples of Christ, Christian Scientists and Congregationalists — first took root in the 1895-98 period, but owing to hard economic times they were slow to build, and a Catholic church next thrust a new spire into the city skyline — **St. Thomas Aquinas Church**.

In March 1901, the Rev. Bernard J. McKinnon of Menlo Park gave Lenten lectures in Fraternal Hall. Soon a building known as the White House at Lytton and Ramona was remodeled for Sunday services attended by 100 persons, mostly of Irish descent. Their dream of building was abetted by a ladies' benefit fair that raised funds to buy property at Waverley and Homer for $1,500. On June 8, 1902, the new $12,000 church formally opened with Father McKinnon as pastor.

In 1909, Monsignor Joseph M. Gleason began a 19-year pastorate. A noted historian, he was renowned for his spirited views, and for joining with local Protestant clergy in ecumenical activities.

St. Thomas Aquinas and its handsome interior became known to movie-goers as a setting for the film *Harold and Maude*. It is the oldest original downtown Palo Alto church sanctuary still in use.

In 1987, the Catholic Community of Palo Alto and Stanford was united as St. Thomas Aquinas Parish with the Rev. Alexander C. Larkin as pastor and Newman director. The parish staff, serving five churches — St. Aloysius, the Newman Center (St. Ann Chapel), Our Lady of the Rosary and St. Albert the Great as well as St. Thomas — is headquartered at the parish office at 745 Waverley Street. In 1992, the Rev. Dennis Browne succeeded Father Larkin.

The **First Congregational Church of Palo Alto** began when 31 persons met in 1898 to organize "an ecclesiastical society." The Rev. Cyrus G. Baldwin, retired president of Pomona College, preached to the society and proposed building dormitories for Congregational students at Stanford and maintaining lectureships in Christian evidences and ethics. Mrs. Stanford, however, held firm in this and other cases to the founding intention "to prohibit sectarian instruction, but to have taught in the University the immortality of the soul, the existence of an all-wise and benevolent Creator, and that obedience to his laws is the highest duty of man." Finding no campus interest, the society dropped Baldwin's proposals relating to Stanford and, after being delayed by the panic of 1899, acted in 1900 to organize a Congregational church in Palo Alto. In March 1903 a building committee approved a report calling for investment of $15,500 in lots and an edifice at Waverley and Hamilton. Dedicated September 19, 1905, it seated 800, nearly twice what any other local church could hold. That capacity, and its handy location, made it the center for refugee relief after the 1906 earthquake — fulfilling the founders' vow to be of service to the community, a pledge made to allay fear that a new congregation might sap the vitality of the five existing Protestant churches.

World War I's drain on town and gown was felt keenly at First Congregational; in a 1920 crisis, leaders feared that they might have to merge with another local body. Then a member came to the rescue. The Rev. Rowland Dodge, Home Missionary Society secretary, offered to give the church any funds allocated to mission work at Stanford.

Soon after the Rev. G. Arthur Casaday began his 1947-1973 pastorate, the church adopted a bold Resolution on Church and Race calling for "a non-segregated church in a non-segregated society."

First Congregational foresaw the need to expand and in 1951 acquired a 4 1/2-acre site at 1985 Louis Road at Embarcadero. There its new sanctuary was dedicated in 1956. The half-century-old, ivy-clad, shingled church downtown was razed for a parking lot. Dr. G. Clyde Dodder has been senior minister since 1981.

The **First Christian Church (Disciples of Christ)** began when the church's state evangelist, the Rev. Robert L. McElhatton, launched a 26-member congregation as the Palo Alto Christian Church at Nortree Hall. On December 4, 1896, he baptized four women in the cold waters of San Francisquito Creek near *El Palo Alto*, recording them as "the first baptisms by our people between Santa Clara and San Francisco and. . . the first immersions by any church in the same territory."

In early 1898, the eloquent Rev. Melvin Putnam

conducted a six-week program of dramatic tent revival meetings. One Sunday morning a windstorm compelled folks to flatten the big top, but failed to daunt the ardent revivalist.

Seventy members incorporated the congregation in January 1901. In 1903 a small brick church at Lytton and Florence, built for $3,150, became the congregation's first real home. In 1918, First Christian bought the Playhouse at Channing and Bryant and remodeled it as the new $12,500 Memorial Christian Church, where dramatic protests of liquor license applications were staged.

Early in the Rev. Donald E. Poston's pastorate (1951-75) First Christian decided to move south. A new church on a 5-acre site at 2890 Middlefield Road was dedicated in 1955. The Rev. Steven D. Shepard has been the pastor since 1986.

The **Palo Alto Unitarian Church** can be traced from a newspaper item inviting "all Unitarians and all others interested in that phase of religious thought" to meet at Castilleja Hall. On January 12, 1896, a small group formed the Unity Society of Palo Alto. Nearly ten years later, at Jordan Hall, at the corner of University and Ramona, on November 12, 1905, a faithful few organized the Unitarian Church of Palo Alto. Stanford University President David Starr Jordan, who often filled the pulpit when there was no regular minister, led the list of charter members.

Plans for a church had been approved, but the drawings were destroyed in San Francisco by the fire following the 1906 earthquake. Undaunted, the Unitarians built in 1907 at Cowper and Channing to a design by noted architect Bernard Maybeck.

In 1926-27, the Rev. Leila Thompson served as the first ordained woman to fill a Palo Alto pastorate. But hard times struck, and membership, always rather small, dwindled until in May 1928 the church announced "last services until next fall." The doors never reopened.

In a "second beginning," 47 persons met in 1947 at the Lucie Stern Community Center at the call of Professor Alfred S. Niles and others. They reorganized as the Palo Alto Unitarian Society, meeting at the Woman's Clubhouse and the

1. Christian Science   2. Presbyterian   3. Baptist   4. Congregational   5. Catholic
6. Methodist Episcopal   7. Protestant Episcopal   8. Truth Center   9. Christian   10. Unitarian

PALO ALTO TIMES/FRANK DAVEY

Collage prepared in 1920 shows downtown churches.

Community Center.

In 1949, the Rev. F. Danford Lion began a 26-year pastorate. Worship remained at the Community Center until 1959, when buildings at 505 East Charleston Road were dedicated. The 5-acre site had been bought for $30,000 in 1958; the facility cost $90,000 to build. A unique feature of the grounds is a bridge across Adobe Creek from the church to Adlai Stevenson House, a residence for senior citizens, which the church helped to found. Dr. Kenneth Collier, the present minister, arrived in 1991.

The **First Church of Christ, Scientist, Palo Alto**, began in 1897. Mrs. A.M. Hague and Mrs. Mary A. Kimball instituted the first regular services at the Kimball home, where worshippers met for two years. On May 15, 1899, the First Church was formally organized.

For the next 17 years, meetings were held in a variety of public gathering places. In 1911, the congregation bought a site at the corner of Bryant and Forest. Still, seven moves had occurred before services could at last be held in the church's own building at 661 Bryant Street on December 17, 1916, with the 500-seat auditorium more than filled. By March 25, 1917, the $20,000 building — fully paid for — was dedicated at two services attended by 2,100 Peninsulans.

From the beginning, the congregation has kept up a reading room, usually in the business district, currently at 542 Ramona Street. In the 1920s, the Stanford Christian Science Organization was founded to serve students.

Stanford Memorial Church is not in Palo Alto, but its existence and university policies as to sectarian services have influenced local church development. Senator Stanford said in 1887, "The Church is to be regularly used for the benefit of the students. No creed or dogma will be permitted to be taught within its walls, but ministers of all denominations will be invited to deliver lectures on the fundamental principles of religions."

Memorial Church was completed in 1902 and worship began in 1903 (a Chapel Union had arranged services until then). The 1906 earthquake did massive damage to the church; reconstruction took until 1913. Thus in the university's early years Memorial Church was often unavailable, and students hungry for familiar worship forms sought out agreeable places in Palo Alto, Mayfield or Menlo Park. Many faculty families, whether living on campus or off, also found community church homes.

The 1989 earthquake again severely damaged Memorial Church; it was closed almost three years during a $10 million reconstruction.

Only nonsectarian Protestant services were allowed at Stanford for many years; not until the 1960s did relaxed rules allow churches to have student centers on campus. Because of this, denominations seeking to serve students used bases in Palo Alto for many decades, and some churches chose sites near the campus perimeter.

In Search of a Home

Other religious groups from roughly 1910 to 1925 navigated courses similar to that of the Christian Scientists. They tended to be culturally isolated as ethnic minorities or as believers in a faith with few local adherents. Some rented space or met in homes for decades before they could manage to build. More than a few groups endured slow maturation, yet thrive today as major congregations.

Christian students from Japan attending Stanford University and a few local residents attended the first meetings in 1909 of what became the Palo Alto Japanese Methodist Church — now **Aldersgate United Methodist Church**. In 1911, the mission received a charter and organized with nine members. Served by part-time pastors, it occupied an 827 Ramona Street boarding house basement and, later, houses nearby. In 1931 it moved to a building at 472 Sheridan Avenue that doubled as a neighborhood center and Japanese language school.

In 1935, the church paid $1,200 for an old house and lot at 306 Page Mill Road. Japanese-American members raised $6,000 of a $10,000 building campaign goal; contributions of $2,500 from the Palo Alto community and $1,500 from a Methodist board closed the gap. The new church was dedicated in March 1940 as Page Mill Methodist Church.

Two years later the congregation was ordered away to World War II relocation centers. When members began to return in May 1944 from Heart Mountain, Wyoming, worship resumed.

Later, construction of Page Mill Expressway cut off parking, and in 1963 the congregation bought a 3-acre site at 4243 Manuela Avenue, where a new church was built and dedicated in 1965. At that time it took its present name, Aldersgate, after the street in London where John Wesley received the Holy Spirit. The Rev. Maryellen Sawada conducts separate Sunday services in Japanese and English.

The **Palo Alto Buddhist Temple** began in the spring of 1914. Bishop Koyu Uchida met with about 10 Palo Alto area *issei* (first-generation settlers) at Alta Mesa Memorial Park for a Hanami Bosan Kai (flower viewing), the now-traditional Memorial Day service. After the Palo Alto Buddhist Temple was founded, the bishop commuted from San Francisco to lead monthly services in homes. As membership grew, weekly services were conducted at the Kaneda Home Laundry on Emerson Street. In 1927, the temple purchased a Ramona Street house.

War with Japan caused the evacuation of the temple members from the West Coast in 1942. Despite strong bonds with other Palo Altans, the Japanese community feared that its organizations might be deemed subversive. The temple burned letters, documents and records, and stored its sacred articles in San Francisco.

After returning from relocation centers, most of the Japanese-Americans were penniless, but members of the Palo Alto Fair Play Council, the Society of Friends and former employers offered them assistance. In 1946, Methodists and Buddhists joined in a memorial service at Alta Mesa for members who died in the war years.

In 1951, several Buddhists acquired a site at 2751 Louis Road. The temple was incorporated in 1953 and took over the site, and on December 4, 1954, its new building was dedicated. The Rev.

PALO ALTO TIMES/JOE MELENA

The Rev. Keisho Maloyama stands in front of the altar of the Palo Alto Buddhist Temple in 1974.

Hiroshi Abiko has been the resident minister since 1983. Since 1951, temple members have put on an annual Obon Festival that draws large crowds.

The **University African Methodist Episcopal Zion Church** began in wartime 1918. Early services were in Fraternal Hall. In late 1923, the 22 members began planning to build on a lot they owned on Ramona near Homer Avenue — the first black church between San Mateo and San Jose. The 200-seat, $6,000 structure was dedicated April 5, 1925.

The Depression brought on a threat of the mortgage being foreclosed. A strong appeal in Dallas Wood's *Palo Alto Times* column sparked efforts that, over several years, relieved the debt burden.

Post-World War II growth prompted the AME Zion Church to buy a larger site at 3549 Middlefield Road in 1966 and build anew. Sale of the old church to the Palo Alto Medical Clinic financed the move.

Palo Alto's **First Lutheran Church** began as a Swedish Lutheran church called the Evangelical Lutheran Bethlehem Church. It was formally organized by 41 charter members on August 20, 1920, in Memorial Christian Church. Mission work by the California Conference of the Augustana Synod had paved the way.

C.B. Swanson, a theological student, preached in Swedish on Sunday afternoon. In mid-1922, the first official pastor arrived, and two years later a quarter of the $12,000 sought for a church building was in hand. Services presented alternately in Swedish and English were at the Christian Church, then in 1925 moved to the Masonic Hall.

In January 1926, the congregation changed its name to the First Evangelical Lutheran Church of Palo Alto, and laid the cornerstone of a sanctuary at Homer and Webster. Dedicated December 12, 1926, the church at 600 Homer Avenue remains in use after remodeling in 1991.

In the Rev. Theodore E. Johnstone's time as pastor (1951-67), First Lutheran built its educational wing and reached its membership peak. The Rev. P. Kempton Segerhammer, pastor since 1988, has said that First Lutheran seeks to contribute to the wider community, and that he sees an upsurge of spiritual interest in the younger generation.

Today's **Palo Alto Seventh-day Adventist Church** began in 1921 when a group of 15 persons organized a branch Sabbath School of the Mountain View Adventist Church in Palo Alto. They met on Saturday afternoons in Ostrander Hall and later in the Woman's Clubhouse and the Native Sons Hall. Two years later Elder M.C. Wilcon helped reorganize the school into a church. Its $8,700 building was erected in 1923 at 786 Channing Avenue at Guinda, and dedicated debt-free. Leslie G. Wallace helped to found the church and, when no ordained minister was on call, ran it as a lay preacher until about 1945. The Rev.

Loren G. Seibold has been the pastor since 1986.

Trinity Lutheran Church can claim a remarkable continuity: Since 1925 it has had essentially only two pastors and one sanctuary, although the building has stood in two places.

English Lutherans organized at the Woman's Clubhouse on May 10, 1925. In December of that year, the Rev. Paul H.D. Lang arrived to begin his 40-year ministry. In 1928, Trinity Lutheran broke ground at Hamilton Avenue and Byron Street for its sanctuary.

Starting in 1944, Lang led the faculty for Palo Alto's four-year experiment with "released time" from public schools for religious education, then permitted under state law but later declared illegal.

Trinity Lutheran acquired an eight-lot site at University Avenue and Middlefield Road in 1948. However, the congregation opted for another location, at 1295 Middlefield, across Melville Ave-

PALO ALTO TIMES/GENE TUPPER

Trinity Lutheran Church rolls slowly on a day-long trip in August 1953 to its new site at Melville and Middlefield.

nue from the Lucie Stern Community Center. As the 100-ton edifice was being moved there during the summer of 1953, dollies on which it was rolling broke, tying up Middlefield Road traffic for 24 hours.

The Rev. Martin R. Taddey became pastor in 1965, and like his predecessor, has had a lengthy tenure. Trinity Lutheran Church is affiliated with the Lutheran Missouri Synod.

The Church of Jesus Christ of the Latter-day Saints has grown in Palo Alto like the biblical tribe of Abraham since the first Mormon settlers, John and Josephine McHale, came in 1904. Initially, growth was slow. Not until 1919 did a dozen people form a mission branch of the San Jose LDS branch. They met in homes, and later in Ostrander's Hall, then in Masonic Hall. They became an independent branch in 1923. In 1931 a chapel at 771 Addison Avenue was dedicated. In 1935, Arthur V. Thulin became the first LDS bishop in Palo Alto.

Reorganization in 1946 created the Palo Alto Stake. Its 1,200 members so crowded the church facilities that a $100,000 building program was undertaken at the Addison-Guinda site to provide a new chapel, social hall, Scout room and classrooms. Meanwhile, some Sunday School classes met at Miss Harker's School.

The LDS chapel at 865 Stanford Avenue was dedicated in 1965, and the chapel at Middlefield and Charleston in 1978. The latter has an open gymnasium and multipurpose room arrangement with a stage that faces two ways, facilitating an emphasis on activities for youths.

As of 1992, six wards of the Menlo Park California Stake (renamed in 1974) consisted wholly or partly of Palo Alto residents.

In one early local religious body, the **Palo Alto Friends Meeting**, more than half a century elapsed between initial gatherings in 1900 and erection of a permanent meeting house. The Society of Friends of Palo Alto began as an offshoot of the San Jose College Park Meeting. The Palo Alto Friends Meeting became an independent entity in 1928. A site at 957 Colorado Avenue was purchased in 1951, and largely through the labor and efforts

of 50 members a meeting house built there was dedicated May 5, 1952. A new meeting house farther back on the property was finished in 1980.

One founder, Professor Augustus Murray, served as clerk for 39 years. At the invitation of President Herbert Hoover, a Quaker, Murray became founder and clerk of the Friends Meeting House on Florida Avenue in Washington, D.C., which Hoover often attended.

Josephine Duveneck, who with her husband Frank owned Hidden Villa Ranch in Los Altos and who co-founded the San Francisco office of the American Friends Service Committee, was a member of the Palo Alto Friends Meeting for about 40 years.

Although two **Assemblies of God** once held services in Palo Alto, neither survives. One started in 1925 over a store at 445 High Street. In 1934 the Rev. Robert Ray became its first ordained pastor, and the congregation bought the old Unitarian Church building at 855 Cowper Street and renamed it Glad Tidings Tabernacle. In the early 1950s one congregation planned to develop a site at Loma Verde Avenue and Middlefield, but instead sold the land and moved to Cupertino.

A custom of that church — using buses — also showed up in an Assembly that grew from a revival meeting at 2846 Middlefield Road, Gospel Lighthouse Church. This congregation bought a 2 1/2-acre plot at 525 San Antonio Road and in 1953 built the Christian Life Center. In 1991 the church closed but the operation remained as a large day care center for children and seniors — employing a big fleet of buses.

Depression Tests Staying Power

Forming new churches grew more difficult in the 1930s, and many of those already established struggled to survive. In Palo Alto, only a couple of new ones managed to take root and grow during the '30s.

The **Church of the Nazarene** was organized in March 1937. The Nazarenes rented the old brick Christian Church building at Florence and Lytton and in 1939 purchased it. Two years later the congregation sold the building to help finance purchase of a site at Marion Avenue and Middlefield for construction of a $40,000 complex. The chapel at 2490 Middlefield was dedicated October 7, 1951. A new sanctuary was added in 1968. During the building era, the Rev. Donald Farrand was pastor (1953-71). Dr. Lee W. Baker became pastor in 1990. In 1987 the church started the Love 'n Care Christian Preschool/Day Care School.

The forerunner of **Bethel Pentecostal Church of God** was born in a commercial building at 2372 El Camino Real in May 1932, and met there until 1935, and later in other California Avenue district stores and homes. In 1945, a new church at 367 Sherman Avenue was dedicated.

Growth in the 1950s and '60s caused need for a larger site, and on March 3, 1963, the members dedicated the Bethel Pentecostal Church of God at 3585 Middlefield Road. Pastors Carl and Trella Hatton, the present leaders, began in 1989. Bethel Pentecostal shares part of its space; Berkland Baptist Church conducts services there in Korean.

Jehovah's Witnesses had met in a Palo Alto home as early as 1924, but for company meetings usually traveled to the Mountain View Kingdom Hall. In June 1942 a group of 30 members, led by John Laier, rented a building at 123 Addison Avenue and began the fourth Jehovah's Witnesses congregation on the Peninsula.

The Kingdom Hall at 4243 Alma Street, completed in 1953 and remodeled in the 1970s and in 1984, and rebuilt in 1993, houses what is now called the Palo Alto South Congregation of Jehovah's Witnesses, and also the Mountain View Spanish Congregation of Jehovah's Witnesses.

In 1975, the Palo Alto North Congregation of Jehovah's Witnesses built the Kingdom Hall at 429 High Street, with men, women and children all sharing the work. The property was bought and the hall built for $54,000. It, too, is also used by a Spanish-speaking congregation.

Jerusalem Baptist Church began in March 1938 when the Rev. E.W.D. Morton recognized the need for a black Baptist church to serve Palo Alto's growing black community. Through the Pilgrim Baptist Church of San Mateo, a mission was started. Seven residents of Palo Alto organized a church on January 7, 1945, renting space, then buying a small building on Emerson Street. Many years later a pastor praised Deacon Edmon Stevens for persisting in starting the church downtown "in a day when our tribe was neither welcome or wanted."

In September 1947, Jerusalem Baptist bought oat-covered land at 398 Sheridan Avenue in the California Avenue district and erected a $40,000 edifice. In the late 1960s and early '70s the church acquired property on Grant Avenue and on the corner of Ash and Sheridan. In 1985 a capital funds campaign was launched, culminating on Mother's Day 1989 when an overflow turnout of past and present members and friends marched from the old to the new sanctuary. The Rev. Emil M. Thomas has been the pastor since 1982.

A Rising Energy Level

Fresh energies galvanized Palo Alto's religious life soon after the Second World War ended. By 1948, three major congregations were getting started south of Oregon Avenue — one a breakaway from a downtown church, one a new Bible-based fellowship and one an offshoot of a church with limited space. From 1949 through 1961, no fewer than 14 new churches and two Jewish temples were founded, while a dozen older congregations moved to new sites. The main thrust of growth ran out Middlefield Road, a thoroughfare nicknamed "Brotherhood Way," bounded by fecund new subdivisions. The Baby Boom went hand-in-hand with a rising interest in religious life.

A group of families who saw a need for an Episcopal parish serving South Palo Alto and sought a chance to play a more active role in church life, particularly in Christian education, began **St. Mark's Episcopal Church** at 600 Colorado Avenue, a block off Middlefield, in 1948. Many of them had attended All Saints' Church.

From the outset they created a self-supporting mission, and before 1948 ended had qualified as a parish, hired a rector and built a chapel and

The Rev. Emil M. Thomas baptizes a young person at the Jerusalem Baptist Church in 1990. The church has made its home in the California Avenue district since 1947.

1   PALO ALTO HISTORICAL ASSOCIATION/GLORIA BROWN

2   PALO ALTO HISTORICAL ASSOCIATION/GLORIA BROWN

3   PALO ALTO HISTORICAL ASSOCIATION/GLORIA BROWN

4   PALO ALTO HISTORICAL ASSOCIATION/GLORIA BROWN

5   PALO ALTO HISTORICAL ASSOCIATION/GLORIA BROWN

6   PALO ALTO HISTORICAL ASSOCIATION/GLORIA BROWN

1. Peninsula Bible Church
2. Church of Christ
3. First Christian Church
4. Palo Alto Baptist Church
5. Church of Jesus Christ of the Latter-Day Saints
6. Bethel Pentecostal Church of God
7. Unity Palo Alto Community Church

After World War II, the main thrust of Palo Alto church growth was out Middlefield Road, along which these and other churches were built.

7   THOMAS HISE

classrooms. In 1952 St. Mark's completed a parish hall seating 400 and moved services there. The 600-seat sanctuary was dedicated in March 1957.

In 1961, St. Mark's experienced one of the most dramatic of a covey of splits in local churches. The Rev. Canon Edwin E. West, rector since 1951, resigned in a theological dispute with Bishop James Pike, complicated by West's distaste for the parish's popular rummage sales. Later West joined the Serbian Orthodox rite and, with numerous ex-St. Mark's members, founded a church in Los Altos Hills.

In 1992, St. Mark's moved to divest part of its site for single-family housing and reconfigure its campus and perimeter buildings. The Rev. Joe Morris Doss was the rector from 1985 to 1993.

Peninsula Bible Church began in 1948, when Ed Stirm felt a need for a biblical ministry to Palo Alto people and Stanford students. He enlisted four other businessmen, Harry Smith, Cecil Kettle, Gus Gustafson and Bob Smith, and they began the Peninsula Bible Fellowship, a Sunday evening study group taught by visiting pastors. During the next two years, they added a Sunday morning service and a Sunday School — all without an official pastor. Then, in September 1950, they called Ray Stedman, who was about to graduate from Dallas Theological Seminary, as executive director. The fellowship developed into the first interdenominational evangelical Protestant church on the Peninsula. Some meetings were in homes, others at the YWCA. Peninsula Bible Church built its auditorium at 3505 Middlefield Road in 1951. A fellowship hall, with classrooms above, was added in 1971.

In PBC's early years, some members began recording and publishing Pastor Stedman's messages, ultimately through Discovery Publishing of Sunnyvale. This ministry now serves over 5,000 people in the United States and overseas.

Varied groups for each age level are hallmarks of Peninsula Bible Church, which grew throughout the 1970s when most congregations leveled off or declined. Pastors/Elders Ron Ritchie (1969), Steve Zeisler (1971) and Doug Goins (1978) share the team leadership.

Grace Lutheran Church began after the First Lutheran Church, seeing potential in fast-developing South Palo Alto, started a Sunday School and an adult Bible class in March 1948 at the Beaudoin Dance Studio at Colorado and Cowper. The powerful response soon persuaded First Lutheran that it could not continue the program or start a new congregation, so it asked the Evangelical Lutheran Church to assume the task. The Rev. Harold J. Brown of San Francisco was called to organize what became Grace Lutheran Church, starting August 5, 1951.

Plans for a permanent location and church home were developed early. Three acres at 3149 Waverley Street, at the corner of Loma Verde Avenue, were purchased and in 1952, with a loan from the synod, construction began. The first unit of the fellowship hall was dedicated September 28, 1952. The sanctuary was dedicated in 1961, when the Rev. Ray Farness (1959-77) was pastor. The Rev. Randall Wilburn became the pastor in 1991.

Unity Palo Alto Community Church at 3391 Middlefield Road grew out of what began in 1949 as the First Church of Religious Science. After meeting first at homes, the church met from 1950-60 at the Woman's Clubhouse. In 1960 it dedicated its first buildings at the present site. In 1990, the old structures were razed and worship was conducted at Gunn High School. A wholly new building complex was completed in 1991.

Docia Norris was a leading figure in the 1953-68 period. She was succeeded by Dr. Raymond K. Lilley (1968-81). In 1980, he announced that he was spiritually guided to leave the Religious Science affiliation. The congregation voted to become independent *with* Dr. Lilley; its name then changed to Palo Alto Community Church. Dr. Lilley died the following year.

The Rev. V. Stanford Hampson was selected as the new minister in 1982, and soon undertook an extensive radio ministry. In 1983 the members voted to affiliate with the Unity School of Christianity.

Like some other churches, Unity makes a

payment to the city in lieu of fire and police service taxes. Many Palo Alto service groups are recipients of its tithing of 10% of the church income.

What was first called Temple Baptist Church, now **Palo Alto Baptist Church**, was formally organized in June 1950 with 12 charter members at the downtown Masonic Temple.

In the early 1950s the congregation met at the former First Baptist Church parsonage at 305 Hamilton Avenue. In 1955, Temple Baptist changed its name to First Southern Baptist Church and relocated to Forest and Waverley in the old Presbyterian Church. A roaring four-alarm fire destroyed that structure on December 13, 1960.

About a month later the pastor, the Rev. Leonard Ross Rhoads, was charged with arson. Although his flock offered to support him pending trial, he resigned and ultimately pleaded guilty and was given probation on condition that he receive psychiatric treatment. His was the most flaming instance of a local minister's fall, but hardly the only one.

While the Rev. Clifford Hodsdon (1960-68) was pastor, the renamed Palo Alto Baptist Church built new facilities at 701 East Meadow Drive, on the corner of Middlefield. The sanctuary was dedicated in 1964. Under the leadership of the Rev. Jack McDaniel, pastor since 1968, the church

In December 1960 fire consumes the First Southern Baptist Church at Waverley and Forest. The pastor later confessed to arson.

PALO ALTO TIMES/GENE TUPPER

became host in 1976 to the Palo Alto Area Senior Day Health Program, donating facilities rent-free. It is also host to English-language devotions of the **Palo Alto Berkland Baptist Church**, a Korean Southern Baptist body.

St. Ann Chapel, located on Melville Avenue at Tasso Street, is the prime example of the effects of past Stanford University policy regarding Catholic and other sectarian services on campus. The chapel was the gift of Clare Booth Luce, congresswoman, wife of Time-Life publisher Henry Luce and later U.S. ambassador to Italy, in memory of her daughter, Ann Brokaw, a student at Stanford who was killed in a Palo Alto automobile accident in 1944. It was built and dedicated in 1951 to provide a place for Mass at a time when Stanford did not allow denominational services on campus (as the university now does). The adjacent former home of writers Charles and Kathleen Norris is the Newman Center for Stanford students.

Covenant Presbyterian Church, planned to serve the South Palo Alto area, opened in fall 1951. Its launching culminated 18 months of preparation sponsored by the First Presbyterian Church. The Rev. Arthur Brown Jr. had been filling the pulpit at First Presbyterian while it sought a new pastor when he accepted a call to lead Covenant Presbyterian in October 1951 and served until 1974. Twenty-two First Presbyterian members formed the core of the new congregation. Covenant Presbyterian was chartered in 1952 and in 1953 occupied its first building on a 2-acre site at 670 E. Meadow Drive, near Middlefield. Other expansions were in 1954, 1958 and 1965, with the sanctuary dedication in 1966.

The **Second Church of Christ, Scientist, Palo Alto**, was formed because the downtown First Church was becoming overcrowded. From October 1952 until 1954, Second Church met in Carpenters Hall at 3056 Middlefield Road. It was recognized as a branch of The Mother Church in January 1953. In 1954, members moved into the first unit of the present building at 3045 Cowper Street. After completion of the initial building plan, the church was dedicated—debt-free—in 1967.

Second Church maintains a reading room at 459 California Avenue.

Jewish Congregations Become Established

Prior to 1954, the nearest place of worship for Jews living in Palo Alto was Temple Beth Jacob, then in Menlo Park, now in Redwood City. Within a few years, Reform and Conservative congregations started up in Palo Alto. A third, Chassidic congregation came later.

Congregation Beth Am was founded in Palo Alto in 1955. In November of that year the Reform congregation began regular Friday evening services in the main sanctuary of the First Methodist Church at the invitation of that body's trustees and membership. "This invitation is a splendid expression of brotherhood in action," founding Rabbi Irving A. Mandel said at the time.

High holiday services continued to be at First Methodist through 1960. From 1959-61, Shabbat services were at the Unitarian Church.

After considering sites in Palo Alto, Beth Am selected acreage just outside the city, at 26790 Arastradero Road, Los Altos Hills. The first major construction there was executed and dedicated in 1961, and in 1968 the temple completed its sanctuary and social hall.

Rabbi Sidney Akselrad succeeded Rabbi Mandel as the senior rabbi in 1963 and served until 1987, when he attained emeritus status and Rabbi Richard Block became senior rabbi. Akselrad led Beth Am in viewing myriad social-action issues. He took part in many interfaith endeavors, helping Christian clergy and laity to understand the Judaic aspects of their heritage and to break down racial barriers.

Congregation Kol Emeth, founded in 1957, was hosted by the First Presbyterian Church and housed in other temporary quarters downtown in its early years. The congregation is affiliated with the United Synagogue as part of the Conservative movement within Judaism.

Kol Emeth dedicated its first building at 4175 Manuela Avenue in 1965, and completed a second stage in 1973 and the final stage, including the

PALO ALTO HISTORICAL ASSOCIATION

At Congregation Beth Am, Rabbi Sidney Akselrad and
Cantor Dora Krakower examine the Torah in 1975.
Rabbi Akselrad led Beth Am for 24 years.

sanctuary, in 1988. Rabbi Sheldon J. Lewis, presiding rabbi since 1973, has said that "we embrace an ideology which reveres and tries to transmit faithfully our religious heritage while maintaining an openness to change and evolution." Learning the skills of leadership, in which every role is shared by men and women, has been an emphasis in the congregation.

Congregation Ahavas Yisroel-Lubavitch, based at 3070 Louis Road, formerly was called Congregation Chabad. The synagogue is still a part of the Chabad of Greater South Bay, an outreach and educational organization, but in the early 1990s took its own name and identity. Psychologist Judah Landes was the primary force behind the founding of the Chassidic congregation in 1975. Rabbi Yosef Y. Levin, who has served since 1980, is also the Chabad's executive director.

The synagogue was based at 830 East Meadow

Drive from 1978-83 and later at the Hoover School on Middlefield Road until 1985.

The **Palo Alto Orthodox Minyan** meets at 453 Sherman Avenue. "Minyan" refers to the quorum of 10 adult Jews required for communal worship.

Other Denominations Take Root

The **Russian Orthodox Church** at 3455 Ross Road began in 1958 as a chapel in a garage. The church was dedicated in January 1966 by Archpriest Nicholas Ponomarev. The Rev. Vladimir Derugin became the pastor of the onion-domed Palo Alto church in 1978. Persons of Russian heritage make up most of the congregation.

St. Andrew's United Methodist Church, founded in 1958, held worship services at Greenmeadow Community Center until 1961. Its church building at 4111 Alma Street was dedicated in 1960 and first occupied the next year. It was the first Palo Alto church to host Hotel de Zink, a rotating church shelter for the homeless, and sponsored resettlement of 12 Ethiopian refugees. The Rev. Gayle Pickrell became the pastor in 1988.

Our Lady of the Rosary Catholic Church was organized in 1958 by the Rev. John Meehan, and dedicated its sanctuary at 3233 Cowper Street in 1959. Father Meehan was noted for his designs of chalices and other church utensils, which were executed by Dirk Van Erp, a San Francisco silversmith. In 1960 the Rev. John Dermody succeeded Meehan as pastor. Father Dermody became pastor emeritus in 1984.

St. Albert the Great Church at 1093 Channing Avenue was founded and dedicated in 1961, with the Rev. Henry MacEnery (1961-64) as founding pastor. The parochial school that is part of St. Albert's buildings complex operated first as St. Thomas, then as St. Albert, and now as St. Elizabeth Seton. As of 1992, it served minority youngsters from East Palo Alto — 56% Hispanic and 38% black.

The **Palo Alto Church of Christ** was begun in 1960 by a group from the Redwood City Church of Christ, many of whom lived in Palo Alto. Members built the church at 3373 Middlefield

Road, between Meadow and Loma Verde, in 1960-61, meeting there for the first services on February 5, 1961. The church is free, self-governing and Bible-centered, with no ties to any denomination.

The **Palo Alto Christian Reformed Church** was founded in 1960 and dedicated its church structure at 687 Arastradero Road the same year. Classrooms were added and the sanctuary expanded in 1973. The church is affiliated with the Christian Reformed Church in North America, which prior to 1890 was called the True Holland Reformed Church. The Rev. Henk DeYoung became the pastor in 1989.

University Lutheran Church and the Lutheran Campus Ministry at Stanford are based at 1611 Stanford Avenue, just outside the campus. Starting in 1945, the campus ministry was carried on from the First Lutheran Church of Palo Alto. University Lutheran was founded in 1965, and its buildings were dedicated in 1967. The Revs. Rudi Johnson (1965-71) and Manfred Bahmann (1973-81) were earlier pastors.

In addition to Sunday worship at the church, the ministry conducts midweek Lutheran services at Stanford Memorial Church. The members, about three-quarters Stanford students, have been active in establishing South Bay sanctuary congregations. The Rev. Herb Schmidt came as pastor in 1986.

Angelo Roncalli Community, led by the Rev. John Duryea, is named for Pope John XXIII, whose Second Vatican Council (1962-65) was marked by a spiritual renewal for the Roman Catholic Church and a search for reunion with separated Christians. Duryea, the scion of an old Palo Alto family, was ordained in 1943. He began campus ministry at San Jose in 1950, and Stanford in 1961. For 11 years he pastored St. Ann Chapel at a time of high involvement in social-action

issues. In January 1976, Father Duryea was banned from Catholic priestly duties because of his impending marriage to Eve DeBona. He initiated his present ministry in September 1976, with the small congregation meeting early Sunday morning at the University Lutheran Church.

Lord's Grace Church began as a campus Bible study among Chinese students, founded by Dr. H.T. Wu, an education student at Stanford. In 1973 the group moved to the Masonic Hall at 461 Florence Street.

In 1987, Lord's Grace Church acquired its present building at 555 College Avenue. Since 1981 the Rev. Tom Chang, senior pastor, has led the nondenominational congregation — the first church to serve ethnic Chinese locally. Services are in both Chinese and English.

In 1989, **Lord's Grace** became the first Chinese church to host the senior citizen program for the ethnic Chinese in cooperation with the Self-Help for the Elderly organization.

Founded in 1980, the **Ananda Church of God Realization**, a New Age congregation, moved in 1987 to specially built quarters at 299 California Avenue, Room 208. Its ministers are David and Asha Praver. It was the first Bay Area church of the now-worldwide movement.

Other small religious bodies in Palo Alto that have yet to acquire permanent places of worship include the **Abundant Life Christian Fellowship** and the **Vineyard Christian Fellowship of the Peninsula**, both conducting services at the Cubberley Community Center; **Ecclesia Gnostica Mysteriorum**, a Gnostic group based at Alma Plaza; a **Muslim** prayer group meeting in the California Avenue district; **Subud California at Palo Alto**, meeting at 330 Melville Avenue; and **Karma Thegsum Choling of Palo Alto**, a Buddhist body.

Soccer became the dominant youth sports activity in the 1980s.

18

Sports: From Sandlots to Superstars

FOOTBALL FOR MAYFIELD

"The first game of football under the Association rules ever played in California will take place at Mayfield next Sunday when... the California Rangers club... play a fifteen composed of Leland Stanford Junior University employees. The people around Mayfield and Menlo Park may therefore reasonably look for a lively afternoon's amusement."

— *Unidentified clipping, circa 1887, Weisshaar scrapbook*

Mayfield had a baseball team before work at Stanford began, but the coming of the university opened a new era of town-and-gown competition. Along with the abovementioned debut of football, O.L. Elliott, Stanford's pioneer registrar, recorded that after classes began in 1891, "match (baseball) games with schools nearby were played, at first on the indifferent Mayfield grounds."

After their gymnasium was built, women students made basketball their main game — and banned men as spectators. In 1894, Stanford coeds donned gym suits and rode to their first off-campus contest: a game in Palo Alto. They lost to Castilleja Hall, 14 to 13.

Intercollegiate Play Begins

Intercollegiate rivalry began to build in March 1892, when Stanford's football team played the University of California at the Haight Street field in San Francisco, scoring a 14-10 upset. This rivalry, celebrated in Bay Area life and legend as the Big Game, moved to Berkeley and Palo Alto as suitable turfs and bleachers were installed. By 1907, Stanford had a grandstand seating about 12,000, and the Big Game brought an infusion of visitors to Palo Alto on alternate years until World War I, with rugby supplanting football from 1906 through 1914. In 1915, UC switched to American football while Stanford clung to rugby. This led to

a rupture of Stanford-Cal athletic relations. Santa Clara University became Stanford's main rival, but after the 1917 game, play was suspended for the duration of the war.

In 1919, Stanford shifted to American football and resumed play with Cal. At the Big Game that year, Stanford's grandstand seated 17,000 with 3,000 more in temporary seats and 3,000 standing. Again in 1920, Berkeley's grandstand was filled to capacity. This upsurge of interest in athletics and the dawning of postwar prosperity cemented a decision at Stanford to build a new stadium.

Stanford's romance with rugby had a remarkable result in 1920. Rugby was an Olympic sport that year (and in 1924) and the U.S. team, composed predominantly of Stanford players, won the gold medal at Antwerp, defeating France 8-0. Dink Templeton, who had grown up in Palo Alto, contributed a 55-yard drop kick to the scoring. John Patrick was another Palo Altan in the scrum, as were a pair of men who later resided in town: Rudolph Scholz and Charles Doe.

Templeton also was a track and field competitor at Antwerp, and therein lies a tale of Palo Alto's special affinity with the high jump. While Dink was a boy, a jumper named George Horine had developed a new style called the Western roll, first in the backyard of his Channing Avenue home, then at Stanford. Horine went on to set a new world record at 6 feet 7 inches, and in the 1912

269

STANFORD UNIVERSITY ARCHIVES
Stanford Track Coach Dink Templeton.

Olympics he placed third. Templeton adopted the style in his own jumping, becoming a fine competitor, but at the 1920 U.S. Olympic Trials the officials called his jump an illegal dive and disqualified him. He managed to make the team in the broad jump instead, and finished fourth. Feg Murray, another Palo Alto-Stanford product, won the third-place bronze medal in the 110 meter high hurdles at Antwerp.

At the Paris Olympics in 1924, Stanford men, including Patrick, Scholz and Doe, once more made up over half the U.S. rugby team. Again they defeated France, this time 17-3. An injury to a French star angered the Parisian crowd, and the Americans left the stadium under police protection. That was the last Olympic rugby match.

Fierce Diamond Rivalry

Early on, Palo Alto developed a sports life of its own, but typically it has been tinged by the influence of Stanford's presence. El Camino Park, on

Stanford land leased by the city across El Camino Real from the present-day Stanford Shopping Center, served as the cradle for semi-pro Palo Alto Oaks and Junior American Legion baseball, industrial leagues softball, soccer and rugby.

The town-and-gown competition noted at the start of this chapter became town-and-town play as Palo Alto grew large enough to field a baseball nine fit to compete with Mayfield's team. The rivals fought it out on Sundays, first in Mayfield or at the Palo Alto ball park "at the end of University Avenue," and after 1914 at El Camino Park. Hinting a fierce clash, a 1905 announcement of a game matching the North Side against the South Side said: "All doctors are invited to bring their satchels." "Greasy Joe" Larkin and candymaker Sticky Wilson were Palo Alto's stars; Joe Mesa was Mayfield's hero.

Over the years the teams had many names. The best-remembered are two semi-pro clubs: the Black Sox before World War II, and the Oaks after the war. These teams drew from local prep and Stanford talent and sent some standouts on to the major leagues.

The Black Sox became the first team to represent Palo Alto in Sunday play against teams from all over Northern California. Some of the stars were businessmen: Ray Tinney, Ed Zwierlein, Tom Farrell, Bob Richards, John Morey, Monte Pfyl. Pitcher Carl Schnell later played for the Cincinnati Reds. "Potts" Manfredi was their slugger.

A Ground-breaking Event

Building Stanford Stadium was the last large local dirt-moving project employing horses and mules. A hundred wagon teams excavated 232,000 cubic yards of earth to pile up the big bowl's slopes and create a playing field 30 feet below ground level. Six months of toil finished the 60,000-seat stadium, designed by Professor C.B. Wing, in time for the 1921 Big Game. Cal marred the day by winning, 42-7.

Alumni subscribed to $97,000 of the $210,000 stadium construction cost under a plan whereby they received special rights to Big Game tickets.

Mayfield's baseball team, 1898.

Philip M. Lansdale, manager of the Bank of Palo Alto, agreed to advance other funds needed with Stanford's share of the anticipated gate receipts as security. Only $80,000 was needed, and it was paid off in 1924.

UC also set out to build a stadium but it was not ready for the 1922 Big Game, so that too was played at Stanford. The 1923 and 1924 Big Games were played in Berkeley's new bowl in Strawberry Canyon. Since 1925, except during World War II, Stanford has been the home team in odd-numbered years, Berkeley in even-numbered years.

Football grew even more popular in the mid-'20s as Glenn S. "Pop" Warner took over as Stanford coach in 1924 and Ernie Nevers starred. To cash in on the stadium's earning power, Stanford built several additions, boosting seating capacity to nearly 89,000 by the late '20s. (Improvements made in 1984 to prepare for Super Bowl XIX cut back the capacity to about 86,000.)

The huge stadium — for years the largest west of New York — put Stanford and Palo Alto on the U.S. sports map and ultimately on the world sports map. It attracted widespread attention in 1928

Teams of horses and mules were used to construct Stanford Stadium in 1921.

The Big Game and the Axe are featured at Stanford Stadium in odd-numbered years.

when Stanford President Ray Lyman Wilbur invited Herbert Hoover to break with past political custom and accept the Republican presidential nomination in the stadium. Hoover spoke to a near-capacity crowd on August 10, 1928, and his words were broadcast across the land.

In 1932, the stadium hosted the U.S. Olympic Trials. In that same year, Ben Eastman, Stanford Coach Dink Templeton's prize trackman, broke the world records for the 440-yard dash and the 880-yard run within a two-week period. However, Eastman's nemesis, the University of Pennsylvania's Bill Carr, won the Olympic 400 meters. Some critics blamed Templeton, claiming that in an intense rivalry with Carr's coach he talked

COURTESY OF UNIVERSITY OF OREGON

Les Steers set state prep high jump records while at Paly High. Later he set the world record.

Eastman into foregoing the 800, his best event, and running the 400.

Football yielded more thrills as Coach Claude "Tiny" Thornhill's 1933-35 "Vow Boys" kept their pledge never to lose to USC, and won Rose Bowl trips three straight years. In 1940 new Coach Clark Shaughnessy unveiled the T-formation, and the "Wow Boys," led by Frankie Albert, Norm Standlee and Palo Alto's Hank Norberg, beat Nebraska in the Rose Bowl.

Then came World War II and a sports hiatus. Its timing had a major impact on one Palo Alto athlete, high jumper Les Steers, who was destined for the Olympics until the war blocked his path. After bursting into adult competition while still at Mayfield Grammar School, Steers wore Paly High's colors as he raised state prep high jump records for three years in a row. Then, competing for the University of Oregon, he boosted the world record to 6 feet 11 inches. Steers' record lasted a long time: from 1941 until 1953.

Dink Templeton, at the end of his long stint as Stanford track coach, helped Steers develop the "belly roll" he used at the top of his leap. It was an adaptation of the Western roll, the same style that got Templeton disqualified in 1920.

Semi-pros and Amateurs
In 1947, a new semi-pro baseball club formed. The Palo Alto Oaks have been playing ever since. Monte Pfyl managed the Oaks for a time; Tony Makjavich has been the skipper for more than three decades. Oaks stars like Chuck Essegian, Jack Shepard, Dick Stuart and Jim Campbell rose to the majors; others like Al Talboy, Ray Young, Frank Mills and Tony Janovich carved lasting niches on the local scene.

Rugby also has hallowed the El Camino Park turf near the baseball diamond. The Palo Alto Ramblers team, formed in 1937, was coached and sponsored from 1940-56 by businessman Clark Congdon. After that, Sam Halstead put in decades as the Ramblers coach.

Prep Sports Standouts
Under Howard C. "Hod" Ray, its football coach for 33 years, Paly High fielded numerous champion teams, but none superior to the unbeaten teams

273

of 1950 and 1951, except perhaps the North Coast Section champion team of 1928. After Ray's death late in 1951, Coaches Hugh McWilliams, Bob Pederson and others left their marks, as did George Hurley and Len Doster at Cubberley High School in the '50s and '60s and Bob Peters at both Cubberley and Gunn. Ted Tollner, one of Cubberley's first stars, went on to major coaching fame. Jim Harbaugh, a former Paly gridder, became quarterback of the professional Chicago Bears.

In 1992, when the *Peninsula Times Tribune* invited readers to vote on the Peninsula's finest high school athletes ever, those listed from Paly High were Harbaugh, Norm Keeler, Al Talboy, Skip Crist, Emil "Frenchy" LaCombe, Rink Babka, Jim Loscutoff, Stu Pederson, Buddy Traina, Merle Flattley, John Stewart, Les Steers, Rudy Feldman and the wrestling Schultz brothers, Dave and Mark. Gunn High nominees were Bill Norberg, Scott Bunnell and Kelly Coan. Cubberley High was represented by Tollner and Don Castle.

In 1950, Hod Ray had singled out as stars from his teams of the 1920s, '30s and '40s Clarence Dirks, Nelson Smith, LaCombe, Gordon "Toby" McLachlan, Steers, Hank Norberg, Lyle Taggart, Keeler, Traina and Feldman. In the second tier he ranked Bud Shreve, Glenn Millar, Wes Fisher, George Kerrigan, Omar Cowles, Don Smith, Don Patch, Henry Cordes, Dick Misenhemer, Grant Denmark and Harry Plymire.

Before 1921, in the school's earliest years, the stars included Feg Murray, Cy Davidson, Clark Boulware, Grant Olaine, Bert and Ernie Risling, Rick Templeton, Otto Lachmund, John Norton, Gene Snell, Avery Howe, Lockhart Card and Lindley Miller.

From 1945 through 1972, town fans made a traditional visit to Stanford Stadium Thanksgiving morning to see the Little Big Game between Palo Alto and Sequoia high schools. Their long rivalry ebbed as each district opened more high schools. Finally in 1976 a reorganization put Paly and Sequoia in entirely different leagues.

For decades Paly swimmers ranked first or second in the North Coast Section, and in 1952

PALO ALTO TIMES/GENE TUPPER

Hod Ray coached Paly High football teams for 33 years.

Coach Nort Thornton Sr. boasted America's best prep squad. They edged a good Stanford freshman team with the aid of a freak happening: a Cardinal ace began to lose his trunks during a hotly fought freestyle sprint and quit the race.

State Champions!

Paly High came up with what may have been its finest basketball team ever in 1992-93. Coached by John Barrette, the Vikings ran up a 31-0 record, taking the Santa Clara Valley Athletic League, Central Coast Section (CCS) and California Interscholastic Federation Division III titles on the way. (Schools with 750 to 1124 students in grades 10-12 play in Division III.)

The starting five — David Weaver, Grant Elliott, Chad Smith, Mark Thompson and David Bennion — had been friends and teammates since they all attended Duveneck Elementary School. Top substitutes David Jefferson and Mikey Smith shared in the fast-break, touch-passing attack that blew away all opposition. In the finale, Paly

Players on Palo Alto High School's undefeated basketball squad pose happily with trophies collected on the way to the 1993 state championship.

PALO ALTO HISTORICAL ASSOCIATION/CHET LOY

defeated Morningside of Inglewood, the defending state titlists, by a 79-59 score. Weaver won honors as the Peninsula Player of the Year.

The Vikings' surge to the championship galvanized community support as no prep team had for many years. " ... I'll never forget the unbelievable support we got from the school and community," Elliott said. The cagers won an off-court honor, too, with the highest collective scholastic grade-point average in the CCS, 3.70.

The basketball crown capped a vintage year for Paly, as its tennis team ran an undefeated string through a third season (see page 278) and its water polo squad went unbeaten, giving John Williams, veteran coach and athletic director, a rousing sendoff into early retirement.

Girls Sports Stars

Paly, Gunn and Cubberley also produced some superior female athletes. Kate Latham, Paly '70, played on the women's professional tennis tour from 1977-84 and now coaches at Gunn High. Pam Blackburn, Cubberley '79, competed in the high jump in the state meet.

Several women's soccer stars went on to earn

All America honors as collegians: Sheila Jack, Paly '82, University of Colorado; Mary Harvey, Gunn '83, goalkeeper for the University of California, Berkeley, and a member of a U.S. women's Olympic demonstration soccer team; and Mei-ling Yee, Paly '80, also a Cal goalie.

Mei-ling Yee (now Okuno) gave up soccer for badminton and won a second in national singles competition. She placed first in 1990 exhibition play before badminton became an official Olympic sport.

Two others from Paly's vintage Class of '82 soccer crop were fullback Heather Hughes, who played for Cal and later became a teaching golf pro, and wing Nancy Slocum, a high school All America who later played on a University of North Carolina team that won the NCAA championship. She now coaches at UC Davis.

An outstanding swimmer, Karen Cramer, Paly '88, went on to Stanford and won All America honors for three years in the freestyle and individual medley.

Local Olympians

Palo Alto high schools produced a couple of

275

Walt Gamage, center, led the PALO Club in promoting local sports. He is flanked by pro quarterbacks Y. A. Tittle, left, and John Brodie.

Olympians in track: discus-thrower Rink Babka of Paly High and 400-meter runner Bill Green of Cubberley. Babka was the 1960 silver medalist in Rome. Green won the 1980 U.S. Trials but the American team didn't reach the Moscow Games because President Jimmy Carter invoked a boycott to protest the Soviet invasion of Afghanistan.

Among those watching their feats closely were earlier Olympians who settled in Palo Alto: Harlow Rothert, shot put silver medalist in 1932, and James LuValle, 400 meters bronze medalist in 1936.

Two locally grown freestyle wrestlers, brothers Dave Schultz, 163 pounds, and Mark Schultz, 181 pounds, won Olympic gold medals in 1984 at Los Angeles.

In 1968, Susie Jones Roy, a 1966 Paly graduate who attended USC, swam in the Olympics, placing ninth in the 100-meter breaststroke. Earlier, in 1960, Anne Warner Cribbs took fifth in the 200-meter breaststroke and won a gold medal on the U.S. 400 medley relay team. Originally from Menlo

Park, Cribbs has worked and resided in Palo Alto for many years. Terry Baxter, Paly '73, went on to the University of Arizona and made the 1980 U.S. Olympic team in the 100 breaststroke, but, like Bill Green, did not compete in the Moscow Games owing to the American boycott.

PALO Club Promotes Sports

A major factor in local sports promotion has been the Palo Alto Live Oaks, or PALO Club, founded in 1946 by Verne Johnson, Jim Rafferty, Stan Troedson and Jimmy Saitta with *Palo Alto Times* sports editor Walt Gamage as a sparkplug. Since 1949 the club has sponsored the Pop Warner Award for the outstanding Pacific Coast senior gridder, presented at one of America's largest sports banquets. The PALO Club boosted many improvements in sports facilities, such as the Palo Alto Municipal Golf Course and the Baylands Recreation Center baseball-softball complex on Geng Road. The club also obtained the original franchise in 1950 for

PENINSULA TIMES TRIBUNE/TED FINK

Scoring a run, 1987 Palo Alto Bobby Sox All Stars catcher Kate Shilstone, right, swaps high-fives with Jody Peterson. Their team, district American Girl Division champs, ranked seventh nationally.

local Little League baseball, which has blossomed into today's profusion of youth leagues for both boys and girls, including Willie McCovey and Babe Ruth baseball, Bobby Sox softball, Pop Warner football, and AYSO and CYSA soccer.

As a forum for dialogue and banter by sports figures at Stanford and other Bay Area colleges and from professional and local ranks, the PALO Club built a lively sports community. This, in turn, became a magnet drawing stars, coaches, team officials, broadcasters and writers as residents or frequent visitors.

A Municipal Golf Course

Palo Alto Muni, the 18-hole public golf course along Embarcadero Road east of Bayshore, owes its existence to public demand — and to city ownership of the land. An engineer named Walt Hensolt first broached the idea in a Toastmasters speech, and went on to make a hobby of planning the course. In 1952, Mayor J. Pearce Mitchell named a Citizens' Committee of 100, headed by William J. Miller, that recommended the proposal after a six-month study. The City Council approved the idea, provided $75,000 could be raised by subscription for the $217,000 project.

In a whirlwind campaign from July to October in 1953, sponsors raised $83,000, paced by a $25,000 gift from the Lucie Stern estate. The council then gave construction a green light. When homebuilder Joseph Eichler appeared before the council with an offer to donate a $45,000 clubhouse, Councilman Robert Cummings, who disliked "modern design," walked out so the offer could be accepted unanimously. Another tussle involved the right to sell beer at the clubhouse, which prohibitionist and church groups protested but the council cleared 12-2.

Mayor Clifford Simpson drove the first ball when the Muni course opened in May 1956. Despite ongoing salt problems with the low-lying links, it began to make a steady profit after a few years. In 1975 usage peaked at 104,227 rounds, and plans emerged for major improvements. Extensive course remodeling in 1978 cost $1.8 million and upgraded the course to a 6,200-yard par 72 with a new and larger clubhouse. Play continued during the work, but was off about 50%.

PALO ALTO HISTORICAL ASSOCIATION

Palo Alto's Municipal Golf Course, opened in 1956, continues to provide recreation for residents and others.

After that the course ran at a net loss to the city for a string of years. Finally, in 1990, play of 110,000 rounds at a $250,000 profit was reported — and profit was projected to hit $1 million in the year 2000 due to growing demand for tee reservations. The council OK'd $57,000 in 1992 for lines

Seaman "Pop" Harris operated his shoeshine stand at the trolley station on the Stanford campus for many years.

19

Toward Integration

*"I believe the social picture is fine here. These children have
a nearly 100% record of cooperation, for the young are
intolerant only of bad sports. . . . they are liked or disliked for
their own merits — and not for their minority status."*

— *Hester Kinnard Harrison, playground supervisor,*
quoted in the Palo Alto Times, *March 17, 1951*

As Mayfield became settled and Stanford University took shape, a broad ethnic mix built up in what today is Palo Alto. People of English, Irish, Scotch, French, German, Swiss, Italian, Portuguese, Swedish, Danish, Slavic and other national origins could be detected in the populace, along with *Californios* of Spanish or Mexican descent, a number of whom had intermarried with *Americanos* by 1890.

A sizable Asian element — mostly Chinese — was also present at first. The Gold Rush had set off a major migration from Canton. Many Chinese men had been employed as early as fall 1864 in construction of the western leg of the transcontinental railroad. Others had filtered into strawberry growing and other local agriculture. Leland Stanford's renowned Palo Alto Stock Farm had a large corps of Chinese employees, and Timothy Hopkins' estate in Menlo Park and others like it employed Chinese cooks, maids and gardeners. Some of them resided in workers' quarters on the estates. Some lived in Mayfield's Chinatown, a group of shanties facing El Camino Real between College and Stanford avenues.

Other non-whites included a few blacks — Seaman "Pop" Harris, who as a rail depot porter and campus bootblack became something of a Stanford institution, arrived in 1892 — and Japanese, who filled janitorial jobs at the university from the time it opened.

Beside being kept in menial jobs, these minorities faced white neighbors' prejudice in varying degrees. Anti-Chinese tensions had been rising since 1877, when 25 Chinese washhouses were burned in San Francisco. In 1878 a Chinese man was denied naturalization by the circuit court; in 1879 California's second constitution was enacted with a section prohibiting employment of Chinese by public agencies. In 1882, Congress passed the Chinese Exclusion Act; after that, vigilante actions soared. Immigrants from Japan also faced virulent hostility at times, although on a different statutory basis. Not until 1924 did a change in the law entirely halt any inflow from Japan.

A Few Pioneer Blacks

Blacks, few in number, seemed to be seen more as individuals. Some, with a lot of "sweat equity," became home owners. Pop Harris, after saving money for nine years, bought a newly built house on Fulton Street and sent for his family in North Carolina — a wife and 13 children. Still, newspapers of the 1890s and 1900s spoke of Asians and "colored" alike in terms appalling to modern readers, even in sympathetic news stories and editorials.

Palo Alto had not yet incorporated when, in November 1893, an attempt to establish a Chinese washhouse prompted the weekly *Palo Alto Times* to editorialize:

NO CHINATOWN WANTED

Palo Alto is not in the ordinary sense an anti-Chinese town. The class of people residing here are too intelligent and independent for that.... On one point, ...we are positively unanimous: We are solidly determined that that vile combination of bad odors, bad women and bad habits known as Chinatown shall not find a lodgment within our limits. There is a place for everything — even for a nuisance, and the place for a Chinatown is as far as possible from Palo Alto.

On the same day, the *Palo Altan* put it even more bluntly:

No Saloons for Palo Alto! No Chinese for Palo Alto! Clean town, clean morals.

The cry in other towns: "The Chinese must go!" In Palo Alto the motto is: "The Chinese must not come!"

Incidents of Prejudice

When Mayfield incorporated in 1903, getting Chinatown off Main Street (now El Camino Real) was near the top of the town agenda. The trustees succeeded in moving Chinese residents to the area that later became the Foon cannery, then Sutter Packing Company, then Maximart, now Fry's Electronics.

Juveniles and college boys alike regarded Chinese peddlers and deliverymen as fair game for malicious hectoring. In 1899, the *Times* reported, a group of young men out for a lark met a couple of quiet and inoffensive Chinese men on the road south of Mayfield, and beat them without provocation. In 1903, nine grammar school youths faced assault charges for throwing stones at a Chinese vegetable vendor and inflicting a severe scalp cut.

A deadlier incident in September 1897 resulted in one of the town's first petitions expressing mass moral outrage. One hundred prominent signers, including three marked as eyewitnesses and "S. Harris," demanded the resignation of Palo Alto Township Constable R.S. Spaulding for "the disgraceful act of shooting down a man [identified as 'the Negro Johnson'] on the streets" at midday. The constable retorted that the man he arrested was guilty of vagrancy "and by his appearance I believed he was a man wanted for some greater offense." It was an accident, Spaulding said: "When he broke and ran I demanded him to stop, and only shot so as to frighten him." The constable refused to resign.

The Slave Girl Case

Even greater community rage, this time adding Stanford's to Palo Alto's, welled up over a Chinese slave girl case in 1900. Among those playing heroic roles were Miss Donaldina Cameron, or "Lo Mo," director of a Presbyterian Chinese mission in San Francisco (who later lived for decades in retirement in Palo Alto), Dr. Charles Gardner, Stanford chaplain and former Palo Alto rector, and druggist B.F. Hall.

Drawing on Carol Green Wilson's account in the book *Chinatown Quest, Times* Editor Elinor Cogswell briefed the story this way:

Kum Quai, an escaped slave girl, was arrested on a ruse — a warrant charging petty theft. Refusing to let the girl go alone with her captors, Miss Cameron became an unwelcome addition to the party on the train down the Peninsula.

In Palo Alto, the men took Kum Quai off the train, locked her and her protector in a hotel room and then moved them to a shack sometimes used to house drunks. Miss Cameron barricaded the door with a beam, but about 2 a.m. the men chopped their way in and snatched the girl. When Miss Cameron climbed into the buggy with them, they threw her roughly to the roadside.

A justice of the peace held night court and turned the girl over to her tormentors, but Miss Cameron had told her story to druggist B.F. Hall and the community — Stanford and Palo Alto — was aroused.

FROM *CHINATOWN'S ANGRY ANGEL* BY MILDRED CROWL MARTIN
Donaldina Cameron and Kum Quai were participants in a 1900 Palo Alto kidnapping case.

Students and townsfolk burned the jail shack and an effigy of the offending justice.

Later the girl was found and given a new trial. Miss Cameron won her freedom by a surprise coup. [Chaplain Gardner, questioning the girl in Cantonese, adduced the fact that she had no immigration card and thus was a federal ward.] Kum Quai's frustrated captor snatched her and tore off again in a buggy, but druggist Hall lost no time in taking after him in a two-wheel cart. Knowing the roads better, he won the race and returned Kum Quai to a safe home and happy future.

Japanese Janitors Become Scholars

Unrelenting toil soon made Japanese youths more than successful janitors at Stanford — they became scholars as well. The fact is recorded in an item in the student newspaper, the *Daily Palo Alto*, in 1892, saying: "The ubiquitous Jap has found his way even into the library. One is now employed cutting the pages of new books." Before long, Stanford had a number of Japanese students.

In 1909, Josaburo Okado founded the Palo Alto Laundry Company, which later became a base for forming a Japanese Methodist church. Although not the first *issei* (first-generation immigrant) to settle in the town, Okado was noteworthy for his proprietorship. Often an immigrant found it useful to have two callings: Naoharu Aihara, designer of the showplace Hakone Gardens in Saratoga, had a tailor shop in Palo Alto from 1911 on.

By 1914, Minnie Ruth Kimura (later Mrs. Kiyo Sue Inui), who had attended Palo Alto High School, became the first Japanese graduate of Stanford or any large Pacific Coast university. Born in Nevada and orphaned early, she had been adopted by Mrs. Mary Gallagher Kimura, the widow of a missionary in Japan, who settled in Palo Alto after her husband's death.

Against All Odds

The notion of Chinese eateries or washhouses downtown was reviled anew in 1905 when the city clerk refused to issue a license to Mock Wo and Ah Fong to open a restaurant. J.F. Parkinson signed an editorial in his paper, *The Citizen*, subheadlined "Chinese Merchants, Restaurants and Laundries Must Go." Said Parkinson, "It seems too bad that a young town, prosperous and progressive, should meet cases and obstacles that require stringent measures to right." He referred back to 1893 and the face-to-face pressure citizens had applied to drive out a would-be washhouse operator.

The *Times* suggested a boycott, saying:

What kind of an impression would a stranger get from our avenue as a Chinese quarter? Mayfield got rid of its Chinese after they had been established there for years. What is Palo Alto going to do about the matter?

The *Palo Altan* said the clerk denied the license request "with the approbation of a majority of the board of trustees." The case went to court and delays ensued; finally the proprietors quietly opened the Cardinal Cafe. The dining public must have disagreed with the trustee majority. Two years later a second Chinese restaurant, the City Cafe, opened downtown. The hosts at the two eateries spent most of their lives feeding Palo Altans.

Winning a Place in Palo Alto Hearts

A smoother approach to the laundry and restaurant matter brought the city its first Chinese family owning residential property in 1912. But the story began much earlier.

Sew Sing, a young man from Shantung, China, arrived in San Francisco to seek his fortune, perhaps as early as the 1870s. Accepting a job as a cook at a farm near Palo Alto, Sing stepped off the train and found Leland Stanford's stable surrey waiting to take him to the mansion. For several years he cooked for Mrs. Stanford. Finally he decided to seek a more profitable venture. In 1898 he opened a small business in Menlo Park, calling it Yow Sun Laundry.

Ngum You Jew (Jew Ngum You, Chinese style), Sing's nephew, joined him at the laundry in 1908. A middleman arranged Jew's marriage to Rose Tong, whose father, Tong Tom Sing (or Tong Hau Gee), was an unusually progressive leader in San Francisco's Chinatown. Tong had won respect as a translator in Pacific Coast courts and immigration offices; he also owned a cigar factory and stores. Believing in the value of education, he had seen to it that his seven daughters and one son learned to speak English and stayed in school. That bucked contemporary custom, which was to give girls less schooling than boys.

The Jews' first son, Paul, was born in Menlo Park in 1912. Sing retired, and Ngum You moved the laundry and his family to a storefront-style Palo Alto home at 647 Emerson Street. Eight more children were born to the couple: Lillian, Vivian, Doris, Thomas, Albert, Louis, Mary Jane and Barbara.

A Toast to Friendship

In 1914, Rose's father staged a public relations coup. He and the young couple put on a chop suey dinner for more than 30 "American guests" at the laundry building. The Chinese New Year event got a front-page newspaper writeup, detailing the full menu and how Rose's three younger sisters and brother "sang several sweet songs in the American style" and led everyone in singing "America." Toastmaster Tong said his people desired to "obey all the laws of the town and to have the protection of their friends."

Good feelings thus generated not only boosted the laundry business and establishment of the City Cafe that same year, but also helped a few months later in a pinch. The police chief raided Yow Sun Laundry late one night and arrested 19 Chinese on gambling charges after finding dominoes and money. They went on trial with "Mrs. Yow Sun" (apparently Rose) testifying, and a jury acquitted them.

"My father was really kind-hearted," Doris Yep of Palo Alto recalled. "When immigrants came over and didn't have a place, he let them stay there until they could get on their feet. Many times he helped the Stanford students who came from the Orient to start. That's how we got our Chinese education — some of them taught us."

Rose Jew became the liaison between the town and its Chinese community. She translated for immigrant wives who saw physicians and learned they were pregnant, assisted at births, arranged housing. Teased as "the employment agency" by her family, she often filled residents' requests to find a cook or maid. She never took any pay.

The laundry prospered, and Ngum You acquired two restaurants in Palo Alto and a third in Redwood City. All of the children graduated from Palo Alto High School except Vivian, who died in her teens. Paul, class of 1932, won renown as a sports star and self-taught dancer who earned three encores at the Boys Stunt Show. He went on to a career as Paul Wing, "the Chinese Fred Astaire," performing all over Europe and America.

Ngum You Jew and Rose Tong Jew pose for their wedding photograph.

Paul Jew performed worldwide as Paul Wing, the "Chinese Fred Astaire."

had acquired a "paper name" (the documents of a U.S.-born Chinese) in order to enter the United States as a returning citizen — a common practice at the time.

The Jew offspring said they never encountered prejudice in Palo Alto, but did in other places. "We spoke English all the time," Doris Yep explained. "I know there are many families that did feel prejudice, and I think that's probably because they spoke Chinese in front of Caucasian children." Paul Jew said he and his siblings knew nothing of Chinese gambling and opium dens that were raided in Menlo Park and elsewhere now and then.

The Mock and Leung families, other early Palo Alto settlers, can relate kindred successes. For other minorities, it wasn't so easy.

Dancing into his upper 70s, he added comedy routines. The film *Forbidden City* featured him.

His brothers and sisters hewed more closely to their parents' examples of enterprise, homemaking and volunteerism, achieving solid if less flamboyant success: Doris as manager of a take-out food service for a time, Tom as owner of Jay Realty, Albert as co-owner of Alfred Electronics, which employed 150 when it was sold to the Singer Company, Louis as a Richmond auto dealer, Lillian as an accomplished artist who is active in civic and social service projects, Mary Jane in a number of managerial positions in the hospitality industry and Barbara as a tireless community volunteer who has worked on behalf of youth and senior citizen projects.

A "Paper Name"?

Business setbacks and ill health blunted the father's hope of retiring to China as a millionaire. He died shortly before Paul, Tom and Louis returned from World War II service overseas. An obituary said Ngum You had been born in Mayfield. But Tom later insisted that his father was born in China, and

A Friend to All

Before turning to the tribulations of the '20s, mention must be made of an ambassador of good will who was one of a kind: Emanuel B. "Sam" McDonald. Born a black preacher's son in Louisiana, he came to Mayfield at age 17, toiled as a farm hand, and won a place in the hearts of a local family who dubbed him a "svart Svensk" (black Swede). He progressed to work as a teamster and straw boss, doubled as Mayfield's deputy town marshal and finally advanced to the position of superintendent of the Stanford Athletic Department's buildings and grounds, a job he did assiduously for nearly 50 years.

Humble, charming, generous and loquacious, Sam McDonald made thousands of friends throughout the Stanford-Palo Alto-Mayfield community and the whole Bay Area. His autobiography, *Sam McDonald's Farm*, published in the mid-1950s, presented a beloved figure's rare perspective on people and events. He became a man of means and owned a substantial amount of property. His charities — most notably the Stanford Convalescent Home — knew no racial bounds.

Gestures of Good Will

Between 1910 and 1920, the Japanese community

PALO ALTO HISTORICAL ASSOCIATION

Emanuel "Sam" McDonald was an institution for nearly 50 years at Stanford.

became the city's dominant minority. It tended to represent itself through corporate group actions, such as buying war bonds. In 1917, the Japanese Labor Association of Palo Alto advertised labor rates within town of one hour, 40 cents; half-day, $1.50; one day, $2.80; slightly more outside town; cooks and waiters, 75 cents for the first hour, 50 cents each additional hour. In 1918 and 1919, similar ads ran; the rates went up a bit each year.

During the 1919 flu epidemic, a temporary hospital was established at the Japanese mission school on Ramona Street. That same year, more than 300 local Japanese attended a play titled "Hototogisu" in honor of the emperor's birthday. In 1920, the Nippon-Gakum organization bought a building in Mayfield for a school. The community marched in annual spring parades on Middlefield Road.

The Japanese group's repeated gestures of good will ran into the antipathy of some other residents. U.S.-Japan diplomatic tensions over Pacific Island disputes exacerbated matters, and some World War I veterans focused their resentment on the resident aliens and their children — American-born citizens. In 1920, a school census showed 70 Japanese students and 10 Chinese. The next year, 208 persons registered, 150 of them Japanese, for the new state alien poll tax.

Segregated District Rejected

A highly insulting confrontation began late in 1920. The Palo Alto Chamber of Commerce passed a resolution advocating "a segregated district for the Oriental and colored people of the city." The American Legion, Native Sons of the Golden West and Palo Alto Carpenters Union collaborated on the proposal. George F. Morell, publisher of the *Palo Alto Times* and a Legionnaire, identified himself as a backer of the segregated zone and of a campaign being mounted by the California Japanese Exclusion League. The proponents promised that if Japanese residents discouraged immigration of their countrymen to the locality and took steps to concentrate their population in a restricted district, they in turn would work for a more harmonious feeling between whites and Japanese.

Palo Alto's Japanese and black communities both repulsed the proposal, for different reasons stemming from unlike legal statuses.

Acting through the local Japanese Association, the Japanese rejected a restricted district, saying it would leave no opportunity for the assimilation they desired.

Commenting editorially, the *Times* said the assimilation reason was "disputed by the prevailing habits of the Japanese who live in social exclusion from the white race, even though homes of the two colors may be next door." It contended that the after-public-school Japanese school aimed to maintain homeland ideals, and concluded: "Socially and biologically, the two races are non-assimilable."

Although the Colored Citizens' Club of Palo Alto took longer to respond, it was more outspoken. Through its president, Henry Dodson, the group declared that "agitation for such an ordinance will only create race prejudice and cause race friction, and engender strife and discord where all before was peace and harmony, thereby lowering the morals of the community."

The black response pointed to a U.S. Supreme Court case, *Buchanan v. Warley*, saying the decision had sounded the death knell for all proposed segregation ordinances in America. It went on:

There are in this city more than 80 colored people among whom there are no loafers, gangsters or anarchists; colored people who have answered every call to arms that this government and her institutions (the greatest yet conceived and created by the genius of man) may not perish from the earth, whose patriotism is too strong to be contaminated by the hellish influence of race prejudice.

Shame on a race that carries in its brain the accumulated culture of the centuries and holds in its hands the wealth of the continent and yet, not only refuses to lift his less fortunate fellow man to the level of enlightenment and virtue, but seeks through humiliating, illegal ordinances and discrimination to sink him to the lowest depths of ignorance and vice.

We believe the best people of this city in unison with the great majority of the people of this state dissent from such an undemocratic doctrine, and we respectfully call upon you to make that dissent known...

Less formally, Dodson said members of the African Methodist Episcopal Zion Church had recently given up a chance to buy a $7,000 meeting house at a $3,000 bargain price because the property was in a white neighborhood and the black citizens did not wish to risk stirring racial animosity. He said 10 of the black residents owned local property, aggregating $100,000 in value — none of it mortgaged — and added that one was a bank director.

No segregated zone was ever legislated by city officials.

Alarums About Filipinos and Hindus Fizzle

Early in 1921, at about the time these rejections became known, a group of white residents sought municipal relief from the "menace" posed by a Filipino Club at 711 Cowper Street occupied by a small number of college-student lodgers and some meeting-day drop-ins. The neighborhood protest drew a strong defense of the club by its prestigious board, led by Dr. Effie York, a practicing physician who had befriended students from the Philippines for about ten years. The petition foundered when the Planning Commission said it lacked the legal power to rezone the street. As for an alarum that Hindus were looking for rooms in the neighborhood, that too came to naught.

Protests were also raised in Mayfield to Japanese and black property acquisitions. In 1919, Mayfield residents were aroused by the sale of an entire block to a Japanese buyer. Fear billowed again in 1920, according to real estate sources, when a Japanese group purchased a 34.5-acre farm tract. In 1923, a protest against an influx of blacks was led by Dollie de Mesa, a descendant from Secundino Robles. (Presumptive evidence implies, incidentally, white exclusion of Hispanics in early Mayfield social life.)

Black Community Social Center

Black residents built the AME Zion Church on Ramona Street near Homer in 1924-25, helped by donations solicited from businesses. It became their social center for a quarter-century. An influx of new settlers swelled the congregation. J.R. "Jerry" Harrison, a World War I Army veteran, and his wife Ruth came in 1922 and after renting for a time bought a Fife Avenue lot and put up a 27-piece "beginner's house" he bought used for $250. Harrison worked at a variety of jobs until 1935 when he became a Southern Pacific redcap at the

Palo Alto station. He stayed 22 years, setting a proud no-lost-baggage record. Beside being charter members of the AME Zion Church, the Harrisons were co-organizers in 1942 of the Santa Clara County branch of the National Association for the Advancement of Colored People (NAACP).

Felix Natis, son of Mrs. Maud Natis, one of the town's first black residents, trained as a musician at the New England Conservatory of Music in Boston. Active in the NAACP's county branch in its early years, he missed election to the Palo Alto City Council in 1947 by fewer than 100 votes.

Americus and Celeste Neely became residents in 1929; he hooked up a Ford motor and a wood saw and set up a wood yard on Forest Avenue between Emerson and High streets. In 1933, Neely opened a bicycle shop at 414 California Avenue. Mrs. Neely became the city's first black realty agent in 1948.

Community Builders

There were other effective black community builders. Hester Kinnard Harrison came to Palo Alto in 1924 when she married cabinet-builder John Harrison (no relation to J.R.). John Harrison studied at night school and landed a Hewlett-Packard

COURTESY OF FRAN'S MARKET

Fran Hinson in his market on Lytton Avenue.

job; Hester gave music lessons, played the AME Zion organ for 40 years, worked as a city recreation leader and did a lot to promote scholarships and self-esteem for black youngsters. Frank "Mac" and Pearl Moulden also won a place; Mrs. Moulden chose the town because she sought good schools, and she and her son William graduated from Palo Alto High together in 1934. The Hinsons (descended from Pop Harris) were another leading family — Isaac and his son Fran, who ran a newsstand at Lytton and Cowper still known as Fran's Market.

In a lean Depression year, 1935, *Times* Editor Dallas Wood wrote in his column that the AME Zion Church mortgage faced foreclosure. White and Asian citizens joined in helping the black community raise rescue money, though it took four years. Historian Guy Miller called it one of the community's brightest brotherhood-in-action episodes.

Like the blacks, the Japanese had been gaining status and economic power in the later '20s and '30s. Alarmed by Japan's militarism and invasion of China in 1937, the Palo Alto Japanese responded by showing their Americanism. In one dramatic demonstration in 1941, they marched carrying a huge American flag during the University Avenue underpass dedication.

"We Are Loyal to This, Our Country"

They more than shared the nation's shock over the Imperial Navy's December 7, 1941, attack on Pearl Harbor, despite not knowing all it foreboded. On December 9, the Palo Alto Japanese-American Association said in a statement in the *Times*:

We..., having lived in Palo Alto and Menlo Park throughout 40 years, and having enjoyed the privileges of citizenship and participation in civic affairs, and having been raised in the tradition of American freedom, are deeply shocked at the news of

The 1941 parade celebrating the opening of the University Avenue underpass featured the Japanese Association of Palo Alto.

the outbreak of hostilities between Japan and the United States.

At this trying moment we wish to make our stand clear. Without reservation, we are loyal to this, our country, the United States of America.

We shall continue, as in the past, by every thought, word and action, to demonstrate our loyalty to the end that the barriers of suspicion and distrust may be scaled, and we may continue to enjoy this freedom which we all cherish so much.

Arthur Okado, association president and successor to his father as head of the Palo Alto Laundry, pointed out that members had bought $2,700 in defense bonds, staunchly supported Red Cross, USO and other community fund drives, assisted the Japanese Methodist Episcopal Church and the Buddhist Church and sent seven youths to Army duty.

Yet war jitters swept the Pacific Coast, anti-Japanese passions flared and rumors of acts of sabotage surfaced. By late February 1942, the FBI and local officers had seized Arthur Okado, his father and other leaders of the association.

"The Loss Will Be Ours"

As Charles C. Kubokawa of Palo Alto put it almost 40 years later, "The reports of *nikkei* (Japanese Americans of any generation) loyalty proved 100 percent correct." There was not a single case of sabotage or spying by the Americans of Japanese ancestry. Moreover, the battle record of the all-*nisei* 442nd Regimental Combat Team, the most decorated U.S. Army outfit of World War II, was peerless.

On March 2, General DeWitt, using executive-order authority delegated by President Roosevelt, ordered all people of Japanese descent evacuated from California, Oregon, Washington and part of Arizona. The sudden order left friends of the victimized group with little to do but try to ease the wrenching relocation. Josephine Duveneck later wrote:

It all happened so quickly and so conclusively that the people who knew and loved the Japanese were caught napping. Church people, teachers, university presidents (like Sproul at Berkeley and Wilbur at Stanford), social workers, county and city officials, YWCA, YMCA workers protested by telegram, letters, meetings, newspaper articles. But it was too late. ... The largest single forced migration in American history was under way.

On May 26, 1942, four large buses carried 144 men, women and children away from Palo Alto. Their baggage was limited to what they could carry. Their homes, vehicles and some other property had been hurriedly sold or turned over to friends for safekeeping. Other possessions had been stored in the Page Mill Methodist Church or at the police department. Tears brimmed in the eyes of the older men and women, a reporter noted — and in the eyes of some of the Caucasian friends waving farewell.

The evening before, the *Times* — its attitude long since changed from its assimilation pronouncement 20 years before — said "the loss will be ours as well as theirs. . . Our hearts go out to them in the sorrow and hardship of their uprooting. We wish them well and pray for the peace which will make it possible for them to return." The paper asked officials having to do "with the relocation of these our neighbors and friends to consider them as loyal Americans sharing in the national emergency . . ." That, sadly, was not to be.

"Sun-Spoiled Californians" Shiver

Once bused to San Jose, the 144 Palo Altans entrained for a temporary stay at Santa Anita Racetrack, and after that, went to Heart Mountain, Wyoming. In that desolate high-desert locale, John Kitasako wrote to the *Times*, the "sun-spoiled Californians" shivered during chill nights — penned in and guarded. Arthur and Josaburo Okado, cleared and freed from FBI detention, soon joined their kin.

Some others from the Palo Alto area went to Tanforan Racetrack and on to Topaz, Utah, or another concentration camp. The relocation centers soon began to leak inhabitants — to college, to military service, to essential jobs inland. But it was November 1945 before the last incarcerated families left Heart Mountain.

Not all *nikkei* evacuated from Palo Alto returned to the city, but those who did arrived penniless, amid a severe housing shortage. The Palo Alto Friends Meeting and the Fair Play Committee, led by Mrs. Duveneck and Gerda Isenberg, did much to help the returnees find shelter, funds and acceptance, backed up by the *Times* and James Edmiston of the War Relocation Authority. Still, it was a bitter homecoming. The Japanese Methodists and the Buddhists joined in a memorial service at Alta Mesa cemetery to mourn those of the community who died during the war.

Wartime Jobs for Blacks

World War II's impact on Palo Alto's black community was quite different. Defense jobs opened up, and blacks from the South arrived to work in Bay Area shipyards. Mainly from rural backgrounds, these newcomers ran into culture shock in their abrupt shift to urban life.

Late in 1942, Roy Wilkins, then the NAACP's young assistant national secretary, spoke in town and gave Palo Alto a pat on the back for its tolerance. He encouraged the community "to volunteer experimentally to teach people how to live together; not to expect overnight changes, but not to slip backward."

Almost a year later, Mary Weymouth of the local NAACP branch stated that the war had almost doubled the black population, but that only 10 additional houses had become available. Nationally, more than 1 million African Americans were in the service, some in all-black units honored for distinction in battle.

V-J Day and the war's end in August 1945 afforded no real relief from the housing crunch. Competition for space escalated as veterans with GI Bill benefits came home to finish college, start

families and buy homes. In Palo Alto, people of minority races lived mainly near the downtown and California Avenue business districts or in a few other enclaves. The city's earliest subdivisions had had no racial covenants barring non-whites, but more than a dozen subdivisions set up after 1925 did. The usual racial-restriction clause stated:

> *No person not wholly of the white Caucasian race shall use or occupy such property or any part thereof unless such person or persons are employed as servants by an occupant of some portion of the property.*

In 1948, the U.S. Supreme Court ruled that federal and state courts could not enforce such covenants. Palo Alto Real Estate Board President Hoyt Rohrer and other brokers opined that the decision would not change the situation in Palo Alto materially. Rohrer said:

> *Most of the minority groups do not want to live in sections where they are not wanted any more than the prospective seller wants to get them in if the adjacent property owners are unfriendly to the proposal.*

It apparently did not occur to the reporter assigned to sample local reaction to the decision to ask black, Chinese and Japanese residents what they thought. Events of the next decade or so spoke for their desire for fair play. Test cases involving black and Chinese buyers arose, typically just outside of Palo Alto proper, in East Palo Alto and other south San Mateo County areas. Some incidents involved acts of violence or terror, others only verbal strife. Japanese American leaders, intent on proving their loyalty all over again, said little publicly about relocation or the discrimination they felt.

Whatever biases adults may have had, students at Jordan Junior High School in 1946–47 evidently did not share them. In three successive student body elections they voted the top office to Alice Kwong, Carol "Bunky" Bowman and Haskins

"Chuck" Kashima, youngsters of Chinese, African and Japanese heritage, respectively.

"Color Line" Battles

As early as 1939, two couples had sued to eliminate "color line" restrictions at Lincoln and Fife avenues. Their contention was that no racial covenant was in the original subdivision restrictions.

Postwar cases tended to be fought more in the arena of public opinion, where fair-play advocates could seize the moral high ground. But it started slowly. In 1946, a fair employment practices law was defeated by California voters 3 to 1. In 1947, a real estate broker floated a "white Peninsula" theory, with little response.

In 1950, Lawrence Lane off Greer Road near Colorado Avenue was set up as an interracial housing development with black, Asian and white residents. The sponsoring Palo Alto Fair Play Committee took pains to prepare neighbors carefully. It became a quiet success.

The same committee reported a survey in 1952 showing that only 68 Palo Altans polled would rent to persons of good character regardless of race while 198 would rent to Caucasians only. A year before, "KKK" had been painted in red letters near the black Jerusalem Baptist Church. The Palo Alto-Stanford NAACP branch, with 159 members, broke away from the Santa Clara County NAACP in 1952.

In 1954, the year of the *Brown v. Topeka* school desegregation decision, it was revealed that a Chinese family headed by a research chemist had decided not to buy in a new Palo Alto subdivision because of pressure from residents.

"Block busting," an ugly real estate practice manipulating fear that minority buyers would ruin property values, began in Menlo Park's Belle Haven district and later spread to East Palo Alto, which over a few years changed from a largely white area to one mostly populated by people of color. In 1954, residents of the Palo Alto Gardens subdivision divided on whether to buy out a black family that was acquiring a home, starting a deluge of letters to the *Times*.

Supporting the Alabama Bus Boycott

In 1956, when Rosa Parks refused to move to the back of a bus in Montgomery, Alabama, a bus boycott resulted. The boycott won the support of the Palo Alto-Stanford NAACP, which adopted the Montgomery chapter and paid its $1,000 national dues. Franklin Williams of Barron Park, NAACP western regional counsel, spoke locally on "The Changing Status of the Negro in U.S. Society." A pro-racial tolerance stand was announced that year by the First Methodist Church.

In 1957, the local NAACP chapter backed fair employment practices legislation and asked Stanford to disavow racial bias in its land leases for housing. The university declined, saying it "has always received into its midst qualified students, faculty and staff of all races, religions and national origins." Willis Williams, a black educator, became principal of Addison School about that time, a symbol of the Palo Alto Unified School District's effort to better balance its staff racially.

Standing Up for Civil Rights

Franklin Williams had a new topic in 1958: how to prevent minorities from being denied the right to buy homes in any neighborhood. Over a dozen Palo Alto churches mounted an open housing campaign.

When the Congress on Racial Equality began its Freedom Rides in 1961, the notion of witnessing the demonstrations in Alabama or Mississippi as a buffer against suppression by local authorities took hold among Palo Alto's bolder clergy and attorneys. A number of them walked in symbolic marches in the South.

Dentist Leroy Lucas headed the local NAACP from 1963-65 and took a visible role in fair housing campaigns. In '65, the year of the Watts riot and a new national voting rights act, NAACP leader Tarea Hall Pittman said in Palo Alto, "There is more segregation in California today than 10 years ago. It's all gone underground." Purging it in the state would take much longer than in the South, she forecast. The chapter she addressed had 1,400 members, mostly white.

1967 brought riots in Newark and Detroit and a foray by Black Panthers into the Legislature at Sacramento. By 1968, Cubberley teacher Ray Fleming denounced gradualism in a talk at a church and NAACP branch President Stanley Puryear led a group of black militants who sought to change the end of the organization's name to "Black Persons." Puryear personally was trying to adopt a Muslimized name.

Then came the assassination of the Rev. Martin Luther King Jr. in Memphis. In Palo Alto, a large, mournful procession formed quickly and marched from University Avenue up Palm Drive, carrying flowers.

Multiculturalism in Schools

In the schools, multiculturalism thrived from 1969 to 1976. But it had a rocky start, as when Black Panther Eldridge Cleaver's wife Kathleen spoke at a faculty retreat, touching off a public furor. Then things settled down.

Electronics manufacturer Roy Clay served three years on the City Council in the late 1970s — the only minority member ever. Horace Anderson, a black engineer, won a school board seat. But

gradually, as substantial equality gains piled up and the Vietnam War protest took center stage, the civil rights movement's intensity waned.

Meanwhile, relocated *nikkei* residents had recouped somewhat from their wartime battering. Spurred by the rising generations and strong Palo Alto area leadership, they at last spoke out. They denounced their detention by the U.S. government for the wholesale violation of constitutional rights that it was. The nationwide redress movement won a presidential apology and token redress in 1988. But payment ($20,000 per person) dragged; many aged *issei* died before receiving their cash.

Palo Alto's Indian Chief

After the Mission era, Palo Alto never had enough American Indians for them to be even deemed a minority group. However, the mother of Ernest Risling of Palo Alto was of Karok Indian blood; he used to say his father was a "stubborn old German." Risling and his brothers were sports stars at Palo Alto High and Ernest's abilities won him election by fellow soldiers as an officer of Company L of the National Guard. He became supervisor of mails in Palo Alto and in 1946 was elected

The Risling brothers, Bertie, Jay and Ernest (L to R), were sports stars during their days at Paly High. Ernest later served as chief of the California Council of Indians.

COURTESY OF ERNESTINE FAXON

chief of the California Council of Indians. As chief, Risling spent nearly two decades overseeing a federal lawsuit through which 36,000 California Indians sought compensation for land taken from their tribes from 1852 on. The U.S. government finally paid about $30 million.

Finding a Voice in Public Life

To give Asian concerns a resounding political voice, Palo Alto psychiatrist Allan Seid and his wife Mari Chan hosted the formation in 1973 of Asian Americans for Community Involvement of Santa Clara County. It brought leaders of the Chinese and Japanese communities together in an activist stance and gained them places on official bodies. Dr. Seid, a fourth-generation Californian born in San Francisco's Chinatown, was appointed to the State Board of Education.

Meanwhile, annual Japanese and Chinese cultural festivals presented by the respective communities with Recreation Department co-sponsorship became Palo Alto traditions. The Chinese Community Center of the Peninsula, founded in 1968, has occupied several Palo Alto locations. The Hua Kuang ("Light of China") Reading Room containing 6,000 Chinese language works compiled by chemist Ernest Hung was housed first at the Chinese Community Center and then moved to Cubberley Community Center.

Coming Full Circle

Changing trends in immigration from mainland China, Hong Kong and Taiwan, particularly in the 1970s, brought Palo Alto new residents with marked high-technology or entrepreneurial skills, a sizable bloc of them speaking Mandarin rather than Cantonese. The 1990 Census showed that the city's 2,897 residents of Chinese ancestry were by far its largest Asian group — an instance of coming full circle round, although in much larger numbers, from the Census count in 1890. Those of Japanese descent numbered 1,302. Filipinos, Asian Indians and Koreans made up the next-largest groups of Asian origin — roughly 400 each.

The 1990 Census put Palo Alto's self-identi-

Local columnist and reporter Loretta Green.

SAN JOSE MERCURY NEWS/
KERRY PAUL AND RON COCHRAN

fied Hispanic population at 2,792, or about 5%. Black population stood at 1,612, or 2.9%, a group composed mainly of successful middle class families. (Poorer blacks and Hispanics, many employed in Palo Alto, tended to live across the county line in East Palo Alto or East Menlo Park.) Perhaps the black community's best-known voice was that of *Peninsula Times Tribune* and now *San Jose Mercury News* columnist Loretta Green, a gifted human-interest writer whose work has been a bridge of understanding connecting residents of various backgrounds. She and a locally developed journalist, Sharon Noguchi, now with the *Mercury News*, have played major roles in recording the history of Palo Alto people of color in addition to their fine all-around reporting and commentary.

Despite their ordeals, minority people generally have thrived in Palo Alto. Through access to good schools, a latter-day fairer break in jobs and housing and their own hard work, many have climbed into professional and managerial ranks. Intermarriage with Caucasians or other minorities has grown increasingly common. Although much remains to be accomplished in enhancing equality, assimilation has advanced farther than many residents once imagined possible.

Votes for Women

Club of Palo Alto

President, Mrs. A. L. Park
611 Gilman Street

Secretary-Treasurer, Miss Vallance Arnott
424 Seneca Street

Auditor, Mrs. M. C. Wilbur
309 Alma Street

Platform

We demand votes for women.

For the long workday,
For the taxes we pay,
For the laws we obey,
We want something to
say.

We are living under a government falsely called a democracy, a government under which only half the people—the men—have anything to say. We want our share in a government of men and women people, by men and women people, for men and women people.

We believe it to be our duty to vote, and since the present laws prevent our voting we believe it to be our duty to demand our share in self-government.

We declare the time has gone by for humble petition. Two million five hundred thousand of our children are now child laborers, and the number is increasing steadily in the face of protests. While child labor continues, patience ceases to be a virtue.

We demand votes for women.

Alice Park was Palo Alto's foremost woman of causes.

20

Saving the World and Other Causes

*"Palo Alto has more going on per square inch
than anywhere in the world."*
— *Virginia Satir, psychotherapist and author, 1987*

Palo Altans have manifested a keen interest in causes and reform from the start. Good schools, clean government, reliable utilities, better health care, easier travel, a climate of temperance, moderate politics and cultural advances all had their moments as causes, as detailed in preceding chapters. So did efforts to sustain a thriving economy and to broaden tolerance.

Other great late 19th and 20th century causes and reforms have also paraded across the city stage again and again. Broadly, they can be grouped as striving for equality and justice, conserving a beneficial environment and promoting world peace.

Some movements sprang from specific hometown events; others localized broader issues. The major ones generated Palo Altans' ardent interest, manifested in marches, rallies, petition drives, letters to the editor and demands on legislators. Often, Palo Alto has become a nerve center through which zealous concerns have been spread regionally, nationally, even globally.

From the inception of the city's voluntary organizations to the present day, Stanford University faculty members have provided vital input, whether by reporting and commenting on captivating new issues or by applying professional expertise to problems. Another local earmark has been the steady proliferation of groups with overlapping interests — affinity networks ready to join in cries for reform.

"The Women… Ask for the Ballot"

In 1870, the year all male U.S. citizens (not just whites) achieved the right to vote, Sarah Wallis organized the Mayfield Woman's Suffrage Association and became its president. Then she was elected to head the first statewide group, incorporated in 1873 as the California Woman Suffrage Educational Association. With the encouragement of her husband, Judge Joseph S. Wallis, a former state senator, she succeeded in getting civil law changed to allow women to make contracts. When Susan B. Anthony visited Mayfield in 1871, Mrs. Wallis was her hostess, even staging a ball and midnight supper.

Late in 1895, as the women's voting issue was about to reach the state ballot, the weekly *Palo Alto Times* commented:

MAY THE GODS PRESERVE US.
We hoped we might escape, but we have caught it. A Woman's Suffrage Club is to be permanently organized Saturday afternoon. We suppose we must pray for grace and be reconciled in the thought that as colic, mumps and measels [sic] are common to childhood, so every new town has its infantile mental diseases. Fathers, husbands, sons and brothers should observe a strict quarantine in this crisis, and we may experience only a light attack of the epidemic.

In the next issue, the editor ran for cover. "It is

COURTESY OF PENINSULA TIMES TRIBUNE

Women were invited to edit a special woman suffrage edition of the Daily Palo Alto Times in October 1911.

indeed a poor cause that cannot stand ridicule and we think that the cause of woman's suffrage is able to take any stray shot that we might fling," he said. Then he offered to publish "signed articles of reasonable length from the ladies of the town which would enlighten us and the public at large on that very pertinent question."

Taking up his offer, members of the Political Equality Club and the Woman's Club of Palo Alto — the latter with over 100 members — saw to it that local campaign activities were amply covered. Five articles prepared by the Equality Club ran before the election. One said: "We hold that the interests of men and women are not divided but identical. . ." Another squib reported: "More than two-thirds of the women of Palo Alto, by actual count, ask for the ballot." The *San Jose Mercury Herald* quoted that claim. In addition, the Equality Club made a concerted effort to familiarize women with all issues of the day so that if they won the vote, they could use it knowledgeably.

When Palo Alto men voted, 71% favored woman suffrage; 161 voted yes, 67 no. Statewide, however, the noes easily prevailed. The *Times* laid the loss to a hostile stand by liquor dealers, "opposition of women themselves and the lack of enthusiasm among the ministers." The paper encouraged trying again along new campaign lines.

The 1911 Suffrage Campaign

Not until 1911 did woman's suffrage in California reach the ballot again, and by then Palo Alto suffragists were even better prepared. Mrs. Jennie Arnott of Palo Alto presided over the county suffrage association, Mrs. Emily S. Karns headed the Palo Alto Independent Suffrage League and Mrs. Etta Waring led a Mayfield unit. Many prominent men spoke out, including Stanford President David Starr Jordan. Monsignor Joseph Gleason of St. Thomas Aquinas Church declared: "We believe that for women to pass judgment on public issues not merely in the press and on the platforms, but also in the ballot, is justly due them not only as citizens but as taxpayers."

At a mass meeting in early August, lawyer Egerton Lakin said, "California women should have the vote to help the men correct the evils of civic life, especially in San Francisco." Two weeks later at a banquet for more than 100 people, Mrs. M.A. Buchan, one of many speakers, offered a wry toast to "Men," saying it had become custom for women when they look upon the lords of creation to become lost in admiration, and she hoped women might be able to admire the men's behavior at the October 10 election.

This time the *Times* turned over an entire edition to the Suffrage League on October 5, and the guest editors said "no newspaper in California has been more generous." The banner headline read: "GIVE CALIFORNIA WOMEN A SQUARE DEAL." Many advertisers used their paid space to state reasons for a favorable vote.

In the showdown, Palo Alto men voted 420 yes, 90 no, and the measure carried all but three precincts. Statewide, it won by the scant margin of 3,587 votes.

Women Soon Outregister Men

Four days later, in the afterglow of victory, Dr. Clelia Duel Mosher, M.D., a Stanford professor, became the first local woman to register to vote — and as a Democrat! (Because of a technicality, however, she soon learned she would have to re-register.) By the 1912 primary election season, Palo Alto women were outregistering men, 594 to 422. Their party affiliations ran Republican 469, Democratic 62, Socialist 23, Prohibition 30 and declined to state 10.

At Roble Hall, Dr. Jordan noted that California, as the first rich and populous state to give the vote to women, would be watched closely. In Palo Alto, the Woman's Club took new steps to educate members in citizenship. So did the Women's Christian Temperance Union, which had stood back during the campaign for fear of stirring up "wet" opposition. Historian Yvonne Jacobson has pointed out that umbrella suffrage leagues of 1911 were organized from the many affiliated women's clubs of that era and overlapped the WCTU.

After 1911, the intensity of the suffragists' long campaign naturally waned. But not in everyone. Alice Park, whose family had settled in Palo Alto as San Francisco refugees of the 1906 earthquake and fire, blossomed as the town's foremost woman of causes. Jonathan Bell, in a student paper on radicalism in Palo Alto from 1912 to 1929, quoted a reporter who interviewed her on the Henry Ford Peace Ship in 1916 as describing Mrs. Park's views this way:

Mrs. Park does not stop with advocacy of woman suffrage [still a national issue until 1920]. She is prominent in the movements for single tax, simplified spelling, and the four-hour day. She believes that women should be economically independent of their husbands. She believes in labor unionism, in socialism, and has been prominent in many fights against child labor.

Bell went on to say:

It might be added she was a pacifist, vegetarian, for birth control and the WCTU, against child-beating, cruelty to animals, and eating too much in hot weather, and for so many other causes that she was thought to be a bit "nutty." Her first interest was always in rights for women, from which she said all her others stemmed. She signed guest registers, "Alice Park, California, where women vote."

Every Cause but One

As a bicycling enthusiast, Mrs. Park stood aloof from one cause: saving oak trees growing in Palo Alto streets. But she did advise, if a tree must be cut, plant two in its place. An absolute pacifist, Mrs. Park once protested a Woman's Club meeting because it was at the National Guard Armory. Scholars studying her life have said her most significant contribution to the peace movement was as a disseminator of information. She carried on a vast correspondence, often inserting a slo-ganeering card for some cause with each letter.

Perhaps her finest work as a feminist was a leaflet, issued first in 1910, comparing the disadvantaged rights of women as against those of men under California law. Its leadoff section, titled "Fathers sole guardians," led to passage in 1913 of a law she wrote granting women equal rights to guardianship of their own children. Her style often had a tinge of ironic humor, as shown in this sample from a section titled "Age of Consent":

. . .The codes protect clams and lobsters and fish and birds, but they fail to protect girls sufficiently, and the courts have failed to punish those who trade in girls as sex slaves. The maximum penalty for stealing a pig is five years. Until 1911 it was the same penalty for stealing a girl. Now girl stealing may be punished by ten years, the same as stealing a mule or calf.

Mrs. Park was involved in the town's last suffrage demonstration on April 24, 1919, when U.S. Senator James Phelan came to speak to the Chamber of Commerce. Park and other Women's Peace Party members picketed him, claiming he hadn't voted for national woman suffrage. Phelan explained later that he was "paired" — his yea vote was matched with a colleague's nay, a Senate practice. The women's bad taste horrified the *Times*, but picketing remained a protest tactic.

Save the Redwoods!

As author and environmentalist Wallace Stegner pointed out, "Virtually all conservation activity up to the mid-20th century was concerned with saving something precious in our national heritage." These efforts, initially aimed at saving wildlife, had barely begun when Stanford University opened in 1891, and it was natural that President Jordan and the life scientists he had recruited followed them closely. Jordan and ten others from Stanford and/or Palo Alto, along with Timothy Hopkins, became founding members of the Sierra Club in 1892, and Jordan and later botany Professor William Russell

Dudley played starring parts in its early publications. As early as 1895, Dudley made a plea to the club for setting aside state groves of redwoods, referring particularly to the magnificent trees in the Big Basin. (Ralph S. Smith, a Redwood City newspaperman, had first raised the cry in 1886-87, shortly before a subscriber shot and killed him — for an unrelated reason.)

Big Basin became the first land conservancy in California acquired by public-private financing, but not before some classic melodrama. Andrew P. Hill, a photographer and artist who operated a branch studio in Palo Alto in 1892-94, became the catalyst. In 1899, Hill paid an entrance fee and took pictures at Felton Big Trees Grove to illustrate an account of a nearby redwoods fire. Arriving later, the grove's owner tried to take away the photographic plates, but Hill refused to give them up. Awaiting a train home, Hill had the idea of campaigning to make the place a public park. He later wrote:

I argued [to himself] that as I had been furnishing illustrations for a number of writers, whom I knew quite well, that here was a latent force which, when awakened to a noble cause, would immediately respond, and perhaps arouse the press of the whole country. Thus was born my idea of saving the redwoods.

Hill consulted with Dr. Jordan, who agreed and called a meeting of interested people on May 1, 1900, at the Stanford library. Its focus became whether to try first to save the redwoods at Big Basin rather than those at Felton. A survey committee assigned to scout Big Basin found hitherto-unknown treasures there; they also befriended the largest stockholder among the owners and learned that some of the biggest first-growth redwoods (*Sequoia sempervirens*) there were about to be cut. At a campfire one night, Hill proposed forming a forest club to preserve the Big Basin; it was quickly named the Sempervirens Club.

A Classic Campaign

The club enlisted members throughout central California, secured vigorous newspaper support and lined up backing from the Sierra Club and other groups. Jordan and Dudley wangled a one-year option on 14,000 acres to quell the threat of immediate cutting. Rather than vie with a rival bill in Congress involving the Calaveras Big Trees, the club switched its target to the state government. A classic drive for legislative approval went on in 1901, almost stalling several times before Hill and his supporters pulled through with tactics that modern pressure groups would readily recognize.

Finally both houses passed the measure, but Governor Henry Gage had two forest bills on his desk awaiting signature, and felt his party could afford only one. He called on Jordan for advice, and the Stanford president argued successfully for Big Basin, saying the other measure — to set up a forestry commission — could wait, but "any delay in connection with the proposed [park] might be fatal."

The Sempervirens Club organized at Big Basin in 1901.

Thus was consummated the first big set-aside of coast redwoods, and the first in California sparked by a concerted citizens' effort. The Stanford-Palo Alto involvement had been crucial.

This beginning gave the Palo Alto community a big stake in the conservation movement. When its national champion, President Theodore Roosevelt, spoke at Stanford in 1903, he hailed the Sierra Club but also praised the possession of Big Basin as "a source of just pride to all citizens jealous of California's good name."

Early Ecological Efforts

Later on, a Sierra Club bid to preserve Yosemite's twin valley, Hetch Hetchy, split the ranks of local members. Professor Charles D. Marx and his brother, Professor Guido Marx, were in a club minority that was sympathetic to San Francisco's water interests. So was Professor Charles B. Wing. All three, of course, were deeply involved in Palo Alto government, and likely foresaw even before the Raker Act of 1913 firmed up San Francisco's Hetch Hetchy rights that Palo Alto would one day need to draw on the mountain water source.

During Palo Alto's first several decades as a city, concerns about preserving resources rarely rose to the surface. Residents were preoccupied with development. However, the Woman's Club undertook the planting of trees along University Avenue in its early days. Mary S. Lakin, one of its "pioneer mothers," used to tell of driving a horse and buggy along and watering saplings.

In 1905, the Political Equality Club issued "A Plea for the Preservation of the Flowers." The pamphlet advocated "sidewalk gardening" to beautify Palo Alto, along with parental vigilance against the depredations of "mischievous children, careless tradesmen and out-of-town visitors." Dr. Jordan and Luther Burbank were quoted, and University of California botany Professor Willis Jepson denounced the wholesale gathering of decorative shrubbery and wildflowers. Professor George J. Peirce of the Stanford botanical laboratory remarked, "An increasing civilized population entails a decrease among all wild things. Beyond this unavoidable destruction of plants and animals people are not likely to go once their attention has been called to the permanent injury temporary thoughtlessness may cause."

Many years passed, however, before residents became alarmed about balancing "progress" and its environmental cost. For example, after the city acquired its baylands in 1926, there came a flash of recognition that in certain conditions untreated sewage spilled intolerably near dairies. So the first sewage treatment plant was built. But most ecology action waited until after World War II.

Early Peace Campaigns

David Starr Jordan stood as the university's, and the town's, leading peace campaigner for most of the years until his death in 1931. Even before he left the Stanford presidency in 1913 to devote more

PALO ALTO HISTORICAL ASSOCIATION/NEWTON
Stanford President David Starr Jordan.

effort to peace promotion, he spoke locally on the topic many times. Peace was on the agenda of the women's clubs, the WCTU and suffrage groups, so he received a respectful hearing — but no mass action. However, as Jonathan Bell noted, Jordan had opposed the Spanish-American War until it was declared, and then "supported his country." Therein lay a harbinger.

Through 1914, Palo Altans generally respected pacifism, and often took stands against intervention abroad. But as anti-German feelings grew, public opinion shifted and desperate notes entered the dialogue. Peace groups decried "the hysterical demand for preparedness" sweeping the land, and boasted of defeating a state compulsory military training bill, but supported more physical training for boys and girls. At Stanford, President Ray Lyman Wilbur emphasized preparedness and put himself at odds with Jordan.

When Palo Alto's National Guard Company L entrained for Mexican border duty in June 1916, calls for backing "our boys" multiplied.

Company L Is Called to the Colors

In March 1917 the *Times* called for war *and* for conscription, and Company L, home from Arizona, was ordered into federal service. Jessie Knight Jordan — Mrs. David Starr Jordan — called for an emergency peace campaign, but on April 3 President Woodrow Wilson asked for war. Congressman E.L. Hayes of San Jose voted against declaring war because Wilson had talked of conscription, but later favored all other war measures.

Military drills began at Stanford and Palo Alto High School, whose principal, Walter Nichols, received a few criticisms. Camp Fremont in Menlo

During World War I, Palo Altans raised money for the Belgian War Relief with street fairs.

Park became an Army base in August, and from then on free speech grew more and more severely restricted and spy scares ran wild. Bell asserted that this poisonous climate stemmed from the fat profits Palo Alto merchants made off the Camp Fremont trade.

In March 1918 the City Council passed an ordinance against "seditious utterances." Police Chief Noble instructed all officers on ending pro-German talk and arresting anyone found berating the government or the president.

Palo Alto also showed its compassionate side. Many months before the U.S. joined in the war, townspeople rallied behind Herbert Hoover's Belgian war relief leadership, ultimately raising more than $50,000 to aid innocent victims of the bloody battles in Belgium. Residents also closely followed Hoover's postwar food relief efforts.

War Ends but Words Still Fly

The war ended in November 1918, and Camp Fremont closed in April 1920. The American Legion protested the use of Palo Alto Community House — a memorial to the war dead — for a meeting concerning amnesty for political prisoners. Peace forces concentrated on getting the last conscientious objectors freed from prison.

At a county schools meeting at San Jose in October 1921, Palo Alto High School Principal Nichols rose to say:

I wear upon my wrist the watch of my son [Alan, an aviator], killed in France in the service of our country. I ask that a committee be appointed to determine whether this Alice Park on the program is the one whose home in Palo Alto is a center of sedition.

The chairwoman diverted the request, but Nichols' remark stood.

Peace Sentiments Rise Anew

Peace sentiments surged again in the '20s. In December 1922, the city's Catholic and Protestant congregations reported that more than 2,500

members had ratified resolutions to outlaw war. The stand, prepared by an interchurch committee chaired by retired U.S. Navy Captain Edward L. Beach, pledged the churches to the teaching of international and interracial friendship and justice for all races.

The Women's International League for Peace and Freedom organized a Palo Alto branch in April 1922, and Alice Park remained active in it until her eyesight failed a few years before her death in 1961 at age 100. Never the largest local women's group, the WILPF was the most absolute in its stands against militarism and for free speech. Writer Kathleen Norris often addressed its meetings.

To inspire thoughts of world peace, the WILPF gave a children's peace fountain, done by sculptor Robert Paine and placed in Rinconada Park in 1926 with a dedication ceremony involving children from six schools. In 1949, Mrs. M.S. Alderton lamented its relocation when the Lucie Stern Community Center was built, and its later deterioration.

Late in the '20s, public opinion had swung around to where arms limitations won strong support from high school students, the press and even the American Legion. But in the '30s, tensions mounted anew as totalitarian states rose to imperil democracy. The 1914-19 cycle repeated, though less virulently. After Pearl Harbor, public support for America's part in World War II solidified; the WILPF merely urged widespread education about U.S. war aims.

Another group active in the '20s and '30s, the Palo Alto Housewives' Union, first came out fighting post-World War I profiteering and inflated living costs. Before long its interests veered from consumer issues to labor union militance. It opposed the state criminal syndicalism law, took stands on strikes and protested "the presence in Chinese waters of American war vessels for the purpose of interference in Chinese internal affairs."

"An Effective Guardian of Good Government"

Two other women's organizations started in 1929 have proven large and enduring, and have rendered signal public service. Both the Palo Alto League of Women Voters and the Palo Alto branch of the American Association of University Women devote careful study to issues within their purview and seek consensus in presenting facts and stands to the public.

Palo Alto Times Editor Elinor Cogswell once pronounced the LWV "an effective guardian of good government at all levels." Originated to make women informed voters, it has built a record of outstanding analysis and explication of ballot issues. Palo Alto's league has repeatedly produced state presidents, and in more recent years its "graduates" have compiled enviable records as officeholders. In addition, those trained in its ranks have found they had acquired skills suiting them for mid-life jumps into the job market.

The AAUW's focus is broader than matters of citizenship and ballot issues, broad as those are, but it applies similar research techniques with dramatic results. How the Palo Alto branch wrote a best-seller will be related later in this chapter.

Personal Growth and Women's Liberation

Establishing homes and raising families were the dominant roles of most local women from the end of World War II through the 1950s, although the war years greatly enlarged possibilities for working outside the home. By 1960, the placidity of the '50s began to melt — change was, as Bob Dylan sang it, "Blowin' in the Wind," and not solely in civil rights. The advent of the birth control pill, together with Betty Friedan's book *The Feminine Mystique* in 1963, opened a new era that not only led to the sexual revolution but also opened a new drive for women's rights. The National Organization for Women, founded in 1966, struck harmonics in Palo Alto.

Joyce Passetti O'Connor, looking back in late 1974 at the end of her stint as women's editor of the *Palo Alto Times*, wrote:

Women became involved [in the mid-'60s] in controversial causes and in a revolution of their own.

Articles about drug abuse, consumer problems, pollution, sex education, population control, child care, family relations, women's liberation — all found space on the women's pages. . .

The women's movement hit the Midpeninsula in the early '70s and a new breed of woman began making news. She was no longer content just helping others. She started looking at and questioning herself and her goals.

Out of that realization came [NOW] and on the local scene continuing education for women, numerous seminars and lecture series probing the roles of women in today's society, and the establishment in Palo Alto of a Resource Center for Women.

These changes, plus the student-led Vietnam War protests and the civil rights struggle, made for turbulent times — with the added excitement of another new fascination: personal growth strivings. Partly spawned by the postwar evolution of group psychotherapy in the nearby Veterans Administration hospitals, what has been called the human potential movement brought sensitivity training, encounter groups, psychodrama workshops and weekend marathons onto the scene, along with women's consciousness-raising groups. The Midpeninsula Free University — the Free You, for short — mushroomed out of nowhere until by 1970 its catalog listed 50 various encounter groups, and there were many others in town.

The craze cooled off after a few years, but certain elements found more lasting niches. Prometheus, a downtown psychodrama workshop, featured Vic Lovell and associates; in College Terrace, Frieda Porat led a staff of more than 30 at the Center for Creativity and Growth. Virginia Satir of the Mental Research Institute, the author of *Peoplemaking*, became another popular lecturer and guru. Fritz Perls of Esalen and self-actualization theorist Abraham Maslow both were widely followed, especially after their deaths in 1970.

Experimentation — with drugs or without —

was common, and encounter techniques and lingo worked their way into the staidest institutions. The liberated spirit of adventure at length collided with the sociopolitical pendulum's swing to conservatism, tax revolts and the demise in 1982 of the proposed Equal Rights Amendment to the U.S. Constitution. After that, women's rights activists looked to more specific issues, such as sexual harassment in the workplace in the early '90s. Meanwhile, the AIDS epidemic chilled the sexual revolution by a marked degree.

Preservation Collides with Development

Old-style conservation had rocked along well into the '50s with the Save the Redwoods League and creation of parks and recreation facilities its banners. Concerns about protecting air and water quality grew gradually. Suddenly, contests of preservation versus development emerged, in the Bay Area and right in Palo Alto. In several epic battles, lines were drawn that fenced in industry.

The first gambit had a long history, and happened rather quietly. Since 1923, the Santa Clara Valley Audubon Society, which always had an active Palo Alto wing, had been eyeing the baylands for a bird sanctuary. Steps toward creating a "bird preserve" were pushed in 1928, but reached an impasse that lasted until after World War II. Then the duck pond and a modest refuge were dedicated.

In the late '50s, ambitious City Manager Jerry Keithley proposed to create lucrative industrial

PALO ALTO WEEKLY/RENEE BURGARD

Palo Alto's duck pond in the baylands.

sites by filling in the baylands, and to annex the foothills and build high-rise towers on the Skyline.

Enid Pearson and Robert Debs, both council-watchers then, were horrified. They launched a petition drive to stop city land development until a general plan was adopted, and when the city attorney advised the council to disregard them, they went to court and made it stick. A 28-month moratorium on development resulted.

At about this time a Save the Bay campaign arose. It originated in Berkeley, but gained great energy in Palo Alto and neighboring cities when word got out that developers wanted to cut down San Bruno Mountain and use the dirt to fill much of the South Bay. A massive public reaction scotched that plan and led to creation of a three-year Bay Conservation and Development Commission, later extended.

Of Parks and Petitions

In the early '60s, Pearson, an Audubon and Sierra Club activist, became angry when one small informal park on the old Sherman School block and part of the city's Bowden Park vanished. Abetted by John Willits and James Warnock, she surveyed park dedication ordinances in California cities and launched a drive for one in Palo Alto. Its aim was to require a vote by the people before the use of any land dedicated for parks or open space could change.

In 1965, the park initiative and another sponsored by Pearson to reduce the size of a council she considered unresponsive both passed, and Pearson herself was elected to the council. The residentialist era had begun, largely due to environmentalism's growing power. Rachel Carson's 1962 book, *Silent Spring*, had rung alarm bells.

The Audubon Society proposed a larger marshland wildlife preserve in 1965, using a solid ecological rationale. An ad hoc study committee urged the city to adopt this plan and commit other baylands to recreational uses. The preserve was created and the Baylands Nature Interpretive Center opened there in 1969. But not until after a League of Women Voters study in 1971 urged

COURTESY OF THE PHOTOGRAPHER/LEO HOLUB
Wallace Stegner led efforts to keep industry out of the foothills.

leaving the baylands alone did the last threats of industrial uses subside.

The Fight for Factory-free Foothills

On the uplands side of town, meanwhile, the concept of industry in the foothills had aroused opposition. A group of residents tried in a 1959 referendum to keep "factories out of the foothills" west of what is now Foothill Expressway. They lost, but in 1962 a group of 26 led by Lois Hogle and Ruth Spangenberg organized the Committee for Green Foothills. Wallace Stegner agreed to be its first president.

In subsequent campaigns, CGF did manage to keep industry from encroaching west of Interstate 280, and to defend the foothills and coastside generally from excessive development. The *Palo Alto Times* and its sister papers had long pursued a policy of keeping the Skyline open, which fit in with CGF's goals and helped fuel a broadly supported 1972 drive to create the Midpeninsula

Regional Open Space District. Other foothills-saving actions were large-lot zoning in the hills and open space easements for Coyote Hill on Stanford land.

Stegner, a Pulitzer Prize-winner novelist who lived just across a country road from Palo Alto, voiced a lyric appreciation of the foothills and their rare "waterfall" fog in *20-20 Vision: In Celebration of the Peninsula Hills*, published by CGF in 1982. He wrote, in small part:

All you have to do to feel the hills as a blessing is to live within sight of them, within the reach of their climatic controls, and under the influence of their watershed. From the Golden Gate to Monterey Bay, the low Santa Cruz Mountains form a barrier, northeast to southwest, between cold ocean and hot inland valleys. They catch twice as much rain from Pacific storms as do the lowlands on either side, and so feed both the surface and subsurface water channels that distribute water throughout the year. They intercept the prevailing westerlies and mediate between Pacific fog and inland sun, forming a marvelous air conditioner nearly a hundred miles long that guarantees the Peninsula the finest year-round climate in the whole round world.

The baylands and foothills triumphs, with their accompanying educational impact, put the community ahead of the learning curve by the time of Earth Day 1970. So did two Stanford biologists, Professors Paul R. Ehrlich, author of *The Population Bomb*, and John H. Thomas, whose doctrine was preached by Los Altos-based Zero Population Growth. In 1969, Thomas argued that Palo Alto should post a "No More People" sign; he said he thought he and Ehrlich had talked to practically every high school student in Palo Alto that year.

Rep. Paul N. "Pete" McCloskey, then the area's congressman, played a national role in the first Earth Day, which was coordinated in Washington, D.C., by a Stanford graduate, Denis Hayes. The

PALO ALTO WEEKLY/RENEE BURGARD
Earth Day's Denis Hayes.

focus then was on clean air and water, and a movement became a revolution.

Starting at Home

For a couple of years, the Palo Alto AAUW had been studying "This Beleaguered Earth." A few months after Earth Day 1970 the AAUW branch issued a booklet titled *If You Want to Save Your Environment. . . START AT HOME!*, with practical tips on ecologically sound things to do at home, in the garden, in the community and in lobbying government. The timely little environmental handbook sold 85,000 copies, according to Carroll Harrington, whose idea it was. Another of the authors, Joyce Leonard, said its advice on recycling broke hitherto-unplowed ground.

How pervasive was the new environmental consciousness? In 1973, looking ahead to the U.S. Bicentennial, the City Council endorsed Mrs. Billy Prior's proposal to create a Palo Alto grove of redwoods in Big Basin as a gift to the nation. It was done through the Sempervirens Fund, established in 1968 in the spirit of the early-day club. Companies, schools, individuals and the council itself all raised funds to help buy trees in the 10-acre grove.

Another catalyst for local action since 1969 has been the Peninsula Conservation Center, which moved its base for a half dozen environmentally oriented organizations and its library to Palo Alto in 1972. Debbie Mytels, its director in 1992, has called the high level of environmental consciousness in every age group in Palo Alto a hopeful sign for the movement's future. "Palo Alto can be. . . a place where things get worked out," Mytels said. "We can set an example, like we did with recycling."

Earth Day 1990 made the city its world headquarters. Denis Hayes interrupted his law career to be its chairman. This time problems requiring international cooperation for a solution held the spotlight: protecting the earth's ozone layer, reducing acid rain and halting the pell-mell destruction of tropical forests.

"We Are Deeply Concerned. . . "

World War II's awesome ending in the atomic bombing of two Japanese cities, Hiroshima and Nagasaki, imparted a major new concern to the postwar peace movement. The Cold War and the rise of the Soviet Union and other powers to nuclear capability heightened it. As periods of war tension marched across the years — Korea, the Berlin Wall, Vietnam, the Persian Gulf — strife about training, conscription, U.S. involvement and the propriety of a great nation engaging in an arms race and using its armed might in little wars has peaked and ebbed.

The Conference on International Organization at San Francisco in 1945 gave Peninsulans a stake in the framing of the United Nations Charter, and added to a longtime local cosmopolitan consciousness. Hopes for some form of world government have often been a debate subject. In 1968, M. Douglas Mattern, chairman of the anti-war

PALO ALTO TIMES/GENE TUPPER

A Vietnam War protest march on Waverley Street.

Emilia and Harry Rathbun, leaders of groups that became Beyond War.

Concerned Citizens of Palo Alto, made the city the Bay Area headquarters for a militant organization espousing world government.

Protests have been sporadic, except when the combined local forces of opposition to the Vietnam War became a seismic wave that threatened to close Stanford University and Palo Alto's high schools, halt city and federal government activities and paralyze defense production in Stanford Industrial Park and nearby facilities. In the fall of 1969, the Peninsula Vietnam Moratorium Committee was turning out crowds of 5,000 or more for protest actions. Nerves rubbed raw; ordinarily even-tempered Mayor Ed Arnold once denounced a "Meal for Peace" sponsored by a number of ministers.

The Cambodian incursion stoked new outrage in May 1970, yielding full-page political advertisements with hundreds to thousands of signers placed by groups not normally so engulfed in a national issue — physicians, school district faculty and staff and an elite set of city leaders who appealed for donations to run a *Washington Post* ad saying: "We are deeply concerned about Cambodia. We urge the Congress to exercise its constitutional power to stop the spread of the Asian War." A three-page *Post* ad resulted.

Peace marches, imperative ads and mega-petitions continued through 1971 and 1972 and into 1973. On January 8, 1973, petitions signed by 4,000 Midpeninsulans were delivered to Congressman McCloskey. A week later 34 ministers signed an open letter to Richard Nixon saying, "We urge you, Mr. President, in the name of God, stop!"

Although war protesters usually stated a negative message, some peace activists tried positive approaches. Beyond War became the most cohesive and most effective of these. Others acted through the Palo Alto Peace Center, later renamed the Midpeninsula Peace Center.

Based in Palo Alto, Beyond War amassed 25,000 adherents across the nation at its peak in the late 1980s. Its origins traced back to retired Stanford Professor Harry Rathbun and his wife Emilia who conducted "Jesus as Teacher" classes in the 1960s. Out of the classes grew Woman to Woman Building the Earth for the Children's Sake (Build the Earth, for short), which sought to enhance a healthy world for children by safeguarding the environment, averting war, improving race relations and championing other causes, including upgrading its members' skills as mates and parents. An affiliated group, Creative Initiative Foundation, made room for men to join in.

Out of this, in 1982, developed Beyond War, which worked in varied ways to promote peaceful resolution of conflicts. Harry Rathbun declared:

Our message is that nuclear war is obsolete in competition between the great powers. It is

PALO ALTO WEEKLY/RENEE FADIMAN
Both sides demonstrate at a St. Aloysius Church prayer walk in 1992.

time to use the same intellect and resources that developed nuclear weapons to find a way to eradicate warfare between nations.

Beyond War avoided direct clashes with governmental authorities and did not make league with protest groups, except for Physicians for Social Responsibility, which also stuck to a positive approach. With original stage productions, satellite TV links, peace promotion prizes and other strategies, Beyond War established people-to-people ties in the former Soviet Union and Eastern Europe. Hundreds of its leaders left their homes and jobs to work, often full-time, as volunteers for the cause.

Toward a Global Community

In April 1992, after the Berlin Wall fell, the Soviet Union broke up and communism collapsed, the group changed its name from Beyond War to Foundation for a Global Community. Joe Kresse, one of the foundation's three executive directors, said Beyond War had reached its goal of implanting a widespread belief in war's futility.

"While war has not ended, there is a greater consciousness that war doesn't work," Kresse said. Now the Foundation for a Global Community is looking ahead to what it sees as a new and larger task: laying a foundation for a world in which humans everywhere, fully recognizing their interdependence, will begin to act for the long-term well-being of their shared planet. The new task is seen as figuring out, on a personal basis, what individuals must do to help the global community survive and thrive. Unlike Beyond War, FGC expects to team up with many other organizations in that task.

While this may be the most dramatic of the Palo Alto-spawned "save the world" groups, it is not the only one. Causes — some still local, others globalized — continue to command the attention of the people who live and interact in the city.

Epilogue: Will Somebody Always Care?

Looking back, significant mileposts of Palo Alto's history stand out clearly.

The village that sprang from the stubblefield of the early 1890s grew apace with Stanford University. Its people suffered while legal proceedings strapped the campus, then prospered as the threat lifted.

By 1909 enough municipal groundwork had been laid so that citizens felt comfortable adopting a charter government designed to insure local independence and stability. A decade later World War I broke up old patterns. In its aftermath the municipality became owner of a hospital, and public services such as police and fire protection grew more professional. The citizenry cheered the hope of lasting peace, and new prosperity dawned. Over about twenty years, the school system was unified and Mayfield and Palo Alto merged.

With the Depression of the 1930s slowing progress, the college town was lucky to receive Lucie Stern's heartwarming gifts of new cultural facilities, with an emphasis on children.

World War II commanded another refocusing. New energies released after the war caused a great expansion of the city in acreage and populace, helped along by a shift to the city manager system of local governance. Electronics, born of Palo Alto radio research triumphs in the 1908-18 era, grew lustily. It led to a surge of light industry that broadened into other fields of high technology — the phenomenon summed up today in the nickname "Silicon Valley."

During the 1960s growth met determined resistance. Residents rose up in fear that the city's attractive living qualities might be paved under. A burst of devotion to environmentalism dovetailed with their fight. Not much later, the forces of industrial expansion based in large part on defense work ran into the stiff opposition of the Vietnam War protesters. Town and gown alike had to deal with crisis conditions. Meanwhile, Stanford had bought out Palo Alto's stake in their joint hospital. School enrollment peaked near 16,000 in 1968, then declined by half over the next two decades. Taxpayer rebellions beginning in 1978 clobbered both the schools and the municipality.

Readjustment marked the 1980s as inflationary interest rates were curbed and business boomed. It became manifest that Silicon Valley's production plants had shifted south, although headquarters activities, research and prototype development kept bases in Palo Alto. Related legal, finance and accounting specialists made the city their location of choice and bolstered its revenues.

Recession in the late '80s and early '90s took a toll. When the city's daily newspaper — its oldest business — abruptly shut down in March 1993, worry about Palo Alto's future surfaced anew. An aging populace, a decline from peak real estate prices and a flattening of business revenues compounded the fears.

Is Palo Alto "over the hill"? Asked just that, David Packard replied, "No, but I don't think it will change very much." Some agreed, but others saw prospects far more promising — or much worse. A year before dying, the *Peninsula Times Tribune* had run a "Paradise Threatened" series that evoked a wide spectrum of opinion on the city's pluses and minuses. Among the refrains were that:

— *the city seemed to be losing its sense of community*

— *other places were outclassing some of its once-unique amenities such as the Stanford Research Park and Shopping Center*

— *it was not welcoming to new businesses and*

— *it feathered its own nest at the expense of neighbors.*

Hardly anyone said Palo Alto was perfect, although there seemed wide recognition of its distinctions and its central position on the Peninsula. Few saw it teetering on the brink of doom.

Assorted straws in the wind may be harbingers of change. For instance, 1993 broke at least one "glass ceiling" as a black woman with exceptional organizing skills became city manager. The schools chief said a new elementary school may be needed soon, hinting a new enrollment climb. Local research labs kept parading out discoveries. Business operations free to locate anywhere were choosing Palo Alto — for example, Paramount's "media kitchen" for Hollywood and Andersen Consulting's technology center, a unit of global accounting and computer services firm Arthur Andersen & Co.

Early in 1993 a 28-member committee began a three-year process of shaping a new comprehensive plan. It is to cover not only the usual land-use guidelines but also a vision of what the city wants to be. Issues to be addressed are expected to include ethnic and cultural diversity, Palo Alto's role within the region and maintaining economic growth in a built-out city.

For the voters, June 1994 will bring a ballot — not the first of its kind — on changing the size of the City Council. This time a reduction from nine members to seven is proposed.

Also under re-examination is the relationship of the university and the city. Seemingly it is in a new stage after the protest-control imperatives of much of Richard W. Lyman's Stanford presidency and the surge of campus expansion, capped by Stanford's centennial and the research overhead controversy that marred the end of Donald Kennedy's tenure.

A task group is looking at the physical interface of campus and city along the community's historic axis, El Camino Real. Meanwhile, new Stanford President Gerhard Casper has triggered debate on the compression of the undergraduate years from four to three — an idea not far removed from Ray Lyman Wilbur's efforts in the 1920s to shift the freshman and sophomore years to local junior colleges.

High technology's pace of change gets faster and faster. And the winds it stirs are felt keenly in the public schools, where the stress of staying on the cutting edge is reportedly high. Judging from what is now in place, Palo Alto companies figure to continue to be prominent in the convergence of computers, video, data transmission, artificial intelligence and virtual reality. The same is true of expeditions to other Earth planets and probes of the vast cosmos beyond. Still other new thresholds promise to be crossed.

At the grass-roots level, recycling of reclaimed water may be the next big ecological step under the municipal aegis. In the effort to overcome the contamination of chemical leaks, Barron Park residents have developed a model for citizen participation — and without much help from city hall, they add pointedly.

On the health front, the Palo Alto Medical Clinic is taking steps toward a major move from its present downtown fringe location to a site to the west, extending from the railroad tracks to El Camino Real between Town & Country Village Shopping Center and the Holiday Inn. What will become of the Clinic's two blocks along Homer? A few land developers who have, in a sense, been returning Palo Alto to local ownership may have ideas.

Mayor Jean McCown, who incidentally speaks Mandarin Chinese fluently, said in her April 1993 State of the City address:

> ... I believe we all understand that Palo Alto is extraordinarily well-educated, financially successful, older and more homogenous than the region and state in which we live. I believe the differences between the city and our surroundings present one of the biggest challenges we face in how we choose to define our "community."

The mayor boldly encompassed Stanford in *her* definition, noting that by doing so she includes Stanford Professor John Gardner, a distinguished former Cabinet officer and a foremost thinker about community and a vision for the future. McCown made clear her interest in closer communication with neighbors on all sides, specifically naming East Palo Alto. She spoke of city limits as "historical jurisdictional barriers that are, at times, more of a hindrance than a help in solving the problems that face us."

Mayor McCown quoted Gardner's dictum that "a community of diverse elements has a greater capacity to adapt and renew itself in a swiftly changing world." She went on to say:

To achieve this, Gardner's point is that we must be inclusive, we must welcome and incorporate diversity, fight fragmentation and polarization of positions, build coalitions across sectors, and create mechanisms to resolve and negotiate disputes. I see this as a philosophy to be applied in relationships between the public and private sectors, between neighborhoods and developers, between cities and across traditional jurisdictional boundaries, between Town and Gown and maybe between Cal and Stanford, except not on Big Game day!

Pointing to the city's tradition of widespread citizen participation in public affairs, McCown called for applying the thrust of this volunteerism and residents' expertise in working out solutions to problems. Neighborhood associations and other groups have an important role to play, she suggested.

Two oft-quoted economists who call Palo Alto home consider the community's present base strong and its long-term prospects chancy but most likely good.

Richard C. Carlson of Spectrum Economics Inc. calls the place "an island of stability in a sea of chaos." One big issue, he said, is keeping the problems of surrounding areas near and far from impinging on Palo Alto's strength, which draws competition for sales tax dollars and employment, as well as raids by other money-hungry government units.

He alluded to the problems of crime building off economic and social changes and "an economy moving strongly in a white collar direction" to the distress of blue collar workers.

Despite Palo Alto's "astonishingly high property tax base per person," Carlson predicted, its ability to maintain a very high level of social services will be tested increasingly. He saw the graying of the citizenry bringing a rather massive turnover of housing stock in the second half of the 1990s. Newcomers moving in (with an average annual family income exceeding $100,000) will include significantly more high-income Asians attracted by the school system, he forecast. A crucial issue will be whether the school system can maintain itself, for high home prices depend on it and if it falters, there is danger of "a self-reinforcing downward spiral."

Increases in density probably will be forced in locations ripe for redevelopment, such as the Page Mill-El Camino Real area, Carlson said. Such changes can be directed but not stopped, in his view.

Appraising Palo Alto's attractions and the concentrations of intellectual capital and major corporate headquarters they have drawn, Carlson remarked, "It doesn't get much better than this, but we've got a real good shot at keeping it."

Robert K. Arnold, director of the Center for the Continuing Study of the California Economy, recently projected that between 1993 and 2005 California has a good chance of outperforming the U.S. economy. Foreign trade, high technology, professional services and tourism and entertainment — all Palo Alto strengths — will lead the growth, according to the center's study.

Looking 50 years ahead, Arnold said internal combustion-powered automobiles that have dominated suburban growth in the last 50 to 75 years will probably be gone. Palo Alto's cityscape will change greatly as a result, with University Avenue perhaps becoming a downtown promenade with moving sidewalks. Arnold expects small electric cars with a lot of main-line connections to replace today's private autos.

A point of interest to Arnold is whether the existing housing stock will last another half century, as it very well may. If it does, he said, residential districts may look much the same as today; if not, he would expect more density.

Arnold sees Silicon Valley as being in a tremendously strong leadership position. With the constantly accelerating pace of change, it might take a wrong turn somewhere and become sidetracked, he observed, but "my guess is that Silicon Valley will be a very, very key economy in the world over the next 50 years."

Fifty-year projections are undependable, Arnold noted, observing that Palo Altans in 1943 could not have foreseen the city's status today. However, a couple of comments from the even more distant past may still be applicable to tomorrow's directions.

During the World War I era, the *Palo Alto Times* remarked editorially on the town-and-gown relationship, saying in part:

Palo Alto's reputation is bound up with the reputation of Stanford. The city now could go ahead on its own course if Stanford were removed, though it would lose an incalculable amount and would not be the same city. [It] is vitally interested in the progress and prestige of the university. Every citizen of Palo Alto should therefore be an intelligent booster of Stanford...

In the mid-1920s, Frank J. Taylor, writing in *Sunset* magazine on why he considered Palo Alto the best little city in the West, extolled its virtues and then remarked:

... the real reason for Palo Alto's place at the head of fine places to live is the spirit of the people. ... Somebody has always cared about civic affairs. Somebody always saw to it that they ran a little better than was necessary, or better than a professional officeholder would run them. Somebody always saw to it that the city got full value for its money. ...

What magic wand waved over this particular "sea of mud" and changed it... into a community... that is the model of civic development the country over? I thought, of course, of some rich man of vision with nothing to do but be "father" to Palo Alto. I spent some time looking for this mythical character and talked to many old-timers of the town. I never found him. He didn't exist. Palo Alto is a community proposition. The town was pulled out of the mud by teamwork. Everybody pulled at the harness when his time came. The thing that put the city on the map as a fine place to live was that somebody always cared how civic affairs ran.

Somebody cared!

Keep that refrain humming.

Appendix A

Palo Alto Buildings on the National Register of Historic Places

Downing House	706 Cowper Street
Squire House	900 University Avenue
Hostess House	25 University Avenue
Fraternal Hall	140 University Avenue
Peck House	860 University Avenue
Pettigrew House	1336 Cowper Street
Norris House	1247 Cowper Street
Pedro de Lemos House	110 Waverley Oaks
U.S. Post Office	300 Hamilton Avenue
Dunker House	420 Maple Street
Kee House	2310 Yale Street
Professorville Historic District	
Ramona Street Architectural District	

State of California Registered Historical Landmarks

Squire House	900 University Avenue
Hostess House/MacArthur Park Restaurant	25 University Avenue
Site of Cyril Elwell/Lee de Forest Radio Lab	903-905 Emerson Street
Hewlett-Packard Garage	367 Addison Avenue
Site of Juana Briones House	4155 Old Adobe Road
Site of Sarah Wallis House	La Selva Drive
Site of Co-Invention of Integrated Circuit	844 E. Charleston Road

Additional Sites Marked by City of Palo Alto and the Palo Alto Historical Association

First school in Mayfield	Birch and Sherman
Antonino Buelna Adobe	San Francisquito Creek and Willow Road (About 1850 Willow)
Middlefield Crossing	San Francisquito Creek at Middlefield Road
Indian Mounds	Near Middlefield Road south of Marion Avenue
Uncle Jim's Cabin	El Camino Real and California Avenue
Clarke's/Wilson's Landing	On Mayfield Slough near Palo Alto Harbor
First Elementary School	Bryant Street near University Avenue
First Hospital	Lytton Avenue and Cowper Street
Secundino Robles Adobe	Alma Street and Ferne Avenue
Rafael Soto Home Site	East side of Middlefield Road just north of Oregon Avenue
El Palo Alto	On south bank of San Francisquito Creek at Palo Alto Avenue and railroad bridge
Delmar Ashby House	1145 Forest Avenue
St. Thomas Aquinas Church	745 Waverley Street
Fire/Police Building	450 Bryant Street (now the Senior Center)
Harbormaster's Adobe	2500 Embarcadero Road

Appendix B

Members of the City Council and Board of Trustees
(Those listed as "mayor" were, prior to July 1, 1909, president of the Board of Trustees)
Source: City Clerk's Office

Name	Service	Years	Mayor
Ackley, Edward	1911-17	6 years	
Allen, B.G.	1912-13	7 months	
Andersen, Ron	1990-		
Arbuckle, Edward	1965-65	5 months	
Arnold, Edward	1962-71	10 years	1968-70
			1965-66
Ball, John	1959-61	2 years	1960-61
Baugh, Dicy	1929-31	2 years	
Beahrs, John	1963-77	14 years	
Bechtel, Betsy	1980-89	9 years	1983
Beene, Adron	1946-47	1 year	
Bentrott, E.H.	1939-51	12 years	
Bertsche, G.G.	1917-33	14 years	
Berwald, John	1967-77	10 years	
Bishop, Stanley	1951-63	12 years	
Blair, Emma	1919-25	6 years	
Blois, J. Byron	1934-53	19 years	1940-48
Bolander, E.H.	1945-51	6 years	
Bonham, W.R.	1933-39	6 years	
Bonn, S.G.	1925-28	3 years	
Bowden, Jerome	1943-52	9 years	
Brenner, Frances	1977-81	4 years	
Brown, W.H.	1935	3 months	
Butler, J.S.	1895-1902	7 years	
Byxbee, J.F. Sr.	1906-09	3 years	
Byxbee, Robert	1953-65	12 years	
Carey, George J.	1905-08	3 years	
Carey, Scott	1975-79	4 years	1978-79
Cashel, Edward	1937-55	18 years	
Cathcart, A.J.	1949-52	3 years	
Cathcart, A.M.	1918-36	18 years	1920-24
Christensen, C.H.	1927-35	8 years	1929-32
Clark, William	1967-73	6 years	
Clay, Roy	1973-79	6 years	
Cobb, Mike	1982-93	12 years	1986
			1990
Collins, Henry	1931-39	8 years	
Comstock, Kirke	1969-77	14 years	1971-74
Congdon, H.F.	1909-18	9 years	
Cooley, Charles P.	1915-27	12 years	1916-19
Cooley, Robert	1963-68	5 years	
Corbet, Burke	1921-22		
	1902-03	3.5 years	
Corcoran, Mildred (Justesen)	1953-59	6 years	
Cornish, H.J.	1942-47	5 years	
Costello, Lorenz	1935-41	6 years	1939-40

Name	Service	Years	Mayor
Cottrell, Edwin	1923-29	6 years	1924-25
Cramer, Frank	1915-17		
	1894-95	3 years	
Crandall, Berton	1933-35	1.5 years	
Cresap, Dean	1962-65		1963-64
	1955-59	7 years	
Cummings, Robert	1953-57	4 years	
Curry, David A.	1902-06	4 years	
Cypher, Clark	1937-44	7 years	
Davis, Burt	1955-61	6 years	
Dean, William	1904-09	5 years	
Debs, Robert	1961-67	6 years	
Dias, Frances	1961-71	10.5 years	1966-68
Dobbel, Charles	1944-44	11 months	
Downing, T.B.	1909-13	4 years	
Drysdale, George	1951-57	6 years	
Duryea, Edwin	1906-09	3 years	
Duveneck, Josephine	1923-27	4 years	
Easterday, O.M.	1918-27	9 years	
Evans, Daniel	1931-34	3 years	
Evans, Stanley	1957-61	5 years	
Eyerly, Fred	1975-83	8 years	1982
Fazzino, Gary	1990-93		1992
	1978-83	9 years	
Ferguson, A.S.	1904-06	2 years	1904-06
Fisher, H.B.	1918-19	7 months	
Fletcher, Ellen	1977-89	12 years	
Flint, Philip	1963-67	4 years	
Freedman, J.C.	1944-51	7 years	
Fuller, T.N.	1902-04	2 years	
Gallagher, Frank	1967-71	4 years	
Gaspar, Walter	1947-52	5 years	1948-51
Giffin, Clifford	1955-61		
	1939-39	6 years	
Goddard, Glenn	1935-41	6 years	
Green, George	1934-35	8 months	
Gullixson, Conrad	1968-69	1 year	
Haight, David	1959-63	4 years	1961-63
Hanley, Donald	1953-55	2 years	
Hare, M.H.	1923-23	6 months	
Henderson, Alan	1977-81		1979-81
	1971-75	8 years	
Henry, W.F.	1909-19	10 years	
Hettinger, E.A.	1909-15	6 years	
Hill, Walter	1948-53	5 years	
Hobart, A.C.	1921-31	10 years	1926-28
Hoge, Frank	1927-29	2 years	1928-29

Name	Service	Years	Mayor
Hoy, Andrew	1939-43	4 years	
Huber, Joseph	1992-		
Huston, Paul	1952-55	2.5 years	
Hutchinson, Joseph	1894-1902	8 years	1894-1902
Hyde, W.F.	1909-12 1903-06	6 years	
Jackson, Hugh	1952-53	6 months	
Johnson, A.W.	1928-34	7 years	
Jordan, C.E.	1909-29	20 years	1925-26 1911-13
Judson, C.H.	1930-37	7 years	1935-37
Kelly, W.H.	1925-35	10 years	
Klein, Larry	1981-89	9 years	1989 1984
Kniss, Liz	1990-93	4 years	
Lakin, E.D.	1913-15	2 years	
La Peire, E.A.	1909-15	6 years	
Lausten, B.P.	1921-33 1905-06	15 years	
Lesley, E.P.	1917-18	1 year	
Levy, Leland	1979-91	13 years	1985
Linder, Ivan H.	1943-51	8 years	
Lund, W.C.	1896-97	1.5 years	
Marshall, James G.	1951-63	12 years	
Marx, Charles D.	1896-1904 1908-09	10 years	1908-09
McCown, Jean	1990-93	4 years	1993
Mendenhall, D.A.	1921-25	4 years	
Merner, Frances (Bower)	1937-53	16 years	
Miller, H.C.	1919-21	2 years	
Miller, Raup	1951-53	2 years	
Miller, W.F.	1913-19	6 years	
Millis, H.A.	1909-12	3 years	
Mitchell, J. Pearce	1930-61	31 years	1951-53
Mitcheltree, Fayette	1904-05	1 year	
Montrouil, Phillip	1947-53	6 years	
Morten, A.B.	1941-51	10 years	
Mosher, G.W.	1929-39 1909-19 1898-1904	26 years	
Navis, Herbert	1955-61		
Norton, Stanley	1969-77	8 years	1975-77
Parkinson, B.	1894-98	4 years	
Parkinson, J.F.	1906-09	3 years	1906-08
Patitucci, Frank	1985-89	4 years	
Pearson, Enid	1965-75	10 years	
Peterson, H.C.	1913-21	8 years	
Porter, Noel E.	1953-65	10 years	1955-60
Radford, William A.	1941-42	1 year	
Reed, E. James	1939-43	4 years	
Renzel, Emily	1979-91	13 years	
Reynolds, H.B.	1929-30	1 year	
Richards, Robert L.	1935-47	12 years	
Rodgers, Lee W.	1959-65	12 years	
Rohrs, Raymond F.	1961-67	6 years	
Roller, A.C.	1915-23	8 years	
Rosenbaum, Richard	1992- 1971-75	6+ years	
Ruppenthal, Karl	1953-59	6 years	
Rus, William P.	1961-67	6 years	
Salsman, Byrl R.	1935-39	4 years	1937-38
Seman, Sylvia	1971-73	2 years	
Sher, Byron	1965-80	14 years	1977-78 1974-75
Simitian, Joe	1992-		
Simkins, H.W.	1908-09	1 year	
Simpson, Clifford	1951-57	6 years	1954-55
Sloan, D.L.	1896-1904	8 years	1902-04
Smith, Emory E.	1894-96	2 years	
Snyder, H.J.	1915-18	3 years	
Snyder, J.O.	1917-22	5 years	
Southwood, W.E.	1939-46	7 years	
Spaeth, C. Grant	1967-71	4 years	
Spencer, John C.	1909-11	2 years	1909-10
Stephens, Carl S.	1957-63	6 years	
Stephens, J.S.	1931-37	6 years	
Sutorius, Jack	1984-91	8 years	1991 1988
Swain, Robert E.	1912-25	13 years	1914-16
Terwilliger, H.L.	1922-24 1919-21	4 years	
Thoits, E.C.	1909-43	40 years	1920 1913-14
Thomas, Denison W.	1919-23	4 years	
Thomas, Margaret B.	1925-31	6 years	
Thomas, Earl C.	1929-48	19 years	1932-35
Truesdale, William	1904-05	1 year	
Umphreys, A.N.	1909-13	4 years	
Vail, W.E.	1909-19	10 years	
Vandervoort, E.T.	1911-15	4 years	
Warren, F.W.	1894-96	2 years	
Wells, J.B.	1952-53	1 year	
Wheatley, Jack R.	1967-71	5 years	1970-71
Wheeler, Lanie	1992-		
Whisler, George H.	1927-30	3 years	
Wickett, Fred A.	1947-55	8 years	
Williams, Thomas M.	1923-26	3 years	
Wilson, Ernest	1909-11	2 years	
Wing, Charles B.	1909-29	20 years	1910-11
Witherspoon, Anne	1975-85	10 years	
Wood, Granville N.	1926-45	19 years	
Woodward, Bertrum	1957-67	10 years	1964-65
Woolley, Gail	1984-91	8 years	1987
Worthington, Edward	1965-71	6 years	
Zweng, H. Christian	1959-65	6 years	

Bibliography

Allen, Peter C., *From the Foothills to the Bay*, Stanford, Stanford Alumni Association and Stanford Historical Society, 1980.

Arbuckle, Clyde, *Clyde Arbuckle's History of San Jose*, City of San Jose, San Jose, Smith & McKay Printing Co., Inc., 1985.

Butler, Phyllis Filiberti, *The Valley of Santa Clara: Historic Buildings, 1792-1920*, with Architectural Supplement by the Junior League of San Jose, San Jose, Junior League of San Jose, 1975; second edition, Novato, Presidio Press, 1981.

Cavalli, Gary, *Stanford Sports*, principal photography by David Madison, Stanford, Stanford Alumni Association, 1982.

Clark, Birge, *An Architect Grows Up in Palo Alto*, Palo Alto Historical Association files, Palo Alto Main Library, 1982.

Coffman, Arthur, *An Illustrated History of Palo Alto*, Palo Alto, Lewis Osborne, 1969.

Cumming, Bruce C., *A History of the Palo Alto Police Department*, (unpublished), Palo Alto Historical Association files, 1990.

De Forest, Lee, *Father of Radio — The Autobiography of Lee de Forest*, Chicago, Wilcox & Follett Co., 1950.

Duveneck, Josephine Whitney, *Life on Two Levels — An Autobiography*, Los Altos, William Kaufmann, Inc., 1978.

Elliott, Ellen Coit, *It Happened This Way*, Stanford, Stanford University Press, 1940.

Elliott, Orrin Leslie, *Stanford University: The First 25 Years*, Stanford, Stanford University Press, 1937.

Fowle (Cameron), Eleanor, *Cranston, the Senator from California*, San Rafael, Presidio Press, 1980.

Golobic, Robert, *Mayfield: Its Development and the Annexation*, (unpublished), Stanford University student manuscript in Palo Alto Historical Association files, 1957.

Griffith, Michael, Christian G. Fritz and Janet M. Hunter, editors, *A Judicial Odyssey: Federal Court in Santa Clara, San Benito, Santa Cruz, and Monterey Counties*, San Jose, Advisory Committee — San Jose Federal Court, 1985.

Gullard, Pamela, and Nancy Lund, *History of Palo Alto: The Early Years*, San Francisco, Scottwall Associates, 1989.

Harrington, Carroll, Marie Niemeyer, Joyce Leonard and Linda Fischman, *If You Want to Save Your Environment … START AT HOME!* (booklet), Palo Alto, American Association of University Women, Palo Alto California branch, Peninsula Press, Inc., 1970.

Historic Environment Consultants, *Historical and Architectural Resources of the City of Palo Alto: Inventory and Report*, Palo Alto, City of Palo Alto, 1979 (revised 1982, 1986).

Hoover, Herbert Clark, *The Memoirs of Herbert Hoover: Years of Adventure, 1874-1920*, New York, Macmillan Company, 1951.

Jacobson, Yvonne, *Passing Farms, Enduring Values: California's Santa Clara Valley*, Los Altos, William Kaufmann, Inc., in cooperation with the

California History Center, De Anza College, Cupertino, 1984.

Jordan, David Starr, *The Days of a Man: Being Memories of a Naturalist, Teacher and Minor Prophet of Democracy*, Yonkers on Hudson, N.Y., World Book Company, 1922.

Liebendorfer, Don E., *The Color of Life is Red: A History of Stanford Athletics, 1892-1972*, Stanford, Department of Athletics, Stanford University, 1972.

Margolin, Malcolm, *The Ohlone Way: Indian Life in the San Francisco-Monterey Bay Area*, Berkeley, Heyday Books, 1978.

Martin, Mildred Crowl, *Chinatown's Angry Angel: The Story of Donaldina Cameron*, Palo Alto, Pacific Books, Publishers, 1977.

McCaleb, Charles S., *Tracks, Tires and Wires: Public Transportation in California's Santa Clara Valley*, Glendale, Interurban Press, 1981.

McDonald, Emanuel B., *Sam McDonald's Farm: Stanford Reminiscences*, Stanford, Stanford University Press, 1954.

Miller, Guy C., and Hugh Enochs, *Palo Alto Community Book*, Palo Alto, Arthur W. Cawston, 1952.

Mitchell, J. Pearce, *Stanford University: 1916-1941*, Stanford, Stanford University Press, 1958.

Morgan, Jane, *Electronics in the West: The First 50 Years*, Palo Alto, National Press Books, 1967.

Nagel, Gunther W., *Iron Will: The Life and Letters of Jane Stanford*, Stanford, Stanford Alumni Association, 1985.

Nilan, Roxanne, and Margo Davis, *The Stanford Album: A Photographic History, 1885-1945*, Stanford, Stanford University Press, 1989.

Olmsted, Roger R., *Scow Schooners of San Francisco Bay*, Cupertino, California History Center, 1988.

Palo Alto AAUW, ... *Gone Tomorrow?: "Neat Cottages" & "Handsome Residences,"* Palo Alto, American Association of University Women, Palo Alto California branch, 1971 (revised 1986).

Palo Alto Historical Association, *The Tall Tree — The Story of Palo Alto and Its Neighbors* (booklets), Palo Alto, 1949- , including *Early Vehicular Travel*, 1950; *Public Schools*, 1951; *Private Schools*, 1952; *Dawn of the Electronics Age*, 1955; *Indians of the Mid-Peninsula*, 1957; *The First 50 Years of Electronics Research*, 1958; *Palo Alto — Its Backgrounds, Beginnings and Growth*, 1960; *Palo Alto Firsts*, 1963; *Portola Discovers San Francisco Bay*, 1967; *From Portola to Palo Alto*, 1969; *Mayfield*, 1976; *Streets of Palo Alto*, 1979; and *Parks of Palo Alto*, 1983.

Regnery, Dorothy F., *An Enduring Heritage: Historic Buildings of the San Francisco Peninsula*, photos by Jack E. Boucher, sponsored by the Junior League of Palo Alto, Inc., in cooperation with the Historic American Buildings Survey of the National Park Service, Stanford, Stanford University Press, 1976.

Regnery, Dorothy F., "Portraits of Sarah [Wallis]," *The Californian: Magazine of the California History Center Foundation*, Cupertino, December 1986.

Smith, Frances Rand, *A History of Early Palo Alto: Rancho Rinconada del Arroyo de San Francisquito* (unpublished manuscript), Palo Alto Historical Association files, 1937.

Stedman, Kathryn Imlay, et al., *Trees of Palo Alto*, Palo Alto, City of Palo Alto and Palo Alto Chamber of Commerce, The National Press, 1959.

Stegner, Wallace, and Committee for Green Foothills members, *20-20 Vision: In Celebration of the Peninsula Hills*, Phyllis Filiberti Butler, editor, Palo Alto, Green Foothills Foundation, 1982.

Stegner, Wallace, "It All Began With Conservation," *Smithsonian* magazine, April 1990, 35-43.

Taylor, Frank J., "Why I Think Palo Alto, California, Is the Best Small City in the West," *Sunset*, June 1926.

Turner, Paul V., Marcia E. Vetrocq and Karen Weitze, *The Founders and the Architects: The Design of Stanford University*, Stanford, Department of Art, Stanford University, 1976.

Tutorow, Norman E., *Leland Stanford: Man of Many Careers*, Menlo Park, Pacific Coast Publishers, 1971.

Varian, Dorothy, *The Inventor and the Pilot — Russell and Sigurd Varian*, Palo Alto, Pacific Books, Publishers, 1983.

Wilbur, Ray Lyman, *The Memoirs of Ray Lyman Wilbur, 1875-1949*, Stanford, Stanford University Press, 1960.

Williams, James C., "Frederick E. Terman and the Rise of Silicon Valley," *Technology in America*, 2nd ed., edited by Caroll Pursell, Cambridge, Mass, M.I.T. Press, 1990, pp. 276-291.

Williams, Sylvia Berry, *Hassling*, Boston and Toronto, Little, Brown and Company, 1970.

Wilson, Carol Green, *Chinatown Quest*, Stanford, Stanford University Press, 1949.

Winslow, Ward, "David Packard in His Own Words," *Peninsula Times Tribune*, Palo Alto, October 20, 21, 22, 1991.

Wood, Dallas E., and Norris James, *History of Palo Alto*, Palo Alto, A.H. Cawston, 1939.

Yu, Connie Young, *Profiles in Excellence — Peninsula Chinese Americans*, Palo Alto, Stanford Area Chinese Club, 1986.

Zurcher v. Stanford Daily, 436 U.S. 539 (1978).

Randy Baldschun and Assistant Fire Chief Reuben Grijalva. Betty J. Rogaway, former coordinator of the Palo Alto Unified School District's early childhood education program and a past president of the Historical Association, has done outstanding oral interviews with many leading school district figures. Bob French's persistent research pinned down elusive facts.

Careful oversight of early electronics history by Don Koijane and George Durfey of the Perham Foundation and their help in obtaining related photographs is gratefully acknowledged.

Prominent city leaders who consented to be interviewed in depth were Mary Balch Kennedy, David Packard, Leonard Ely, Templeton and Catherine Peck, Bishop R. Marvin Stuart, William Alhouse, the Rev. Harold Bjornson, Emilia Rathbun, Enid Pearson and Rabbi Sidney Akselrad. Their vivid recollections, stories and insights into the reasons Palo Alto developed as it did broadened the writer's appreciation of our past.

Doris Yep and other members of Rose and Ngum You Jew's family, especially Lillian Wong and Paul Wing Jew, gladly retold their saga.

Others interviewed more briefly were Bill Reller, Emily Renzel, Albert Wilson, George "Tad" Cody, Bill Busse, Harry Rodda, Lloyd McGovern, George Hurley, Stephanie Adcock, John Williams, Ron Skillicorn, Jeanne McDonnell, Claude "Tony" Look, Larry McDonnell, Nonette Hanko, Ellen Wyman, Sara Chaney, Lester Hodgins, Charles G. Schulz and Judges Ed Scoyen, Bart Phelps, James W. Stewart and William A. Ingram.

Also Harry Sello, Joe Ehrlich, Robert A. Kreutzmann, Allan F. Brown, Robert V. Brown, John C. Northway, John Brooks Boyd, Roger E. May, Alan Winterbotham, Malcolm Dudley, Marion Sellers and Bob Burgess of Lockheed, Steve Witmer of Watkins-Johnson, Pete Waller of NASA, Dave Kirby of Hewlett-Packard.

In addition, Florance Paulsen Minard, Lucy Hill, Doris McLachlan Whalen, Ellen Bergren, Alfred Werry, Fred Hoehn, Dorothy Dewing, Mary Edith Jones Clifford, Diana Steeples, John Santana Jr., Keith Clark, Ken White, Judy Leahy, Kay

Muranaka, Ryland Kelley, Ambassador L.W. "Bill" Lane Jr., Patricia Faber Eaves, Pearl Hannah, Alf Brandin, Jan Puthoff and retired Fire Marshal Herbert Nelson.

David Matson and Dave Hatunen of the Public Works Department supplied a much-improved map of annexations to Palo Alto.

Gordon Moore of Intel Corp. helped locate a photograph of an early flip-flop integrated circuit designed by now defunct Fairchild Semiconductors. Joan O'Connor of Stanford Management Company provided photographs, as did Mary Chanchanian of Hoover Associates and Bill Alhouse. Robin Templeton Quist Gates supplied family photographs. Betty Land graciously allowed access to her writing on the human potential movement — and threw in poppy seeds. The writings of Kathy Akatiff and Nita Spangler about Sarah Wallis added vital details.

Carl B. Moerdyke reviewed the writing agreement. Among those who gave publishing know-how were Harry Press and Bob Beyers. At Keeble and Shuchat, Barbara Wright and Kristin Jacobson gave special help in photo copying, as did Dorothy Willis at Willis Photo Lab.

Leonard Ely provided sound advice on raising funds to finance the publication. Leland D. Levy headed a marketing committee that succeeded in soliciting funds and publicizing the book. Serving with him were Crystal Gamage, Gene Nickell, Marge Collins, Liz Hogan, Warren Kallenbach, Michael Litfin, Sue MacDonald, Keith Clark, Debbie Ford-Scriba, Frank Livermore, Cyanne McElhinney, Judy Leahy, Gain John, Gloria Brown and Betty Rogaway. Desktop publisher Carroll Harrington rendered outstanding *pro bono publico* services, assisted by Siobhan Jones Facey. Faith Bell gave important counseling on marketing points.

If the newspaper is indeed the first draft of history, many staffers of the *Palo Alto Times* — literally hundreds — contributed heavily by their past reporting and editing. Among those whose original work provided significant source material for this book are Harold R. Stevens, Monte Linsley, Dan Endsley, Walt Gamage, Frances Moffat, Glenn

Brown, Al Bodi, Richard M. Stannard, Art German, Mary Madison, Robert E. Burgess, Paul Emerson, Mary Grant Hager, S.J. Moffatt, Dick O'Connor, Joyce Passetti O'Connor, Mary Ann Seawell, Don Webster, Bob Slayman, Marge Scandling, Ron Goben, Myron Myers, Terry Hansen, Derek Schoen, Jack Rannells, Jay Thorwaldson, Marc Salgado, Mary T. Fortney and Paul Voakes.

Gene Tupper rightfully leads the list of photo credits, along with his veteran *Times* associates Joe Melena and Ken Yimm. All of them bridged over to the *Peninsula Times Tribune*, there joining such other top-flight photographers as Bob Andres and Sam Forensich.

Times Tribune staffers who made signal contributions include Leonard Koppett, Robert Lyhne, Bill Shilstone, Roy Hurlbert, Tom Rosenstiel, Christina Kenrick, Mark Simon, Linda Jacob and Ruthann Richter. Again, hundreds of others wrote city history. The author is especially grateful to six top executives of the paper. Bill Harke, the last editor, was of enormous help in that and his earlier post as managing editor. Editors Mike Kidder and Kevin Doyle and Publishers Tom Culligan, Peter Heraty and Robert E. Wood granted the run of the files and copying privileges. Sports Editor Danny DeFreitas and Keith Peters, now *Palo Alto Weekly* sports editor, assisted liberally.

Unsung heroines of local history are to be found in the "morgue" — the newspaper library. We are deeply indebted to Pamela A. Allen for her patient help — and for giving up precious farewell moments with associates on the paper's final day to smuggle out previously requested photo prints and deliver them at a taco stand rendezvous. Joan Merritt and Elizabeth R. Miller also aided greatly.

At the *Weekly*, Publisher William S. Johnson and his staff have done fine reviews of local history by the decades and from other angles. Paul Gullixson, now associate editor after a stint as *Times Tribune* editorial page editor, has often brought facts about Palo Alto's past to public notice in his columns. Don Kazak, Diane Sussman, Jock Friedly and many other writers have helped residents to see the community in retrospect.

Many pictures herein are by photographers whose work has graced the *Weekly* — Carolyn Clebsch, first and foremost, Renee Fadiman, Renee Burgard and others. Other illustrations trace to cameramen of up to a century ago who got excellent results with rudimentary equipment, such as W.H. Myrick, Andrew P. Hill, Frank Davey and Dan Baker. More recently, the gifted Carolyn Caddes followed them by donating segments of her work to the Association.

At the *San Jose Mercury News*, Publisher Larry Jinks, Executive Editor Robert Ingle, Managing Editor Jerome Ceppas and his assistant Tom Brew and Library Director Gary Lance all have graciously aided this project. News stories by Carolyn Jung and many other reporters were informative, as were history pieces by Joanne Grant and Patricia Smith. Inspiration also came from two former Palo Alto colleagues of the author now at the *Mercury News*, Deputy Managing Editor/Features Ann Hurst and Special Sections Editor Carolyn Snyder, and from Lou Calvert, Bob Drews, James Braly, Jane Abbott Anderson, Willys Peck, Heather Urquhart, Patrick Murphy, Harry Farrell and Bill Strobel.

Special thanks are due to Gain and Jane John and Gloria Brown for making their homes available for committee meetings, and to the persevering spouses who endured the strains of this process: Holly Winslow, Jay Wilson, Jane John and Luana Staiger.

Whatever errors remain in this book are of course the responsibility of the author and the Publications Committee. Many others who gave their assistance have necessarily been omitted here, but not because those who shaped the book are ungrateful. Thanks to everyone, named or unnamed, who contributed.

List of Illustrations

Index